3rd Edition

COMPUTERS

BRIEF

Understanding Technology

Floyd Fuller

Appalachian State University
Boone, North Carolina

Brian Larson

Modesto Junior College
Modesto, California
California State University—Stanislaus
Turlock, California

Senior Developmental Editor: Christine Hurney
Production Editor: Courtney Kost
Cover Designer: Leslie Anderson
Text Designer and Page Layout: David Farr, ImageSmythe; Leslie Anderson, Petrina Nyhan
Illustrator: Precision Graphics
Copy Editor: Rosemary Wallner
Proofreader: Kathryn Savoie
Indexer: Ina Gravitz

Care has been taken to verify the accuracy of information presented in this book. However, the authors, editors, and publisher cannot accept responsibility for Web, e-mail, newsgroup, or chat room subject matter or content, or for consequences from application of the information in this book, and make no warranty, expressed or implied, with respect to its content.

Trademarks: Some of the product names and company names included in this book have been used for identification purposes only and may be trademarks or registered trade names of their respective manufacturers and sellers. The authors, editors, and publisher disclaim any affiliation, association, or connection with, or sponsorship or endorsement by, such owners.

Image Credits: Chapter 1. *Page 2:* Corbis; *Page 3:* Dex Images/Corbis; *Page 4:* (top) PhotoDisc/Getty Images, (middle) Corbis, (bottom) AP Photo/Peter M. Fredin; *Page 6:* (top) © Intel Corporation, (bottom) Corbis; *Page 7:* Bettman/Corbis; *Page 8:* T. Kevin Smyth/Corbis; *Page 9:* Corbis, Courtesy of the National Human Genome Research Institute; *Page 10:* © Paradigm Publishing, Inc.; *Page 12:* (top) © Paradigm Publishing, Inc., (bottom) screenshot reprinted with permission from Microsoft Corporation; *Page 13:* Screenshots © Google Inc., and are used with permission; *Page 16:* © Paradigm Publishing, Inc.; *Page 18:* (top) © Paradigm Publishing, Inc., Corbis; *Page 19:* (left) Courtesy of Dell Inc., © Hewlett-Packard Company; *Page 20:* (left to right) © Maxell Corporation Inc, © Memorex Products Inc, © Memorex Products Inc; *Page 22:* AP Photo/Karsten Thielke; *Page 25:* Corbis, Rainer Holz/zefa/Corbis; *Page 26:* © Ed Kashi/Corbis, Toshiyuki Aizawa/Reuters/Corbis; *Page 27:* Ausloeser/zefa/Corbis; *Page 28:* © Motorola, Inc.; *Page 29:* Courtesy of Dell Inc.; *Page 30:* AP Photo/Hewlett Packard Company; *Page 31:* (top) Courtesy of Dell Inc., (bottom) Royalty-Free/Corbis; *Page 32:* Kimberly White/Reuters/Corbis; *Page 33:* Markowitz Jeffrey/Corbis Sygma. *Image Credits continue following Index.*

We have made every effort to trace the ownership of all copyrighted material and to secure permission from copyright holders. In the event of any question arising as to the use of any material, we will be pleased to make the necessary corrections in future printings. Thanks are due to the aforementioned photographers and agents for permission to use the materials indicated.

Softcover Edition:
ISBN 978-0-76382-937-7 (Text & CD)
ISBN 978-0-76382-929-2 (Text)

Hardcover Edition:
ISBN 978-0-76383-369-5 (Text & CD)
ISBN 978-0-76383-368-8 (Text)

© 2008 by Paradigm Publishing, Inc.
875 Montreal Way
St. Paul, MN 55102
E-mail: educate@emcp.com
Web site: www.emcp.com

Printed in the United States of America

16 15 14 13 12 11 10 09 08 07   2 3 4 5 6 7 8 9 10

CONTENTS

CHAPTER 1
Our Digital World 1

Cyber Scenario 2
Immersed in Digital Technology 2
Digital Information 5
Computerized Devices vs. Computers 5
The Computer Advantage 7
Speed 8
Accuracy 8
Versatility 9
Storage 10
Communications 10
How Computers Work 13
Data and Information 13
The Information Processing Cycle 15
Computers and Computer Systems 15

e-THICS > **Pick up the Phone 17**

Components of a Computer System 17
Computer Hardware: An Overview 17
Computer Software: An Overview 20

Tech Visionary > **Konrad Zuse 22**

Categories of Computers 23

Globe Trotting > **Nano City 24**

Personal Computers 24

Cutting Edge > **The Computer Weight-Loss Diet 27**

Hot Spot > **Fly-by-Wireless Technology 28**

Workstations 28
Midrange Servers 29

Tech Visionary > **William Hewlett and David Packard 30**

Mainframe Computers 31
Supercomputers 32

On the Horizon 33
Chapter Summary 35
Key Terms 36
Chapter Exercises 37

TECH INSIGHT
Buying and Installing a PC TI-A1

CHAPTER 2
Input and Processing 45

Cyber Scenario 46
Input Technology 47
The Keyboard 47
Touch Screens 49
The Mouse and Other Point-and-Click
Devices 49

Globe Trotting > **The Telepathic Typewriter 52**

Pens and Tablets 53

Tech Visionary > **Gordon E. Moore 54**

Optical Scanners 54
Bar Code and Optical Readers 56
Graphic and Video Input Devices 57
Audio Input Devices 61

Tech Visionary > **John Eckert and John Mauchly 62**

Data Processing by Computers 63
Data Representation: Bits and Bytes 64
ASCII and EBCDIC Coding Schemes 64
Unicode 65

The System Unit 65
The Power Supply 65
Storage Bays 67
The Motherboard 68
   The Central Processing Unit 69

e-THICS > **The Chip Debate 74**

Tech Visionary > **Jack S. Kilby 77**

   System Clock 77
   Random Access Memory 78
   Read-Only Memory and Flash Memory 81
   Expansion Slots and Expansion Cards 83
   Ports 85
   Buses 86

On the Horizon 87
Chapter Summary 90
Key Terms 91
Chapter Exercises 93

TECH INSIGHT
Adding Software and Hardware
Components to Your PC TI-B1

CHAPTER 3
Output and Storage 99

Cyber Scenario 100
Output 101
   Types of Output 101
   Output Devices and Media 102
Display Devices 103
   Cathode Ray Tube (CRT) Monitors 105
   Flat-Panel Displays 105
   Monitor Performance and Quality Factors 105

Tech Visionary > **Steven Jobs 106**

   Monitor Ergonomics 110
   Wearable Computers 110
   Television Displays 110
   Screen Projectors 112

Printers 113
   Dot-Matrix Printers 114
   Line Printers 115
   Ink-Jet Printers 115
   Laser Printers 117
   Thermal Printers 118
   Plotters 119
   Special-Purpose Printers 119
   Multifunction Devices 121
Audio Output 123
   Speakers and Sound Systems 123

Cutting Edge > **Techno Eyes 124**

   Voice Output Systems 124
Storage Devices and Media 124
   File Types 125
   Secondary Storage Systems 126
Magnetic Storage Devices and Media 126
   Floppy Disks and Disk Drives 127
   Hard Disks and Hard Drives 128
   USB Flash Drives 130
   Tape Cartridges and Tape Drives 130
Optical Storage Devices 131
   CD-ROMs 133

Cutting Edge > **Keeping It Personal 134**

   CD-Rs 134
   CD-RWs 135
   DVD-ROMs 135
   Caring for Optical Discs 136
Large Computer System Storage Devices 137
   Magnetic Storage Devices for Large
     Computer Systems 137

Globe Trotting > **Freedom in the Desert 140**

   Optical Storage Devices for Large
     Computer Systems 140

On the Horizon 141
Chapter Summary 143
Key Terms 144
Chapter Exercises 145

TECH INSIGHT
Telecommunications and Networks TI-C1

CHAPTER 4
System Software 153

Cyber Scenario 154
The Function of System Software 155
The Function of the Operating System 156

Globe Trotting > **Booting Up Bhutan 157**

　Booting (Starting) the Computer 157

Hot Spot > **Coming Soon—
　　　　Transistors on Steroids! 159**

　Managing Memory 159
　Configuring and Controlling Devices 160
　Managing Essential File Operations 161
　Monitoring System Performance 161
　Providing Basic Security Functions 162
Software User Interfaces 162
　Command-Line Interfaces 162
　Graphical User Interfaces 163

Tech Visionary > **Bill Gates 170**

Personal Computer Operating Systems 170
　Windows 171
　Macintosh Operating System 175
　OS/2 176
　Linux 176
Server Operating Systems 177

Tech Visionary > **Linus Torvalds 178**

　Novell Netware 179
　Windows 179
　UNIX 180

Cutting Edge > **Sharing Code through Krugle 181**

Operating Systems for Handheld Devices 182
　Palm OS 182
　Windows Mobile 182
Utility Programs and Translators 182
　Utility Programs 183
　Translators 188

On the Horizon 189
Chapter Summary 191
Key Terms 192
Chapter Exercises 193

TECH INSIGHT
The Internet and the World Wide Web TI-D1

CHAPTER 5
Application Software 201

Cyber Scenario 202
Types of Application Software 203
　Commercial Application Software 204
　Other Application Software Models 205

Globe Trotting > **To Stop a Moving Target 206**

　Application Software for Individual Use 207
Productivity Software 208
　Word Processing 208

Tech Visionary > **Bill Atkinson 212**

　Desktop Publishing 213
　Spreadsheets 214
　Database Management 217
　Presentation Graphics 221
　Software Suites 223
　Personal Information Manager (PIM) 223
　Project Management 224
Software for Household Use 225
　Personal Finance 225
　Tax Preparation 226
　Legal Documents 227
　Games and Entertainment 228
　Educational and Reference Software 229

Cutting Edge > **To Catch a Plagiarist 230**

Graphics and Multimedia Software 231
　Painting and Drawing Software 231

Tech Visionary > **Dan Bricklin 232**

　Image-Editing Software 233
　Video and Audio Editing Software 233
　Web Authoring Software 234
　Computer-aided Design Software 235
Communications Software 235
　Electronic Mail 235
　Web Browsers and Search Engines 236
　Instant Messaging Software 236

Hot Spot > **Can You Meet Me Now? 238**

Groupware 238
Webconferencing 239

On the Horizon 240
Chapter Summary 243
Key Terms 244
Chapter Exercises 245

TECH INSIGHT
Computer Ethics TI-E1

APPENDIX Troubleshooting Your PC A-1

Windows Tutorials WT-1

Internet Tutorials IT-1

Glossary G-1

Index I-1

PREFACE

FOR MILLIONS OF PEOPLE WORLDWIDE, the computer and the Internet have become an integral and essential part of life. In the home, we use computers to communicate quickly with family and friends, manage our finances more effectively, enjoy music and games, shop online for products and services, and much more. In the workplace, computers have become an almost indispensable tool. With them, workers can become more efficient, productive, and creative, and companies can connect almost instantly with suppliers and partners on the other side of the world.

Studying this book will help prepare students for the workplace of today—and tomorrow—in which some level of computer skills is often an essential requirement for employment. Employees who continually try to improve their skills have an advantage over those who do not. Some would even argue that understanding technology has become a survival skill. This book will help students become survivors.

What's New in the Third Edition?

As with the previous editions, the goal of this new edition of *Computers: Understanding Technology* is to introduce students to the key information technology concepts and the vital technical skills that can help improve their personal and professional lives. In planning the changes for the third edition, we conducted reviews and focus groups and used that feedback to create a state-of-the-art computer concepts product that will enhance the teaching and learning experience.

Like the previous edition, this third edition is offered in three divisions of identical chapter content to match the three most common computer concepts course lengths. The Comprehensive book consists of Chapters 1–15, the Introductory book consists of Chapters 1–9, and the Brief book includes Chapters 1–5. In response to the increased need to understand issues related to security and the need to cover this important topic early in the course of study, the Security Issues and Strategies chapter has been moved to the Chapter 8 position, which allows it to be included in both the Introductory and Comprehensive titles. Also, this new placement allows the presentation on security to appear directly after Chapter 7, The Internet and the World Wide Web. The new topic order is as follows:

Chapter 1, Our Digital World
Chapter 2, Input and Processing
Chapter 3, Output and Storage
Chapter 4, System Software
Chapter 5, Application Software
Chapter 6, Telecommunications and Networks

Chapter 7, The Internet and the World Wide Web
Chapter 8, Security Issues and Strategies
Chapter 9, Database and Information Management
Chapter 10, Information Systems
Chapter 11, Electronic Commerce
Chapter 12, Programming Concepts and Languages
Chapter 13, Multimedia and Artificial Intelligence
Chapter 14, Computer Ethics
Chapter 15, Information Technology Careers

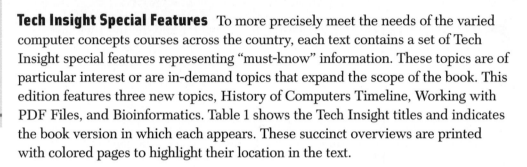

Tech Insight Special Features To more precisely meet the needs of the varied computer concepts courses across the country, each text contains a set of Tech Insight special features representing "must-know" information. These topics are of particular interest or are in-demand topics that expand the scope of the book. This edition features three new topics, History of Computers Timeline, Working with PDF Files, and Bioinformatics. Table 1 shows the Tech Insight titles and indicates the book version in which each appears. These succinct overviews are printed with colored pages to highlight their location in the text.

Additional Application Exercises: Windows and Internet Tutorials Recognizing the crucial need for students to be able to use Windows efficiently and effectively, we have developed a set of 15 Windows Vista tutorials that teach the core computer management skills. Students can work through the group of tutorials in one sitting, or they can work through them one at a time as the first activity in the end-of-chapter exercises. The Windows Tutorials appear with the seven

Table 1 Tech Insight Special Features

Tech Insight Title	Comprehensive	Introductory	Brief
Adding Software and Hardware Components to Your PC		✔	✔
Bioinformatics	✔		
Buying and Installing a PC	✔	✔	✔
Computer Ethics		✔	✔
History of Computers Timeline	✔	✔	
The Internet and the World Wide Web			✔
Telecommunications and Networks			✔
Using XML to Share Information	✔		
Working with PDF Files	✔	✔	

Note: All of the Tech Insight special features are available in the Library section of the Internet Resource Center at www.emcp.net/CUT3e.

Internet tutorials at the end of the book. All of the tutorials are included in the three versions of the text.

Chapter Features

All of the chapter features are designed to engage the students and to help them learn the concepts presented.

Cyber Scenarios Cutting-edge developments related to the chapter topic are illustrated in a realistic, practical portrayal of how technology may affect students' lives now and in the near future. These engaging scenarios allow students to connect with the concepts that will be covered in more depth in the chapter.

CyberScenario

JENNA WINBON IS AWAKENED BY UPBEAT MUSIC playing and her window blinds opening to let in the morning sunshine. The smell of fresh-brewed coffee gradually makes it to her end of the house as she ponders her upcoming day at the office. A computer system called a home information infrastructure manages the MP3 player and stereo system, window blinds, and cof-

Opening the door from the utility room to the garage automatically starts Jenna's car and opens the garage door simultaneously. As she backs out of the garage, she notices the car's interior temperature is approaching the

New, Interesting, and Informative Topic Boxes All of the intra-chapter topic boxes have been updated for this edition. All of these boxes expand the text discussion and present high-interest applications of the topic. Chapters contain four to six topic boxes of varying types.

- Hot Spot, new to this edition, focuses on wireless technology and the interesting twists, perspectives, or uses of wireless technology and the related communications and community-building issues.
- Tech Visionary honors the current drivers and prominent pioneers in IT.
- Cutting Edge showcases hot new technologies.
- Globe Trotting features innovative IT applications worldwide.
- e-THICS highlights ethical issues and situations in IT.

Expanded Content Throughout the book, icons appear in the textbook's margins identifying where additional, related content can be found to support chapter study. Each chapter is supported by animated, Flash-based Tech Demos on the Encore CD as well as articles and supporting activities on the Internet Resource Center.

Tech Demo 3-4
Laser Printer

Go to this title's Internet Resource Center and read the article titled "Internet Social Networks." www.emcp.net/CUT3e

On the Horizon Each chapter ends with a brief overview of some exciting new developments to watch.

OnThe**Horizon**

THE TOPIC OF SECURITY IS AT THE TOP of legislative and corporate agendas due to concerns that criminal and terrorist organizations could exploit insecure communication networks, including the Internet. New developments in biometrics and cryptography show great promise in meeting coming security needs.

Improved Chapter Summaries and Key Terms Listing To help students review the concepts and terminology presented in the text, the chapter summaries include questions and answers that directly relate to the main concepts presented in each chapter. These summaries are also available in an interactive format on the text's Internet Resource Center, hotlinked with corresponding terms and definitions. Key terms are grouped, allowing students to better understand the relationships between the terminology and the larger, organizing concepts in the chapter.

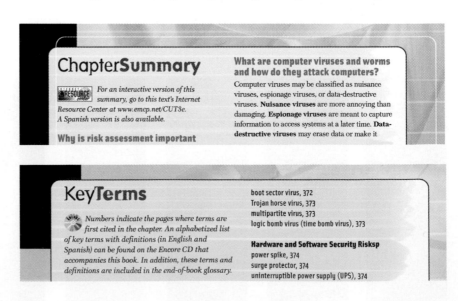

ChapterSummary

For an interactive version of this summary, go to this text's Internet Resource Center at www.emcp.net/CUT3e. A Spanish version is also available.

Why is risk assessment important

What are computer viruses and worms and how do they attack computers?

Computer viruses may be classified as nuisance viruses, espionage viruses, or data-destructive viruses. **Nuisance viruses** are more annoying than damaging. **Espionage viruses** are meant to capture information to access systems at a later time. **Data-destructive viruses** may erase data or make it

KeyTerms

Numbers indicate the pages where terms are first cited in the chapter. An alphabetized list of key terms with definitions (in English and Spanish) can be found on the Encore CD that accompanies this book. In addition, these terms and definitions are included in the end-of-book glossary.

boot sector virus, 372
Trojan horse virus, 373
multipartite virus, 373
logic bomb virus (time bomb virus), 373

Hardware and Software Security Risksp
power spike, 374
surge protector, 374
uninterruptible power supply (UPS), 374

New End-of-Chapter Concepts Exercises As in previous editions, this text includes end-of-chapter exercises that assess the students' comprehension of the chapter content using a variety of approaches to maintain interest, foster creative and critical thinking, and address different learning styles. These exercises are also available on the Internet Resource Center at www.emcp.net/CUT3e along with supplemental information there and on the text's Encore CD. Icons identify where the student can find additional content.

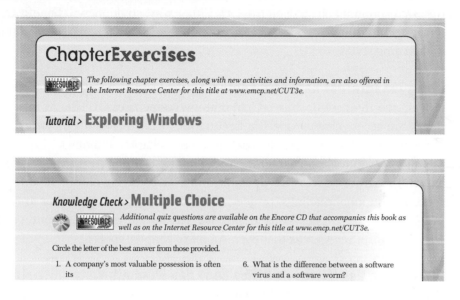

Student Courseware

Because of the ever-changing nature of the IT industry, and because students learn in many different ways, *Computers: Understanding Technology, Third Edition* is supported by an Encore CD, a Web site, and hands-on tutorials.

Using the Encore CD Included with the textbook is a multimedia CD that adds an experiential and interactive dimension to the learning of fundamental computer concepts. For every chapter, the Encore CD offers the following features.

- **Tech Demos:** These brief, animated Flash segments bring key topics to life. To highlight them for the instructor and student, the text includes a margin note and Encore CD icon next to the related chapter discussion.
- **Quizzes:** The Encore CD includes a rich bank of multiple-choice quizzes available in both practice and reported modes. In the practice mode, students receive immediate feedback on each quiz item and a report of his or her total score. In the reported mode, the results are e-mailed to both the student and instructor. Book-level and chapter specific quizzes are available.

- **Glossary:** Key terms and definitions, with audio support are combined with related illustrations from the text. New to this edition, the glossary terms and definitions are also available in Spanish.
- **Image Bank:** Illustrations of concepts and processes are accompanied by the related terms and definitions.
- **Key Terms Flash Cards and Acronyms Flash Cards:** Flash cards are a fun way to learn terms and acronyms, and each chapter is supported by this interactive, game-like feature.

Additionally, the Encore CD includes a comprehensive set of computer literacy tutorials called Tech Tutors, which are accessible at any time and within any chapter.

The Encore CD may be used as a preview or as a sequel to each chapter—or both. That is, a student can play each chapter's Flash animations to get an overview of what is taught in the book and then study the text chapter before returning to the CD for its enriching content and interactivity. Or, a student can complete the reading of a chapter and chapter exercises and then work through the corresponding chapter on the CD. Either way, students will benefit from working with this integrated multimedia CD and will find an approach that suits all learning styles.

Using the Internet Resource Center Students will find other useful learning aids on the Internet Resource Center at www.emcp.net/CUT3e. At this site, students can access chapter-specific Lecture and Study Notes documents, PowerPoint presentations, quizzes, interactive chapter summaries (in English and Spanish), terminology crossword puzzles, and key terms and acronyms flash cards. To further address the dynamic and ever-changing nature of computer technology, additional readings, projects, and activities for each chapter are also provided. The text includes icons identifying articles and activities found on the Internet Resource Center that correspond to chapter content.

Learning to Use Microsoft Office 2007 and Windows Vista To supplement this title and to provide hands-on learning, 50 additional interactive tutorials teaching the basics of Microsoft Office 2007 and Windows Vista are available. Using realistic simulations, which come with audio and Flash animations, student can quickly learn the basic operations of Word, Excel, Access, and PowerPoint 2007.

Instructor Resources

Instructor support for the third edition has been expanded to include a Curriculum Planner and Resources binder with CD. This all-in-one print resource includes planning resources such as lesson blueprints, teaching suggestions, and sample course syllabi; presentation resources such as lecture notes, student study notes, PowerPoint presentations and handouts, and additional discussion questions and enrichment activities; and assessment resources including an overview of available assessment venues, answer keys for end-of-chapter exercises, and sample midterm and final exams. Contents of the Curriculum Planner and Resources supplement are also available on the password-protected section of the Internet Resource Center for this title at www.emcp.net/CUT3e.

This edition is supported by an ExamView test generator. Instructors can use the bank of over 1,500 multiple choice, true/false, short answer, and graphics-based items to create customized, Web-based or print tests.

Instructors can use SNAP Training and Assessment to access banks of concept items for each chapter, or to build new test items. Exams delivered by SNAP over the Web are reported and graded automatically. Tutorials teaching the basics of Office and Windows are also available on the SNAP Tutorials CD.

Acknowledgements and Appreciation

Writing and publishing a book is a complex and expensive task that requires the dedicated efforts of many people. Throughout this project, we authors have had the pleasure and privilege of working closely with the highly skilled and quality-focused professionals at EMC Corporation.

We offer our sincere appreciation to Christine Hurney, Senior Developmental Editor, and Courtney Kost, Production Editor, for their diligence and for their many contributions to this book. Their excellent editorial efforts and their attention to detail contributed greatly to the successful completion of this work. Working closely with Christine and Courtney has been a privilege and a pleasure. A special thanks is in order to Sonja Brown, Editorial Director, for her professional insights and contributions to this edition. To the entire staff at Paradigm Publishing, we offer our sincere gratitude.

We are indebted to technical writer and consultant Deborah Merz, whose careful attention to accuracy and relevancy proved invaluable. Thank you to Denise Seguin, co-author of the *Marquee Microsoft Office 2007* series, for creating the Windows Vista tutorials; to Alec Fehl, co-author of *Internet: Systems and Applications, Second Edition*, for creating the Internet Tutorials; and to Carolyn Reser for writing many new thought-provoking and informative topic boxes. We also thank John Baker, co-author of *Internet: Systems and Applications, Second Edition*, for his preparation of the chapter articles and activities for the Internet Resource Center.

Our families deserve special credit. Our wives, Edith and Alma, and our children, Cindy and Michael, and Amanda and Keith, were constant sources of love, support, and encouragement. Although we can never repay them for their sacrifices on our behalf, we are truly grateful to each, without whose support we could not have written this book.

Consultants and Reviewers We are indebted to three individuals who served as technical consultants and reviewers for the first edition, which provided the solid foundation for this and future editions:

David Laxton, industry consultant, Cincinnati, Ohio
Deborah Merz, technical writer and consultant, West Bloomfield, Michigan
Mary Kelley Weaver, instructor, St. Johns River Community College

Additionally, we thank the instructors and other professionals who participated in shaping the revision plan for this edition. As instructors who teach introductory computer courses, and as practicing professionals who are knowledgeable about the latest computer technologies, they brought a real-world perspective to the project.

Lynn Bowen
Valdosta Technical College
Valdosta, Georgia

Joy Bukowy
Robeson Community College
Lumberton, North Carolina

John P. Cicero, PhD
Shasta College
Redding, California

Bruce Collins
Davenport University
Holland, Michigan

Reet Cronk, PhD
Harding University
Searcy, Arkansas

Heather Crosthwait
Enersource Hydro Mississauga Information Systems
Mississauga, Ontario

Marvin Daugherty
Ivy Tech Community College
Indianapolis, Indiana

Joan Davis
Centennial College
Toronto (Scarborough), Ontario

Phillip Davis, PhD
Del Mar College
Corpus Christi, Texas

Angie Davison
Lake Land College
Mattoon, Illinois

Mary Beth Graham
Carroll Community College
Westminster, Maryland

Wade T. Graves, EdD
Grayson County Community College
Denison, Texas

Saeed Molki
South Texas College
McAllen, Texas

Pam Silvers
Asheville-Buncombe Technical Community College
Asheville, North Carolina

Joyce Thompson
Lehigh Carbon Community College
Schnecksville, Pennsylvania

Kenneth Weimer
Kellogg Community College
Battle Creek, Michigan

Dedication

The moment I met the young lady who would later become my wife, I knew that
my life would be changed forever. And, it has been. She has been my devoted
companion, my closest friend, the mother of our children, and my enduring source
of encouragement and inspiration. For her devotion to our family and to so many
others to whom she has given so freely of her time and energies, I dedicate this
book to my wife, Edith Mizelle Fuller.

—Floyd Fuller

For all the times the kids climbed on the computer or poured juice on the keyboard,
for all the times she took care of things while I typed, and for all the times she was
understanding and thoughtful, I dedicate this book to my wife, Alma Larson.

—Brian Larson

CHAPTER 1

Our Digital World

Learning Objectives

> Explain and give examples of digital technologies

> Discuss the advantages of using computers

> Briefly explain the computing process

> Distinguish between computers and computer systems

> Identify the components of a computer system

> Describe the categories of computers

> Differentiate between wired and wireless computing

CyberScenario

IT'S 8:30 A.M. AND MARC HANSON'S FLIGHT has just taken off from Dallas, heading for Chicago's O'Hare International Airport. After the Boeing 767 reaches its cruising altitude, the flight attendant announces that passengers are now permitted to use personal electronic devices, including their computers.

Marc reaches under his seat to retrieve his notebook computer, and a few keystrokes later, his computer is connected to the Internet. Marc logs into his company's network and reviews the sales presentation he will be making today. He makes a few updates and e-mails it to his Chicago contact in preparation for the meeting.

Marc sends an e-mail message to remind his supervisor that he will not be in the office today. He sends another e-mail to Steve Reminger at Teledex Company in Chicago confirming their meeting at 3 p.m. He sends four more messages during the next few minutes, each one to a branch office in another part of the country.

He carefully reviews his investment portfolio by accessing his broker's Web site. Caterpillar is down $0.50, Dell Computer is up $1.25, Microsoft Corporation is up $2.21, and Disney is up $1.13. All in all, not bad! After placing an order to buy 100 more shares of Disney, Marc moves on to check the news.

Marc scans the latest headlines by accessing *USA Today's* Web site. One article announces that a major competitor is having difficulty with its proposed acquisition of a smaller company. From another article,

Marc learns about the latest alternative-fuel vehicles being introduced next year. Before he shuts down his computer, he pays his electric bill and checks the current price of an item he is selling in an online auction.

Returning the laptop to his briefcase, Marc retrieves his smartphone and sends an instant message to Helen Ramirez to notify her of the flight's updated arrival

Immersed in Digital Technology

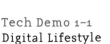

Tech Demo 1-1
Digital Lifestyle

Computers and other digital devices permeate our daily lives. High-definition televisions (HDTVs) display amazingly clear and colorful images of sports events, reality TV shows, and other popular programs. Electronic coffeemakers, digital alarm clocks, and cell phones quicken and simplify daily routines. Automobile manufacturers use computerized robots to build cars and trucks. Businesses increasingly rely on electronic mail (e-mail) to communicate internally and with vendors and customers. Electronic freeway information signs and traffic monitor-

Shelly sends a photo of her softball team after a victory while Marc has been traveling. Marc saves the picture on his phone and promises to be at her next game.

Marc's e-mails are among the billions of e-mail messages sent daily throughout North America. The Web sites he accessed are part of the millions of Web sites on the Internet in the year 2007, which has grown exponentially since the World Wide Web's birth less than two decades ago. During the hour and a half it took Marc to fly from Dallas to Chicago, he accomplished the following tasks:

- updated a sales presentation and distributed it for a same-day meeting
- communicated with at least six different people at diverse locations
- reviewed his appointments for the day
- read the latest national and regional news
- checked the day's trading prices of his stock investments and placed a trade
- transferred money from his bank account to the electric company
- checked the status of an auction item
- viewed a photo taken at his daughter's school while he was traveling

In the not too distant future, Marc and millions of other consumers will regularly use the Internet from anywhere, at anytime, using smaller and smaller Internet-enabled devices. Business, household, and personal activities are becoming more accessible from any location through devices that connect through the Internet without wires.

time. She responds that she will meet him upon his arrival at 10:30 a.m. Marc looks for updates to his schedule and sees that after a quick debrief over coffee, it will be time for lunch with Mirax Corporation's purchasing agents, when he will present his company's marketing suggestions. Following the Teledex appointment in the afternoon, his busy day will end with dinner at the Lough Bispo Restaurant on Chicago's North Side before he takes an evening flight back home.

Marc then calls his daughter, Shelly. When she answers, her image appears in color on the small LCD screen of Marc's phone, as does his image on hers.

ing devices help drivers navigate our busy highways and alert drivers to emergencies, such as missing or abducted persons. And some 65 percent of U.S. children ages 2–17 use the Internet from home, school, or some other location, according to a report from the Corporation for Public Broadcasting. In today's world, living even a day without some type of digital interaction is highly unlikely for most people. What about you? How digital is your life? Complete the survey in Figure 1-1 to get a sense of the number of digital interactions you have every day. Place a check mark next to each activity you have experienced in the past 24 hours.

Digital coffeemakers offer options for start time, temperature, and even varied flavors for different days of the week.

Cell phones have become so common in everyday life that most people would be lost without them.

ROAD MAY BE ICY IN AREAS

Sharing up-to-date information with morning commuters allows drivers to take alternate routes or make other plans.

Like most people, you are probably aware that you interact with electronic devices every day, but perhaps you were surprised by the large number of your digital experiences. The extent to which computers and digital technology drive daily life has led historians to characterize today's world as a "digital world." You know the term *digital* has something to do with computers. But what does the term mean and why is it important?

- driving a car
- tracking appointments on a personal digital assistant (PDA)
- calling or text messaging (also called texting) on a cell phone
- depositing or withdrawing money at an ATM
- working on a desktop computer or laptop
- sending information via a fax machine
- filling up the gas tank in your car
- creating copies with a photocopier
- riding an elevator
- shopping online
- playing video games
- answering a telemarketing call
- manipulating numbers with a calculator
- buying groceries in the self-serve checkout line
- riding on the subway
- retrieving a voice mail message
- snapping a photo on a digital camera or a camera phone
- watching a movie on a DVD player
- cooking with a microwave
- operating an electronically controlled dishwasher
- adjusting an electronic thermostat
- buying food or soda from an electronic vending machine
- entering a locked building with a security card
- purchasing an item with a debit card
- researching airline ticket prices on the Internet
- buying or selling an item on eBay
- downloading music from a Web site

Figure 1-1 Digital Interaction Survey
Check all of the activities that you have experienced in the last 24 hours.

Digital Information

Digital refers to a type of electronic signal that is processed, sent, and stored in discrete parts (bits), rather than an analog signal, which is a series of electronic pulses in a continuous wave. These discrete parts are represented by "on" and "off" electrical states, which in turn correspond to the digits 1 (on) and 0 (off). In a computer, this system of 1s and 0s corresponding to on and off electrical currents represents all information. Thus, computers use digital information, and computer technology in general is considered digital technology. You will learn more about this fundamental information technology concept in the chapters that follow, but for now, remember that *digital* refers to information represented by numbers and that all of the interactions listed in the survey in Figure 1-1 used digital information.

Tech Demo 1-2
Analog vs. Digital

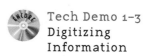
Tech Demo 1-3
Digitizing
Information

Computerized Devices vs. Computers

Digital processing occurs within miniature electrical circuits etched onto a tiny square of silicon (or another material) called a **chip**, and digital cameras, cell phones, electronic coffeemakers, and computers all contain electronic chips.

The first dual-core Itanium processor was released by Intel in July, 2006. Intel and its partners claim the processor increases performance by a factor of two, while reducing power comsumption by approximately 20 percent compared with the previous single-core version.

However, the chips within computerized devices differ considerably from the chips within computers in terms of power and capability, a distinction that separates electronic devices into two broad groups: special-purpose, or embedded computers, and general-purpose computers, or simply computers. The manufacturer has programmed the chip within an **embedded computer** to perform a few specific actions. For example, an embedded chip in a digital camera automatically controls the speed of the camera's lens so the right amount of light enters through the lens. An embedded chip in a bar code scanner reads the bar code on clothing tags and identifies the item and its price. A tiny computerized chip in a digital thermometer determines the body temperature of patients at a medical clinic.

The electronic chips within a **general-purpose computer**, on the other hand, contain programs that allow the user to perform a range of complex processes and calculations. For example, a computer containing a word processing program allows a user to create, edit, print, and save various kinds of documents, including letters, memos, and brochures. A **computer**, therefore, is defined as an electronic device that:

- operates under the control of a set of instructions, called a **program**, that is stored in its memory
- accepts data that a user supplies
- manipulates the data according to the programmed instructions
- produces the results (information)
- stores the results for future use

A digital thermometer is an example of an embedded computer, which contains a chip that the manufacturer programs to perform a specific function.

The Computer Advantage

Prior to the early 1980s, computers were unknown to the average person. Many people had never even seen a computer, let alone used one. The few computers that existed were relatively large, bulky devices confined to secure computer centers in corporate or government facilities. Referred to as mainframes, these computers were maintenance intensive, requiring special climate-controlled conditions and several full-time operators for each machine. Because the early mainframes were expensive and difficult to operate, usage was restricted to computer programmers and scientists, who used them to perform complex operations, such as processing payrolls and designing sophisticated military weaponry. Other than a few researchers or technicians having security clearances, most employees were prohibited from entering areas where the computer was housed and operated.

Beginning in the early 1980s, the computer world changed dramatically with the introduction of the **microcomputer**, also called the personal computer (PC) because this computer was intended to be operated by an individual user. These relatively small computers were considerably more affordable and much easier to use than their mainframe ancestors. Within a few years, ownership of personal computers became widespread in the workplace, and today, the personal computer is a standard appliance in homes and schools. A 2005 U.S. Census Bureau report stated that, by 2003, 76 percent of U.S. households with school-aged children owned a computer, and 83 percent of children had access to a computer at school. In terms of business spending, the information technology (IT) sector now accounts for more than 50 percent of capital expenditures.

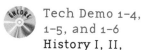

Tech Demo 1–4, 1–5, and 1–6 History I, II, and III

Today's computers come in a variety of shapes and sizes and differ significantly in computing capability, price, and speed. For example, a powerful business com-

Early mainframe computers, such as the one shown above, were large, bulky devices that were difficult to operate.

puter capable of processing millions of customer records in a few minutes may cost millions of dollars while an office desktop computer used for creating correspondence and budget forecasts may cost less than a thousand dollars. Whatever their size, cost, or power, all computers offer advantages over manual technologies in the following areas:

- speed
- accuracy
- versatility
- storage capabilities
- communications capabilities

Speed

Computers operate with lightning-like speed, and processing speeds are increasing as computer manufacturers introduce new and improved models. Contemporary personal computers are capable of executing billions of program instructions in one second. Some larger computers, such as supercomputers, can execute trillions of instructions per second, a rate important for processing the huge amounts of data involved in forecasting weather, monitoring space shuttle flights, and managing other data-intensive applications.

Accuracy

People sometimes blame human errors and mistakes on a computer. In truth, computers are extremely accurate when accurate programs and data are entered and processed. A popular expression among computer professionals is **garbage in, garbage out (GIGO)**, which means that if inaccurate programs and/or data are entered into a computer for processing, the resulting output will also be inaccurate. It is the user's responsibility to make certain that programs and data are entered correctly.

Computers, such as those found on communication satellites, can process information with speed and accuracy.

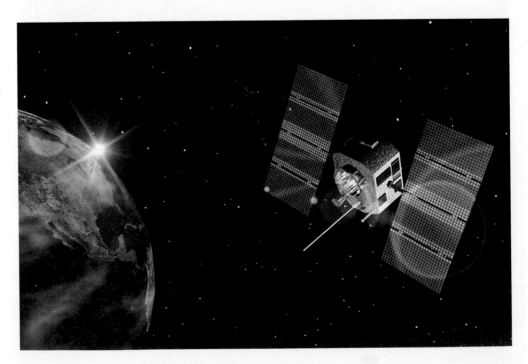

CHAPTER 1 Our Digital World

Versatility

Computers are perhaps the most versatile of all machines or devices. They can perform a variety of personal, business, and scientific applications. Families use computers for entertainment, communications, budgeting, online shopping, completing homework assignments, playing games, and listening to music. Banks conduct money transfers and account withdrawals via computer. Retailers use computers to process sales transactions and to check on the availability of products. Manufacturers can manage their entire production, warehousing, and selling processes with computerized systems. Schools access computers for keeping records, conducting distance-learning classes, scheduling events, and analyzing budgets. Universities, government agencies, hospitals, and scientific organizations conduct life-enhancing research using computers. Perhaps the most ambitious computer-based scientific research of all time is the Human Genome Project, which was completed in April 2003, more than two years ahead of schedule and at a cost considerably lower than originally forecast. This project represented an international effort to sequence the 3 billion DNA (deoxyribonucleic acid) letters in the human genome, which is the collection of gene types that comprises every person. Scientists from all over the world can now access the genome database and use the information to research ways to improve human health and fight disease.

Members of a family may use computers for a varity of purposes, including entertainment, communications, budgeting, online shopping, paying bills, completing homework assignments, viewing and printing photos, playing games, and listening to music.

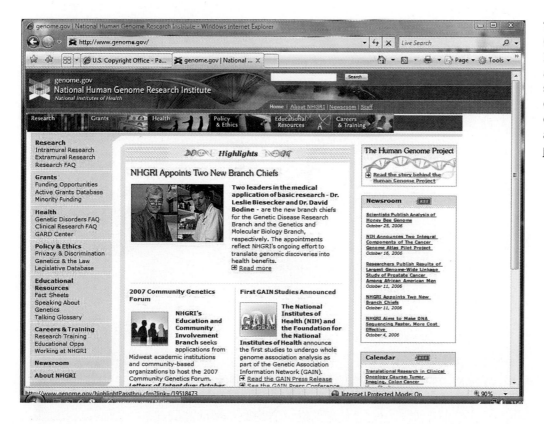

The National Human Genome Research Institute funds genetic and genomic research, studies the related ethics, and provides education to the public and to health professionals.

A flash drive can hold a large amount of data in a very small amount of physical space. Flash drives are portable, allowing users to easily move information from one computer to another.

Storage

Storage is a defining computer characteristic and is one of the features that revolutionized early computing, for it made computers incredibly flexible. A computer is capable of accepting and storing programs and data. Once a program is stored in the computer, users can access it again and again to process different data. For example, a user repeatedly can access a spreadsheet program such as Microsoft Excel to track budget expenditures and to project possible outcomes if income and expenses change. Computers can store huge amounts of data in comparably tiny physical spaces. For example, one compact disc can store about 109,000 pages of magazine text, and the capacities of internal storage devices are many times larger.

Communications

Most modern computers contain special equipment and programs that allow them to communicate with other computers through telephone lines, cable connections, and satellites. Computers having this capability are often linked together so users can share programs, data, information, and equipment such as a printer. The structure in which computers are linked together using special programs and equipment is called a **network**, as shown in Figure 1-2. Newer communications technologies allow users to exchange information over wireless networks using wireless devices such as personal digital assistants (PDAs), notebook computers, cell phones, and pagers.

A network can be relatively small or quite large. A **local area network (LAN)** is one confined to a relatively small geographical area, such as a building, factory, or

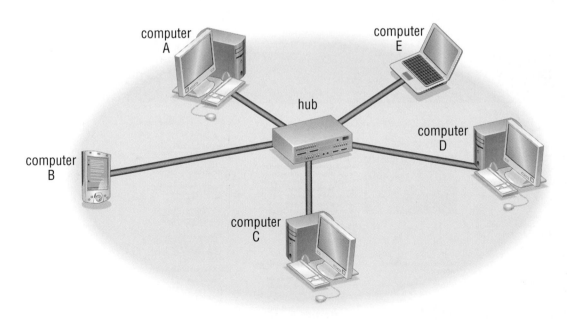

Figure 1-2 A Network

This type of network, called a star network, is a collection of computers and devices linked together by software and communications devices and media.

college campus. A **wide area network (WAN)** links many LANs and might connect a company's manufacturing plants dispersed throughout the United States. Constant, quick connections along with other computer technologies have helped boost productivity for manufacturers such as Timken Company, an industrial bearing maker headquartered in Canton, Ohio. All of its tooling machines are networked, and the factory itself is networked to 76 other company locations in the United States and worldwide. Using digital designs and networked machines, the company can produce a customized bearing product in 15 to 30 minutes, which took half a day using older methods.

The Internet: A Super Network   The network you are most likely familiar with is the Internet, which is the world's largest network. The **Internet**, also called the Net, is a worldwide network made up of large and small networks linked together via communications hardware, software, telephone, cable, and satellite systems for the purpose of communicating and sharing information (see Figure 1-3).

In 2005, research firms reported that an exciting milestone was achieved: One billion people around the world were using the Internet for various purposes, including:

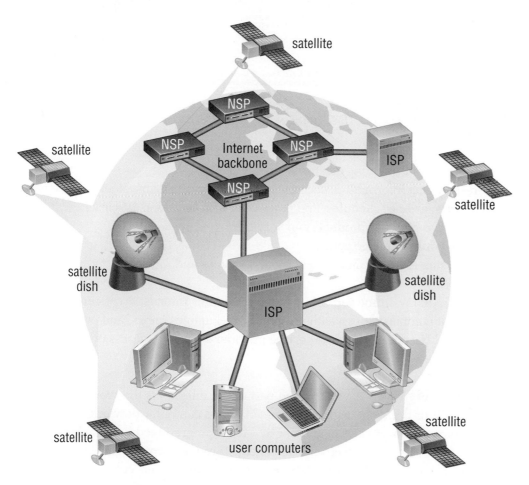

Figure 1-3 The Internet
The Internet is a worldwide network of large and small networks linked together via communications hardware, software, and media for the purpose of communicating and sharing information.

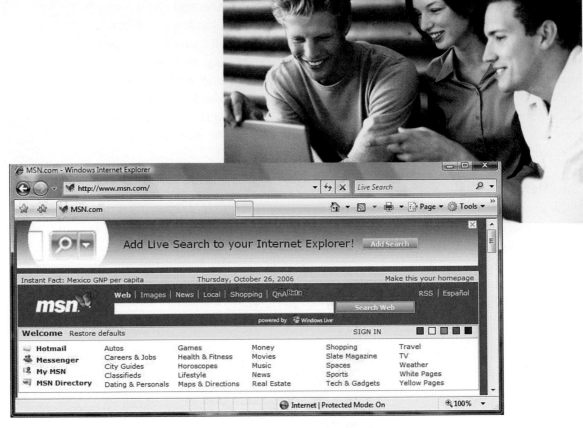

An online service such as MSN provides users with Internet access, daily weather reports, stock quotes, and other types of information.

- sending and receiving electronic mail (e-mail)
- researching information, such as weather forecasts, maps, stock quotes, news reports, airline schedules, and newspaper and magazine articles
- buying and selling products and services
- taking online college courses
- accessing entertainment, such as online games and music

There are many online service providers that offer Internet access and provide a portal that contains daily weather reports, stock quotes, news, and other types of information. Users can leave the service provider's portal to access other Web sites of interest.

The World Wide Web A widely used part of the Internet is the **World Wide Web** (**WWW** or the **Web**), a global system of linked computer networks that allows users to move from one site to another by way of programmed links on Web pages. A **Web page** is an electronic document stored on a computer running the Web site. The document may contain text, images, sound, and video, and it may also contain links to other Web pages and other Web sites. Web visitors find information using a **search engine**, which is a software program that locates and retrieves requested information. For example, suppose you entered the topic of "feeding habits of brown bears" into the program's search box. Within moments, the search engine would display a list of information sources on the Web.

A search engine such as Google is a software program that enables a user to search for, locate, and retrieve information available on the World Wide Web.

All network and Internet activities begin with individual computers, and it is at the computer level where the information that drives our economy originates. Understanding the broad steps in the processing of information is key to recognizing the significance of computer technology.

How Computers Work

Computers are designed to accept data a user enters, process the data according to program instructions, and then output the processed data in a useful form—as information. Note that data and information are not the same thing. Information is a product of a recurring series of events called the information processing cycle.

Data and Information

Data is raw, unorganized facts and figures. By itself, a piece of data may be meaningless. For example, the fact that an employee has worked 40 hours in one week may be useless to the payroll department staff. However, by entering additional data, such as the employee's pay rate, number of exemptions and deductions, and then processing the data, department personnel can generate useful information, including paychecks, earnings statements, and payroll reports. Therefore, **information** is defined as data that has been processed (manipulated, organized, or arranged) in a way that converts it into a useful form. Once created, information can be displayed on a computer screen or printed on paper. It can also be stored for future use, such as for processing periodic payroll reports.

Data entered into a computer can be one type or a combination of two or more of the following types, illustrated in Figure 1-4:

- **Text data** consists of alphabetic letters, numbers, and special characters. These data are typically entered to produce output such as letters, e-mail messages, and reports.
- **Graphic data** consists of still images, including photographs, mathematical charts, and drawings.
- **Audio data** refers to sound, such as voice and music. For example, using a microphone a person can enter a voice message that the computer stores in digitized form. Or, a user can download music from a Web site and listen to the songs over speakers connected to the computer.
- **Video data** refers to moving pictures and images, such as a videoconference, film clip, or full-length movie. For example, a user may record a home movie using a digital video camera. The user then connects the camera to a computer, which plays the video and displays it on the computer screen.

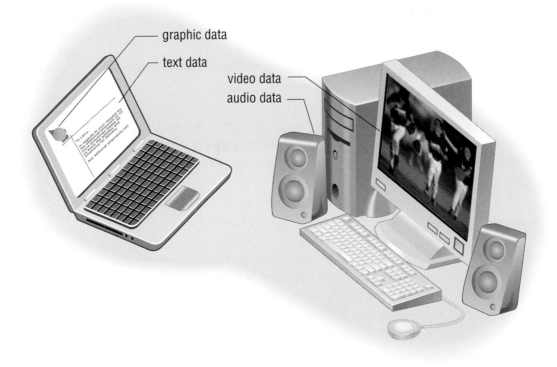

Figure 1-4 Types of Data Combined to Provide Information
Combining types of data can improve the level of presentation quality of a message. Text data and graphic data are combined to create a professional business letter (left). Audio data and video data are combined to create a movie (right).

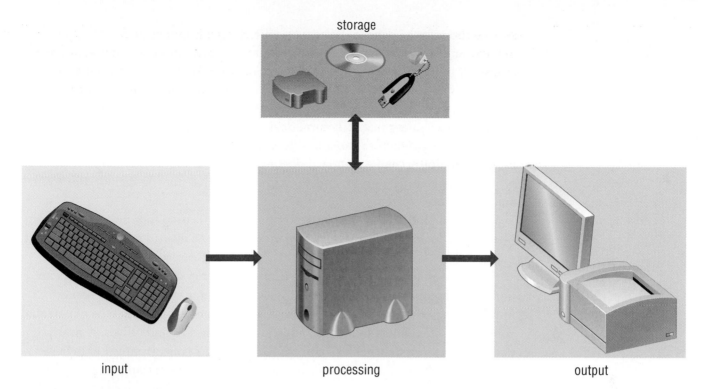

storage

input   processing   output

Figure 1-5 Information Processing Cycle
During the information processing cycle, data is entered into a computer, processed, sent as output, and stored (if required for future use).

The Information Processing Cycle

Using a computer to convert data into useful information is referred to as **information processing** (also called data processing). Processing data into information involves four basic functions: input, processing, output, and storage. During processing, these four functions are often performed sequentially, but not always. The steps of input, processing, output, and storage are collectively known as the **information processing cycle**, which is illustrated in Figure 1-5.

Data entered into a computer is called **input**, which also is the name of the first step in the information processing cycle. Once entered through an input device such as a keyboard or mouse, the data is manipulated, or processed, according to the programmed instructions. **Processing** occurs in a computer's electrical circuits. This results in the creation of information called **output**. Output is then sent to one or more output devices, such as a monitor or a printer. Usually, it is also sent to **storage** media such as a hard drive, compact disc, or flash drive for future use. Information a computer processes can be output in a variety of forms:

- written, or textual form, as in research reports and letters
- numerical form, as in a spreadsheet analysis of a company's finances
- verbal or audio form, as in recorded voice and music
- visual form, such as photos, drawings, and videos

Computers and Computer Systems

Technically, the term *computer* identifies only the **system unit**, the part of a computer system that processes data and stores the information. A **computer**

system, however, includes the system unit along with input devices, output devices, and storage devices. The number and kinds of devices included are a matter of individual need or preference. For example, a buyer shopping for a new personal computer would expect to purchase an entire system, including the system unit, keyboard, mouse, monitor, storage devices, and perhaps a printer. An engineer in a structural design firm might need a more powerful system unit capable of running building design software, along with a larger monitor, a plotter, and a standard document printer. Figure 1-6 shows a variety of input, processing, output, and storage devices that may be included in a personal computer system.

In the remainder of this book, the term *computer* is used to refer to a computer system that includes all necessary devices that allow a user to input programs and data, process the data, output the results, and store the results for future use.

Some computer systems are single-user computer systems whereas others are multi-user computer systems. A **single-user computer system**, as the name implies, can accommodate a single (one) user at a time. This is the type of personal computer system found in homes and in small businesses and offices. A **multi-user computer system** can accommodate many users concurrently. Large businesses typically use these systems to enable several managers and employees to simultaneously access, use, and update information stored in a centrally located system. For example, using computers at their respective workstations, a payroll clerk can access and view an employee's payroll record while a shipping clerk is tracking a customer's shipment. In addition, the users can interact with each other

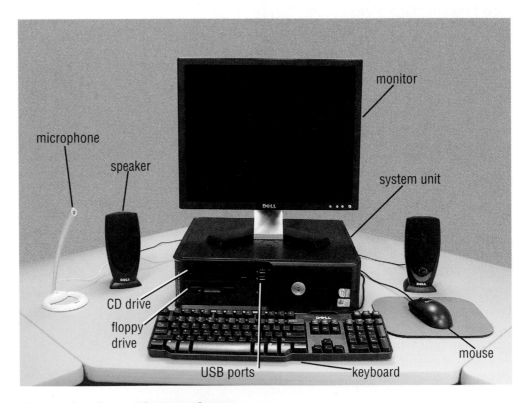

Figure 1-6 A Personal Computer System

At a minimum, a computer system consists of more than just the system unit. It also includes a monitor, keyboard, mouse, a hard disk drive, videoprocessor, CPU, motherboard, and power supply. Users can add a variety of other input, output, and storage devices.

Pick up the Phone

THE YEAR 2000 MARKED THE BEGINNING of the new millennium, a good time to set up resolutions for the future. In that spirit, the United Nations established lofty goals to improve the lives of people around the globe: to diminish poverty and hunger, reduce infant mortality, increase gender equality, fight disease, and establish universal primary education.

Thanks to tremendous innovations in science and communication, solutions seem to be close at hand. The difficulty remains in getting the technology that could be a lifeline to those who need it the most. It may be hard to believe, but one in six people worldwide still do not even have access to a telephone. That means 800,000 villages—1 billion people—are without any type of connection to the outside world.

The gap between developing countries who are being empowered by access to a global network of knowledge and those that are still virtually in the dark is widening. Getting even the remotest village connected will be essential to meeting the United Nations' Millennium Goals.

As the Secretary-General Kofi Annan stated, "...we are truly the first generation with the tools, the knowledge and the resources to meet the committment ... to making the right to development a reality for everyone and to freeing the entire human race from want."

Source: Sandrasagra, Mithre J. "Development: Digital Divide Becoming a Vast Chasm," *Inter Press Service News Agency*, September 14, 2005. December 2006 <http://ipsnews.net/news.asp?Idnews=30263>.

---

easily and quickly. The main focus of this book is on general-purpose, single-user computers—personal computers—that enable users to complete a variety of computing tasks. These are the computers you will most likely work with in your home, in your school's computer lab, and on the job.

Components of a Computer System

A computer system consists of two broad categories of components: hardware and software. The combination of hardware and software that makes up a particular system depends on the user's requirements, and given the number of hardware devices and software programs available in the marketplace, users can configure all kinds of possible setups. Manufacturers typically offer a system unit, monitor, and keyboard package, leaving the choice of mouse, printer, and other hardware devices up to the buyer. PC system units are usually preloaded with the Microsoft Windows operating system software plus some basic programs such as a word processing program.

Computer Hardware: An Overview

Hardware includes all of the physical components that make up the system unit plus the other devices connected to it, such as a keyboard or monitor. These connected devices are referred to as **peripheral devices** because they are outside, or peripheral to, the computer. Examples include a keyboard, mouse, camera, and

Go to this title's Internet Resource Center and read the article titled "Major Advances in the History of Computing." www.emcp.net/CUT3e

printer. Some peripheral devices, such as a monitor and hard disk drive, are essential components of a personal computer system. Hardware devices are grouped into the following categories:

- system unit
- input devices
- output devices
- storage devices
- communications devices

The System Unit   The system unit is a relatively small plastic or metal cabinet housing the electronic components that process data into information. Inside the cabinet is the main circuit board, called the **motherboard**, which provides for the installation and connection of other electronic components (see Figure 1-7). Once installed on the motherboard, the components can communicate with each other, thereby allowing data to be processed into information.

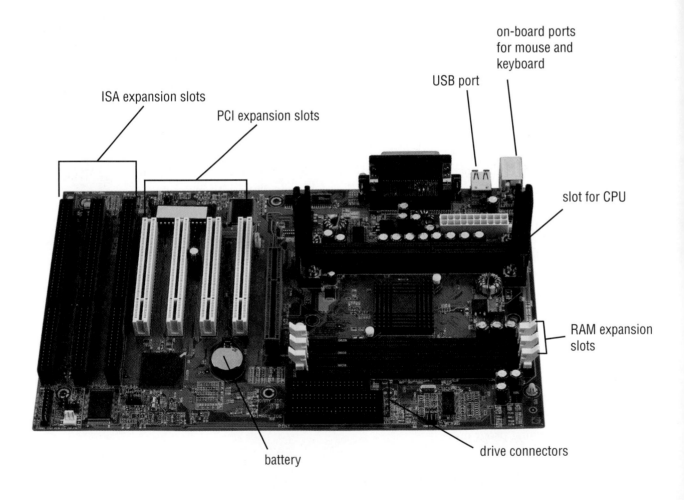

Figure 1-7 Parts of a Motherboard
This empty motherboard is ready for the chips and cards to be placed in the open slots.

The microphone, keyboard, and mouse are common types of input devices.

The main components of the motherboard are the **central processing unit (CPU)**, also called the microprocessor (or simply processor), and internal memory. The CPU processor consists of one or more electronic chips that read, interpret, and execute the instructions that operate the computer and perform specific computing tasks. When a program is executed, the processor temporarily stores the program's instructions and the data the instructions need into the computer's memory. **Main memory**, also called primary storage or random access memory (RAM), consists of small electronic chips that provide temporary storage for instructions and data during processing.

Go to this title's Internet Resource Center and read the article titled "Enterprise Computing Trends." www.emcp.net/CUT3e

Input Devices   An **input device** is a hardware device that allows users to enter program instructions, data, and commands into a computer. The program or application being used determines the type of input device needed. Common input devices are the keyboard, mouse, and microphone.

Output Devices   An **output device** is a device that makes information available to the user. Popular output devices include display screens (monitors), printers, television screens, and speakers. Some output devices, such as a printer, produce output in **hard copy** (tangible) form, such as on paper or plastic. Other output devices, such as a monitor, produce output in **soft copy** (intangible) form that can be viewed, but not physically handled.

Monitors and printers are the most common output devices for personal computers.

Most new personal computers contain a combination CD/DVD drive that can read a variety of CD and DVD formats.

Storage Devices   Unlike memory that stores instructions and data temporarily during processing, a **storage device**, often called storage medium or secondary storage, provides for the permanent storage of programs, data, and information. Once stored, information can be retrieved, modified, displayed, imported, exported, copied, or printed.

A storage device itself records programs, data, and/or information to a storage medium and retrieves them from the storage medium. For example, a CD drive (storage device) would write data to a CD (storage medium), and the CD drive would retrieve data from the CD later.

Communications Devices   A **communications device** makes it possible for a user to communicate with another computer and to exchange instructions, data, and information with other computer users. The most popular communications device is a **modem**, an electronic device capable of converting computer-readable information into a form that can be transmitted and received over communications systems, such as standard telephone lines. Due to increased speeds, broadband Internet access (via cable and DSL) has been replacing dial-up acess over the past few years. The Pew Internet and American Life Project reported that as of March 2006, only 22 percent of adults in the U.S. had a dial-up connection, while 42 percent had a broadband connection.

Computer Software: An Overview

Software consists of programs containing instructions that direct the operation of the computer system and programs that enable users to perform specific applications, such as word processing. The three main classifications of software are system software, application software, and communications software.

System Software   **System software** tells the computer how to function and is divided into two categories: operating system software and utility software. The **operating system** is the most important piece of software in a computer system. It contains instructions for starting the computer and coordinates the activities of all hardware devices. Most personal computers use one of the Microsoft Windows operating systems, while Apple Macintosh computers use either the Macintosh operating system or Microsoft Windows.

Utility software consists of programs that perform administrative tasks, such as checking the computer's components to determine whether each is working properly, managing disk drives and printers, and checking for computer viruses.

Macintosh OS X is the most common operating system for the Macintosh platform.

Application Software   **Application software** consists of programs that perform specific tasks, such as word processing, spreadsheet preparation, database searching, and slide show presentation. Thousands of commercially prepared application programs are currently available for managing personal and business activities.

Communications Software   **Communications software** makes it possible for a computer to transmit and receive information to and from other computers. To communicate over the Internet, a user needs an account with an **Internet service provider (ISP)**, a company that has a permanent connection to the Internet and

Windows Vista is a popular operating system that can be used on the PC platform.

INVENTOR OF THE FIRST COMPUTER
Konard Zuse

MANY SCHOLARLY SOURCES CREDIT Howard Aiken and his team of researchers for building the first computer in 1944. American researchers such as Aiken would find out only after World War II ended that a German engineer had finished building a computer almost three years ahead of them. What took a *team* of researchers in the United States to accomplish was finished three years earlier by one man named Konrad Zuse. Most researchers were unaware of his achievements for many years due to the poor communication between Germany and the rest of world. This confused the issue of where and by whom the first computer was actually built. Now most scholars agree that Zuse's Z3 was the first reliable, freely programmable computer based on binary floating-point number and switching systems. Essentially, the world's first computer!

Zuse was born June 22, 1910, in Berlin, Germany, and graduated with a degree in civil engineering from the Technical University of Berlin in 1935. His distaste of the routine, but complex, calculations he encountered as an engineering student led him to dream of a machine capable of automatic calculation.

In 1938 he quit his job with the Henschel aircraft factory and moved in with his parents so he could work full time on creating his dream machine. In their living room he first built the Z1, a prototype for the Z3. The Z1 was a binary, electrically driven mechanical calculator that used thin metal sheets instead of relays. The method of storing data on metal sheets was entirely novel and considerably cheaper than relays. The only electrical unit was a small engine used to provide 1 Hertz.

From the beginning, Zuse believed that computers should be freely programmable. He also realized they should work in a binary number system. This would allow binary switching elements to run the whole computer. This semilogarithmic mechanism allowed the machine to compute very small and large numbers with precision. He also developed a punch tape memory to accompany these systems. These tools were all used in the Z1, leading to a very sophisticated machine. The Z3 used generally the same architecture as the Z1, but instead of punch-tape-controlled memory it used electronic relays, which are much more reliable.

The Z3 utilized the binary number system and could perform floating-point arithmetic at a time when the rest of the world was still speculating about it being theoretically possible. He also started a company in 1941 called Zuse-Ingenierbüro Hopferau and created the Z4, the first commercially sold computer, beating the commercial Harvard Mark I to market by five months. The Z4 was a fully functional, automatic, digital computer.

In 1986, Zuse decided to rebuild the Z1. He was 77 when he started, and the project ran from 1987 to 1989. The first Z1 was financed by Zuse, his family, and his friends. The reconstruction project required about 800,000 Deutsche Marks; a group of companies interested in the project financed it. The replica is now on display in the Museum for Transport and Technology in Berlin, Germany. Zuse died December 18, 1995, but left behind a world reshaped by his innovations.

Source: Zuse, Horst. "The Life and Work of Konrad Zuse," *EP Online.* December 2006 <http://www.epemag.com>.

provides temporary access to individuals and others, usually for a fee. Some ISPs provide communication software that is installed on a subscriber's computer to enable the user to send and receive electronic mail messages to other similarly equipped computers. The software also provides access to the massive storehouse of information on the Internet and the World Wide Web. Other ISPs allow subscribers to simply use standard e-mail software and a **Web browser**, a special program for viewing Web pages, to accomplish the same functions.

Categories of Computers

Rapid advances in computer technology often blur the differences among types of computers, and industry professionals may disagree on how computers should be categorized. Typically, they use criteria based on differences in usage, size, speed, processing capabilities, and price, resulting in the categories named in Table 1-1:

- personal computers
- handheld computers
- workstations
- midrange servers
- mainframe computers
- supercomputers

Note, however, that personal computers and midrange servers both may be used for the same purpose in networking and that the processing capabilities

Go to this title's Internet Resource Center and read the article titled "Enterprise vs. Personal Computing." www.emcp.net/CUT3e

Table 1-1   Categories of Computers

Category	Size	Instructions Executed per Second	Number of Accommodated Users	Approximate Price Range
personal computer	fits on a desk, in a briefcase, on a laptop, or is worn	600 million to about 3 billion, or more	a single user, or a part of a network	a few hundred to thousands of dollars
handheld computer	fits in hand(s); some may be carried in a pocket	depending on device, a few hundred	a single user, or a part of a network	depending on the model, $99 to several hundred dollars
workstation	similar to a desktop PC, but larger and more powerful	depending on the type, 3 to 5 billion	a single user, or a part of a network	a few thousand up to several thousands of dollars
midrange server	fits into a large cabinet or a small room	billions of instructions	hundreds of users concurrently	$5,000 to hundreds of thousands of dollars
large server or mainframe computer	with needed equipment, occupies a partial or full room	billions of instructions	hundreds or thousands of users concurrently	several thousands up to millions of dollars
supercomputer	with equipment, occupies a full room	trillions of instructions	thousands of users concurrently	several million dollars

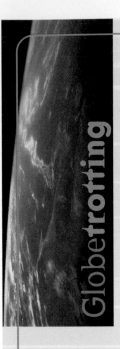

among the different groups may overlap. Handheld computers are given their own category, although technically they are a subset of personal computers. Their growing market and importance for business and home users warrants treating them as a separate category.

Personal Computers

A **personal computer (PC)** is a self-contained computer capable of input, processing, output, and storage. A personal computer must have at least one input device, one storage device, one output device, a processor, and memory. The processor, or microprocessor, is contained on a single chip. Recall that the chip is a thin piece of silicon containing electrical circuitry. About the size of a postage stamp, the processor chip serves as the computer's central processing unit (CPU), performing calculations and processing data. Think of the CPU as the "brain" of the computer. The three major groups of PCs are desktop computers, portable computers, and handheld computers.

Desktop Computers   A **desktop computer** is a PC designed to allow the system unit, input devices, output devices, and other connected devices to fit on top of, beside, or under a user's desk or a table. This type of computer may be used in the home, a home office, a library, or a corporate setting. Desktop computers are typi-

Go to this title's Internet Resource Center and read the article titled "Continuing Evolution of Personal Computing Technology." www.emcp.net/CUT3e

A desktop computer, as the name suggests, is designed to fit on top of a user's work area. Users can place tower-type system units on the floor.

cally connected to a network (or an Internet connection) with cables. Wires or cables also connect keyboards, monitors, speakers, printers, and other peripheral devices to the system unit.

Although wires and cables are likely to be a feature of the computer world for some time to come, newer computing technologies that communicate wirelessly, without physical connections, increasingly are replacing them. The mobility of today's workforce and the need for Internet access anytime, anywhere have driven the demand for portable computers.

Portable Computers A **portable computer** is a personal computer that is small enough to be moved around easily. As its name suggests, a **laptop computer** can fit comfortably on the lap. As laptop computers have decreased in size, this type of computer is now more commonly referred to as a **notebook computer**.

Manufacturers recently began introducing a new type of notebook computer called the **tablet PC**. A tablet PC has a liquid crystal display (LCD) screen on which the user can write using a special-purpose pen, or **stylus**. The handwriting is digitized, and the tablet PC can convert it to standard text or it can remain as handwritten text. Tablet PCs also typically have a keyboard and/or a mouse. Tablet PCs rely on **digital ink technology**, where a digitizer (a grid of

A notebook computer is a portable computer designed for mobile users, people who frequently move about in their work.

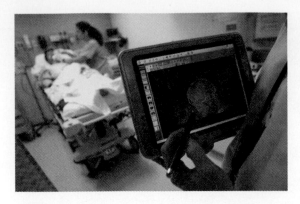

A tablet PC is a type of notebook computer that has a liquid crystal display (LCD) screen on which the user can write using a special-purpose pen, or stylus.

tiny wires) is laid under or over an LCD screen to create a magnetic field that can capture the movement of the special-purpose pen and record the movement on the LCD screen. The effect is like writing on paper with liquid ink. Once captured, the digitized information can be entered into a computer for processing. In the past, tablet PCs use a special operating system designed for tablet PC technology, such as Microsoft Windows Vista includes tablet PC functionality.

Another type of portable computer, the **wearable computer**, is in its early stages. As the name implies, a wearable computer is worn somewhere on the body, thereby providing a user with access to mobile computing capabilities and information via the Internet. Futurists predict that wearable computers may be incorporated into clothing items such as the Java Jacket invented in 2000 by Doug Sutherland, a staff engineer at Sun Microsystems. His jacket computer lets him monitor his e-mail, adjust the water temperature in his aquarium, and operate the lights at his home. A six-button keypad is embedded in the cuff.

A wearable computer, such as this portable eyewear viewer, allows for hands-free computing capability.

CHAPTER 1 Our Digital World

The Computer Weight-loss Diet

IF RUNNING ACROSS AIRPORTS with that heavy laptop is getting you down, you may want to switch to computer-lite. More and more travelers are replacing that cumbersome computer bag with a combination of cell phone, handheld device, and foldable keyboard.

The OQO-01, for example, is a full-featured PC that runs Windows. Weighing in at only 14 ounces, it is barely bigger than a pack of index cards. The latest palmtops are designed to handle software for Web surfing, e-mailing, or working with Word, Excel, or PowerPoint files, although the small screens may have you squinting. With wireless technology, a mouse, keyboard, headphone, digital camera, or even a GPS system can be added.

To cut back even more, replace the foldable keyboard with the Bluetooth Laser Virtual model. At a mere 3 ounces, it outlines a keyboard on a surface with a ruby laser and monitors finger movement with a motion detector.

Of course, laptops themselves keep shrinking in size and weight. Panasonic's R5 tips the scale at just 2.2 pounds. But the beauty of using wireless parts to form the whole is that you can tote with you only the pieces you need for a trip. The downside: Each piece needs its own charger, so be ready to untangle all those cords in your suitcase when you reach your hotel room.

Source: Wayner, Peter. "Laptop Getting Heavier? Assemble Your Own—Much Lighter—Device," *The New York Times*, June 6, 2006.

Handheld Computers Even smaller personal computers can fit into the hand. This type of computer is known as a **handheld computer**, also called a handheld, pocket PC, or palmtop. The display and keyboard of this type of computer is quite small due to space limitations. Some handheld computers contain chips in which both programs and data are stored, eliminating the need for disk drives.

Handheld computers are popular with business travelers. Once back in the office, a user can connect a handheld computer to a larger computer for exchanging information. In recent years a type of handheld computer called a **personal digital assistant (PDA)** has become widely used. With a PDA, a user can perform calculations, keep track of schedules, make appointments, and write memos. Some PDAs use wireless transmitting technology (in the form of radio waves), which allows Internet access from almost any location.

A handheld computer is small enough to fit in the palm of a user's hand.

Fly-by-Wireless Technology

ENGINEERS IN PORTUGAL have successfully carried out test flights of the AIVA, an aircraft that, when complete, will rely entirely on a wireless network to connect its engines, navigation system, and onboard computers. The unmanned, nine-foot-long prototype uses Bluetooth technology to send messages between its critical systems. Older aircraft use mechanical links and cables to connect components, but the "fly-by-wireless" approach will allow planes to use less power and be lighter in weight.

Number one for the engineers is to make the wireless aircraft safe from electromagnetic interference or jamming caused by chance or by terrorist design. The world will probably see wireless used for brakes and steering in cars long before it is fine-tuned enough to meet the high standards of aviation regulations and nervous fliers.

Source: Graham-Rowe, Duncan. "'Fly-by-Wireless' Plane Takes to the Air," *New Scientist*, May 16, 2006. December 2006 <http://www.newscientist.com/channel/tech/dn9176.html>.

A variety of Internet-enabled devices allows users to access the Internet, send and receive e-mail messages, and browse the World Wide Web.

Because of their small keyboards and displays, many PDAs require a pen or stylus for data entry and are known as **pen computers**. Like the tablet PC, a pen computer uses a special kind of software that recognizes human handwriting. Utility meter readers, package delivery persons, and other workers who need to continually move about on their jobs use pen computers to process and store data on the spot.

Some handheld computers are Internet-enabled, meaning they can access the Internet without wire connections. For example, a **smartphone** is a cell phone that connects to the Internet to allow users to transmit and receive e-mail messages, send text messages and pictures, and browse through Web sites on the phone display screen. Some PDAs with similar Internet capabilities also have built-in phone capabilities. The similar capabilities of multifunction PDAs and smartphones illustrate the convergence that is occurring as different types of devices take advantage of Internet technology.

Workstations

Workstations resemble desktop personal computers but provide users with more processing power and greater capability. A **workstation** is a high-performance single-user computer with advanced input, output, and storage components that can be networked with other workstations and larger computers.

A workstation is a high-performance, single-user computer with advanced input, output, and storage components that can be networked with other workstations and larger computers.

Workstations are typically used for complex applications that require considerable computing power and high-quality graphics resolution, such as computer-aided design (CAD), computer-assisted manufacturing (CAM), desktop publishing, and software development. Workstations generally come with large high-resolution graphics displays, built-in network capability, and a high-density storage device. Like personal computers, workstations can serve as single-user computers. However, they are typically linked to a network and have access to larger computers, often midrange servers or mainframes.

Midrange Servers

Linked computers are typically connected to a larger and more powerful computer called a **network server**, sometimes referred to as the host computer. Although the size and capacity of network servers vary considerably, most are midrange rather than large mainframe computers (discussed later). Sun Microsystems, Inc., and Hewlett-Packard Corporation are leading manufacturers of servers.

A **midrange server**, formerly known as a minicomputer, is a powerful computer capable of accommodating hundreds of client computers or terminals (users) at the same time. Users can access a server through a terminal or a personal computer. A **terminal** consists of only a monitor and keyboard, with no processing capability of its own. Because it has no processing power and must rely on the processing power of another computer, terminals are often referred to as dumb terminals. Midrange servers are widely used in networks to provide users with computing capability and other resources available through the network, such as Internet access, software, data, printers, scanners, and other peripherals.

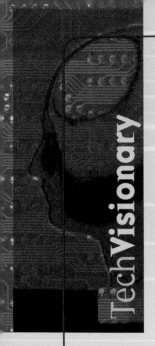

COFOUNDERS OF HEWLETT-PACKARD CORPORATION

William Hewlett and David Packard

FEW INDIVIDUALS, IF ANY, have had a greater impact on the computer industry than William Hewlett and David Packard. The business they founded together in Hewlett's garage in 1939 spawned the California high-tech corridor that became known as Silicon Valley. The business was the Hewlett-Packard Corporation, which designs and builds a variety of state-of-the-art computer products, perhaps the best-known being computers and printers. Today, a visitor to almost any computer store will quickly spot Hewlett-Packard products ranging from electronic calculators to Web servers and systems. The "Hewlett" name appears first in the corporate name and on HP products as the result of a coin toss when the two men formed their original partnership.

Hewlett was born May 20, 1913, in Ann Arbor, Michigan. Packard was born September 7, 1912, in Pueblo, Colorado. Both attended Stanford University and were awarded bachelor of arts degrees in 1934. Packard stayed at Stanford to earn a master's degree in electrical engineering, while Hewlett received his master's in electrical engineering at the Massachusetts Institute of Technology.

HP's first product was a resistance-capacitance audio oscillator based on a design developed by Hewlett when he was a graduate student. This first product was sold to Walt Disney, who used eight of them in the production of *Fantasia*. The company's first "plant" was a small garage in Palo Alto, California, with an initial capital investment of $538.

Through the years, both Hewlett and Packard held various corporate offices and government positions and also served as trustees on corporate and college boards. Each received numerous awards both in this country and abroad. In 1993, Packard retired as chairman of the board at Hewlett-Packard Corporation at which time he was named Chairman Emeritus, a title he held until his death in 1996. Hewlett served as company president and vice-chairman of the board and was named Director Emeritus in 1987. He died in July 2000 at the age of 87.

Both men leave behind a remarkable legacy of technological innovation and business strategy. Together they built a company known worldwide for innovation and for computer products that, through the years, have been models widely envied among computer engineers.

Source: The Biography Channel.

William Hewlett (left) and David Packard

A midrange server is a powerful computer that can accommodate (serve) multiple users in a network. Midrange servers come in a variety of shapes and sizes, but even the smallest ones are several times more powerful than a personal computer.

Mainframe Computers

In a small business environment, a personal computer can be used as a server. Large businesses needing more powerful servers may use mainframe computers. Larger, more powerful, and more expensive than midrange servers, a **mainframe computer** is capable of accommodating hundreds of network users performing different computing tasks. A mainframe's internal storage can handle hundreds of millions of characters. Mainframe applications are often large and complex. These computers are useful for dealing with large, everchanging collections of data that can be accessed by many users simultaneously. Like midrange servers, a mainframe computer can also function as a

A mainframe computer is a large, powerful, and expensive computer system that can accommodate multiple users at the same time. Mainframes and midrange servers are differentiated by their processing capabilities.

network server. Government agencies, banks, universities, and insurance companies use mainframes to handle millions of transactions each day.

Supercomputers

Supercomputers are the Goliaths of the computer industry. A **supercomputer** is the fastest, most powerful, and most expensive of all computers. Many are capable of performing trillions of calculations in a single second. Performing the same number of calculations on a handheld calculator would take a person two million years.

Supercomputer designers achieve stunning calculation speeds by joining hundreds of separate microprocessors. Many of the machines provide enough disk storage capacity for hundreds of terabytes of data (1 **terabyte** is the equivalent of 1 trillion alphabet letters, numbers, or special characters). In a move to expand supercomputing into the realm of the unimaginable, IBM continues developing the BlueGene supercomputers. BlueGene/L, currently the fastest computer in the world, processes 280.6 trillion calculations per second, a measure of speed called a **teraflop**. BlueGene/P is scheduled for completion in 2008, performing 1 quadrillion calculations per second, a measure of speed called a **petaflop**. The next system, BlueGene/Q, is targeted for speeds of 3 petaflops. Primary applications include weather forecasting, comparing DNA sequences, creating artificially intelligent robots, and performing financial analyses.

Supercomputers are the world's fastest, most powerful, and most expensive computers, capable of processing huge amounts of data quickly and accommodating thousands of users at the same time. IBM's BlueGene supercomputer was completed in 2005 and is at the top of the TOP500 supercomputer list.

OnThe**Horizon**

COMPUTERS, NETWORKS, THE INTERNET, AND THE WEB are unquestionably among the most important technological developments in history. Cell phones, wireless personal digital assistants, and the use of the Internet for communications are becoming commonplace. But what about the future? Where is computing technology heading? Social thinkers, futurists, and computer experts may not agree on specific predictions, but their thoughts tend to converge in the area of technology trends we can expect to occur in the first decade of the twenty-first century.

Embedded Computers Everywhere

The rapid increase in embedded computers in all areas of personal and work life will continue. Consumers will be able to scan foods and other types of products embedded with special chips to get information on product content, age, and freshness. Before long, every citizen will probably carry a small plastic card housing a tiny microchip that contains complete medical, credit, military, and driving records. Many more "smart highways" embedded with millions of tiny sensors will alleviate driving worries because they will guide cars speeding along at 120 mph, all the time aware of surrounding traffic.

Futurists predict that before long, people will carry a "personal history" card embedded with a microchip that contains one's medical, credit, military, and driving records.

On-Demand Computing

Some computer industry leaders, including strategists at IBM and American Express, contend that information technology is maturing and entering a phase in which corporations will buy computing resources the way they purchase utilities—paying only for as much as they use. No doubt the downturn in IT spending in the early 2000s helped pave the way for this buy-as-you-go approach, but the ready availability of computing resources over the Internet has also played a role. Called "on-demand computing," the trend means reduced fixed costs and greater flexibility for businesses.

Convergence

Convergence is the combining of separate technologies into a single package, resulting in a product featuring all the benefits of the individual technologies as well as additional benefits derived from the merger of the component technologies. The trend towards convergence in computer technologies is driven by companies eager to attract customers by offering products with novel features and one-stop shopping.

The Voice over Internet Protocol (VoIP) network known as Skype offers a perfect example of the trend toward convergence in computer technologies. When Skype first appeared it offered computer-to-computer telephony using a peer-to-peer networking arrangement. Since its debut, Skype has rapidly incorporated different technologies in order to offer its users a number of additional features, including video calls and conferencing, group chats, SMS, call forwarding, and the ability to call ordinary telephones. Convergence has allowed Skype to continue to attract customers and maintain its status as the leading VoIP network. You can expect to see similar examples in the coming years as companies pursue convergence to produce more feature-laden products.

Faster Communication and a Shrinking Global Community

Within the present decade, almost-instant Internet connections will become the norm throughout the United States and worldwide, allowing information to be accessed in fractions of a second. Broadband penetration to U.S. households was predicted to exceed 80% by 2007, with the rate of growth increasing rapidly. This rapid growth in not limited to the U.S.—China's broadband connectivity growth rate is now twice that of the U.S.

Faster Internet connections affect the way we use the Internet. High-speed Internet facilitates synchronous (real-time) distance eduction through the Internet, now frequently known as online learning. Within the next 10 years one expert has predicted that the number of college students taking courses online will increase from the current 7% to 25%.

High-speed Internet connections will increase the number of online shoppers as well. Experts predict that by the year 2010, the dollar amount of online shopping will represent more than 40 percent of all sales.

Eventually almost everyone in the world will have access to high-speed Internet. For the twenty-first century, it is safe to say that *virtually* anything is possible.

Chapter**Summary**

How has digital technology infiltrated your daily life?

We are living in a **digital** world in which computer technology increasingly powers the devices of daily life, including high-definition televisions (HDTVs), microwave ovens, watches, cell phones, and automobiles. Embedded chips, computers, networks, and the Internet and World Wide Web enable us to communicate globally. No digital device has exerted a greater impact on our lives than computers. A **computer** is an electronic device that operates under the control of programmed instructions stored in its memory, accepting data (input) that is manipulated (processed) according to the instructions and output as information, which may be stored for future use.

What advantages do computers offer?

Computers offer advantages in the areas of speed, accuracy, versatility, storage, and communications. As a result, they are widely used in homes, schools, the workplace, and in society for communicating, managing finances, analyzing data, planning, researching, and for hundreds of other purposes and applications. The **Internet** and the **World Wide Web**, in which networks of computers around the world are linked together, continue to play a dominant role in all areas of human activity.

How do computers convert data into useful information?

Data is raw, unorganized facts and figures. Data entered into a computer consists of one or more of the following types: **text**, **graphic**, **audio**, and **video**. **Information** is data that has been processed (manipulated, organized, or arranged) in a way that converts the data into useful forms.

Using a computer to convert data into useful information is called **information processing** (also called data processing). The **information processing cycle** involves the actions of **input**, **processing**, **output**, and **storage**.

What is the difference between a computer and a computer system?

The term *computer* identifies only the **system unit**, the part of a computer system that processes data into information. A **computer system** includes the system unit along with input, output, storage, and communications devices.

What are the primary components of a computer system?

Computer system components can be divided into two broad groups: hardware and software. **Hardware** includes all of the physical components of the computer and the **peripheral devices** connected to it. The main hardware components are the **system unit**, **input devices**, **output devices**, **storage devices**, and **communications devices**.

   Software consists of programs containing instructions that direct the operation of the computer system and programs that enable users to perform specific applications. The main types of software are **system software**, consisting of the **operating system** and **utility software**; **application software**; and **communications software**.

What are the basic categories of computers and their distinguishing characteristics?

A **personal computer** is a self-contained computer capable of input, processing, output, and storage. A **handheld computer** fits comfortably in a user's hand. A **workstation** is a high-performance single-user computer with advanced input, output, and storage components that can be networked with other workstations and larger computers. A **midrange server**, is a powerful computer capable of accommodating hundreds of client computers or terminals (users) at the same time. A **mainframe computer** is capable of accommodating hundreds of network users per-

forming different computing tasks. A **supercomputer** is the fastest, most powerful, and most expensive of all computers.

KeyTerms

Numbers indicate the pages where terms are first cited in the chapter. An alphabetized list of key terms with definitions (in English and Spanish) can be found on the Encore CD that accompanies this book. In addition, these terms and definitions are included in the end-of-book glossary.

Immersed in Digital Technology
digital, 5
chip, 5
embedded computer, 6
general-purpose computer, 6
computer, 6
program, 6

The Computer Advantage
microcomputer (personal computer or PC), 7
garbage in, garbage out (GIGO), 8
network, 10
local area network (LAN), 10
wide area network (WAN), 11
Internet, 11
World Wide Web (WWW or the Web), 12
Web page, 12
search engine, 12

How Computers Work
data, 13
information, 14
text data, 14
graphic data, 14
audio data, 14
video data, 14
information processing (data processing), 15
information processing cycle, 15
input, 15

processing, 15
output, 15
storage, 15

Computers and Computer Systems
system unit, 15
computer system, 16
single-user computer system, 16
multi-user computer system, 16

Components of a Computer System
hardware, 17
peripheral devices, 17
motherboard, 18
central processing unit (CPU, microprocessor, or processor), 19
main memory (primary storage or random access memory [RAM]), 19
input device, 19
output device, 19
hard copy, 19
soft copy, 19
storage device (storage medium or secondary storage), 20
communications device, 20
modem, 20
software, 20
system software, 20
operating system, 20
utility software, 20
application software, 21
communications software, 21
Internet service provider (ISP), 21
Web browser, 23

Categories of Computers
personal computer (PC), 24
desktop computer, 24

portable computer, 25
laptop computer, 25
notebook computer, 25
tablet PC, 25
stylus, 25
digital ink technology, 25
wearable computer, 26
handheld computer (handheld,
    pocket PC, or palmtop), 27
personal digital assistant (PDA), 27
pen computer, 28

smartphone, 28
workstation, 28
network server (host computer), 29
midrange server (minicomputer), 29
terminal (dumb terminal), 29
mainframe computer, 31
supercomputer, 32
terabyte, 32
teraflop, 32
petaflop, 32

ChapterExercises

 The following chapter exercises, along with new activities and information, are also offered in the Internet Resource Center for this title at www.emcp.net/CUT3e.

Tutorial > Exploring Windows

Tutorial 1 demonstrates how to start up a Windows-based PC and log in with a user name, if required. It also explains the proper way to shut down the PC to avoid data loss and file corruption. (See the Exploring Windows tutorials section at the end of the book.)

Expanding Your Knowledge > Articles and Activities

Visit the Internet Resource Center for this title at www.emcp.net/CUT3e, read the articles related to this chapter, and complete the corresponding activities. The article titles include:

- Topic 1-1: Major Advances in the History of Computing
- Topic 1-2: Enterprise Computing Trends
- Topic 1-3: Enterprise vs. Personal Computing
- Topic 1-4: Continuing Evolution of Personal Computing Technology

Terms Check > **Matching**

 For additional practice, go to the Internet Resource Center for this title at www.emcp.net/CUT3e for a chapter crossword puzzle.

Write the letter of the correct answer on the line before each numbered item.

a. network
b. Web page
c. Internet
d. data
e. software

f. personal computer
g. information
h. computer
i. operating system
j. hardware

____ 1. A collection of raw, unorganized content in the form of words, numbers, sounds, or images.

____ 2. A worldwide network of computers linked together via communications software and media for the purpose of sharing information.

____ 3. Data that is organized to be meaningful and potentially useful.

____ 4. The most important piece of software in a personal computer system.

____ 5. An electronic document stored at a location on the Web.

____ 6. A computer designed for use by a single individual and capable of performing its own input, processing, output, and storage.

____ 7. Programs containing instructions that direct the operation of the computer system and the documentation that explains how to use the programs.

____ 8. A computer's physical components and devices.

____ 9. An electronic device that accepts input (programs and data), processes the data into information, stores programs and information, and delivers output (information) to users.

____ 10. A group of two or more computers, software, and other devices connected by means of one or more communications media.

Technology Illustrated > **Identify the Process**

What process is illustrated in this drawing? Identify the process and write a paragraph describing it.

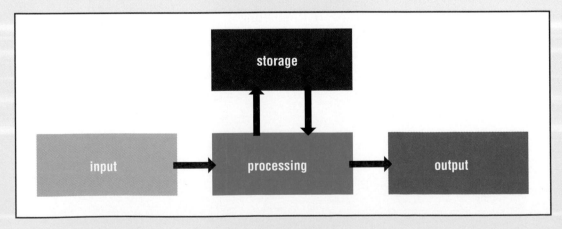

Knowledge Check > Multiple Choice

  Additional quiz questions are available on the Encore CD that accompanies this book as well as on the Internet Resource Center for this title at www.emcp.net/CUT3e.

Circle the letter of the best answer from those provided.

1. A small electronic chip a manufacturer programs for use in another product, such as a digital camera or microwave oven, is called a(n)
   a. programmed chip.
   b. embedded chip.
   c. component chip.
   d. storage chip.

2. The usefulness of computers can be attributed to their speed, accuracy, versatility, reliability, storage, and
   a. communications capabilities.
   b. peripheral components.
   c. decreasing prices.
   d. connectability.

3. Technologies that consist of two or more computers, devices, and software connected by means of one or more communications media, such as telephone lines, are called
   a. computers.
   b. communications.
   c. information processing.
   d. networks.

4. A self-contained computer capable of performing its own input, processing, output, and storage is called a(n)
   a. embedded computer.
   b. digital chip.
   c. dual-purpose processor.
   d. personal computer.

5. A computer component contained on a single chip, or thin piece of silicon containing electrical circuitry, and serving as the computer's central processing unit is called a
   a. wired component.
   b. silicon chip.
   c. microprocessor.
   d. circuit chip.

6. The fastest, most powerful, and most expensive of all computers is the
   a. personal computer.
   b. supercomputer.
   c. mainframe computer.
   d. midrange server.

7. Data that has been processed into a useful form is called
   a. digital data.
   b. input.
   c. information.
   d. output.

8. According to this chapter's Cyber Scenario, which of the following activities did Marc perform using his smartphone?
   a. sending an instant message
   b. buying stock
   c. reading news headlines
   d. receiving a photo

9. The main circuit board inside the cabinet of a personal computer that provides for the installation and connection of other electronic components is the
   a. modem.
   b. secondary circuit board.
   c. motherboard.
   d. attachment board.

10. The most important piece of software in a computer system is the
    a. operating system.
    b. application software.
    c. utility software.
    d. communications software.

Things That Think > **Brainstorming New Uses**

In groups or individually, contemplate the following questions and develop as many answers as you can.

1. Futurists hold that computers will be every-where. For example, bridges will have comput-ers that will alert city planners when part of a bridge is weakening or too stressed and in need of repair. What other objects can you think of that should have the same type of warning or notice capability built into the device?

2. Many futurists claim that we will be wearing computers in the future. What workplace dilemmas, problems, or limitations could be addressed if we start wearing computers that are capable of collecting and analyzing data (tracking inventory, for example)?

3. Computer literacy is extremely important as the use of computers has become commonplace in many occupations. What are some examples of how computers are used in your field of study or future career?

Key Principles > **Completion**

Fill in the blanks with the appropriate words or phrases.

1. The term _____ refers to infor-mation represented by the numbers 1 (on) and 0 (off).

2. In a personal computer, the term *computer* identifies only the _____, the part of a computer system that processes data into information.

3. A(n) _____ , also called the host computer, is a computer to which other computers are connected and on which programs, data, and information are stored.

4. Memory, also called _____ , consists of small electronic chips that provide temporary storage for instructions and data during processing.

5. A monitor produces output in _____ form, a type of output that can be viewed, but not physically handled.

6. Software that tells the computer how to oper-ate is called _____ .

7. Software that consists of programs that per-form administrative tasks, such as checking the computer's components to determine whether each is working properly, is called

_____ .

8. A type of software program that locates and retrieves requested information from the Web is called a(n) _____ .

9. The processor and memory chips are housed on a computer's _____ .

10. CD drives, hard disk drives, and floppy disk drives are examples of _____ devices.

Tech Architecture > Label the Drawing

In this illustration of a computer system, label the devices as input, output, processing, or storage devices.

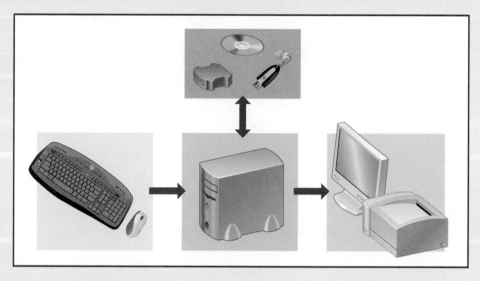

Techno Literacy > Research and Writing

Develop appropriate written responses based on your research for each item.

1. Assume you are offered a free personal computer system of your choice and you are to select the input, output, and storage devices you want. Create a list of uses for your new computer. Then research various computer systems and components advertised in magazines and on the Internet. Choose a computer system that will meet your needs and write a paragraph explaining why you selected a particular personal computer system.

2. Knowing that handheld computers vary in operating system (Palm, PocketPC, etc.), memory, weight, price, and in other ways, create a table or chart that includes the manufacturer's name, handheld model, operating system, wireless capabilities, and price. Visit a computer store in your area and examine three handhelds. Using the chart you prepared, record information about each model. Based upon your analysis of the handheld computers you examined, which would you prefer as your own? Are there additional features that affected your decision? Explain the reasons for your decision.

3. The Internet provides easy access to a wealth of information and is considered to be a time-saver for busy people. Prepare a written report explaining what aspects of your life have been simplified or improved by the use of the Internet. Include your predictions for additional Internet capabilities that you expect to use in the next five years.

4. Many projects are under way to expand the use of wearable computers in the workplace, in military applications, and for personal use. Using your school library or other sources of information, research the uses of wearable computers. Based on your findings, write an article describing the application of wearable computers to enhance our daily lives.

Technology Issues > Team Problem-Solving

In groups, brainstorm possible solutions to the issues presented.

1. Today's classrooms are made up of more diverse students and students with a wider range of performance capabilities compared to previous decades. In fact, some theorists claim there is a 200 percent differential in the learning rate in our classrooms today. Imagine how computers will help instructors teach so many different types of students. Consider both traditional and distance learning modes.

2. Artificially intelligent robots are likely to play a large role in our future. What are some possible new applications of this technology in the areas of manufacturing, health care, and home maintenance?

3. Since computers were first introduced, there has been considerable debate concerning their effect on employment. For example, some people argue that computers have replaced many workers and are, therefore, a social evil. Others argue that the computer industry has created many new high-paying jobs in the technology field. In your group, discuss both sides of this issue: Have computers had an overall good effect or bad effect on society?

Mining Data > Internet Research and Reporting

Conduct Internet searches to find the information described in the activities below. Write a brief report summarizing your research results. Be sure to document your sources, using the following format, which is recommended by the Modern Language Association (MLA):

- author's name (if known)
- title of document, in quotation marks
- title of Internet page or online periodical, in italics (if not titled, put Home Page or give the name of the organization that created and maintains the page)
- date of publication (for an article) or date site was last updated, if available
- date you accessed the site
- URL, in angle brackets < >

Example: Sanders, Jill M. "The Space Agency Launches a Winner," *NASA News*, January 2004. March 2004 <http://www.mit.edu:000/people/glenn.html>.

1. Using online news sources, select a specific event that occurred in one country (other than the United States) within the past year. Find three separate news reports of the event and describe how each media source perceived the event. What are the similarities? What are the differences? What are the possible reasons for the differences?

2. What kinds of information are available at the Web site of your state government? Your summary should discuss the information available on a particular date.

3. Research the topic of high-tech stock investments as discussed in online news sources. What is the current trend as of the date of your research?

Technology Timeline > Predicting Next Steps

Look at the timeline below outlining the major benchmarks in the development of computing. Research this topic and fill in as many steps as you can. What do you think the next steps will be? Complete the timeline through the year 2030.

1937 Dr. John Atanasoff and Clifford Berry design and build the first electronic digital computer.

1958 Jack Kilby, an engineer at Texas Instruments, invents the integrated circuit, thereby laying the foundation for fast computers and large-capacity memory.

1981 IBM enters the personal computer field by introducing the IBM-PC.

1993 World Wide Web technology and programming is officially proclaimed public-domain and available to all.

2004 Wireless computer devices, including keyboards, mice, and wireless home networks, become widely accepted among users.

2006 Five million subscribers connect to BlackBerry Internet services for work and personal communications.

Ethical Dilemmas > Group Discussion and Debate

As a class or within an assigned group, discuss the following ethical dilemma.

The term *plagiarism* refers to the unauthorized and illegal copying of another person's writing or creative work. For example, a student may copy an author's writing from a magazine article or from a Web page and submit the report without giving the original author credit. Also, an individual can illegally retrieve an artist's recordings from Web sites and replay the music again and again, thereby depriving the original artist of royalties.

In your group, discuss the issue of downloading commercial movies from the Internet for one's personal use. Should such practices be legal or illegal? Should the user be required to pay the production studio or the movie stars each and every time the movie is watched? Should there be legal penalties involved?

Buying and Installing a PC

SHOPPING FOR A PERSONAL COMPUTER (PC) can be enjoyable, if you are well informed. Some shoppers think all personal computers are alike so their main objective is to find the cheapest one. Doing so can be a mistake. Many first-time buyers have discovered that the computer they purchased lacked components and features they needed. Avoid making this mistake by arming yourself with information and careful planning. This Tech Insight provides some useful guidelines to help you find the right desktop, notebook, or handheld PC and then install it.

Buying a Desktop Personal Computer System

The decision to buy a PC represents a major investment in both time and money. Chances are that you will use your computer for at least three years, perhaps even longer. Before making the final purchasing decision, complete each step outlined in the following process.

Step One: Identify Your Needs

Before spending your money, prepare a written list of your computing needs and how and where you will be using your new system. Answering the following questions will help you identify your needs.

1. Where will I use my new PC? If you will be using it only in your home or office, a desktop computer may be suitable. However, if you travel for business or if you need mobility in general, you should consider purchasing a notebook (laptop) computer weighing five pounds or less. See the "Buying a Notebook Computer" section for additional guidelines.
2. For what purposes will I use my computer? For example, will you use your PC to prepare letters and reports? Analyze numeric and financial data? Prepare visual presentations? Access the Internet? Listen to music? Create and work with graphics? List all possible uses since these will determine the software and hardware you need. Generally, if you will use multimedia and/or graphics programs, you will need greater storage and processing capabilities.
3. How long will I keep this computer? Try to estimate the number of years you will use your computer before buying the next one. If you expect to use your PC for several years, consider buying one that has expansion slots so you can add new components, such as a modem, printer, or add-on memory boards.

Step Two: Establish a Budget

Ask yourself how much you can realistically afford to pay for a computer. Prices of desktop personal computers range from a few hundred to thousands of dollars. Faster and more feature-rich PCs are usually more expensive. Also, personal computers soon become obsolete. Within a few years you may need a faster and more versatile model.

Step Three: Choose Software to Match Your Needs List

Every computer must have software, including system software and applications software. System software, such as Microsoft Windows or Mac OS, allows a computer to manage its computing resources, including the system unit and input and output devices. Most PCs come with the system software already installed. For general business or academic situations, Windows-based systems are more widely used, but for graphics applications, a Mac platform may be preferable.

Determine the total storage space and processing power you will need for the programs you intend to use. These calculations will drive your hardware choices. Note, too, that some PCs arrive from the factory with a software suite, such as Microsoft Office, already installed. The suite includes word processing, spreadsheet, database management, e-mail, and other applications.

Step Four: Select the Hardware Components

Hardware refers to all of the equipment that makes up a personal computer system (see Figure 1): the system unit, input devices, output devices, secondary storage devices, and all peripheral devices, such

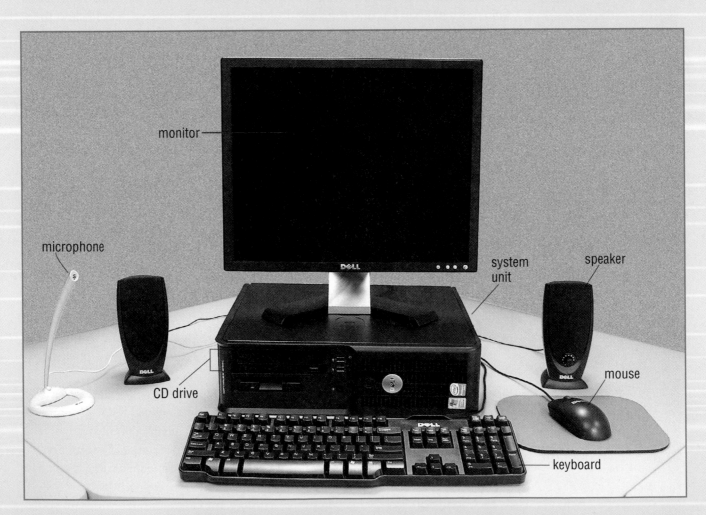

Figure 1 Hardware Components of a Personal Computer System

A complete personal computer system includes not only the system unit, monitor, keyboard, and mouse, but also a printer and speakers and possibly a webcam.

as printers. Following are some guidelines for selecting PC hardware components.

The System Unit   The system unit is typically a metal cabinet containing the essential components for processing information. Along with other standard components, the system unit contains a microprocessor, main memory (RAM), and slots for installing a graphics board, sound board, modem, or other peripherals. Hard disk drives, CD drives, and DVD drives are also housed in the system unit. Increasingly, PC manufacturers are not including a floppy disk drive in new computers.

- **PC architecture**. PC architecture refers to the design and construction of the PC and its system unit, and not all architectures are the same. For example, the architecture of an Apple Macintosh differs from that of an IBM or IBM-compatible PC. Therefore, software written for an Apple Macintosh PC may not run on an IBM or IBM-compatible PC. However, some newer Macintosh PC models can run both types of software. Although some users prefer a Macintosh PC, more software is available for IBM and IBM-compatibles.
- **Microprocessor**. Selecting the right microprocessor is extremely important. Processing speed, typically measured in gigahertz (GHz), is probably the first consideration. The higher the number of GHz, the faster the processor can access and process programs and data. If speed is important, consider choosing a microprocessor with a speed of 2.0 GHz or more. PCs containing microprocessors with speeds up to 3.0 GHz and higher are available.
- **Main memory**. Main memory (RAM) is needed for the temporary storage of programs and data while the data is being processed. Some application software requires a considerable amount of RAM to function properly, and newer software versions usually require more RAM than older versions. Newer desktop PCs typically come with 512 MB of RAM, or more. Make certain the PC has sufficient RAM to run the software you will be using. For example, if you will be working with newer, larger, and more complex applications, such as video and graphics editing, watching movies, or listening to music, consider buying a PC with 2 gigabytes (GB) of RAM.

- **Secondary storage**. What type(s) and amounts of secondary storage are you likely to need? Think of your hard drive as a storage cabinet. The more stuff you have, the more storage you need. Start with a hard drive with 80 GB. If you'll be storing many photos and tunes, move up to 160 GB. Storage capacity of newer hard drives go up to 500 GB. Most computers come with a CD drive and a hard disk drive already installed. A standard compact disc can store up to 750 MB of data, and certain DVDs provide even greater storage capacity. A hard disk drive contains one or more rigid storage platters and provides for the permanent storage of considerably more data. However, the disk itself cannot be removed from the drive. The storage capacity of a hard disk is an important consideration because it is used to store all system and application software, such as Microsoft Word. Typical hard disk capacities are 80 GB, 160 GB, and up to 500 GB.

Other secondary storage devices and media are available. If you will use your PC to play movies, your purchase should include a DVD drive. If you will work with large files, consider purchasing a computer that includes a CD-RW drive. A CD-RW disc is a reusable high-capacity disc that allows you to store huge amounts of data and to erase data no longer needed. Flash drives are also easy to use and are portable.

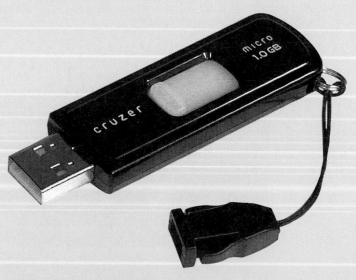

A flash drive is an easy-to-use and portable secondary storage device that provides reusable memory.

- **Ports**. A port on a personal computer is a connection you can use to connect a device, such as a mouse or printer. A personal computer has internal ports and external ports. An internal port allows for the connection of components such as disk drives. External ports (see Figure 2) allow you to connect peripheral devices such as modems, printers, digital cameras, and mice. The number of available ports determines the number of devices and add-on boards that can be connected to the system unit.

Most PCs have at least one of the three basic types of ports: parallel, serial, and Universal Serial Bus (USB). A parallel port connects an external device, such as a printer. A serial port is a general-purpose port that can be used to connect almost any type of device, including modems, mice, and printers. A USB port connects various devices, including keyboards, mice, monitors, and printers. USB ports are particularly important if you need to connect a digital camera, connect to the Internet via a cable modem, or use a flash drive. A USB port located at the front of the system unit provides easy access if you will be plugging in a flash drive or connecting a digital camera.

Some manufacturers label external ports to make it easy for users to locate where devices are to be connected to the system unit. For example, printer, mice, and keyboard ports are often labeled. Many new PCs come with instructions and diagrams that identify the ports to which specific devices are to be connected.

Input Devices   Typical input devices are a keyboard and a mouse, although other kinds of input devices are available. Most keyboards and mice operate similarly. However, there are slight differences in how each "feels" to the user. Before buying a PC, examine the keyboard and mouse for comfort and ease of use. Some sellers will allow you to exchange the keyboard or mouse that comes with the computer for a different one of comparable value.

Output Devices   Output devices produce output in either soft copy or hard copy form. Most PCs come with a monitor (for soft copy output), but you may have to purchase a hard copy device, such as a printer, separately.

- **Monitors**. Slim, lightweight, flat-screen liquid crystal display (LCD) monitors have virtually replaced the older and bulkier cathode ray tube (CRT) displays. The resolution of most LCD monitors is quite good and they take up less desktop space. There are wide differences among PC monitors, with resolution being perhaps the most important variable. Resolution refers to the clarity of the text and images being displayed on the screen. Higher resolutions, such as a resolution of 1,024 by 1,024 pixels, display text and images with exceptional clarity. High-resolution monitors are typically more expensive, but may be worth the extra cost.

Monitor size is another important consideration. Viewing areas range from 15 diagonal inches to 21 inches and higher. Larger monitors are usu-

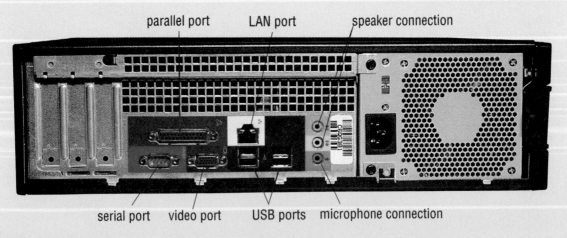

Figure 2 System Unit Ports
Ports are typically visible on the back of the system unit.

ally more expensive, but may be a priority if you work with graphics or if your vision is weak.

- **Printers**. Two popular types of printers are ink-jet and laser, both of which are versatile and capable of producing high-quality output in color. Examine a variety of printers and models and check the price, print speed, and output quality of each.

    Most ink-jet printers are quiet, produce high-quality output, and are relatively affordable, although the ink cartridges they use can be expensive. Print resolution is an important factor to consider. Some offer impressive resolution and can produce output of amazing color.

    Laser printers are fast and can produce high-quality output in both black and color tones. Color laser printers are more expensive than those using only black toner. The cost of color laser printers ranges from a few hundred to thousands of dollars.

    If you will print pictures or graphics, a photographic printer is preferable to an ordinary ink-jet or laser printer. Most photographic printers are reasonably priced and are capable of producing highly detailed and brilliantly colored photographs and graphics.

Buying a Notebook Computer

A notebook (or laptop) computer is a portable personal computer that contains the components and

Notebook computers provide the same basic functionality as a desktop computer and are portable.

devices people use most often. However, various brands and models are available, and you should select the notebook that will match your list of needs, as described in the preceding section. Following are guidelines for buying a notebook computer.

Compatibility

As a buyer, you have a choice between a Windows and Macintosh computer. If you already have a Windows desktop PC and will share programs and data between the two, consider buying a Windows notebook. If, on the other hand, you will be working with graphics applications, you may want to check out Macintosh notebook models. Regardless of the operating system you choose, make sure it is the most recent version available. If a new version will soon become available, you may want to consider waiting for the new version before making a purchase.

Computer Size and Weight

Notebooks vary in weight from about four pounds to more than eight pounds. If you will be carrying it with you, a 7- or 8-pound computer can be quite burdensome so you should consider a notebook weight in the 4 to 6 pound range. For portability you will need a carrying case for your notebook computer. Some sellers offer a free carrying case with the computers they sell. If you will purchase a carrying case, choose one with separate compartments for storage media, such as CDs and DVDs. Make sure the case is lightweight and sufficiently durable to protect your computer.

Processor

Consider notebooks with different processor speeds, and determine which speed will best fit your needs and your budget. Most users prefer a minimum processor speed of 1.6 GHz. For computer games, a faster processor makes playing games more enjoyable.

Keyboard and Pointing Devices

Check out a variety of notebooks and the keyboard and pointing device each offers. Are you comfortable working on a small keyboard? Select a notebook that has a keyboard and pointing device that feels the most comfortable. You might decide not to use the built-in mouse but will use a wireless mouse instead.

Display Screen

Before you buy, examine the size and clarity of the computer's display screen. Screens range from about 12 inches up to 20 inches, measured diagonally. Larger screens typically offer better viewing but they are heavier and usually more expensive. Also, some screens must be viewed directly whereas other types can be viewed from various angles. If you will use your notebook for displaying graphics or playing games, you may want a larger, active-matrix display screen.

Disk Type and Capacity

Choose the type and capacity of disk drives. Will you need a hard disk drive? A CD-ROM or CD-RW drive? A flash drive? A notebook hard disk should have a minimum capacity of 40 GB. If you will use the computer to watch movies and/or listen to music, you will need speakers and a DVD drive.

Internal Memory (RAM)

Internal memory capacity is an important consideration. Select a computer with at least 1 GB of RAM. Less RAM will limit the kinds of software you use and the applications you can run on your computer.

Wireless Capability

Consider the option of built-in wireless capabilities. If you will travel and take your notebook with you, having wireless capability is essential. Many hotels, airports, restaurants, and other facilities now provide wireless access. To take advantage of wireless capability, you will need a built-in modem.

Buying a Handheld Computer

The popularity of handheld computers has ballooned, particularly for mobile workers and people who want computer access anytime, anywhere. Depending on the specific handheld model, these lightweight, pocket-sized computers that fit in the palm of one's hand offer a range of features, including an appointment book, notepad, calculator, calendar, phone, video player, and music player.

Handheld computers offer organizer features such as an appointment book, notepad, calculator, and calendar. Additional software, including a word processing program, can be added to some models.

Many are Web-enabled, allowing owners to access information and to send and receive e-mail. Some handhelds also are preloaded with basic application software, including word processing and spreadsheet programs. Data entry and command selection are accomplished with a pen-like stylus or a built-in keyboard.

If you are in the market for a handheld, follow these guidelines to narrow the field of choices:

- Decide how much you are willing to pay. Prices range from less than $100 to about $1,200, depending on the type of handheld and the features offered. For example, about $250 will buy a handheld with a color 320-by-320 pixel screen, about 25 MB of memory, and a 200 megahertz processor. For about $400, you can get a 400-megahertz chip, 50 MB of free memory, and a screen display of 320 by 480 pixels.
- Determine which applications you want to run on your computer. Read available literature and talk with other handheld users to get their opinions and suggestions. For business purposes, you may want programs such as Microsoft Word, Excel, and PowerPoint. For personal use, you may want MP3 capability in addition to the basic organizer functions.

A keyboard can be added to a handheld device to expand its functionality.

- Visit a computer retailer and ask a sales associate to demonstrate the various models available. With the employee's supervision, practice using the computer's touch screen and the device's keyboard and stylus (if available with the computer).
- Decide whether you want a color or monochrome (black and white) screen. Most users prefer color, and color-screen resolutions have improved markedly in recent years. A black-and-white display may be acceptable for buyers who will use only the calendar and appointment book features.
- Check out battery life and accessories. A long battery life may be a top consideration if your handheld is your only computer or your main work device. Think of the accessories you may need, such as an extra battery, battery charger, and carrying case for your computer. If you travel frequently, you may need a modem, removable storage, and a portable keyboard.
- Decide whether you need Internet access and wireless capability. Some handhelds come equipped with a modem and software that provides for wireless connections and Internet access. If you will need these capabilities, make sure the device you are considering offers them.

Before you make a purchase, learn whether the device is upgradeable so you can add additional capability in the future. Memory Sticks, for example, offer a quick and easy way to boost power and performance.

Installing a Desktop Personal Computer

Because most notebook computers and handhelds are self-contained, the computer installation process mainly applies to desktop computers. Installing a new desktop PC requires following a few basic steps that should take less than an hour.

Prior to bringing your new PC to your home or office, or having it delivered, you need to decide where to position it. Estimate the total space the system will require. You will want to find a comfortable location near one or more electrical outlets. Avoid placing your PC where it will be exposed to direct sunlight or dampness. If your computer contains a dial-up modem and you will be connecting to an Internet service provider (ISP), your computer should be located near a telephone jack. If you will be using a cable connection, position your computer near the cable connection.

Step One: Unpack Your Computer System

While unpacking your new computer and components, locate all items, including computer components, power cords and cables, manuals, assembly instructions and diagrams, and warranty cards. Keep these items together. Be sure to fill out all warranty cards and mail them to the respective manufacturers to register your purchase in case you need to return the computer or contact the manufacturer for technical assistance. Store the containers and padding materials in case you need to return the computer or a defective component to the manufacturer. As you continue unpacking, carefully place each component on your desk or table.

Step Two: Connect the Components

After unpacking and placing the system unit at your workplace, look closely at the various ports on the front and back of the system unit. Usually, ports are labeled or color-coded to help you match each device with its port. Also, some manufacturers enclose written instructions and illustrations for connecting system devices. Locate these documents and carefully follow the instructions.

Because some system devices and peripherals, including the system unit, monitor, and printer,

A surge protector guards computer components from damage during electrical power surges.

require electrical power, each uses a power cord. Locate the cord for each device and plug it into the device. Some devices have a permanently attached cord.

You can protect components from damage that can result from power surges by using a surge protector. Plug the power cords into the device. Later, you will plug the surge protector into a wall outlet. (Caution: do not plug the surge protector into an electric outlet until you are ready to boot up the computer system.)

Each device that comprises your computer system needs to connect to the system unit by means of a cable. To connect a device, connect one end of the cable into the device itself and the other end into the appropriate port on the system unit (usually located at the back of the system unit). In addition to color coding cables and ports, some manufacturers package a color-coded chart or diagram showing how cables are to be connected. Typically, cable connectors are physically designed to fit a particular port.

Step Three: Boot the Computer

After connecting all devices, plug the surge protector into a wall outlet, turn it on, and then turn on the computer. Check to make sure all components and devices work properly. If a device does not work, check first to see if the device is properly connected to the system unit, turned on, and plugged into the surge protector. If the computer, device, or component still fails to work properly, you can get help from an experienced user or from the seller's or manufacturer's Help Desk.

A Final Word

Although prices are declining, a computer still represents a major expenditure, whether you are buying a desktop, notebook, or handheld PC. Do your homework. Ask for recommendations from friends or colleagues. Carefully examine various computer makes and models and then choose wisely. Chances are, the choice you make is one you will live with for a long time. Making the right decisions results in the purchase of a highly effective and efficient tool you will enjoy using in your home, at the office, in school, or on the road.

Input and Processing

Learning Objectives

> Define the terms *input* and *processing*

> Categorize input devices for personal computers and explain their functions

> Identify the main components of the system unit and explain their functions

> Explain the four basic operations of a machine cycle

> Describe the different types of computer memory and their functions

> Discuss the importance of expanding a computer's capabilities and explain how it can be accomplished

CyberScenario

JENNA WINBON IS AWAKENED BY UPBEAT MUSIC playing and her window blinds opening to let in the morning sunshine. The smell of fresh-brewed coffee gradually makes it to her end of the house as she ponders her upcoming day at the office. A computer system called a home information infrastructure manages the MP3 player and stereo system, window blinds, and coffeemaker, along with many other appliances and electronic devices in her home.

Sitting at her bedside, she hears the shower start. She knows that in two minutes it will be ready for her at the temperature she programmed. Jenna glances at today's news headlines scrolling across the bottom of the flat-screen TV on the wall. Turning her attention to the morning show in progress, she sees that a segment on caring for aging parents is about to start. Walking toward the closet, Jenna instructs the TV to record the segment for her to view tonight. As Jenna opens the closet door, a voice informs her that today will be sunny and 78 degrees. She chooses a silk-blend suit and hangs it just outside the bathroom.

Before returning to her get-ready-for-work ritual, Jenna types a brief message on her smartphone. She wants to make sure that her company's purchasing manager orders new notebook computers for the three new sales associates before the local vendor's special offer expires.

Thirty minutes later, Jenna gathers her briefcase and smartphone and heads for the garage. As she passes the wall clock in the utility room, she is reminded on a digital display that she needs to go to the Marietta office today instead of her normal Peachtree Center office.

Opening the door from the utility room to the garage automatically starts Jenna's car and opens the garage door simultaneously. As she backs out of the garage, she notices the car's interior temperature is approaching the 72 degrees she had selected on the Preferences menu of the controls system. Feeling a

bit thirsty, Jenna asks her built-in navigation system to find the Starbucks closest to the Marietta office. After noting the location displayed on the retractable screen in the dashboard, she turns her attention to the satellite radio station she had selected, enjoying the music and anticipating the taste of a latte.

"Now," she thinks, "if only my appointments and meetings at the office will go as smoothly."

Computer systems similar to the one in Jenna's home may soon become a reality within reach of average consumers. Increasingly, builders are including high-speed cables in the walls of new houses to allow for networked media systems throughout the home. Called "structured wiring," this hidden cable system allows flexibility in room design and accommodates state-of-the-art technology such as video and audio monitoring and remotely controlled lighting, cooling, and heating.

In addition to having outdoor sprinklers that automatically shut off when it is raining, this technology can be used for safety and security. Alerting home occupants when someone enters the perimeter of the yard, viewing inside and outside video images of the home, and detecting motion (or lack of motion) in an elderly parent's house are examples of how houses will be able to communicate with their owners through smartphones or other communication technologies. Home systems such as these will add yet another dimension to the term *cyber space*.

Input Technology

Chapter 1 explained that the process of turning data into useful information is called the *information processing cycle*, and that the four steps of the cycle are input, processing, output, and storage. Performing each step involves the use of specific components and devices, all of which are grouped under the term *hardware*. In this chapter you will learn about many of the devices for entering data and programs into the computer and about the computer itself—how it processes data into information and which hardware components are involved in that process. But first, it is important to better understand the first step in the information processing cycle and the technologies that support that function.

Tech Demo 2-1
External Parts of a PC

The term *input* refers to any data or instructions entered into a computer enabling the computer to perform a desired task. Users can input data and instructions using a variety of methods and devices, such as typing on the keyboard or speaking into a microphone connected to a computer. In fast-food restaurants, workers input customers' orders by pressing a key that represents a food item or touching a picture of the item on the computer screen.

As defined in Chapter 1, an **input device** is a hardware device that allows users to enter programs, data, and commands into a computer system. The program or application being used determines the type of input device needed. For example, many computer games require a joystick, whereas writing a letter to another person requires a keyboard. Keyboards, point-and-click devices, and scanners are among the more popular input devices. Desktop and notebook computer systems usually include at least two input devices.

The most common way to input data or instructions into a computer is with a keyboard.

The Keyboard

The most common input device is the **keyboard**, an electronically controlled hardware component used to enter alphanumeric data (letters, numbers, and special characters). A keyboard may be plugged into the system unit or connected wirelessly through **Bluetooth** or another radio-frequency (RF) technology. The two main keyboard types are alphanumeric and special-function.

Alphanumeric Keyboards The keys on most alphanumeric keyboards are arranged as they are on a typewriter, although computer keyboards typically contain additional keys. Keyboards for desktop computers contain from 101 to 105 keys that the user presses to enter data into the computer. Keyboards for smaller computers, such as notebook computers, contain fewer keys. In addition to keys for alphabet letters and symbols, most keyboards contain

- function keys
- special-purpose keys
- cursor-control (arrow) keys
- numeric keys arranged in keypad form

Function keys, labeled F1, F2, F3, and so on, allow a user to quickly access commands and functions.

The numeric keypad, which performs the same functions as a calculator, is used for entering numbers quickly.

Special-purpose keys, such as Control, Alternate, and Delete, are used in conjunction with other keys to enter commands into the computer.

Cursor-control keys govern the movement of the cursor on the screen and include the Up Arrow, Down Arrow, Right Arrow, and Left Arrow keys on most keyboards.

Figure 2-1 A Keyboard's Key Groupings
A computer keyboard is organized into several different groups of related keys.

Figure 2-1 shows a typical keyboard with the special key groups and their functions. The placement of the specialty keys varies among hardware manufacturers.

Special-Function Keyboards   A **special-function keyboard** is designed for specific applications involving simplified, rapid data input. For example, many fast-food restaurant cash registers are equipped with special-function keyboards. Rather than type the name and price of a specific sandwich, the employee need only press the key marked "Cheese Burger" to record the sale. Special-function keyboards enable fast-food employees, ticket agents, and retail clerks to enter transactions into their computer systems very quickly.

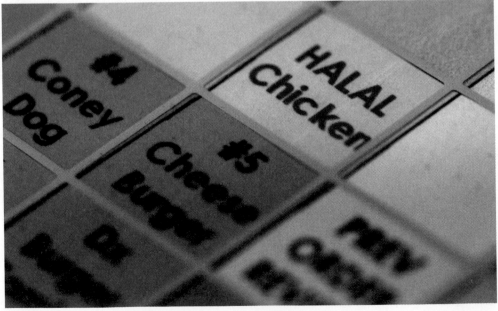

Many businesses use special-function keyboards to increase employee efficiency.

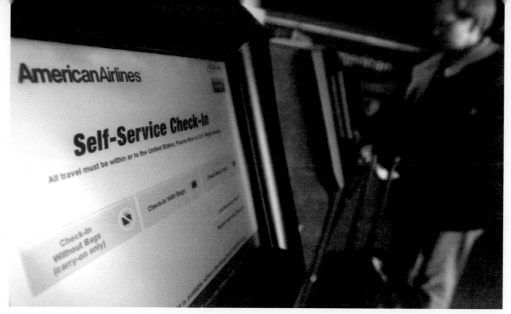

Touch screens are commonly used at airport check-in counters, allowing travlers to obtain boarding passes and check luggage.

Touch Screens

A **touch screen** is another type of input device. Touch screens use sensing technology, allowing a user to make selections from among a group of options displayed on a screen by pressing a finger against the chosen option. For example, a bank customer can begin making a withdrawal by touching the *Withdraw* option on the automated teller machine (ATM) screen. Touch screens are widely used in ATMs, restaurants, airport check-in counters, and kiosks in buildings and stores.

The Mouse and Other Point-and-Click Devices

Operating systems such as Windows and Macintosh incorporate a **graphical user interface (GUI)** containing buttons, drop-down menus, and icons to represent program features and commands visually. The user issues commands by pointing at an icon or menu item with a **mouse**, which after the keyboard is the second most

A mouse is an input device that, when moved about on a flat surface, causes a pointer on the screen to move in the same direction.

common input device. Moving the mouse causes the **mouse pointer** (cursor) on the computer screen to move in a corresponding way (see Figure 2-2). A pointer allows users to make selections from a menu and to activate programs represented by icons displayed on the screen. If you visualize the computer mouse as a small oval with a long cable tail, you can understand how it got its name.

A mouse plugs directly into the computer or is connected wirelessly. A mouse used on the Macintosh generally has one button, while a mouse used on a PC generally has two, although multibutton models are also available. The button on the left side is used to signal a choice by a single click or a double click, depending on the situation. The button on the right side is used to display special options and menus. The user can set up additional buttons to initiate special functions. A scroll wheel is often integrated into a mouse for easier movement up and down documents and Web pages.

On a traditional mouse, the underside of a mouse is a rubber-coated ball that glides over a rubberized pad with a smooth fabric surface, called a **mouse pad**. The most common mouse today, an **optical mouse**, uses a light sensor instead of a mouse ball to track movement. This type of mouse can be moved around on nearly any smooth surface except glass, so no mouse pad is necessary. A **foot**

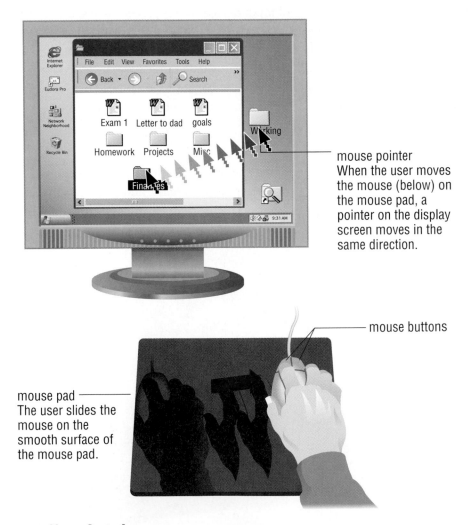

mouse pointer
When the user moves the mouse (below) on the mouse pad, a pointer on the display screen moves in the same direction.

mouse buttons

mouse pad
The user slides the mouse on the smooth surface of the mouse pad.

Figure 2-2 Mouse Controls
Every movement of the mouse corresponds to the movement of the mouse pointer on the display screen.

mouse allows people with carpal tunnel syndrome or other hand or wrist injuries to use a computer.

Trackballs   The trackball is an input device similar to a mouse. A **trackball** consists of a plastic sphere resting on rollers, inset in a small external case. The trackball is often described as an upside-down mouse, although unlike the mouse it remains stationary. Users move the ball with their fingers or palm. One or more buttons for choosing options are incorporated into the design of the trackball. The main advantage of using a trackball is that it requires less desk space than a mouse. A trackball is therefore a good choice for people working in confined areas. Trackballs also require less arm movement, making them useful to those with limited arm mobility.

Touch Pads   A **touch pad**, also called a track pad, is a small, flat device that is sensitive to touch, pressure, or motion. Many portable computers have built-in touch pads, as shown in Figure 2-3. Notebook computers equipped with touch pads enable users to move the on-screen pointer by sliding a finger across the surface of the pad. A touch pad has two parts: One part incorporates two buttons, while the other functions like the smooth surface of a mouse pad. People with carpal tunnel syndrome, a painful condition caused by repetitive movements of the hand and wrist, find a touch pad or trackball easier to use than a mouse.

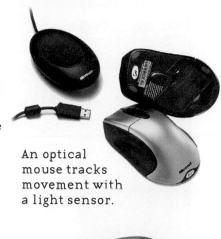

An optical mouse tracks movement with a light sensor.

The ball in a trackball is contained on top of the device or on the side. Rolling the ball moves the pointer on the screen.

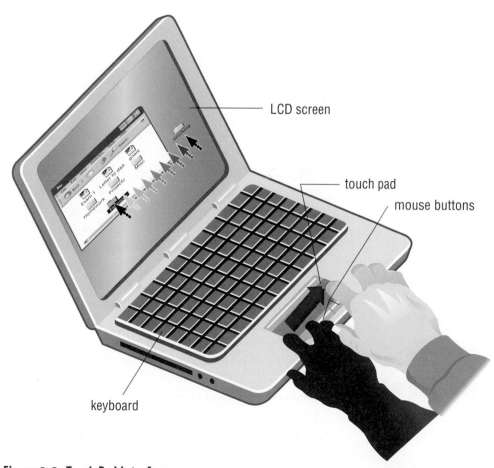

LCD screen

touch pad

mouse buttons

keyboard

Figure 2-3 Touch Pad Interface
With a touch pad, the user traces a finger on the pad, moving the pointer on the screen. Below the touch pad, there are buttons for clicking commands.

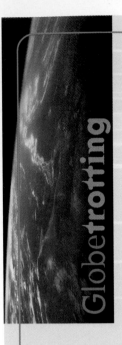
The Telepathic Typewriter

IMAGINE THE FRUSTRATION OF BEING COMPLETELY PARALYZED, unable to speak or motion to caretakers, family, or friends. It would take nothing less than a mind reader to find out your needs and feelings.

Telepathic technology may be in the future for those trapped without communication because of paralysis, disease, or stroke. Scientists in Berlin are working on brain-computer interfaces that would make it possible for a severely paralyzed person to voice thoughts without moving a muscle. Eventually, this research may even make it possible for people who are disabled to use brain signals to drive mechanical devices to move their limbs.

Brain waves are the electrical signals emitted by the firing of millions of nerve cells in the brain. To harness this electrical activity, a volunteer wearing a tight cap fitted with electrodes focuses on a computer screen containing letters. The electrodes pick up the activity and run the information through a computer program that identifies patterns in the brain signals. A la biofeedback, the volunteer learns how to manipulate brain waves into moving the cursor to select a letter.

At present, the process of writing even one thought is slow going. It takes almost an hour to attach the cap to a volunteer's scalp, and even with practice it can take up to ten minutes to create one sentence. Researchers hope to streamline the process so that those suffering paralysis will be freed from their isolation.

Source: "Brain-controlled Device Could Help the Disabled," *Mail&Guardianonline*, March 7, 2006. December 2006 <http://www.mg.co.za/articlePage.aspx?articleid=265991&area=/>.

A joystick is an input device used for moving objects about on the computer screen. Many types of computer games require a joystick.

Joysticks The **joystick** (named after the control lever used to fly fighter planes) is a small box containing a vertical lever that moves the graphics cursor correspondingly on the screen when pushed in a certain direction. It is often used for computer games. Some joysticks have a button in the tip for activation by the user's thumb. Pressing this button performs such actions as firing a game weapon at an object on the screen. Notebook computer users have recently become accustomed to a unique type of joystick, called a "pointing lever," or simply a "pointer." It is about the size of a pencil eraser and fits between the G and H keys of the keyboard. By placing the index finger on top of the lever, users can slightly push or pull it to adjust the pointer on the screen. This type of joystick eliminates a bulky external mouse or joystick and allows the hand to remain close to the keyboard.

Pens and Tablets

Some people complain that drawing with a mouse is like drawing with a bar of soap, although exquisite computer art has been generated using a mouse. Artists, engineers, and others who need precise control over an input device may choose instead to use a **digitizing pen** and a **drawing table**t to simulate drawing on paper. Owners of personal digital assistants (PDAs) such as the Palm handheld and the Handspring Visor also may use a stylus, or special pen, to choose menu options and to write information in the screen.

A **graphics tablet** is a flat tablet mapmakers or engineers use to trace precise drawings. Hundreds of tiny intersecting wires forming an electronic matrix are embedded in the tablet surface. The intersection of two wires represents a specific location, or address, each of which has a value of "0." To capture an image, users grasp a stylus or crosshair cursor and trace an image or drawing placed on the tablet surface. As the user draws on the tablet surface with the pen, the values of intersections the pen touches change to "1"s. During the process, the exact locations of the 0s and 1s are stored in the computer's memory and can be saved on a storage medium. When the drawing is displayed on the screen or on paper, all "1" bits are displayed as tiny dots, which collectively represent the image. After tracing streets, parks, highways, or other images, users can input location labels with the keyboard.

Most PDAs include a stylus for choosing menu options and writing on the screen.

Engineers, drafters, and others who need to create precise, detailed drawings use graphics tablets.

COFOUNDER AND CHAIRMAN EMERITUS, INTEL CORPORATION

Gordon E. Moore

IN 1965 GORDON MOORE PREDICTED that the number of transistors the industry would be able to squeeze onto a computer chip would double every year, while the price per transistor would drop just as dramatically. This pre- diction, now known as Moore's Law, held true until 1975, when he updated the prediction to a doubling every two years. The performance increase is unprecedented in any other industry in human history and plays a large part in driving our modern economy. The total number of transistors on a chip has gone from hundreds to billions since 1970, an improve- ment making today's chips more than 5,000 times more powerful.

Essentially, Moore's Law still holds and will continue to do so for the immediate future. Experts debate how long we can continue to shrink transistors, as some components of the newest transistors (not yet in production) are only three atoms wide. Logically, the smallest possible transistor could be measured in the space of a few atoms, but what will Intel do for an encore after this goal is achieved within the next 10 to 20 years?

Moore was born in San Francisco, California, in 1929. He earned a B.S. in chemistry from the University of California at Berkeley and later a Ph.D. in chemistry and physics from the California Institute of Technology. He is considered a founding father of Silicon Valley, as he was a cofounder of chip maker Intel Corporation in 1968 and originally served as executive vice president. He became president and CEO in 1975, then chairman and CEO in 1979. Currently, his title is Chairman Emeritus.

Source: <http://www.intel.com>.

Optical Scanners

An **optical scanner** (or scanner) is a light-sensing electronic device that uses lasers to read and capture printed text and images, such as photographs and drawings. The scanned text or picture is created and stored as an image rather than as a paper document. Once scanned, the text or image can be displayed, edited, printed, stored on a disk, inserted into another document, or sent as an attachment to an e-mail message. Figure 2-4 shows how a scanner converts a picture into a digital image.

The scanned material is stored as a matrix of rows and columns of dots, called a **bitmap**. Each dot consists of one or more bits of data. The greater the number of bits making up a dot, the clearer the scanned image. The density of each dot helps determine the quality of the captured image. Modern scanners can capture text and images at resolutions ranging from 30 to 48 bits per dot. A scanned picture is often as clear as the original image.

Resolution also depends on the number of pixels per inch. A **pixel** is the small- est picture element (or dot) that a monitor can display. The higher the number of pixels, the sharper and clearer the captured image when displayed or printed.

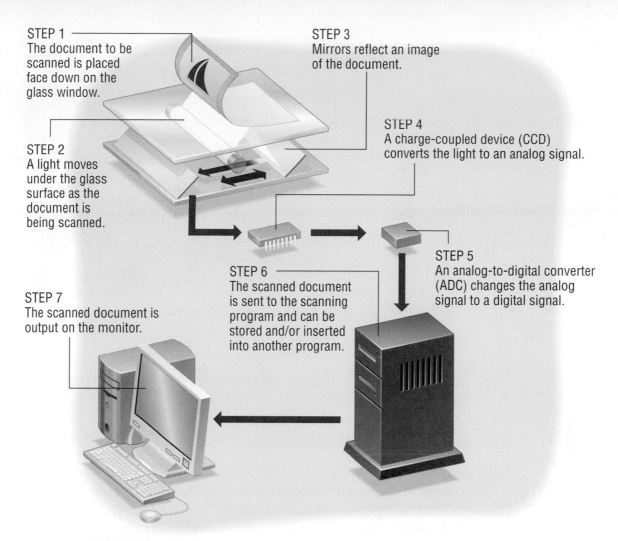

STEP 1
The document to be scanned is placed face down on the glass window.

STEP 2
A light moves under the glass surface as the document is being scanned.

STEP 3
Mirrors reflect an image of the document.

STEP 4
A charge-coupled device (CCD) converts the light to an analog signal.

STEP 5
An analog-to-digital converter (ADC) changes the analog signal to a digital signal.

STEP 6
The scanned document is sent to the scanning program and can be stored and/or inserted into another program.

STEP 7
The scanned document is output on the monitor.

Figure 2-4 The Scanning Process
A scanner captures text and/or graphic images and converts them into a format the computer can understand for display and storage.

Resolution is measured in **dots per inch (dpi)** and expressed as the number of rows and columns. For example, a scanner with a dpi of 600 × 1,200 has a capacity of 600 columns and 1,200 rows of dots. Most modern scanners for home or office use a resolution of at least 1,200 dpi. Commercial scanners offer higher resolutions and are more expensive.

Scanners can process information in two different ways. A **dumb scanner** can only capture and input scanned text and images. Once entered into a computer, the text or image cannot be altered. By contrast, an **intelligent scanner** uses **optical character recognition (OCR)** software that allows captured text or images to be edited with a word processor or other application program. Depending on the scanner model, the OCR software may be included in the package, or it may need to be purchased separately.

The two most popular types of scanners are page scanners (flatbed scanners) and handheld scanners. Personal computer users often use page scanners to capture text, graphics, and other data from printed documents. Pages are either laid face down on the scanner's glass surface or fed through the scanner by means of a side-feed device. While the page scanner remains stationary, the scanning device inside moves back and forth to capture an image of the material on the glass sur-

A flatbed scanner is a very common type of image scanner.

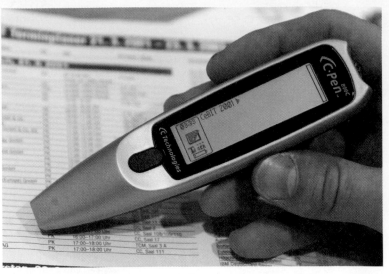

Pen-style scanners are useful in scanning and storing text quickly.

face. With handheld scanners, users manually move the scanner across the material to be scanned.

Bar Code and Optical Readers

Retailers, wholesalers, shipping companies, banks, hotels, and other businesses use a variety of scanning technologies. A **bar code reader** is the most common commercial scanner application. Almost everything for sale today on the retail level is marked with a bar code, also known as a **Universal Product Code (UPC)**. The lines in a bar code contain symbols that can be read by a bar code reader. Sometimes the reader takes the form of a pen. At other times it is placed below a glass cover at the end of a conveyor belt. Bar code readers translate the lines into a number. The computer then uses this number to find information about the product in a database, such as its name and price. Using bar codes greatly increases accuracy in recording sales and enables retail stores to update inventory files automatically. Overnight shipping services such as FedEx and United Parcel Service (UPS) often use bar codes to identify packages.

Nurses use bar code readers to verify that they are giving the right medication to the right patient.

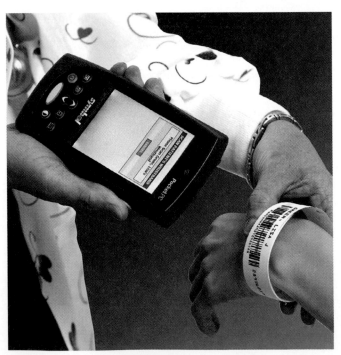

In addition to bar code readers, many retailers have also installed scanners known as optical readers at checkout stations. Similar to the use of credit or debit cards with magnetic stripes, a smart card can be inserted into a slot on an **optical reader**. A **smart card** contains electronic memory and an embedded microprocessor for accessing and updating the card's contents. This allows customers to pay for purchases, verify their identity, and access information such as personal medical records.

Graphic and Video Input Devices

Graphic and video input devices can be directly connected to a computer to upload images and video in their original form. Today's graphic and video input devices are digital cameras and digital video cameras.

Digital Cameras   While conventional cameras record images on film, a **digital camera** captures images in a digitized form that a computer can use. In appearance, digital cameras resemble traditional film-based cameras, although digital cameras are often smaller in size. Most are portable, although some models are stationary and connect directly to a computer.

This bar code reader allows a customer to scan items as they are placed in the shopping cart, making the final checkout process quicker.

Several advantages that digital cameras have over conventional cameras have led to their increased popularity. With a digital camera, the picture is viewable right away, allowing the user to retake the photo if needed. Digital photos are also easier to retrieve, edit, duplicate, and share with others since they are just computer files.

Most digital cameras store captured pictures directly in flash memory (which will be discussed later in this chapter) for transfer to a computer as input. Users can then adjust the color and size of the image using photo-editing software. They can also print the picture, copy it into another document, post it on a Web site, or e-mail it.

A digital camera looks much like a standard camera but captures and stores an image in a digital format that users can view immediately or download to a computer.

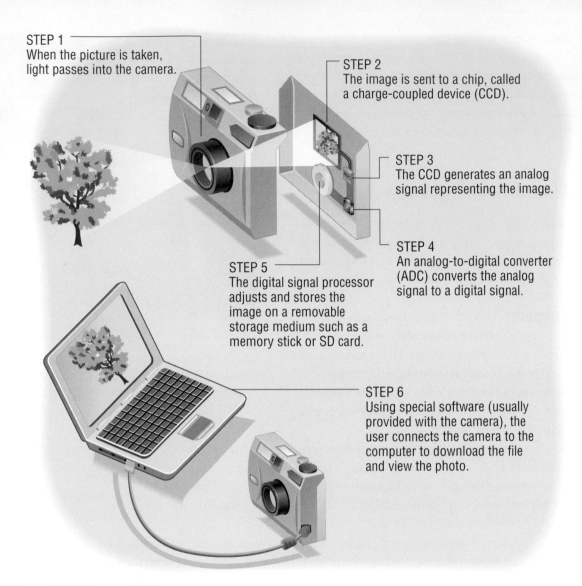

STEP 1
When the picture is taken, light passes into the camera.

STEP 2
The image is sent to a chip, called a charge-coupled device (CCD).

STEP 3
The CCD generates an analog signal representing the image.

STEP 4
An analog-to-digital converter (ADC) converts the analog signal to a digital signal.

STEP 5
The digital signal processor adjusts and stores the image on a removable storage medium such as a memory stick or SD card.

STEP 6
Using special software (usually provided with the camera), the user connects the camera to the computer to download the file and view the photo.

Figure 2-5 How a Digital Camera Works
A digital camera captures images by converting them from analog to digital format and storing them on a removable storage medium. Once users capture and store the pictures, they can print them or insert them into a document such as a sales brochure.

Many digital cameras can also be connected to a television for viewing or connected to a printer for printing. Figure 2-5 illustrates how a digital camera works.

As with scanners, digital photo quality is measured by the number of bits stored in a pixel, or dpi. The resolution of digital cameras is usually advertised in terms of megapixels (millions of pixels). A camera with a resolution of 4.0 or 5.0 megapixels produces high-quality pictures suitable for most consumers. However, professional photographers desire resolution of at least 4,096 × 4,096 pixels (about 16 megapixels), which is about twice the resolution of 35-millimeter film and approximately the same clarity achieved by high-end 4 × 5 film cameras.

Digital camera technologies are now common in cell phones as well. Many cell phone users are able to capture and transmit pictures taken by cameras inside their phones. For example, photographs of a newborn child can be instantly transmitted to family and friends, or a biology student on a field trip can take and store photographs of plants and animals for further study. Some cell phones are even equipped with digital video camera technology that can record short videos.

Many cell phones are equipped with digital camera technology, allowing users to capture and transmit pictures (and sometimes short videos).

Webcams and Video Cameras   **Video input** occurs using a special type of video camera attached to the computer. Both webcams and digital video cameras (camcorders) are devices that capture video input. A **webcam** is a digital video camera that captures real-time video for transmission to others via a Web server or an instant messaging tool.

Most video input now involves the use of high-resolution digital video cameras and camcorders. These capture and store video in digital form that allows images, such as still photos and movies, to be displayed in clear and brilliant color. Unlike analog video cameras, digital video cameras do not require a digitizer. Instead, the video camera can be plugged directly into a computer's Universal Serial Bus (USB) port and used immediately (Figure 2-6). With video-editing software, it is possible to view each frame of the video and edit video sequences.

Businesses, government, and organizations are discovering numerous video-input applications. For example, book publishers can now include a small printed

The SmileCam can automatically track motion and can be controlled remotely through an Internet connection.

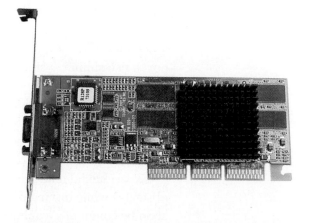

An expansion video card provides improved graphics for high-resolution graphics applications such as digital photos and video.

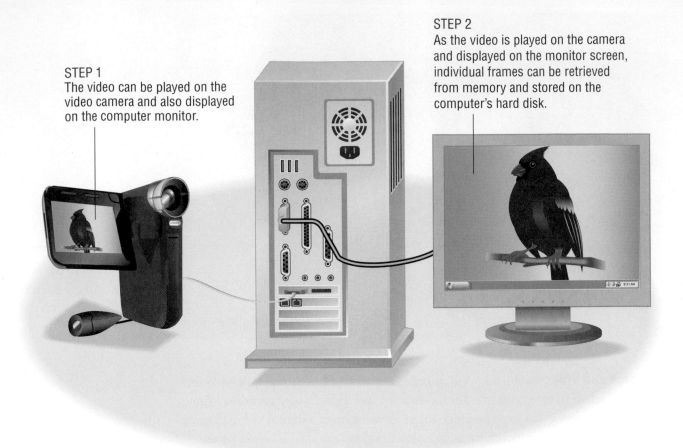

STEP 1
The video can be played on the video camera and also displayed on the computer monitor.

STEP 2
As the video is played on the camera and displayed on the monitor screen, individual frames can be retrieved from memory and stored on the computer's hard disk.

Figure 2-6 Process for Viewing Digital Video
Users can plug a digital video camera directly into a computer to display the recorded video.

image on a book cover or within a magazine ad allowing an order to be placed when a person holds the image up to a video camera on the computer. The camera captures the printed image, enters it into the computer, and transmits the order over the Internet to the publisher.

Some banks have begun using advanced video-input systems to identify customers. A camera captures an image of a customer and quickly compares the image with those stored in a computer, eliminating the necessity of checking a driver's license or other identification. High-security situations that require quick identification, such as military installations, government facilities, and airports, use similar systems that store an image of a person's eye, fingerprints, or facial structure.

Manufacturers use video technology for quality control. For example, a product moving along an assembly line can be photographed and instantly compared with a stored photograph of the "perfect" product. If a missing or broken part is detected, the computer rejects the product before it is packaged for shipment.

Experimental unmanned military vehicles use a vision-input system to avoid obstacles while driving over rough terrain. Similar vision-input technologies may soon be commonly available for civilian vehicles. Vision-input offers great promise for safer driving in the future.

New facial recognition systems in airports can help security and law enforcement personnel identify terrorists by their facial structure.

Audio Input Devices

The process of entering (recording) speech, music, or sound effects is called **audio input**. Personal computers must contain a sound card to record or play sound. They will also need speakers and a sound-capturing device, such as a microphone, audio CD player, or tape player plugged into a port (slot) on the sound card. Finally, special software is required, such as the Windows Sound Recorder utility.

Voice input technologies allow users to enter data by talking to the computer. Newer releases of word processing and spreadsheet applications commonly include voice input. Voice recognition and speech recognition are two types of voice input programs.

A **voice recognition program** does not understand or process speech. Instead, it recognizes only preprogrammed words stored in a database. A word database may contain only a few words, or many millions of words. Voice-activated ATMs, for example, allow customers to conduct financial transactions by speaking into the machine. Voice recognition capability also is included in the most recent releases

Computers equipped with appropriate hardware and software can record sound or respond to voice commands.

John Eckert and John Mauchly

JOHN P. ECKERT AND JOHN W. MAUCHLY INVENTED and improved computers through original designs and profoundly impacted history through their work. They designed the Electronic Numerical Integrator and Computer (ENIAC), which was commissioned by the United States in 1943 to help the military compile tables for the trajectories of bombs and shells. The ENIAC used roughly 18,000 vacuum tubes and measured two-and-a-half meters tall and 24 meters long. It was 1,000 times faster than the electromechanical machines that preceded it, and was capable of up to 5,000 additions per second. It was easily the most complex computer of its generation.

Mauchly was born August 30, 1907 in Cincinnati, Ohio, and studied physics while on scholarship at John Hopkins University. He graduated with a doctorate in physics in 1932. He did some work analyzing the weather and realized that weather forecasts would require compiling large sets of data very quickly. He developed an interest in electrical circuits for computation before beginning to teach at the University of Pennsylvania, where he would eventually begin to build the machines he envisioned.

Eckert was born April 9, 1919 in Philadelphia. He went to William Penn Charter School in

Philadelphia and graduated in 1937 before going to the University of Pennsylvania to study electrical engineering. He started teaching there shortly after graduating in 1941. Mauchly, though 12 years his senior, took Eckert's training course in electronics designed for defense purposes, and they soon became interested in each other's work.

The University of Pennsylvania was already researching early computers. They specifically used a Bush analyzer designed by Vannevar Bush. The machine required too much manual work to be effective for smaller calculations, and Mauchly developed his own ideas on how to construct better computers. Mauchly and Eckert would discuss electronic computer designs for two years before Mauchly's report on the construction of a computer was accepted. Then they were approved by The Ballistic Research Laboratory in Aberdeen, Maryland, to start building the ENIAC. Eckert was appointed chief engineer on the project. The ENIAC was finished in 1946 after World War II ended, and was used chiefly on top-secret problems associated with the development of nuclear weapons.

Eckert and Mauchly then started the Electronic Control Company together and received an order in 1946 to build the Binary Automatic Computer

of the Microsoft Office suite. A voice recognition program is a **speaker-independent program**, which means it can respond to words spoken by different individuals.

A **speech recognition program** provides another type of voice input in which words spoken by a user are stored in a database. A microphone and a type of speech recognition software, such as IBM's Via Voice or Dragon NaturallySpeaking, enable words spoken by the user to be stored in digital form in the computer. Once words are stored, the user can issue commands and enter data by speaking words that exactly match those recorded previously. A computer with speech recognition capability can continue to learn new vocabulary and commands from user voice input. A speech recognition program is usually a **speaker-dependent program**. The computer will recognize words only if they closely match the speech patterns of a previ-

(BINAC). The major advancement of this machine was that instead of punched cards for data storage, it used magnetic tape. They changed their company name to the Eckert-Mauchly Computer

Eckert and Mauchly (center) with the ENIAC at the Moore School of Electrical Engineering in 1941.

Corporation and in 1950 developed the Universal Automatic Computer (UNIVAC), a computer capable of handling numbers and letters with equal ability and meant for business use. It was the first commercial computer produced in the United States. They produced 46 UNIVACs before the Remington Rand Corporation bought them in 1950.

Eckert stayed with the company as an executive until he retired in 1989. He continued to act as a consultant, however, until his death in 1995. After Mauchly left the company, he formed Mauchly Associates. He was president from 1959 until 1965 when he became chairman of the board. Later he was president of Dynatrend Incorporated from 1968 until his death in 1980.

Eckert and Mauchly both received various awards for pioneering the field of computer technologies and their amazing achievements. They shared the Harry M. Goode Memorial Award in 1966 and were elected to the National Academy of Engineering in 1967. Eckert won the U.S. National Medal of Science in 1969, and Mauchly was elected a life member of the Franklin Institute.

Sources: O'Connor, J. J., and E. F. Robertson. *John Presper Eckert.* December 2006 <http://www-history.mcs.st-andrews.ac.uk/Biographies/Eckert_John.html>; O'Connor, J. J., and E. F. Robertson. *John William Mauchly.* December 2006 <http://www-history.mcs.st-andrews.ac.uk/Biographies/Mauchly.html>.

ously recorded word. If another person uses the computer, it may not understand verbal commands because of differences in speech patterns.

Data Processing by Computers

All of the hardware devices discussed so far have dealt with input, the first phase of the information processing cycle. The second phase is processing, which involves another set of computer hardware components, most of which reside in the system unit. The purpose of inputting data into a computer system is to process data into a form that is useful. Recall that information processing, also called data processing or simply processing, refers to the manipulation of data

INTERNET RESOURCE center

Go to this title's Internet Resource Center and read the article titled "Processor Installation and Upgrades." www.emcp.net/CUT3e

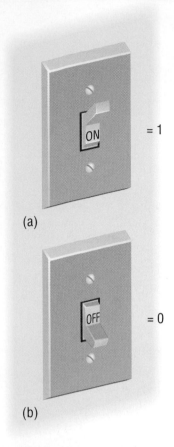

(a)

= 1

(b)

= 0

Figure 2-7 Binary Number System Analogy
The binary number system uses a condition that is similar to what happens when an electrical switch is turned on, causing current to flow. In the binary number system, a one (1) represents an "on" state in which there is an electrical charge (a), and a zero (0) represents an "off" state in which there is no electrical charge (b).

Go to this title's Internet Resource Center and read the article titled "Advances in Chip Architecture." www.emcp.net/CUT3e

according to instructions in a computer program. The program used to manipulate the data may be written by the user or purchased from a software vendor. Data may be manipulated in various ways during processing. For example, a payroll program manipulates data by calculating employee gross pay, taxes to be withheld, deductions, and net pay. The results of those calculations can then be used to print employee paychecks and reports. A commercial word processing program such as Microsoft Word can be used to manipulate text and other data to produce letters, memos, and other documents.

All computers are electronic devices, which means they operate on electricity, and their programs and data are in electronic form. Programs and data are entered and stored in the computer's memory. When a program is executed, the processing unit retrieves the instructions and data as needed throughout the processing period. When processing is finished, the program and the processed data (information) are stored in the computer's memory until the information is output or saved for future use.

So what happens during processing? Physically, electrical currents representing programs and data are moving about very quickly through electronic circuits between components inside the system unit. The currents are created by tiny switches called transistors, which are either on or off, with "on" represented by the number 1 and "off" represented by the number 0. All data used in computers is represented by combinations of ones and zeros, each of which is considered a **bit** (an abbreviation for binary digit). As described in Chapter 1, electrical currents or signals within computers are therefore called digital signals, and data is referred to as digital data.

Data Representation: Bits and Bytes

The first large computers made use of the decimal number system, in which numbers are indicated by the symbols 0 through 9. Engineers soon hit upon a much simpler system known as **machine language** for representing data with numbers. Machine language uses **binary numbers** ("bi" means two), which are constructed solely of the symbols 0 and 1. The **bit** (0 or 1) is the smallest unit of data in the binary system. By itself, a bit is not very meaningful. However, a group of eight bits, or a **byte**, is significant because a byte contains enough possible combinations of 0s and 1s to represent 256 (28) separate characters. These characters include letters of the alphabet, numbers, and special symbols, such as a dollar sign ($), a question mark (?), and a pound sign (#).

To picture the concept of using binary numbers to represent data within the electrical circuits on a computer chip, consider an electric light switch. Flipping the switch to the "on" position causes the current to flow and turns on the light, while flipping the switch to the opposite position turns the light "off" (see Figure 2-7). Various patterns of "on" and "off" could therefore represent alphabet letters and numbers.

ASCII and EBCDIC Coding Schemes

Two widely used data coding schemes based on the binary system are the **American Standard Code for Information Interchange (ASCII)** and the

Extended Binary Coded Decimal Interchange Code (EBCDIC). The ASCII data coding scheme is used on many personal computers and various midsize servers. The EBCDIC scheme is used mainly on large servers and mainframe computers. Figure 2-8 illustrates these two coding schemes and the combinations that represent specific characters. Coding schemes such as ASCII and EBCDIC make it possible for users to interact with a computer. For example, pressing a specific key on a keyboard, such as the letter "J," generates an electrical signal. The generated signal is converted into binary form (a byte) and is stored in memory. The computer then processes the digital signal and quickly displays an image (in this case, a "J") on the screen, as shown in Figure 2-9.

Unicode

Although widely adopted as a standard for personal computers, the ASCII system has proved to be too limited because it cannot deal with certain languages, such as Chinese, which uses more complicated alphabets than does English. To accommodate a larger array of letters and symbols, computer scientists have developed a system called **Unicode**. Unicode uses two bytes, or 16 binary digits, and can represent 65,536 separate characters. Since the first 256 codes are the same in both ASCII and Unicode, existing ASCII-coded data is compatible with newer operating systems, including Windows Vista and Macintosh OS X, that use Unicode.

The System Unit

The main part of a desktop computer, the **system unit**, houses the components that process data into information. System units for PCs come in various shapes and sizes. The modified system unit shown in Figure 2-10 illustrates various system unit components. From the outside, the system unit looks like a metal or plastic cabinet with several button switches and openings in the front and back. The inside is a maze of circuit boards, wires, and cables of various colors, a fan for cooling, and empty slots where more circuit boards can be added. The system unit comprises the power supply, storage bays, and the motherboard.

The Power Supply

Like other electronic devices, a computer requires a **power supply** to supply energy to the computer. Many personal computers use a power cord that connects the computer into a standard alternating current (AC) 115 to 120 volt wall outlet. Because this type of power is unsuitable for use with a computer requiring a

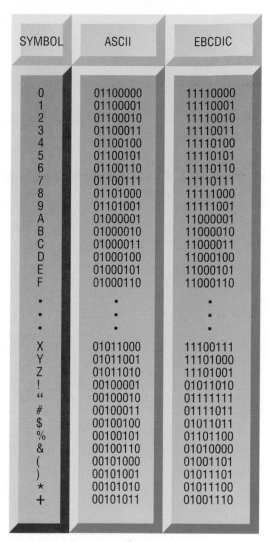

Figure 2-8 ASCII and EBCDIC Coding Schemes
ASCII is a coding scheme many computers, including personal computers, use. The EBCDIC coding scheme is used mainly on large computers such as IBM mainframe computers.

SYMBOL	ASCII	EBCDIC
0	01100000	11110000
1	01100001	11110001
2	01100010	11110010
3	01100011	11110011
4	01100100	11110100
5	01100101	11110101
6	01100110	11110110
7	01100111	11110111
8	01101000	11111000
9	01101001	11111001
A	01000001	11000001
B	01000010	11000010
C	01000011	11000011
D	01000100	11000100
E	01000101	11000101
F	01000110	11000110
.	.	.
.	.	.
.	.	.
X	01011000	11100111
Y	01011001	11101000
Z	01011010	11101001
!	00100001	01011010
"	00100010	01111111
#	00100011	01111011
$	00100100	01011011
%	00100101	01101100
&	00100110	01010000
(	00101000	01001101
)	00101001	01011101
*	00101010	01011100
+	00101011	01001110

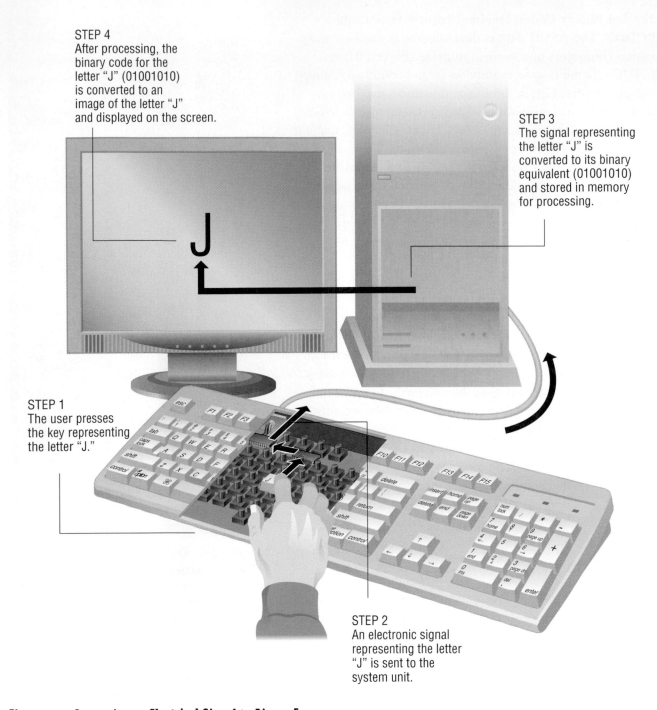

STEP 4
After processing, the binary code for the letter "J" (01001010) is converted to an image of the letter "J" and displayed on the screen.

STEP 3
The signal representing the letter "J" is converted to its binary equivalent (01001010) and stored in memory for processing.

STEP 1
The user presses the key representing the letter "J."

STEP 2
An electronic signal representing the letter "J" is sent to the system unit.

Figure 2-9 Converting an Electrical Signal to Binary Form
Pressing a specific key generates an electronic signal that is converted into binary form (a byte) and stored in memory. The computer then processes the digital signal and quickly displays the character on the screen.

direct current (DC) between 5 and 12 volts, the power supply unit in the system unit converts the incoming current from AC into DC.

In addition to plug-in power, portable computers use battery power when plug-in power is unavailable or impractical. Most portable computer batteries are rechargeable, allowing the battery to be recharged for use again and again.

The power supply typically includes a fan for cooling of the entire system unit. Computer usage generates a lot of heat, but the components inside the system unit

power supply

CD drive

floppy disk drive

hard drive

AGP video card

PCI expansion card

motherboard

Figure 2-10 System Unit Components
The system unit is the main part of a personal computer system, containing the components necessary for processing information.

need to stay cool. Some computers have additional fans for components such as the Central Processing Unit (CPU), but a single fan is usually sufficient.

Storage Bays

A **storage bay** (often just called a bay) is a site where a storage device, such as a floppy drive, hard drive, or CD/DVD drive is installed. The number of bays in a computer determines the number of storage devices that can be installed, an important factor for buyers to consider when purchasing a PC. Figure 2-11 shows the bays in a typical desktop computer.

PC bays come in different sizes, the most common ones being a hard drive and a CD/DVD drive. An internal bay, such as one that houses a hard drive, is concealed entirely within the system unit. An exposed bay is used when direct access

Tech Demo 2-2
Internal PC
Components

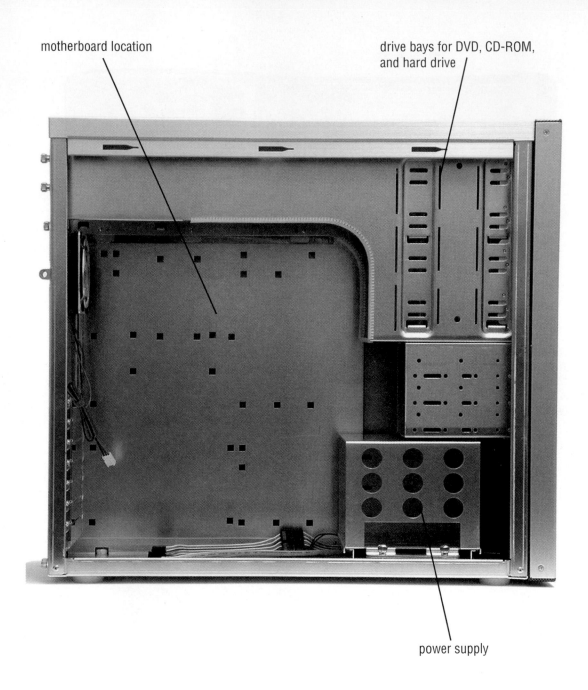

motherboard location

drive bays for DVD, CD-ROM, and hard drive

power supply

Figure 2-11 Bays on a Desktop Computer
The desktop computer shown above contains a CD/DVD drive bay and a hard drive bay.

is required to the device, such as insertion and removal of a CD or DVD in a CD/DVD drive.

The Motherboard

Tech Demo 2-3
Motherboard

A **motherboard** is a thin sheet of fiberglass or other material with electrical pathways. Each **trace** is an etched pathway that connects a component soldered to the motherboard or attached to it by various wires or connectors. Figure 2-12 identifies components typically found on the motherboard in contemporary desktop computers, and their functions are as follows:

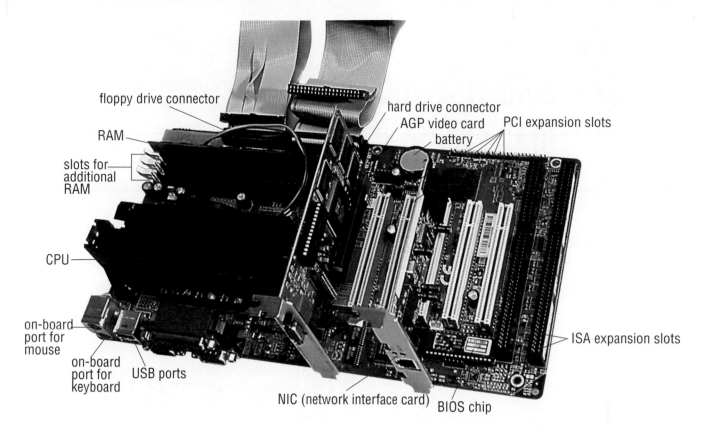

floppy drive connector

hard drive connector

RAM

AGP video card
battery

PCI expansion slots

slots for
additional
RAM

CPU

on-board
port for
mouse

ISA expansion slots

on-board
port for
keyboard

USB ports

NIC (network interface card)

BIOS chip

Figure 2-12 Motherboard Components
The motherboard holds the major processing and memory components,
including the CPU, RAM, and ROM chips.

- central processing unit (microprocessor) for manipulating all types of data
- a system clock (and battery) to synchronize the computer's activities
- slots for connecting the random access memory (RAM) chips that contain the
  temporary memory where programs and data are stored while the computer
  is in use
- one or more read-only memory (ROM) chips that contain the computer's
  permanent memory where various instructions are stored
- expansion slots for attaching expansion cards that add various capabilities to
  the computer, such as the ability to access files over a network or to digitize
  sound or video
- ports for connecting input devices such as a keyboard, mouse, modem, and
  output devices such as speakers and a printer
- buses, which are electronic connections that allow communication between
  components in the computer

The Central Processing Unit

Every computer contains a central processing unit (CPU). The CPU of larger computers often spans several separate microprocessor chips and various circuit boards,
whereas in a personal computer the CPU is a single chip. This **microprocessor
chip**, also called an integrated circuit, is a small electronic device consisting of tiny
transistors and other circuit parts on a piece of semiconductor material. This material is known as a **semiconductor** because it is neither a good conductor of electric-

Go to this title's
Internet Resource
Center and read the
article titled
"Improvements in Chip
Materials and
Manufacturing
Processes."
www.emcp.net/CUT3e

Is There a Doctor in the Chip?

MOST CONSUMERS don't give a passing thought to the fact that the microchips in their electronics have a life expectancy of about three years. The devices are traded in for updated models long before the processor fails. But scientists about to launch a space vehicle on a 10-year mission might start to be more than a little worried that the only backup to a system breakdown is spare parts.

The answer is a field programmable gate array (FPGA). The FPGA is a processor containing chips that could actually fix themselves as they whirl through space. FPGAs, first developed in 1984, use programmable intersections called logic blocks instead of a hardwired pat-tern of circuits. When a processor fails, a backup chip uses an algorithm that keeps trying different configurations until it hits on the one that gets the job back on track.

NASA researchers recently tested a self-healing processor by blasting it with 250 kilo-rads of radiation. Like magic, the zapped system started running 100 configurations per second until it had restored itself.

Researchers are working to not only develop self-repairing chips but also create ones that can grow, adapt, and change with the environment, just as the human body does. In the field of immunotronics, scientists apply what is known about the human immune system to the creation of artificial systems capable of growth and repair.

Source: Bains, Sunny. "Computer, Heal Thyself!" *Wired*, September 2005.

---

ity (like copper) nor a good insulator (such as rubber). Semiconductor material therefore does not interfere with the flow of electricity in a chip's circuits. The most commonly used semiconductor material is silicon, a type of purified glass.

On a personal computer, all processing functions are contained on a single microprocessor chip. Because the functions are housed on a single chip, the terms *CPU* and *microprocessor* are used interchangeably. Recall from Chapter 1 that the CPU, or microprocessor, is often referred to as the "brain" of a personal computer system because it interprets and executes the instructions for most computer operations. The CPU consists of a control unit, an arithmetic/logic unit (ALU), and registers, as shown in Figure 2-13.

These components of the CPU perform four basic operations that are collectively called a **machine cycle**. The machine cycle includes *fetching* an instruction, *decoding* the instruction, *executing* the instruction, and *storing* the result (see Figure 2-14). The machine cycle is the same whether you are using a midrange server or a personal computer.

Control Unit   The **control unit** directs and coordinates the overall operation of the computer system. It acts as a traffic officer, signaling to other parts of the computer system what they are to do. It interprets program instructions and then initiates the action needed to carry them out. These are the *fetching* and *decoding* steps of the machine cycle. **Fetching** means retrieving an instruction or data from memory. **Decoding** means interpreting or translating the instruction into strings

Tech Demo 2-4
How Data Flows
into a PC

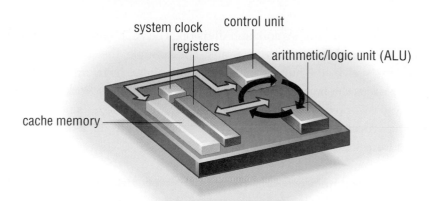

Figure 2-13 Central Processing Unit
The central processing unit (CPU) contains a control unit, arithmetic/logic unit (ALU), and registers.

of binary digits (bytes) the computer understands. The time required to fetch and decode an instruction is called **instruction time**, or **I-time**.

Arithmetic/Logic Unit   As shown in Figure 2-14, the **arithmetic/logic unit (ALU)** is the part of the CPU that performs the *executing* step of the machine cycle. **Executing** means carrying out the instructions and performing arithmetic and logical operations on the data. The arithmetic operations the ALU can perform are

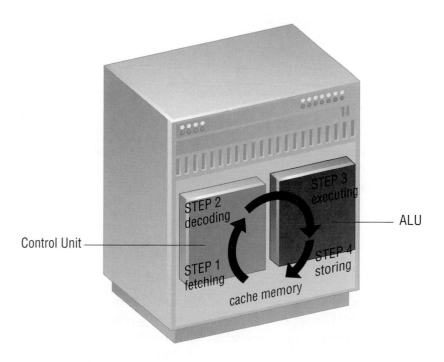

Figure 2-14 Machine Cycle
This process includes the four steps for reading and carrying out an instruction: fetching, decoding, executing, and storing.

addition, subtraction, multiplication, and division. The ALU can also perform logical operations, such as comparing data items. For example, the ALU can determine if one data item, such as the number of hours an employee has worked, is less than, equal to, or exceeds the number of hours in a standard 40-hour work week. If the number of hours worked is less than or equal to 40, the employee's pay is calculated using a particular formula. If the hours worked exceeds 40, a different formula is used for calculating overtime pay.

Registers   To speed up processing, the ALU uses a **register** to temporarily hold instructions and data. This is the *storing* step of the machine cycle. **Storing** means writing or recording the result to memory. Registers are accessed much faster than memory locations outside the CPU. The time required to execute and store an instruction is called **execution time**, or **E-time**.

Various kinds of registers are used, each serving a specific purpose. Once processing begins, an **instruction register** holds instructions currently being executed. A **data register** holds the data items being acted upon. A **storage register** holds the immediate and final results of processing.

Coprocessors   In addition to the main processor, or CPU, a personal computer may also contain one or more coprocessors. A **coprocessor** is a special-purpose chip that assists the CPU in performing certain types of operations. The first mainstream coprocessor was a math coprocessor, which was used to perform mathematical computations more quickly for scientific, engineering, and statistical applications. Math coprocessors have now been integrated into most ALU components of microprocessor chips and are no longer separate chips. A **graphics coprocessor** is designed specifically for handling image-intensive applications, such as Web pages and computer-aided design programs. A **cryptographic coprocessor**, also called a crypto-coprocessor, provides encryption and related processing.

Factors in Microprocessor Speed and Power   The power and speed of microprocessor (CPU) chips are determined primarily by the number of transistors, the clock speed, and the number of bits that can be handled as a single unit. A variety of microprocessors with varying speeds and capabilities are available. Newer microprocessors are extremely fast and powerful and offer exceptional capabilities. For example, Intel Corporation's first Pentium 4 processor, introduced in 2000, contained 42 million transistors and had a clock speed of up to 1.7 gigahertz (GHz). Newer Pentium 4 versions contain even more transistors and operate at speeds of 4.0 GHz or more. Contrast that capability with Intel's 80286 processor introduced in 1982, which had a clock speed of 6 to 12 megahertz (MHz) and a total of 134,000 transistors.

In 2003, Intel introduced the Pentium M chip for notebook computers. When packaged with an Intel Wi-Fi wireless adapter, the chip is called the Centrino. Notebook manufacturers quickly took advantage of the extended battery life and cooler operating temperatures of the Pentium M by offering several new ultralight notebooks that provide high-performance computing and wireless LAN capabilities. The Pentium M is especially useful for the Tablet PC, which needs a longer battery life and more processing power to manage handwriting recognition. Table 2-1 shows the clock speed and number of transistors for several microprocessors, and Table 2-2 lists similar statistics for mobile devices.

Table 2-1 A Comparison of Desktop Personal Computer Processors

Processor Name	Manufacturer	Year of Introduction	Clock	Number of Transitors
80286	Intel	1982	6–12 MHz	134,000
68020	Motorola	1984	16–33 MHz	190,000
80486DX	Intel	1985	16–33 MHz	275,000
68030	Motorola	1987	16–50 MHz	270,000
68040	Motorola	1989	25–40 MHz	1,200,000
Pentium	Intel	1993	75–200 MHz	3,300,000
Pentium Pro	Intel	1995	150–200 MHz	5,500,000
Pentium II	Intel	1997	233–450 MHz	7,500,000
Celeron	Intel	1998	266–633 MHz	19,000,000
Athlon	AMD	1999	1.1 GHz	22,000,000
Pentium III	Intel	1999	1.0 GHz	28,000,000
Pentium 4	Intel	2000	1.3 GHz	42,000,000
Athlon XP	AMD	2001	1.7 GHz	77,000,000
PowerPC 970	IBM	2003	1.8 GHz	52,000,000
Opteron 144	AMD	2003	1.8 GHz	106,000,000
Samprom	AMD	2004	2.0 GHz	68,500,000
Athlon 64 FX	AMD	2005	2.8 GHz	114,000,000
Athlon 64 X2	AMD	2005	2.8 GHz	233,000,000
Pentium D (dual core)	Intel	2005	2.8–3.2 GHz	230,000,000
Athlon 64 (dual core)	AMD	2005	2.0–3.2 GHz	233,000,000

Table 2-2 A Comparison of Notebook Computer and Mobile Device Processors

Processor Name	Manufacturer	Year of Introduction	Clock Speed	Number of Transitors
Pentium Mobile	Intel	1997	200 MHz	55,000,000
Celeron Mobile	Intel	1999	266 MHz	18,900,000
Mobile Duron	AMD	2000	1.3 GHz	25,000,000
Pentium M	Intel	2003	1.3 GHz	77,000,000
Celeron	Intel	2004	1.0 GHz	55,000,000
Mobile Sempron	AMD	2004	1.8 GHz	37,500,000
Turion 64	AMD	2005	2.4 GHz	114,000,000

The Chip Debate

LOYAL CUSTOMERS AT THE BAJA BEACH CLUB in Barcelona can pay for a drink or get immediate access to the VIP lounge with just the wave of an arm—an arm that has been implanted with the VeriChip.

Employees at the Cincinnati video surveillance company CityWatch.com who need to get into the high-security database will now find it off limits unless they agree to have a VeriChip implanted under their skin.

The Pentagon is considering VeriChip implants in place of dog tags for its military personnel.

So what is this VeriChip? It is a glass-encapsulated radio frequency identification (RFID) tag about the size of a grain of rice. Dog and cat owners have used such "smart tags" to ensure that their pet can be tracked down if lost, and companies have used tags in consumer products to track sales and shipping. RFIDs have been promoted as a way to keep Alzheimer patients from wandering and as a way to literally keep medical records within arm's reach while traveling.

But the broadening use of RFIDs in humans has ignited an international debate. There are questions about security. The information on VeriChips is at present unencrypted, and anyone who attains access to it could easily read the data. Also, directions for making a cloning device that could easily swipe the ID number of a chip nearby are on the Internet.

In addition, to a lot of people the very idea of a "spy chip" smacks of Big Brother. These critics see the VeriChip as just another step toward an Orwellian world that already accepts government monitoring of cell phone calls, "black boxes" that collect data on driver behavior in automobiles, and public security cameras everywhere. When VeriChip Chairman Scott Silverman floated the idea on television of using his product to verify the whereabouts of guest workers, it only added to fears of VeriChips being used to control and monitor people. The debate is so heated that Wisconsin recently enacted a law making it a criminal offense to force an individual to have a chip implanted.

There is also the belief of some Christian leaders that the chip is a tool of the devil as prophesied in the Bible. The Book of Revelations tells of a time when no one can buy or sell without a mark on the right hand—the so-called "mark of the beast,"—and that connection could be a public relations nightmare for VeriChip.

Sources: Peale, Cliff. "Firm Implants ID Chips," *The Cincinnati Enquirer*, February 14, 2006; McIntyre, Liz, and Katherine Albrecht. "Wisconsin Bans Forced Human RFID Chipping," *News With Views*, June 1, 2006. December 2006 <http://newswithviews.com/McIntyre/Liz6.htm>; "VeriChip," *Wikipedia*. December 2006 <http://en.wikipedia.org/wiki/Verichip>.

A microprocessor's **word size** also affects its power and speed. In microprocessor terms, a **word** is a group of bits or bytes that a computer can manipulate or process as a unit. Some microprocessor chips are 32-bit chips, meaning they can handle 32-bit blocks of data at a time. Newer microprocessors are designed to handle 64-bit blocks of data at a time. For example, Intel's Pentium 4 chip is designed for 64-bit blocks of data, and the chip's main circuitry also accommodates 64-bit words. This means that a 64-bit data path leads from the CPU to RAM, which translates into faster processing.

Microprocessor Performance Improvements   Since 1971, when Intel Corporation introduced the company's first microprocessor, chip designers have developed many techniques for improving the speed and performance of microprocessors. These techniques center on the raw materials used to make the chips, the density of the circuits on a chip, and changes in the way instructions are executed. Following is a summary of key advances in the development of microprocessors to date:

- **Reduced instruction set computing (RISC).** Many early computers and other devices used processors that contained a lengthy and complex set of instructions for processing data. Most modern computers now use a shortened set of instructions, called RISC, which increases their speed and efficiency.

- **Pipelining**. In older computers the CPU had to completely execute one instruction before starting a second instruction. Modern computers now use a technique called **pipelining**, which allows the CPU to execute instructions faster. Pipelining enables the computer to begin executing another instruction as soon as the previous instruction reaches the next phase of the machine cycle. Figure 2-15 shows the machine cycle with pipelining and Figure 2-16 shows the less efficient cycle without pipelining.

- **Closer circuits.** Newer computers contain chips with circuits packed much closer together than those in earlier chips, thereby decreasing the distance that instructions and data must travel. The closer packing makes them much faster and more efficient.

- **New and better materials.** Most chips consist of electrical circuits etched onto a piece of silicon. Some chip manufacturers are designing copper circuits to replace the aluminum circuits used today, because copper is a better conductor of electricity.

- **Parallel processing.** Despite the many performance improvements, most personal computers still use a single processor. This is primarily because a processor is the most expensive computer component, usually costing hundreds of dollars. With a single processor, instructions are executed *serially*, or one at a time. However, scientists have developed ways for two or more processors and memory components to work together simultaneously (in parallel). **Parallel processing** allows two or more processors to work

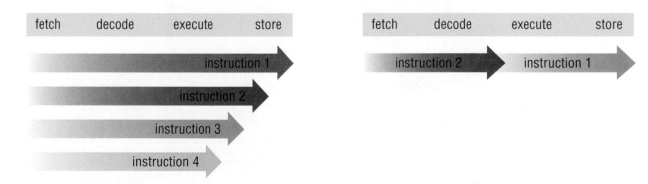

Figure 2-15 Processing with Pipelining
Computer processing speed is improved with pipelining. With pipelining, the computer begins executing a new instruction as soon as the previous instruction reaches the next phase of the machine cycle.

Figure 2-16 Processing without Pipelining
Older computers that did not use pipelining execute an instruction after the previous instruction completes the machine cycle. This is less efficient than when processing is done with pipelining.

concurrently on segments of a lengthy application, thus dramatically increasing processing capability.

- **Multithreading and hyperthreading.** Some newer microprocessors provide multithreading and hyperthreading capabilities that allow operating systems and applications software, such as Windows, to process applications faster. In programming, a thread is a part of a program that can execute independently of other parts. **Multithreading** refers to a carefully designed program that enables several threads to execute at the same time without interfering with each other. Intel has developed a technology called **hyperthreading**, which allows its Pentium series of microprocessors to execute multithreaded software applications simultaneously and in parallel rather than processing threads in linear fashion, thereby greatly increasing processing speed.

- **Dual-core and multi-core processors.** To speed processing, some processors now offer dual-core processors and multi-core processors for personal computers and servers. The word **core** refers to the essential processor components. A **dual-core processor** (Figure 2-17) is a CPU that includes two complete cores per physical processor, meaning a single integrated circuit (silicon chip) contains two processors and their cache memories (discussed later in this chapter). A **multi-core processor** contains more than two separate processors on a single chip. Dual-core and multi-core processors are well suited for multitasking environments in which a user can be working with multiple computing tasks concurrently.

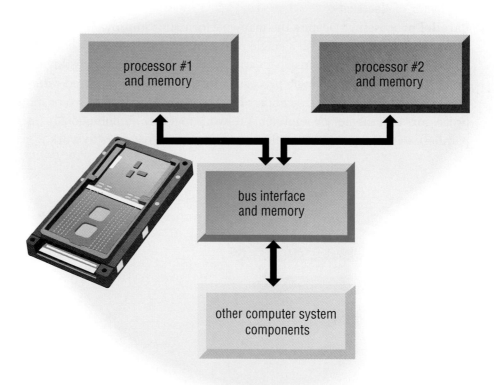

Figure 2-17 Dual-Core Processor
A dual-core processor is a CPU that includes two complete cores per physical processor, meaning that a single integrated circuit (silicon chip) contains two processors and their cache memories.

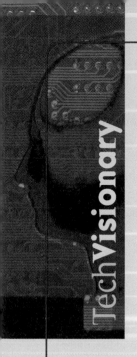

NOBEL PRIZE WINNER

Jack S. Kilby

THE 2000 NOBEL PRIZE IN PHYSICS was awarded to 76-year-old Jack Kilby for his work on the integrated circuit, which paved the way for the technological revolution that became known as the "Information Age." The development of the integrated circuit permitted gigantic gains in computer power.

Kilby's first integrated circuit, about the size of a thumbnail, was built in 1958. His novel idea was to develop the numerous electrical transistors in the chip's circuit from a single block of material, rather than assembling them with wires and other components. Kilby's work led to the integrated circuits of today, shrunk in size and loaded with millions of transistors. Without the integrated circuit, the personal computers of today would not have been possible.

Also credited with coinventing the pocket calculator, Kilby worked for Texas Instruments until 1970 and then became a freelance inventor. He held more than 60 patents and has been awarded honorary degrees from three universities. Kilby said he had no idea how much his microchip would expand the field of electronics. Until his death in 2005, he still listened to music on a turntable and did not own a cell phone.

Kilby received half of the $915,000 Nobel prize. The other half was shared by two physicists who invented semiconductor heterostructures. The Nobel Prize is usually awarded for an abstract theoretical insight or an experimental technique. This is the first time the award was given for engineering rather than pure science.

As a nod to the worldwide impact of the Internet, the Royal Swedish Academy of Sciences gave the prize to three men whose work enabled the growth of computer technology.

Sources: Johnson, George. "The Nobels: Dazzled by the Digital Light," *The New York Times*, October 15, 2000; Glanz, James. "3 Men Vital to Internet Share Physics Prize," *The New York Times*, October 11, 2000; Crissey, Mike. "Texan's Microchip Speeds Info Age," December 2006 <http://www.news.excite.com/news/ap/001010/19/nobel-reax>; Texas Instruments Company Overview, 2006. December 2006 <http://www.ti.com/corp/docs/kilbyctr/jackstclair.shtml>.

System Clock

A computer contains a **system clock** in the form of a small electronic chip that synchronizes or controls the timing of all computer operations. The clock generates evenly spaced electrical pulses that synchronize the flow of information through the computer's internal communication channels.

Pulses of the clock execute or "trigger" instructions. Since an instruction may direct the execution of other events either internal or external to the CPU, the clock pulse provides a way for these events to occur in harmony. Pulse speed is measured according to the number of clock pulses per second, called **hertz**. One hertz is equal to one pulse per second.

One **clock cycle** is equal to two ticks of the clock. A CPU uses a fixed number of clock cycles to execute each instruction. The faster the clock ticks, the faster the CPU can execute instructions. Some personal computers today operate at clock speeds faster than one gigahertz. The speed of the clock affects only the speed of the CPU. It has no effect on the operation of peripheral devices.

Random Access Memory

Random access memory (RAM), also called main memory or primary storage, is the temporary memory in which programs and data are stored while the computer is in use. Programs must first be entered, or input, into RAM before they are executed or data is processed. The CPU then moves information from RAM into its registers for processing. RAM performs these three functions:

- accepts and holds program instructions and data
- acts as the CPU's source for data and instructions and as a destination for operation results
- holds the final processed information until it can be sent to the desired output or storage devices, such as a printer or disk drive

Each memory location has its own unique address, just as each person has a postal mailing address. When the CPU needs an instruction or data from memory, an electronic message is sent to the appropriate address and the instruction or data is transferred to the appropriate register in the CPU.

The CPU must be able to find programs and data once they are stored in RAM. Therefore, program instructions and data are placed at a specific location within RAM, known as an **address**. Each location has its own unique address, just as each person has an individual postal mailing address. When the CPU needs an instruction or data from RAM, an electronic message is sent to the instruction's address and the instruction is transferred to the appropriate register in the CPU.

Random access means that because each RAM location has an individual address, the computer can go directly to the instructions and data it needs, rather than search each individual location one after another (sequentially). RAM memory is both readable and writable, meaning that the contents of any RAM location can be changed and/or read at any time. RAM memory is also **volatile memory**, meaning that it requires a constant charge to keep its contents intact. If a computer loses power, the contents of its memory are lost. Therefore, it is important to save any valuable work frequently to a permanent storage medium.

The temporary nature of RAM is its most important characteristic. When the computer is finished with one set of instructions and data, it can store another set in the first set's place. RAM is reusable, much like a chalkboard. Instructions and data can be written on the chalkboard (or into RAM) and then erased to make room for new instructions and data to be written in the same space.

Types of RAM   Two types of RAM used with early PCs were **Dynamic RAM (DRAM**, pronounced dee-ram) and **Static RAM (SRAM**, pronounced ess-ram). Some personal computers contained either, or both, types. Without a continuous supply of electrical energy, DRAM chips eventually lose their contents. Because of this, DRAM chips must be constantly refreshed by receiving a fresh supply of energy. SRAM is a static type of RAM that is faster and more reliable (and more expensive) than the more common DRAM. The term *static* refers to the fact that SRAM doesn't need to be refreshed like DRAM and it therefore allows a faster access time.

Over the years, newer computers have been introduced that contain faster microprocessors. To accommodate the increased speed, chip manufacturers have designed and built faster RAM chips. **Synchronous DRAM (SDRAM)** divides RAM into two separate memory banks to increase the processing of memory requests. **Double Data Rate SDRAM (DDR SDRAM)** can transfer data twice as fast as SDRAM because it reads data twice during each clock cycle. DDR SDRAM is standard in most computer systems today, and a third generation (called DDR3 SDRAM) is emerging.

The amount of main memory in a computer is important. Large programs, such as desktop publishing and computer-aided design applications, require a lot of main memory. A computer may be unable to use a program if the computer's main memory is insufficient. Additional RAM chips can be installed inside the system unit on most computers.

Measuring RAM Capacities   RAM storage capacities are measured in bytes. Since most personal computers have enough memory to store millions or even billions, of bytes, it is common to refer to storage capacity in terms of **kilobytes** (equal to one thousand bytes), **megabytes** (equal to one million bytes), and even **gigabytes** (one billion bytes). Storage capacities of personal computers are typically quoted as 512 megabytes, or as one or more gigabytes. By contrast, today's

Table 2-3 Measures of Data Storage

Term	Abbreviation	Mathematical Notation	Approximate Number of Bytes	Exact Number of Bytes
bit			0 or 1	1/8
byte		1	1	
kilobyte	KB	2^{10}	1 thousand	1,024
megabyte	MB	2^{20}	1 million	1,048,576
gigabyte	GB	2^{30}	1 billion	1,073,741,824
terabyte	TB	2^{40}	1 trillion	1,099,411,627,7756
petabyte	PB	2^{50}	1 quadrillion	1,125,899,906,842,624
exabyte	EB	2^{60}	1 quintillion	1,151,921,504,606,846,976
zettabyte	ZB	2^{70}	1 sextillion	1,180,591,620.717,303,424
yottabyte	YB	2^{80}	1 septillion	1,208,925,819,614,629,174,706,176

mainframe computer storage is often measured in **terabytes**, or trillions of bytes, and the most powerful supercomputers offer storage capacities expressed in **petabytes**, each of which is approximately 1,000 terabytes. The prefix tera- is derived from the Greek word for monster, an apt association to the tremendous size of a terabyte. Table 2-3 displays the various measurements of storage. Table 2-4 shows the amount of memory typically contained in various types of computers.

Cache Memory   A type of processing storage used with RAM is cache memory. **Cache memory** (pronounced *cash*) is a holding area in which the data and instructions most recently called by the processor from RAM are stored. When a processor needs an instruction or data from RAM, it first looks for the instruction in cache memory. Because some instructions are called frequently, they are often found in cache memory, shortening processing time. Cache memory may be con-

Table 2-4 Computer Memory Comparisons

Type of Computer	Number of Processors	Amount of Memory
handheld computer	usually one	64 MB or more
notebook PC	usually one	256 MB or more
desktop PC	usually one or two	512 MB or more
workstation	one or two	128—1,024 MB or more
midsize server	several	hundreds of GB or more
mainframe	hundreds	hundreds of GB or more
supercomputer	hundreds to thousands	hundreds of TB to several petabytes

tained on the CPU in the form of memory chips hardwired onto the motherboard, or as reserved space on a storage device such as a hard disk. Some operating systems also allow users to set aside a portion of RAM to be used as cache memory.

There are various types of cache memory. **Level 1 cache memory** is built into the architecture of microprocessor chips, providing faster access to the instructions and data residing in cache memory. **Level 2 cache memory** may also be built into the architecture of microprocessor chips, as is the norm for current processors. On older computers, it may consist of high-speed SRAM chips placed on the motherboard or on a card that is inserted into a slot in the computer. **Level 3 cache memory** is available on computers that have level 2 cache, or advanced transfer cache, and is separate from the microprocessor.

Memory Access Time   **Memory access time** is the amount of time required for the processor to access (read) data, instructions, and information from memory. Access time affects the speed at which the computer can process data and therefore the overall performance of the computer. Access time is usually stated in fractions of a second, as shown in Table 2-5. For example, a millisecond (abbreviated as ms) is one-thousandth of a second, and a picosecond is one-trillionth of a second. A processor with a memory access time of 50 nanoseconds would be twice as fast as one with an access time of 100 nanoseconds. However, computer manufacturers usually describe memory in terms of the amount of memory, not its speed. Thus, a manufacturer may specify a computer as having 512 MB of memory that can be expanded to 2 GB.

Read-Only Memory and Flash Memory

A computer's system unit has one or more **read-only memory (ROM)** chips that contain instructions or data permanently placed on the chip by the manufacturer. Figure 2-18 shows the location of RAM and ROM on the motherboard. The contents of a ROM chip can be read only by the user and cannot be altered or erased. ROM chips store nonvolatile memory. **Nonvolatile memory** is memory that is not lost if the power is interrupted. A typical PC contains ROM chips on which essential programs have been stored. One such program is the **basic input/output system (BIOS)**, the program that boots (starts) the computer when it is turned on. The BIOS also controls communications with the keyboard, disk drives, and other computer components. Also activated with the startup of the computer is a **power-on self test (POST) chip**, containing instructions that check the physical components of the system to make certain they are working properly.

Table 2-5 Memory Access Times

Term	Abbreviation	Speed
millisecond	ms	one-thousandth of a second
microsecond	μs	one-millionth of a second
nanosecond	ns	one-billionth of a second
picosecond	ps	one-trillionth of a second

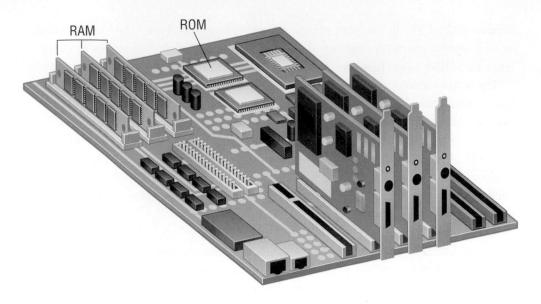

RAM

ROM

Figure 2-18 Location of RAM and ROM on the Motherboard
RAM chips temporarily store programs and data during the processing stage of
the information processing cycle. On some small computers, ROM chips
contain permanent storage of the operating system and the instructions for
managing peripheral devices.

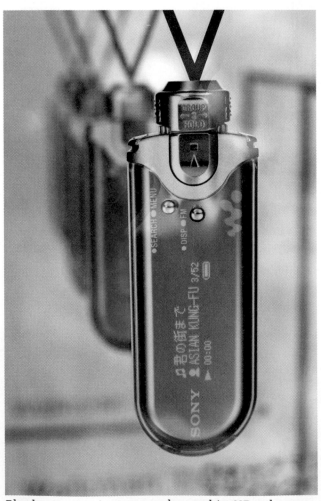

Flash memory is commonly used in MP3 players
and digital cameras.

A computer also may have ROM chips containing permanent instructions that direct the operation of peripheral devices, including the keyboard, monitor, and disk drives. Without these ROM chips, users would need to enter complex instructions each time the devices are used.

Flash memory, also referred to as flash ROM, is a type of nonvolatile memory that can be erased and reused, or reprogrammed. Flash memory is used for storing programs and data on many hand-held computers and devices, such as digital cameras, PDAs, cellular phones, and MP3 players. Some flash memory is portable. With digital cameras, a flash memory card can be removed and inserted into a printer or photo processing kiosk for instant printing. Portable flash drives are becoming increasingly common for transferring files between computers.

Several different types of removable flash cards are in use today, but they are physically different and incompatible with each other. The manufacturer and type of handheld device purchased will dictate the type of flash card used. Different types of flash cards include CompactFlash (CF), SmartMedia, Secure Digital (SD), MultiMediaCard (MMC), xD-Picture, and Memory Stick. The storage capacity of these flash cards typically ranges between 16 MB and 8 GB of data, and capacity is always increasing.

CHAPTER 2 Input and Processing

Flash memory is a small, portable card used to store various kinds of data and can be used in many different electronic devices.

Expansion Slots and Expansion Cards

An **expansion slot** is an opening in the motherboard allowing the insertion of an **expansion card** (also called an adapter). Expansion cards are add-on components to required computer functions. These cards are used to either upgrade basic functionality such as graphics quality or they may be used to add new functionality such as networking.

Although a variety of expansion cards are available, the four main types typically found in today's computers as add-on components are sound cards, video or graphics cards, network interface cards, and modem cards. A **sound card** allows sound input, such as voice, by means of a microphone and sound output via speakers. A **graphics card** (also called a video card) enhances the quality of pictures and images displayed on the monitor. A **network interface card** allows for communication between the computer and a network. A **modem card** enables computers to communicate via telephone lines and other communications media. Newly purchased personal computers typically include many of the necessary cards already installed,

An expansion card is a circuit board that can be installed inside a system unit, usually on the motherboard. Shown here are a graphics card (left), sound card (middle), and a network interface card (right).

Table 2-6 Expansion Cards

Type of Card	Function
graphics card	enables a computer system to process and display high-quality graphics and video
modem card	enables a computer system to use telephone lines for communication between computers
network card	enables a computer system to participate in a local area network
sound card	allows high-quality sound input via a microphone and output via speakers
TV tuner card	allows a PC to pick up television signals
wireless network card	enables a computer to receive nearby wireless network signals

and additional expansion cards may be inserted into slots within a computer to add or upgrade some of the capabilities discussed in Table 2-6.

Notebook and other portable computers are often too small to accommodate large motherboards, expansion boards, and other components. As a result, a type of expansion board called a **PC card** (or PCMCIA card) has been developed specifically for smaller PCs. The standards that are used to monitor this technology have been developed by the Personal Computer Memory Card International Association (PCMCIA). The PC card plugs into the side of a notebook or portable computer. Most are about the size of a credit card, only thicker, and can be unplugged and removed when no longer needed. Type I cards provide additional memory. Type II cards typically provide networking or sound capabilities, and Type III cards provide a removable hard drive. Users can switch back and forth among various types of PC cards while the computer is running.

Expansion cards on small computers, such as notebook computers, are called PC cards. The most common PC cards are network and wireless network cards.

Ports

A **port** (sometimes called an interface) is an external plug-in slot on a computer used to connect to a device such as a printer or a telephone line. Personal computers have ports that are "dedicated," meaning they are reserved for connecting a specific device. For example, a personal computer has a dedicated port for connecting a keyboard and another for connecting a mouse. Personal computers usually contain the following types of ports, as shown in Figure 2-19:

- Dedicated ports for connecting a mouse and a keyboard.
- A **Universal Serial Bus (USB) port** is widely used for high-speed modems, scanners, digital cameras, and other devices. Many keyboards and point-and-click devices are now available with USB ports as well. A single USB port can accommodate more than 100 peripheral devices connected together in sequence.
- A **serial port** (also called a communications [COM] port), is used for connecting some peripheral devices such as a keyboard, mouse, PDA, or external modem. A serial port can transmit data only one bit at a time. Most personal computers have at least one serial port, but dedicated ports and USB ports have largely replaced the use of serial ports.
- A **parallel port** is used for connecting a peripheral device to a computer. Most personal computers have at least one parallel port that is usually used for connecting a printer. A parallel port transmits data eight bits at a time. On personal computers, a parallel port uses a 25-pin connector.
- A **video port** connects a monitor and may be built into the computer or provided by a graphics card placed in an expansion slot.
- A **network port** connects a computer system to a local area network. The cable used to connect to a network has an RJ-45 connector, which is slightly larger than a telephone cable connector.
- A **modem port** connects a modem card to a telephone line. The cable used to connect to a telephone line is a standard telephone cable with an RJ-11 connector.
- An **audio port** connects a sound card to external devices such as speakers, microphones, and headsets.

Tech Demo 2-5
Parallel Cable

Tech Demo 2-6
Serial Cable

A **small computer system interface (SCSI**, pronounced *scuzzy*) is a parallel interface system used by most Apple Macintosh computers, some PCs, and most UNIX systems for connecting peripheral devices to a computer. SCSI interfaces provide for faster transmission rates than standard serial and parallel ports. Users can attach multiple devices to a single SCSI port.

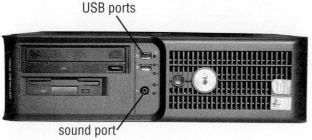

USB ports · sound port · parallel port · LAN port · speaker connections · serial port · video port · USB ports · microphone connection

Figure 2-19 Ports on a System Unit

Ports are external plug-in slots that connect devices such as monitors, keyboards, and printers to the system unit. These ports are visible on the front and back of the system unit.

Due to size constraints, most personal computers have a limited number of ports, restricting the number of devices that can be connected. Some notebook computers can be inserted in a **docking station**, an accessory that provides additional ports plus (typically) a charger for the laptop's battery, extra disk drives, and other peripherals.

Buses

Go to this title's Internet Resource Center and read the article titled "Bus Technology." www.emcp.net/CUT3e

How does data move from one component to another inside a computer? The answer is that every computer contains buses that connect various components and allow the transmission of data. A **bus** is an electronic path within a computer system along which bits are transmitted (see Figure 2-20). The size of a bus, referred to as **bus width**, determines the number of bits the computer can transmit or receive at one time. For example, a 32-bit bus can handle 32 bits at one time, whereas a 64-bit bus can handle 64 bits at one time. The larger the number of bits a bus can handle at one time, the faster the computer can transfer data. One way to visualize a bus is to think of it as a highway allowing data to travel from one location to another, with "bus stops" along the way where data is dropped off or picked up. The more lanes in the highway, the greater the number of "vehicles" ("0s" and "1s") that can travel on the highway at one time.

Computers contain two basic bus types: a system bus and an expansion bus. A **system bus** on the motherboard connects the processor (CPU) to main memory, providing the CPU with fast access to data stored in RAM. An **expansion bus** provides for communication between the processor and peripheral devices. For example, data traveling between RAM and a low-speed peripheral device, such as a printer or scanner, travels along an expansion bus.

A typical personal computer contains a variety of expansion buses. A **local bus** allows for the connection of high-speed devices such as hard drives. A **Peripheral**

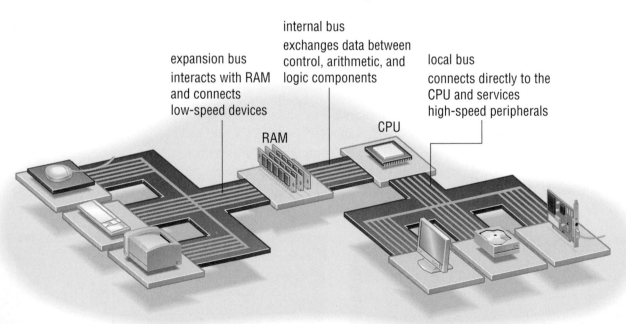

expansion bus interacts with RAM and connects low-speed devices

internal bus exchanges data between control, arithmetic, and logic components

local bus connects directly to the CPU and services high-speed peripherals

RAM

CPU

Figure 2-20 Bus Connections
Data in the form of bits travel along a bus to get from one location in a computer system to another, similar to the way vehicles travel along a highway. Bits travel along a bus from memory to the CPU, from input devices to memory, from the CPU to memory, and from memory to storage devices.

Component Interconnect (PCI) bus allows for the connection of sound cards, video cards, and network cards to a computer system. The speed at which data travels along a PCI bus is much faster than the speed at which data traveled in earlier bus technologies. Most personal computers now contain a PCI bus. An **Accelerated Graphics Port (AGP) bus** increases the speed at which graphics (including 3-D graphics) and video can be transmitted and accessed by the computer. Most newer processors, including Intel's Pentium processors, support AGP technology. For newer PCs, AGP is being replaced by the **PCI Express bus** standard for 3-D graphic cards. PCI-Express provides much faster data transfer rates than the original PCI, making it better suited for applications such as streaming video and computer games. The Universal Serial bus (USB) eliminates the need to install a board into a slot. This means that multiple external devices can be connected together and then connected to the computer's USB with a single cable. One device may be disconnected and another device connected while the computer is running, a capability known as **hot plugging** or hot swapping.

OnThe**Horizon**

THERE CAN BE LITTLE DOUBT new and exciting computer technologies will continue to appear on the computing horizon. A variety of new input and processing technologies will increase the speed and capability of computers, making our lives more enjoyable and exciting. The following paragraphs identify some technologies we may expect to be introduced within a few years, if not earlier.

Advances in Nanotechnology

Researchers in such fields as physics, chemistry, materials science, and computer science are using nanotechnology, which involves crafting machines from individual atoms, to build microscopic, massively parallel computers that are more powerful than the supercomputers of today. These computers could be programmed to replicate themselves and be injected into a human body to hunt down deadly viruses or cancers and destroy them. Scientists have already used the technology to create carbon nanotubes that are 100 times stronger and 100 times lighter than steel. Nanotubes can be used to develop semiconductors, aircraft, automobiles, and many other things. Nanotechnology robots (nanobots) could be used to clean up dangerous environmental spills and perform other tasks not suited well to humans.

Currently the U.S. government spends over 11 billion dollars on nanotechnology research and development, a figure that is undoubtedly exceeded by private sector R & D. These efforts have resulted in a number of real-world applications, and in 2005 sales of products incorporating nanotechnology exceeded 32 billion dollars, with pre-

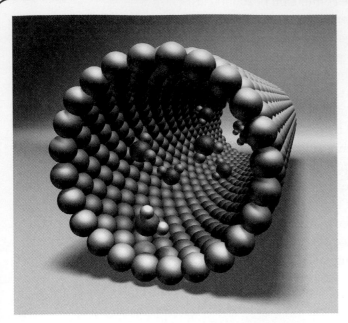

Nanotubes are at the core of nanotechnology, which builds computers at the atomic level.

dictions that sales will reach $2.6 trillion by 2014. Improvements brought about by nanotechnology are the reason for the rapid increase in sales figures. Intel predicts that its processor performance per watt will improve 300 percent by 2010 through the use of nanotechnology. The company is currently using 45 nanometers silicone technology, and plans to reduce that to 22 nanometers by 2011. To give an idea of how small these products are, a single nanometer is one billionth of a meter. The benefits of nanotechnology bring with them some dangers, particularly as the technology is employed in the health and environmental fields. Only 11 million of the 11 billion dollars the U.S. spends on nanotechnology R & D is devoted to studying the risks of the technology, a figure that many government and industry experts feel is far too low.

Cell: A New Microprocessor Architecture

The Internet and Web have created a need for computers capable of handling massive amounts of information. Computers available now are relatively slow in accessing the Internet and downloading information. IBM, along with Sony and Toshiba, has created the first iteration of a new microprocessor architecture called Cell.

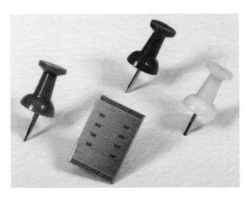

The Cell micro-processor, smaller than a quarter, debuted in the Sony Playstation 3.

Fashioned after supercomputing technology, the Cell microprocessor is based on cellular technology that will allow computers to run on tiny processors that are integrated directly with memory and communications circuits. IBM describes the future state as the equivalent of putting 32 desktop computers on a dime-sized chip. Each of these new chips will contain 32 to 36 cells, each of which will have a 1 GHz processor and up to 1 GB of memory. The expected result will be computers with computing capabilities equal to that of today's mainframe computers.

Cell has already been designed into the Sony Playstation 3, running ten times faster than the latest Intel Pentium chip. As Cell evolves, future applications may include smartphones, high-definition televisions, missile systems, radar, and medical imaging.

Next-Generation Keyboards

Efforts to improve the ubiquitous keyboard continue apace. A Russian company recently announced a unique design featuring keys containing miniature display screens. Each key's screen can be instantly changed to show the function controlled by the key, whether it be alphanumeric characters or symbols. When a key's function changes its display will automatically change as well, making it an ideal keyboard for anyone needing to work with different character sets. The Optimus keyboard also can automatically display the function keys unique to many different programs, or display keys that control access to different software programs.

As computer devices continue to shrink the search for satisfactory input methods continues. Most solutions involve smaller keyboards or keypads, but several companies are now marketing laser keyboards that use both infrared and laser technology to project a virtual keyboard onto almost any surface, allowing users to type away on a full-size QWERTY Keyboard. The virtual keyboard is projected by a small battery-powered wireless device that can be rested in front of any flat surface, and can be attached to portable computers and mobile devices, including PDAs and cell phones.

Virtual keyboards, or projection keyboards, are available as extensions to handheld computers for easier data entry.

Smart Homes

Modern homes are full of labor-saving, entertainment, comfort, and security devices. The long-held dream of linking this equipment so that control can be automated is now being realized, and even updated to include the ability to control functions through the Internet. Homes equipped with the structured wiring and computerized control systems allowing intelligent control of household devices are known as Smart Homes. While it is possible for builders to install the required structured wiring into older homes, it is much easier to install it during the construction process, something that more and more builders are doing. As the technology proliferates the cost of equipping Smart Homes has dropped, and they are no longer confined to the upper levels of the real estate market.

While wiring still predominates as a connection method, home product wireless technologies such as Z-Wave are increasingly being employed. The Z-Wave Alliance is a consortium of independent companies who have adopted the Zensys' Z-Wave open standard. A key feature of Z-Wave products is their compatibility with other products operating to the Z-Wave standard. Current Smart Homes usually contain a combination of structured wiring and wireless technologies, but in the not too distant future it is likely that all household devices will be linked wirelessly.

Chapter**Summary**

 For an interactive version of this summary, go to this text's Internet Resource Center at www.emcp.net/CUT3e. A Spanish version is also available.

What is input?

The term input refers to data and instructions entered into a computer enabling the computer to perform the task desired by the user.

What are some examples of input devices?

An **input device** allows programs, data, commands, and responses to be entered into a computer system. Types of input devices include **keyboards**, **touch screens**, **mice** (plural for mouse), **trackballs**, **touch pads**, **joysticks**, **pens** and **tablets**, **optical scanners**, **bar code readers** and **optical readers**, **microphones**, **digital cameras**, **video cameras**, and **webcams**.

How do computers process data?

Also called data processing or simply processing, the term information processing refers to the manipulation of data according to instructions in a computer program. All computers are digital devices that use the *binary number system*. They are capable of recognizing only "off" and "on" ("0" and "1") states. Each of these "0" and "1" digits is called a bit. A **bit** represents the smallest unit of data in the binary system. A group of eight bits is called a **byte**. Combinations of 0s and 1s are used to represent letters, numbers, and special characters in coding schemes such as **ASCII**, **EBCDIC**, and **Unicode**.

What are the main components of the system unit?

The **system unit** is the component that houses the processing hardware. It consists of the **power supply**, **storage bays**, and the **motherboard**. The power supply converts AC electricity into power that the computer can use. **Storage bays** are used

for installing additional devices such as hard drives and CD/DVD drives. The **motherboard** contains the **central processing unit (CPU)**, **system clock**, **random access memory (RAM)**, **read-only memory (ROM)**, **expansion slots**, and **expansion cards**, **ports**, and **buses**.

What makes up the central processing unit?

The **CPU** within the system unit is the part of a computer where processing occurs. In a personal computer the CPU consists of a **microprocessor chip**, that processes the data. The CPU contains a control unit and an arithmetic/logic unit. The **control unit** controls activity within the computer. The **arithmetic/logic unit (ALU)** performs processing operations on the data. **Registers** are used for storing instructions and data until they are needed for processing.

What types of memory does a computer need?

A computer needs both random access memory and read-only memory to function. **Random access memory (RAM)** chips inside the system unit are used to store programs while they are being executed, and data while it is being processed. The amount of RAM is measured in bytes. A specific type of RAM, called **cache memory**, provides for faster access to instructions and data, speeding up computer applications.

Read-only memory (ROM) refers to chips on which instructions, information, or data has been prerecorded. Usually, once data has been recorded on a ROM chip, it cannot be altered or removed and can only be read by the computer. However, **flash memory** is a special type of ROM that can be erased and reprogrammed.

What are expansion slots and cards?

An **expansion slot** is an opening in a computer where a circuit board, called an **expansion card**, can be inserted to add new capabilities to the computer. A **PC card** is a small expansion card that plugs into the side of a notebook or portable computer.

KeyTerms

Numbers indicate the pages where terms are first cited in the chapter. An alphabetized list of key terms with definitions (in English and Spanish) can be found on the Encore CD that accompanies this book. In addition, these terms and definitions are included in the end-of-book glossary.

Input Technology
input device, 47
keyboard, 47
Bluetooth, 47
special-function keyboard, 48
touch screen, 49
graphical user interface (GUI), 49
mouse, 49
mouse pointer, 50
mouse pad, 50
optical mouse, 50
foot mouse, 50
trackball, 51
touch pad (track pad), 51
joystick, 52
digitizing pen, 53
drawing tablet, 53
graphics tablet, 53
optical scanner (scanner), 54
bitmap, 54
pixel, 54
resolution, 55
dots per inch (dpi), 55
dumb scanner, 55
intelligent scanner, 55
optical character recognition (OCR), 55
bar code reader, 56
Universal Product Code (UPC), 56
optical reader, 57
smart card, 57
digital camera, 57
video input, 59
webcam, 59
audio input, 61
voice input, 61
voice recognition program, 61

speaker-independent program, 62
speech recognition program, 62
speaker-dependent program, 62

Data Processing by Computers
machine language, 64
bit, 64
binary numbers, 64
byte, 64
American Standard Code for Information Interchange (ASCII), 64
Extended Binary Coded Decimal Interchange Code (EBCDIC), 65
Unicode, 65

The System Unit
system unit, 65

The Power Supply
power supply, 65

Storage Bays
storage bay (bay), 67

The Motherboard
motherboard, 68
trace, 68
microprocessor chip (integrated circuit), 69
semiconductor, 69
machine cycle, 70
control unit, 70
fetching, 70
decoding, 70
instruction time (I-time), 71
arithmetic/logic unit (ALU), 71
executing, 71
register, 72
storing, 72
execution time (E-time), 72
instruction register, 72
data register, 72
storage register, 72
coprocessor, 72
graphics coprocessor, 72
cryptographic coprocessor (crypto-coprocessor), 72
word size, 74

word, 74
reduced instruction set computing (RISC), 75
pipelining, 75
parallel processing, 75
multithreading, 76
hyperthreading, 76
core, 76
dual-core processor, 76
multi-core processor, 76
system clock, 77
hertz, 78
clock cycle, 78
random access memory (RAM) (main memory or primary storage), 78
address, 79
volatile memory, 79
Dynamic RAM (DRAM), 79
Static RAM (SRAM), 79
Synchronous DRAM (SDRAM), 79
Double Data Rate SDRAM (DDR SDRAM), 79
kilobyte, 79
megabyte, 79
gigabyte, 79
terabyte, 80
petabyte, 80
cache memory, 80
level 1 cache memory, 81
level 2 cache memory, 81
level 3 cache memory, 81
memory access time, 81
read-only memory (ROM), 81

nonvolatile memory, 81
basic input/output system (BIOS), 81
power-on self test (POST) chip, 81
flash memory (flash ROM), 82
expansion slot, 83
expansion card (adapter), 83
sound card, 83
graphics card (video card), 83
network interface card, 83
modem card, 83
PC card (PCMCIA card), 84
port (interface), 85
Universal Serial Bus (USB) port, 85
serial port (communications [COM] port), 85
parallel port, 85
video port, 85
network port, 85
modem port, 85
audio port, 85
small computer system interface (SCSI), 85
docking station, 86
bus, 86
bus width, 86
system bus, 86
expansion bus, 86
local bus, 87
Peripheral Component Interconnect (PCI) bus, 87
Accelerated Graphics Port (AGP) bus, 87
PCI Express bus, 87
hot plugging (hot swapping), 87

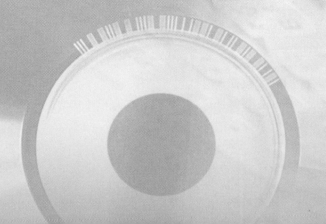

ChapterExercises

 The following chapter exercises, along with new activities and information, are also offered in the Internet Resource Center for this title at www.emcp.net/ CUT3e.

Tutorial > Exploring Windows

In Tutorial 2, you will explore new Vista features by opening the Help and Support Center and viewing an article describing the main features of Vista as well as viewing a demostration on security basics.

Expanding Your Knowledge > Articles and Activities

 Visit the Internet Resource Center for this title at www.emcp.net/CUT3e, read the articles related to this chapter, and complete the corresponding activities. The article titles include:

- Topic 2-1: Processor Installation and Upgrades
- Topic 2-2: Advances in Chip Architecture
- Topic 2-3: Improvements in Chip Materials and Manufacturing Processes
- Topic 2-4: Bus Technology

Terms Check > Matching

 For additional practice, go to the Internet Resource Center for this title at www.emcp.net/CUT3e for a chapter crossword puzzle.

Write the letter of the correct answer on the line before each numbered item.

a. motherboard
b. keyboard
c. arithmetic/logic unit
d. binary
e. port
f. fetching
g. system clock
h. register
i. expansion card
j. mouse

_____ 1. A number system that uses combinations of zeros and ones (0s and 1s) to represent letters, numbers, and special characters.

_____ 2. A circuit board that can be inserted into a computer to give the computer added capability.

_____ 3. Retrieving an instruction or data from memory.

_____ 4. The main circuit board inside the system unit.

_____ 5. A component of the ALU that temporarily holds instructions and data.

_____ 6. A small electronic chip that synchronizes or controls the timing of all computer operations.

_____ 7. An opening in the computer that allows an external component to be plugged into a circuit board.

_____ 8. A handheld point-and-click input device whose movement across a flat surface causes a corresponding movement of its on-screen pointer.

_____ 9. The part of the CPU that carries out instructions and performs arithmetic and logical operations on the data.

_____ 10. The most common input device used to enter alphanumeric characters into a computer.

Technology Illustrated > Identify the Process

What process is illustrated in this drawing? Identify the process and write a paragraph describing it.

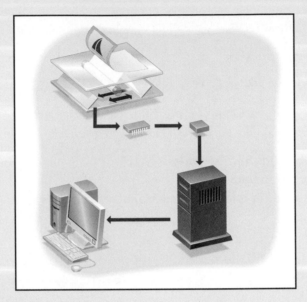

Knowledge Check > Multiple Choice

  Additional quiz questions are available on the Encore CD that accompanies this book as well as on the Internet Resource Center for this title at www.emcp.net/CUT3e.

Circle the letter of the best answer from those provided.

1. Data and instructions entered into a computer that enable the computer to perform desired tasks are called

    a. processing.
    b. input.
    c. storage.
    d. controlling.

2. Data that has been processed in a manner that renders it meaningful and useful to the user is called

    a. input.
    b. information.
    c. a program.
    d. fetching.

3. A CPU contains

    a. a card reader and a printing device.
    b. an analytical engine and a control unit.
    c. a control unit and an arithmetic/logic unit.
    d. an arithmetic logic unit and a card reader.

4. The part of a computer that coordinates all of its functions is called its

    a. ROM program.
    b. system board.
    c. arithmetic/logic unit.
    d. control unit.

5. A byte is equal to

    a. four bits, or one nibble.
    b. six bits and one nibble.

c. two bits.

d. eight bits.

6. The system clock inside a computer ensures that the

a. computer user will always know the correct time.

b. computer will run faster than one without a system clock.

c. activities of the computer will be properly synchronized.

d. computer will be able to address a 32-bit data bus.

7. The parts of the information processing cycle are

a. fetching, decoding, executing, and storing.

b. fetching, comparing, interpreting, and outputting.

c. inputting, interpreting, processing, and outputting.

d. input, processing, output, and storage.

8. Processing speed in microprocessors is measured in

a. megabytes.

b. hertz.

c. kilobytes.

d. bits per second.

9. On a personal computer, all processing functions are contained on a single electronic chip called a

a. microprocessor.

b. data processor.

c. calculation chip.

d. BIOS chip.

10. A holding area that stores the data and instructions most recently called by the processor from RAM is called

a. residual memory.

b. nonvolatile memory.

c. static memory.

d. cache memory.

Things That Think > Brainstorming New Uses

In groups or individually, contemplate the following questions and develop as many answers as you can.

1. Scientists have invented the first prototype of a computerized scalpel that can tell a surgeon when to stop cutting during surgery to remove cancerous tumors so that only the diseased tissue is removed. This technology would allow doctors to save healthy tissue, thus potentially improving the patient's odds for survival. What other fields could benefit from this development? Consider possible uses in various industries.

2. Computers can accomplish many tasks today, but there are still some things they cannot do. Think of some of the things you would like the computers of the future to be able to do. Which of the new uses will be the most popular and why?

Key Principles > Completion

Fill in the blanks with the appropriate words or phrases.

1. A type of input device that allows a user to make selections from among a group of options displayed on a screen by pressing a finger against the chosen option is known as a(n) _____.

2. Material captured by a scanner is stored as a matrix of rows and columns of dots, called a _____.

3. A computer language that uses binary numbers, which are constructed solely of the symbols 0 and 1, is known as _____.

4. A type of code capable of accommodating certain languages having more complicated alphabets than English is called _____.

5. Small electronic devices consisting of tiny transistors and other circuit parts on a piece of semiconductor material are called microprocessor chips or _____.

6. A small electronic chip that synchronizes or controls the timing of all computer operations is the _____.

7. A computer word is _____.

8. Random access memory (RAM) is _____.

9. Cache memory is _____.

10. The four steps or actions in the machine cycle are _____, _____, _____, and _____.

Tech Architecture > Label the Drawing

In this illustration of a computer system, label the devices as input, output, processing, or storage devices.

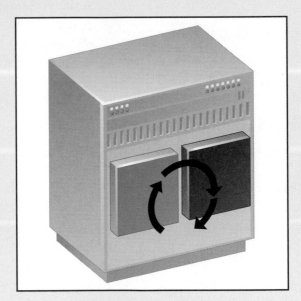

Techno Literacy > Research and Writing

Develop appropriate written responses based on your research for each item.

1. What is inside the computer case? Ask your instructor to allow you to open up a computer in the computer lab and look at the components inside. Using paper and pen, draw the components that you recognize and label each one. At a minimum, include the microprocessor chip, memory chips (RAM and ROM), expansion slots, expansion boards, and ports. Ask your instructor to explain other components you do not recognize. Label each one and write a brief summary of the component's function.

2. How many ways can users input data? Page through a computer magazine such as *PC World*

or visit a computer store and select a personal computer that interests you. Research and describe all of the different input devices that could be used with that particular computer system.

3. What can you do with an expansion card? Describe the various types of expansion boards and their functions. What kind of expansion boards would you like to add to your computer? Why?

4. How do the kinds of computer memory differ? Describe the differences among RAM, ROM, flash memory, and cache memory. Is there any relationship between processing speed and the different types of memory? If so, what?

Technology Issues > Team Problem-Solving

In groups, brainstorm possible solutions to the issues presented.

1. As our population ages, the number of Americans with disabilities will increase. Computers and computer technology offer the potential to make life easier for people who are disabled. What are some of the possibilities? What are some of the ways computer technology may be used to improve their lives in the future? Do you foresee any ethical problems with any of these solutions?

2. Even in today's computerized world there are still people who do not like computers and try to avoid them as much as possible. Why do you think people would feel that way? Do you see this attitude increasing or decreasing in the future? What can be done to combat this computer phobia (fear or dislike of computers), or should anything be done at all?

Mining Data > Internet Research and Reporting

Conduct Internet searches to find the information described in the activities below. Write a brief report that summarizes your research results. Be sure to document your sources, using the MLA format (see Chapter 1, page 42, to review MLA style guidelines).

1. Moore's Law is a famous concept in the information technology industry. Developed around a prediction in 1965 by Gordon Moore, cofounder of Intel Corporation, the law holds that the computing capability of integrated circuits, measured by the number of transistors per square inch, doubles every two years (originally, Moore said 12 months). Research this topic and explain why Moore's Law continues to be accurate or why it has proved incorrect. What are industry leaders predicting for the future?

2. What is the most powerful supercomputer in the world? Where is it located? Who designed and manufactured the computer? What is it used for?

3. Research the topic of spying technologies that countries use to gather information on each other's activities. What are some of the newest devices and how successful are they?

Technology Timeline > Predicting Next Steps

Look at the timeline below outlining the major benchmarks in the development of computing. Research this topic and fill in as many steps as you can. What do you think the next steps will be? Complete the timeline through the year 2030.

1982 Sony releases the first commercial electronic still camera, which was a video camera that took video freeze-frames.

1989 The first true digital camera that stored images with digital signals is introduced.

1994 The first digital cameras for the general consumer market are released.

1995 Sony debuts the first digital camcorder.

2002 Cell phones with digital cameras become available in the United States.

2006 The first feature film to be shot entirely with cell phones is completed.

Ethical Dilemmas > Group Discussion and Debate

As a class or within an assigned group, discuss the following ethical dilemma.

As technology manufacturers look to cut costs, they often consider "outsourcing" production to an offshore company or moving production facilities to countries outside of the United States. Either of these options may result in savings due to lower labor and facilities costs.

In your group, discuss the issues of outsourcing production and moving production facilities to other countries. Are these practices illegal or unethical? Should such cost-cutting measures be considered more important than the employment of U.S. workers? Is it fair for companies to pay workers lower wages in another country? Should there be incentives for companies to maintain their facilities in the United States?

Adding Software and Hardware Components to Your PC

INSTALLING SYSTEM SOFTWARE, APPLICATION PROGRAMS, and hardware components with early PCs was difficult and cumbersome compared with the installation process for modern computers. In the past, users had to enter complex instructions. Thus, an experienced computer technician or other professional was needed to install the software or hardware properly. Today's computer manufacturers have made these activities easier by including installation instructions and diagrams with their products. Additionally, Microsoft Windows includes features that enable users to install software and hardware more quickly and easily. For example, the Windows Control Panel contains utilities for installing and removing application programs and hardware devices. In this Tech Insight you will learn how to install software programs and add hardware devices to your personal computer system.

Manufacturers such as Dell Computer preload most of their new PCs with the Windows operating system, some application programs, and basic hardware devices. Because most PCs use Windows, this Tech Insight assumes you are using a Windows-based computer.

Installing or Upgrading the Operating System

Sometimes situations occur that require you to reinstall the operating system and application programs. An operating system (OS) contains programs that direct a computer's operations and programs that manage the computer's internal and external components. If Windows was not preinstalled on your computer, a CD-ROM containing the OS may have been included in the package, or you can purchase one at a computer store or at another retail outlet.

Installing the OS on your hard disk is relatively simple. With your computer turned off, insert the CD-ROM containing the OS into the CD or CD/DVD drive at the front of the system unit. Turn the computer on. A small ROM chip on the motherboard will search for an operating system and find it on the CD, along with a file of instructions for installing the OS. Installation instructions will be displayed on the screen. Follow the instructions to complete the process.

When a new version of the OS becomes available, you may want to install it on your computer, a procedure known as upgrading. To install the upgraded version, insert the CD-ROM containing the new version in the CD drive. Follow the instructions on your screen to install the new version. The installation should be completed in a few minutes.

Installing Application Software

Application software enables users to perform specific types of activities and tasks for which computers were designed. The type of software purchased depends on the user's intended purpose, and there are application programs available for almost every need. The most widely sold type is productivity software that enables users to improve their efficiency at home and on the job. Examples of productivity software include word processing, spreadsheet, database, desktop publishing, presentation graphics, project management, and computer-aided design.

TIP System requirements for installing the software are usually printed on the software package or box. Among the requirements is the minimum amount of hard disk space (capacity) needed to house the software. Be sure your hard disk has enough unused capacity to store the software. If there is insufficient capacity on your hard disk, you will be alerted to this problem.

Most applications come on CDs or DVDs that run their Setup utility automatically when the disc is inserted into a PC. To install a new application, simply insert its disc and follow the prompts that appear. If AutoPlay is turned on for the CD or DVD drive and it is set to ask what you want to do with each disc, an AutoPlay dialog box appears. Click *Run autorun.exe* to allow the disc to run its automatic setup utility. If you are prompted for an administrator password or confirmation, type the appropriate password or provide confirmation.

If nothing happens when you insert a program disc, try manually activating the Autorun file on the CD as follows (in Windows Vista):

1. Click Start and click Computer.
2. Double-click the drive icon in which the CD or DVD is inserted.

If nothing happens after you do the preceding steps, you might need to browse the disc to find the Setup program. Follow these steps to locate the setup program:

1. From the Computer window, right-click the drive icon for the CD or DVD and choose Explore.
2. Double-click Setup.exe or Install.exe. If these files are not present, consult the documentation for the application to determine the name of the setup program file, and double-click on that file name.

After the software has been installed, you can access the program by clicking the Start button, the Programs option, and then selecting the program you installed, such as Word. (Note: The installation process is the same for almost all application programs.)

TIP If a previous (older) version of the software is already installed on your hard disk and you are installing an upgrade, only the needed parts of the newer version will be installed. Also, files you created using the older version will remain intact, allowing you to continue using those files.

Most software manufacturers include installation instructions with the software programs they sell.

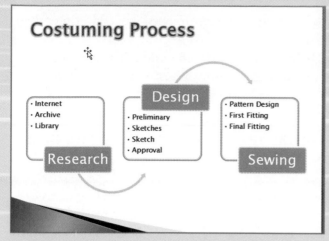

Presentation graphics is an example of productivity software.

Connecting System Components

In addition to the system unit, your PC probably came with basic components such as the monitor, keyboard, mouse, and maybe a printer. These components are referred to as peripherals, because they are external (or peripheral) to the system unit. In the following sections, you will learn about device drivers and plug-and-play features and how to connect add-on peripheral devices to the system unit so that, collectively, all devices and components function smoothly as a computer system.

Device Drivers and Plug-and-Play Features

Every device, whether it is a printer, disk drive, or keyboard, must have an associated driver program. A driver controls the device, translating commands between the device and programs that use the device so that it functions as intended. Each device has its own set of specialized commands that only the driver knows. Most programs access devices by using generic commands. A driver accepts generic commands and translates them into specialized commands for the device.

Some drivers, such as the keyboard driver, are included with the computer's operating system, because the manufacturer assumes you will use the keyboard that came with the computer. Other special devices, such as a scanner or joystick, may come with the device's driver program on a CD-ROM that you will need to load. The operating system will include drivers for a variety of devices, allowing the user to choose the needed ones. A filename of a

driver designed for use in a Windows environment often has a DRV file extension.

Some computer systems will configure devices and expansion boards automatically, a feature known as plug-and-play. With plug-and-play, a user should be able to plug in a device and use it immediately. Newer Apple Macintosh computers are plug-and-play systems, and both Microsoft and Intel use a technology called PnP (short for plug and play) that supports plug-and-play installation.

Your PC probably has the plug-and-play capability. Adding new components is simply a matter of plugging the devices into the appropriate ports on the back of the system unit.

Locating System Unit Ports

The system unit contains several ports (see Figure 1). Many manufacturers label the ports, and some companies include an installation diagram with their computers. Additionally, cables that come with a computer usually will fit into only one port. These aids assist users in setting up a computer system.

Connecting a New Printer

Most printers purchased for home or office use are either ink-jet or laser. Both types require a container of ink called a toner cartridge. If your printer came without a toner cartridge or a printer cable, you'll need to purchase these items.

Use the Autorun built into the application's CD to easily start the Setup program. Shown here is the AutoPlay dialog box in Windows Vista.

Installing a printer is a simple task. To connect the printer to the system unit and to a power source, complete the following steps:

1. With the power turned off, plug one end of the printer cable to the printer and the other end to the port located at the back of the system unit. Most printers are USB models, so they can connect to any available USB port on the PC.
2. Plug the power cord into the power connector on the printer and the other end into a surge protector.
3. Turn on the computer.
4. If Windows automatically detects the new printer and prompts you for its Setup disc, insert that disc and follow the prompts. If not, click Start and click Control Panel.
5. Click Hardware and Sound and then click Printers. Icons for the currently installed printer drivers will appear.
6. Click Add a Printer to open the Add Printer dialog box.
7. Click Add a local printer and then click Next.
8. Follow the on-screen instructions to complete the installation process.

Installing Expansion Boards and Devices inside the System Unit

Most computers are shipped with printed instructions for installing internal components, expansion boards, and other devices inside the system unit. At some time you may want to add one or more of these components to increase your computer's capabilities. For example, you may want to install additional RAM capacity, a modem, or an extra CD or DVD drive. The instructions most likely include a section explaining the procedure for gaining internal access to the motherboard, expansion slots, and other components. Follow the steps carefully.

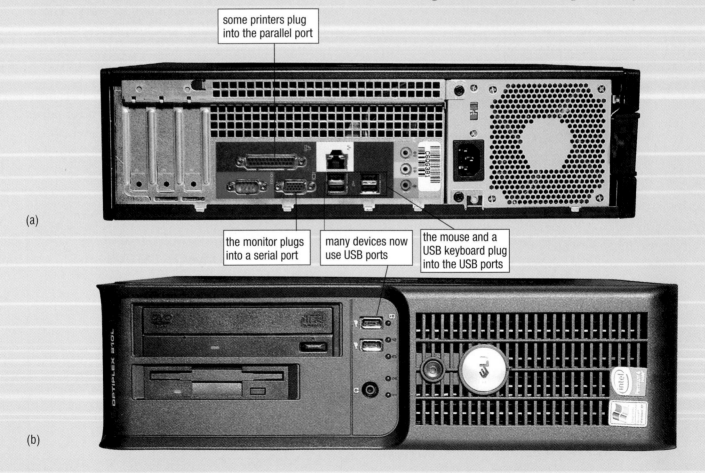

(a)

some printers plug into the parallel port

the monitor plugs into a serial port

many devices now use USB ports

the mouse and a USB keyboard plug into the USB ports

(b)

Figure 1 Ports on a System Unit

A variety of ports located on the system unit provide for the connection of peripheral devices, including monitor, keyboard, mouse, and printer. (a) Back of the system unit. (b) Front of the system unit.

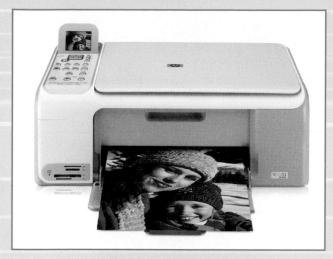

A printer is one example of a peripheral device.

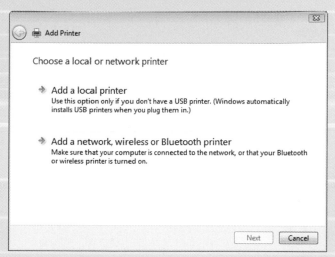

The Windows Vista Add Printer dialog box allows for the installation of a local or network printer.

TIP Computer prices have declined significantly during recent years. If your computer is more than two or three years old, you may find it more cost-effective to purchase a new computer system with more capabilities and greater capacity than to upgrade your present computer.

Precautionary Measures

Before attempting to install any device or circuit board inside the system unit, you should perform the following steps in sequence:

1. Turn off your computer and all other devices.
2. Ground yourself by touching an unpainted metal surface at the back of the computer (system unit) before touching anything inside the computer. While you work, periodically touch an unpainted metal surface to dissipate any static electricity that might cause damage to the computer.
3. Unplug the power cable to your computer and then press the power button to ground the system board.
4. Disconnect all devices connected to the computer, including the monitor, from electrical outlets or a surge protector to reduce the potential for personal injury or shock. Also, be sure to disconnect any telephone or communication lines from the computer.

An extensive variety of devices and circuit boards can be installed inside the system unit to render the computer more useful, including CD drives, DVD drives, graphics boards, sound boards, modems, and memory (RAM) boards. Unless you have training

and experience in the installation of internal devices and circuit boards, you may want to have the work done by a certified PC technician who can perform and guarantee the installation. In such cases, ask questions and make sure the technician or company is one supported by the manufacturer of your computer. Additionally, only a certified technician should install or replace some components. For example, to replace a microprocessor in some computers you need a special tool designed for this purpose. Installing or replacing storage drives involves a series of complex steps that are probably better left to an experienced technician.

Unlike the installation of microprocessors, storage drives, and other components that may require the services of a service technician and typically involve a series of complex steps and special tools, installing expansion boards is relatively easy. Many users prefer to install one or more expansion boards, such as a RAM board, to enhance the computer's capabilities. The user's manual that came with your computer may contain instructions for installing various types of boards, including RAM boards. Also, manufacturers of expansion boards usually include printed installation instructions and illustrations in the package along with the board.

The installation procedures for various types of boards are quite similar. Chances are that after you have installed one kind of expansion board, you will find the installation of other kinds of boards even easier.

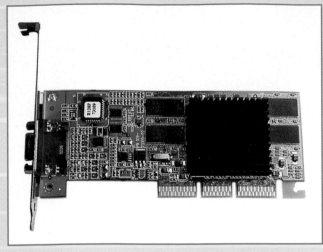

Additional components such as this video card can be installed to add extra functionality to a computer.

Figure 2 Installing a RAM Board
When inserting a DIMM module, the clip fits into the notch on the side of the DIMM. If inserted properly, it snaps into place easily.

Installing a RAM Board

Older PCs came with a type of RAM called SIMM (single inline memory module). Newer Pentium PCs contain a type of RAM called DIMM (dual inline memory module). The user's manual supplied with your computer will specify the type in your system. The main difference in the way the two modules are installed is that SIMM modules are inserted into an expansion board at an angle and a DIMM module is inserted vertically. Assuming your computer uses DIMM modules, you can easily install an additional DIMM module by completing the following steps:

1. Study carefully the printed instructions and illustration(s) that came in the package along with the DIMM module. The illustrations or diagrams identify the slot where you will insert the module.
2. With the system unit panel removed to expose the motherboard, locate the slot where you will insert the module. (Note: Your computer should already contain at least one RAM module and may provide multiple slots for adding more RAM). Select an empty slot, perhaps the one closest to the already installed RAM module, although any available slot may be used.

3. Match the orientation of the DIMM module with the slot. The module will fit only one way because of notches in the slot.
4. Firmly press the DIMM module (board) straight down into the slot, until the clips on both ends fit over the notch in the DIMM module. The DIMM module fits properly if the clip snaps into place (Figure 2). (Caution: Do not exert too much pressure on the DIMM module. The module should easily snap into place when inserted properly.)

A Final Word

A variety of software and hardware products is available to expand the capacity and functionality of your computer. However, you must decide whether to upgrade your old PC or purchase a new one with greater capabilities. Additionally, you need to decide whether you should perform the installation of new software or hardware or use the services of a trained professional. Consider the cost of an upgrade, the reputation of the prospective technician, and whether or not you feel competent in performing an upgrade.

CHAPTER 3

Output
and
Storage

99

Learning Objectives

> Define output, and describe hard copy, soft copy, and the different types of output

> Explain the difference between an output device and output media

> Identify the major types of monitor technologies and how they function

> Describe the various types of printers, their printing processes, and the types of printing jobs they are commonly used for

> Identify the less common types of output devices and their uses

> Explain the types of storage media, how they operate, and how data or information is stored on them

Cyber**Scenario**

ON THE DRIVE TO HER OFFICE, NELL BAKER, vice-president of marketing at a New Jersey import company, contemplates her busy day ahead. First, she has a meeting with the company's district marketing managers, after which she will interview a candidate for a vacant district manager position in San Diego, California, and attend a board meeting via videoconference. Although she can't recall her other appointments, she will access her schedule when she arrives at the office. Pulling into her company's downtown parking deck, she parks in her reserved space, grabs her briefcase, locks her car, and takes the elevator to her office on the building's tenth floor.

As she approaches the door of her office suite, she remembers to pause while a security camera quickly photographs the iris of her right eye and compares the image to a previously captured image stored in the company's computer database. Within seconds a digitized voice greets her with the words, "Good morning, Ms. Baker," and the door to her suite is unlocked.

Entering her office, Nell is greeted by her administrative assistant and informed that her morning tea will soon be ready. Nell proceeds to her desk, settles into her chair, and presses a button underneath the desktop. A large screen connected to the information systems database descends from the ceiling as a voice from two hidden speakers says, "Good morning, Ms. Baker. What can I do for you?" Nell responds, "Get me the November sales reports for all marketing districts." Almost immediately, the report for the Northeast district appears on the screen, followed by the remaining district reports, each of which is displayed for 30 seconds. After a brief inspection of the information, Nell issues a voice command to print all the reports. Within minutes, the printer in the mahogany cabinet behind her desk has produced the documents.

Nell then issues a verbal command to display the application form and résumé of Charles Walker, whom she will interview at 10 a.m. for the vacant marketing position. Both documents are immediately displayed in the order in which they were requested. With Nell's command to print both documents, the laser printer quickly outputs the résumé and application, and Nell prepares to examine them more carefully. Finally, Nell issues a request to see her schedule for the day, which is promptly displayed on the drop-down screen above her desk. She spends the next few minutes carefully reviewing the marketing reports and Charles Walker's employment information.

All in all, it will be a typically fast-paced and productive day for Nell, made possible by modern state-of-the-art computer, storage, and output technologies that provide the information she needs to devise strategies and make decisions. Technologies similar to those Nell uses are rapidly becoming available in the workplace, allowing managers and employees to boost their productivity and enhance their employers' competitive position in the marketplace.

Output

Recall from Chapter 1 that **output** is processed data that can be used immediately or stored in computer-usable form for later use. Output may be produced in either hard copy or soft copy, or in both forms. **Hard copy** is a permanent version of output, such as a letter printed on paper. **Soft copy** is a temporary version and includes any output that cannot be physically handled. For example, the information displayed on a bank teller's computer terminal screen during an account balance inquiry is considered soft copy. Voice output such as the telephone company's computerized directory assistance is another form of soft copy. We depend on all sorts of output in our daily lives.

Types of Output

Computer output may consist of a single type of output or a combination of types. A properly equipped computer system is capable of outputting data in the form of text, graphics, audio, or video.

Text consists of characters and numbers used to create words, sentences, and paragraphs that compose various types of text-based documents including letters, memos, mailing labels, and newsletters. Web pages typically contain text and may also contain other forms of output including graphics, music, voice, and sound.

Graphics are computer-generated pictures produced on a computer screen, paper, or film. Also called graphical images, graphics range from simple line or bar charts to detailed and colorful images and pictures. Graphics are often seen on commercial Web page advertisements.

Soft copy output can be an effective way to share information quickly and efficiently. It can be more dynamic than hard copy output, and more portable as well.

It is common to see people listening to audio output.

Video and audio are often combined when home movies are made. Both the visual and audio components enhance the information that is output.

Audio is any sound, including speech and music. If a computer is equipped with a sound card and speakers, users can insert a CD or DVD into its drive and listen to music while relaxing or working on a project. Numerous Web sites provide sound that allows users to listen to a sales pitch describing a product or to sample selections from an advertised music CD.

Video consists of motion images, similar to those seen on a television or movie screen. Video is often accompanied by audio, making the output even more realistic and lifelike. A popular use of both audio and video is for creating home movies. By attaching a video camera to a computer, anyone can capture and play back movies of family members that record both images and conversation.

Output Devices and Media

An **output device** is any hardware device that makes information available to a user. A computer produces output using the combination of output devices, media, and software available with a particular system. Popular output devices include displays (monitors), printers, plotters, televisions, and speakers. An **output medium** is any medium or material on which information is recorded. Examples of output media include paper, plastic film, and magnetic tape.

Display Devices

A **monitor** is a fundamental component of every single-user computer system and is the most common soft-copy output mechanism for displaying text, images, graphics, and video on a screen. Available in a variety of shapes, sizes, costs, and capabilities, monitors allow users to view information temporarily.

A monitor consists of a plastic case that houses a viewing screen and the electronic components that allow information to be displayed on the screen. Most mobile computers contain a monitor housed in the same case as the computer and other components. For example, the monitor of a notebook computer is attached to the case with hinges, allowing it to be viewed when the case is opened. The monitor of a handheld computer is also an integral part of the computer case.

Monitors are designed to operate smoothly with input devices, such as a keyboard. Information in the form of digital signals is entered into the processor, or CPU, by means of the keyboard or another input device. A **video card** (also called a graphics card or video adapter) converts digital signals into information, including text, pictures, and images, that is immediately displayed on the monitor screen.

While some older monitors displayed information in only one color, called monochrome, today's monitors are capable of displaying output in vivid color. Some are capable of displaying information in thousands of different colors and shades.

A computer monitor is a common soft copy output device.

Full-color displays are available in small, portable devices.

Monitors also come in a variety of sizes, from tiny two-inch screens for handhelds and other mobile devices, to 21-inch (or larger) screens for PCs. Monitor sizes are measured diagonally, from one corner to the diagonally opposite corner. Common sizes for desktop PC monitors are 15, 17, 19, and 21 inches.

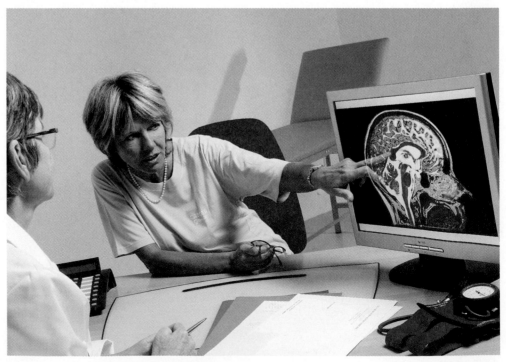

Large desktop displays can present vibrant, full-color images.

Cathode Ray Tube (CRT) Monitors

The original type of monitor for desktop computers was the **cathode ray tube (CRT) monitor**. A CRT is a large, sealed glass tube housed in a plastic case. The front of the tube is the screen. A cable at the rear of the monitor plugs into a graphics adapter board on the motherboard inside the system unit. An electric cord on the monitor plugs into an electrical outlet. CRT monitors use the same cathode ray tube technology used in television sets, so most are fairly large and bulky. Smaller CRTs are used with terminals, such as those found in banks and retail establishments.

The screen of a CRT monitor is coated with tiny dots of phosphor material. An RGB monitor displays dots consisting of red, green, and blue phosphor. Red, green, and blue are primary colors, and they can be combined in various ways to produce a wide range of colors.

When information is sent to a CRT monitor, it is sent as an analog signal through a video card. A video card residing on the motherboard inside the system unit converts the digital signals produced by the computer into analog signals and sends them through a cable to the monitor. The type of display determines how the images appear on the screen.

Flat-Panel Displays

A **flat-panel display** uses a technology that allows the screen to be smaller, thinner, and lighter than CRT monitors. An additional benefit of these lightweight compact screens is that they consume less power compared with CRT monitors. These features make them desirable among users of mobile devices, and they are increasingly found on desktop computers as well.

The majority of flat-panel displays use liquid crystals to produce information on the screen. In a **liquid crystal display (LCD)**, liquid crystals are sandwiched between two sheets of material. Electric current passing through the crystals causes them to twist. This twisting effect blocks some light waves and allows other light waves to pass through, creating images on the screen.

LCD monitors use digital signals, unlike CRT monitors that employ analog signals. Electronic circuitry converts analog signals coming from the video card back into digital signals. The cost of this technology has decreased to the point where LCD monitors are now inexpensive enough to include in new computer system packages sold by manufacturers. Very few CRT monitors are sold today.

LCD monitors feature active-matrix color displays. In an **active-matrix display**, also known as a thin-film transistor (TFT) display, separate transistors control each color pixel, allowing viewing from any angle. Large-size LCD monitors are now available that can be mounted on a wall in a video conferencing room.

Active-matrix displays produce clearer, sharper images compared with those from passive-matrix displays.

Monitor Performance and Quality Factors

The quality and performance of monitors depend on three main factors:

- video card
- resolution
- refresh rate

CEO, APPLE COMPUTER
Steven Jobs

STEVEN JOBS COULD SERVE AS THE PROTOTYPE of America's computer industry entrepreneur. A college dropout fascinated with counterculture and Eastern thought, Jobs transformed himself into a millionaire by the age of 30. Additionally, he is credited with changing the way people think about technology and helping to ignite the personal computer revolution.

Jobs started his career as a video game designer at Atari. After spending time in college and traveling in the Middle East, Jobs returned to the United States and reconnected with friend and fellow technology enthusiast Steve Wozniak, who was working at Hewlett-Packard and building computers in his spare time. Jobs became convinced that Wozniak's latest computer, which became the Apple I, had market potential. Each sold a few prized possessions to raise $1,300, and together Jobs and Wozniak started their computer business in Jobs' garage in 1976, naming the company Apple Computer based on Jobs' fond memories of a summer job in an Oregon orchard.

The Apple I was the first personal computer that appealed to a broad market of businesses, schools, and the public, and Apple Computer quickly became a $335 million company. But by 1981, IBM had joined the race for market dominance with the launching of the IBM PC, and Apple began losing ground. Meanwhile, Jobs was leading a development team that would soon change the face of personal computing. In December 1979, Jobs and his team visited the elite Xerox PARC research center, where they saw the Alto computer, a prototype that featured a graphical user interface and a mouse. Jobs' team rushed back to the office and modified specifications for the Lisa (a computer named after Jobs' daughter). Both the Lisa and its successor, the Macintosh, were launched with a mouse and a point-and-click interface.

Although the graphic user interface radically changed the way people use computers, the Macintosh fell short of its early sales predictions. In 1985, Jobs left the company. In 1986, he founded NeXT Software and purchased Pixar Animation Studios from filmmaker George Lucas. Under Jobs, Pixar produced *Toy Story* (the first wholly computer-generated film), *A Bug's Life, Toy Story 2,* and *Monsters Inc.*, all highly successful ventures.

In a strange twist, Jobs was invited back to Apple in 1996 when Apple bought NeXT for $400 million. Jobs became interim CEO, and helped turn around the company's dwindling market share with the introduction of the tremendously popular iMac and iBook computer lines in the summer of 1998.

In January 2000, Jobs was appointed permanent CEO of Apple Computers Inc. That same month, Apple also announced a $200 million investment in EarthLink, an Internet service provider that works with Apple to bring new online features to computer users. Under Jobs' direction, Apple continues to produce a variety of popular, innovative products, including the iPod and the iTunes music store.

Source: "Steven Jobs Biography," *A&E Television*, July 2006. December 2006 <http://www.biography.com/search/article.do?id=9354805>.

Video Card The display of graphics on a monitor is dependent on the memory and processor contained on the video card (or graphics card). Video cards usually have their own built-in video memory that is separate from the memory contained on the motherboard. Video memory is typically called Video RAM (or VRAM). The amount of VRAM on a video card determines the **bit depth** (also called color depth)—measured as bits per pixel—that drives the number of colors and the resolution of the display. It also dictates the speed at which signals are sent to the monitor. The amount of video memory ranges from 128 megabytes (MB) to 512 MB.

The number of colors a video card can display is determined by the number of bits used by the card to store information about each pixel (the bit depth). An 8-bit video card, often referred to as 8-bit color, uses 8 bits to store information about each pixel, whereas a 16-bit video card uses 16 bits. For example, an 8-bit video card can display 256 colors (28). A 16-bit video card can display 65,536 colors.

The greater the number of bits, the better and more clearly the image will be displayed on the screen. A 24-bit video card can display images more clearly than an 8-bit or 16-bit video card, and in true color. True color refers to any graphics device using at least 24 bits to represent each pixel. **True color** means that more than 16 million unique colors can be represented, a range that accommodates the complex shades and hues of our natural world (hence the term "true"). Since humans can only distinguish a few million colors, this is more than enough to accurately represent any color image.

Resolution As with scanners and digital cameras, the number of pixels in the display determines the monitor's quality, or **resolution**. A **pixel** (short for picture element) is a tiny single point in anything being displayed on the screen. An electron beam moves back and forth across the rear of the screen causing the dots on the front of the screen to glow (see Figure 3-1). The glowing dots produce a character or

Tech Demo 3-1
Resolution

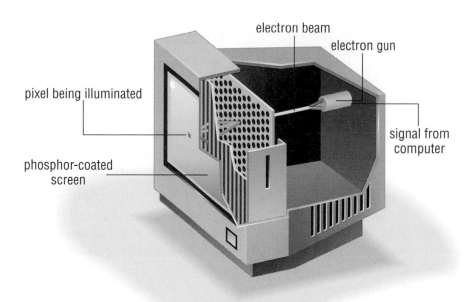

Figure 3-1 CRT Monitor Mechanics
An electron beam moves back and forth across a phosphor-coated screen, causing pixels to be illuminated.

Figure 3-2 Resolution

Images are displayed using pixels on the monitor screen. The greater the number of pixels, the sharper the image.

image on the screen composed of pixels. Each pixel can be illuminated, or not illuminated, to produce an image on the screen, as shown in Figure 3-2.

The greater the number of pixels, the higher the resolution and the more detailed the image. However, higher resolutions result in smaller displayed characters and images, which can be an advantage (more elements can be displayed) or a disadvantage (smaller images and text may be difficult to see). Higher-resolution settings also consume more processing power because additional power is required to continually refresh a larger number of pixels. The increase in power consumption slows down the amount of processing power immediately available for other processing activities.

Screen resolutions typically range from 640 × 480 to 1600 × 1200 pixels or more. Lower resolutions are suitable for displaying draft-quality text and images. Higher resolution allows more accurate images to be displayed on the screen, and may be desirable for users such as artists or Web page designers, who regularly work with higher-quality text, graphics, and other detailed images. For a comparison, look at Figure 3-3, which shows the same desktop displayed in a low-resolution

Figure 3-3 Screen Resolution
In the 800 × 600 pixels screen resolution (left), the desktop icons and the photo are larger than in the 1280 × 1024 pixels screen resolution (right).

and a high-resolution format. Most monitors sold today offer a range of resolution settings, which can be adjusted depending on the user's preference.

Another factor influencing image resolution is dot pitch. **Dot pitch** refers to the distance between the centers of pixels on a display. Less distance between pixels increases the quality of the displayed image. A smaller dot pitch makes text and graphics easier to read. Monitor dot pitch can range from 0.25 millimeters (mm) to 0.31 mm. A monitor having a dot pitch of 0.26 mm will display high-quality text and graphics and is suitable for most applications.

Refresh Rate   Refresh rate is yet another factor affecting monitor quality. Just as light from a flashlight becomes dimmer as the batteries run down, images displayed on a monitor screen become weaker as the current used to produce them diminishes. This causes the screen to flicker. To avoid this problem, power is continually being sent to the monitor to refresh the display. **Refresh rate** refers to the

Tech Demo 3-2
Refresh Rate

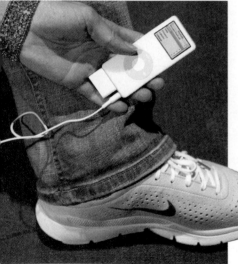

Wearable computers are well suited to today's mobile lifestyle.

number of times per second the screen is refreshed (redrawn). To avoid flickering, the refresh rate should be at least 72 hertz (Hz) or refreshed 72 times per second. High-quality displays have a fast refresh rate that produces a constant, flicker-free image that causes less eyestrain for the user.

Monitor controls are typically located on the front of the monitor and allow adjustment of the brightness, contrast, positioning, height, and width of images displayed on the screen. Monitors usually come with screen settings preset by the manufacturer. The Windows Vista operating system allows users to change monitor settings through the Control Panel options accessed by clicking the Office button (the Start button in previous Microsoft operating systems). Users can change the settings to meet their needs, or easily change back to the preset (default) settings.

Monitor Ergonomics

Ergonomics is the study of the interaction between humans and the equipment they use. Extensive research has shown that the correct use of a monitor can greatly reduce eyestrain, fatigue, and other potential problems.

Many monitors have built-in features that address ergonomics issues. These features allow adjustment of the monitor to make viewing more comfortable, to minimize eye and neck strain, and to reduce glare from overhead lighting. Some have controls that allow adjusting the monitor for the brightness, contrast, height, and width of displayed images. Monitor brightness is a matter of individual preference. Some ergonomic specialists recommend the use of an antiglare screen to reduce glare from the screen. It is important for both users and monitors to be positioned correctly. Figure 3-4 illustrates the correct positioning to provide maximum comfort and ease of use.

Wearable Computers

Some mobile workers need and use a hands-free **wearable computer** that allows them to perform their work without having to stop what they are doing to use a computer. Computers in the form of headsets, eyeglasses, watches, and other accessories are already in use by mobile workers. For example, a work crew can wirelessly connect to the corporate network to send and receive work-related data and information, such as a wiring diagram needed to locate a faulty electric outlet.

The use of wearable computers and displays is becoming widespread due to their cost-effectiveness and ability to eliminate work delays. Future improvements to wearable displays will render them smaller and even more adaptable to a greater variety of work-related, entertainment, and communications applications.

Television Displays

Many home computer users take advantage of their television sets for displaying computer output. To use an older, CRT-style television as a display device for computer output, an electronic device called an NTSC converter was required. Named for the National Television System Committee, an NTSC converter device

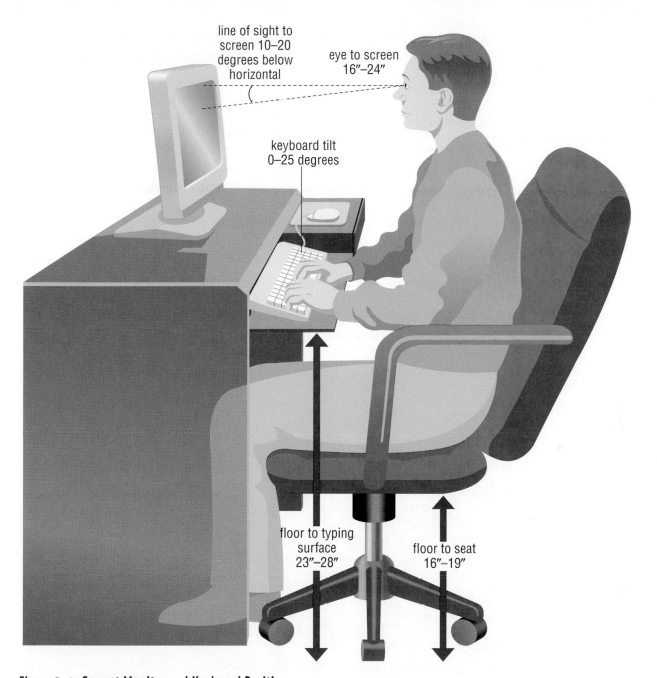

Figure 3-4 Correct Monitor and Keyboard Position
Correct positioning when using a monitor can reduce physical
fatigue and discomfort.

converted the computer's digital signal into an analog signal that could be displayed on the television screen.

Newer television technology, **high-definition television (HDTV)**, does not require an NTSC converter. Because HDTV uses digital signals instead of analog signals, computers can be connected directly to the television set. HDTV sets typically include a wider screen and provide higher resolution than standard television sets. These features make HDTV attractive for presenting information to large groups.

The Federal Communications Commission (FCC) has mandated that all television stations transmit program signals in both analog format and digital format by

2008. As the manufacture of high-definition televisions becomes more competitive, the cost of HDTV sets will almost certainly decline and their overall quality will improve.

Screen Projectors

A **screen projector** is a device that captures the text and images displayed on the computer screen and projects those same images onto a large screen so the audience can see the text and images clearly. It is often used in classrooms so students can see the instructor's presentation, and by speakers making presentations to a large audience at meetings, conventions, and conferences.

Two types of projectors are LCD projectors and DLP projectors. Most of the earlier computer projection systems were based on LCD technology which tends to produce faded and blurry images. A new technology developed by Texas Instruments, called Digital Light Processing (DLP) uses tiny mirrors housed on a special kind of microchip called a Digital Micromirror Device (DMD). The result is sharp images that can be clearly seen even in a normally lit room.

Screen projectors help multiple people view the output on a computer screen.

Printers

A **printer** is the most common type of device for producing hard-copy output on a physical medium, such as paper or transparency film. Almost all printers are capable of printing in either portrait or landscape format (see Figure 3-5). In **portrait format**, a printed page is taller than it is wide. Portrait format is usually used for letters, memos, reports, and newsletters. In **landscape format**, a printed page is wider than it is tall. Landscape format is best suited for financial spreadsheets and other types of tabular reports. These types of reports typically include many columns of data, which the portrait format could not accomodate.

Printers are separated into two broad categories, based on how they interact with the print medium: impact and nonimpact. An **impact printer** prints much like a typewriter, by physically striking an inked ribbon against the paper. Dot-matrix printers and line printers are examples of impact printers. A **nonimpact printer** forms characters and images without actually striking the output medium, using electricity, heat, laser technology, or photographic techniques. Ink-jet printers, laser printers, thermal printers, and plotters are types of non-impact printers.

A computer uses a printer card installed on the motherboard to control printing. The printer card contains a port extending to the rear of the system unit. Most printers connect to the computer by means of a cable attached to the rear of the printer. The other end plugs into the port on the printer board. An electric cord at the rear of the printer plugs into an electric outlet. Some printers have wireless capabilities, connecting to a computer via Bluetooth or Wi-Fi.

(a)   (b)

Figure 3-5 Portrait and Landscape Formats
Portrait format's (a) name comes from the fact that traditional portraits are taller than they are wide. To illustrate a landscape (b), wider images are usually more useful.

Dot-Matrix Printers

A **dot-matrix printer** forms and prints characters in a manner similar to the way numbers appear on a football scoreboard. A close look at a scoreboard will reveal that each number consists of a pattern of lighted bulbs. For a dot-matrix printer, the "lighted bulbs" are tiny dots forming characters and images on the paper (the "scoreboard").

In dot-matrix printing, a print head strikes an inked ribbon and deposits ink on the page, which is why dot-matrix printers are classified as impact printers. Inside the print head are thin wires, and their impact produces tiny dots of ink arranged to represent text, symbols, or images, as shown in Figure 3-6.

The number of dots in a linear inch or dots per inch (dpi), is a measure of the resolution, or print quality. The print head of a dot-matrix printer may contain from 9 to 24 pins, depending on the printer model and manufacturer. The number of pins determines the number of dots the print head can print during one impact. More pins produce more dots in each character, resulting in higher-quality print. Dot-matrix printers print one character at a time. Their speed is measured by the number of characters per second (cps) the printer is capable of printing. These printers range in speed from a few characters to several hundred characters per second, with 450 cps being a typical rate.

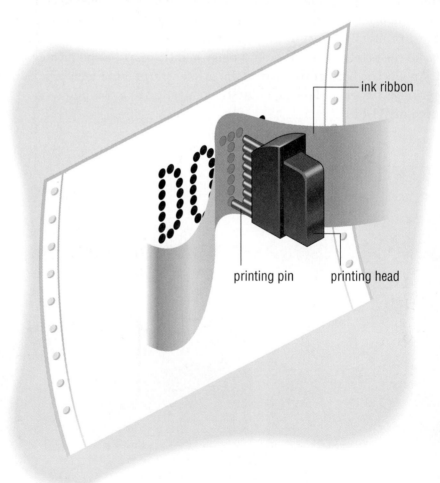

Figure 3-6 Printing Using a Dot-Matrix Printer
Before striking the ribbon, the printer extends the correct combination of pins to form a specific character. As with the display of pixels on a monitor, the more pins the printer uses, the sharper the printed letters.

The print quality of most dot-matrix printers is often inferior to higher-quality printers. The clarity of the printing may be described as **draft quality** (approximately 300 dpi), which is acceptable for some printing. For important business letters and documents, most users prefer **letter quality** (approximately 1200 dpi).

Because dot-matrix printers are impact printers, they are capable of printing multipart forms containing an original and carbon copies. For this reason they are more commonly found in businesses and schools. For example, colleges and universities may use dot-matrix printers for printing class rolls and grade reports. Individuals seldom use dot-matrix printers since they rarely need to print multipart forms and they usually prefer higher-quality print output.

Line Printers

A **line printer** is a high-speed printer capable of printing an entire line at one time. A fast line printer can print as many as 3,000 lines per minute. A line printer contains a chain of rotating characters or pins that print an entire line at one time. They typically use 11 × 17-inch tractor-fed, continuous-form paper. Their fast speed makes them useful when large volumes of printing are needed, such as detailed company documents, reports, and invoices. The disadvantages of line printers are that they cannot print graphics, the print quality is low, and they are very noisy.

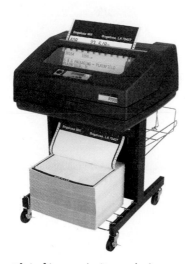

This line printer prints on continuous form paper that is tractor-fed.

Ink-Jet Printers

For applications requiring letter-quality print, most people choose nonimpact printers, such as ink-jet and laser printers. Technological improvements and declining prices have made these two types the preferred printers among personal computer users. An **ink-jet printer** is a nonimpact printer that forms characters and images by spraying thousands of tiny droplets of electrically charged ink onto a sheet of paper as the sheet passes through the printer (see Figure 3-7). The printed images are in dot-matrix format, but of a higher resolution than images printed by dot-matrix printers. This is because the tiny dots produced by high-end printers are much closer together. In fact, the dots are so dense the printed characters and images may appear as letter-quality characters and images, rather than as a group of dots.

Tech Demo 3-3
Ink Jet Printer's
Data Path

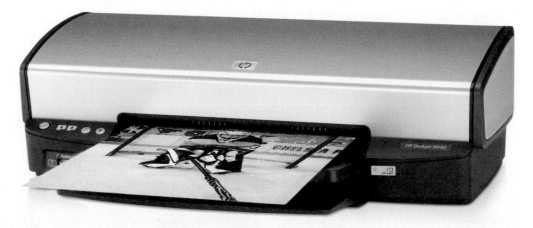

Ink-jet printers provide good-quality, inexpensive output.

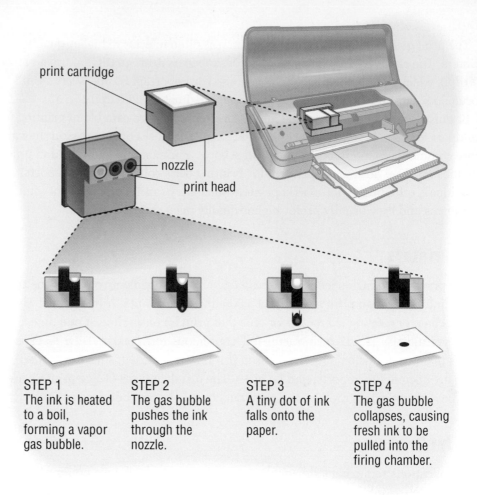

STEP 1
The ink is heated to a boil, forming a vapor gas bubble.

STEP 2
The gas bubble pushes the ink through the nozzle.

STEP 3
A tiny dot of ink falls onto the paper.

STEP 4
The gas bubble collapses, causing fresh ink to be pulled into the firing chamber.

Figure 3-7 Printing Using an Ink-Jet Printer
An ink-jet printer produces output by spraying tiny droplets of ink onto the paper or other medium to form text and images.

Typical resolutions are 600 dpi for black-and-white printing and 2400 dpi for color printing on high-quality paper. Higher resolution means higher-quality characters and images. Some high-end ink-jet printers are capable of producing photographic-quality output almost as detailed and colorful as photos processed using traditional darkroom methods.

Most ink-jet printers use two or more ink cartridges, one for black print and one or more for color printing. Each cartridge has multiple holes, called nozzles. During printing, combinations of tiny ink droplets are propelled through the nozzles by heat and pressure onto the paper, forming characters and images.

The number of pages per minute (ppm) a printer can produce determines an ink-jet printer's speed. Speeds currently range from 1 ppm to 16 ppm for draft-quality output. Printing color photos and other graphical images may slow the printing speed to as few as one or two pages per minute.

The cost of operating an ink-jet printer can vary greatly. A typical single page text document using only black ink may cost from $.02 to $.06 per page. By comparison, the cost of printing a combination of black and color characters and images may range from $.08 to $.20 per page. Printing a full-color photograph may cost $.90 or more.

Unlike dot-matrix printers, most ink-jet printers are relatively inexpensive. Prices of ink-jet printers range from less than $100 to $350. Their inexpensive price and versatility make them popular among personal computer users. They can be used for printing letters, memos, reports, spreadsheets, brochures, and a variety of other printing applications. Some computer manufacturers now bundle an ink-jet printer with each computer they sell.

Laser Printers

A **laser printer** is a nonimpact printer that produces output of exceptional quality using a technology similar to that of a photocopy machine. Laser printers are used for any printing application, including those requiring output of printing-press quality material. Their speed and ability to produce clear, crisp text and images have made them the fastest growing segment of the printer market. Prices range from a few hundred dollars for a black-ink laser printer (monochrome) to a thousand dollars and up for a color laser printer. Laser printers produce text and images of exceptional quality. Figure 3-8 illustrates the way a laser printer works.

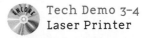

Tech Demo 3-4
Laser Printer

A laser printer creates text and graphics on a rotating metal drum using a laser beam. During printing, components inside the printer read characters and relay them to a printer device called a laser mechanism. A laser beam produces characters and images on a rotating drum inside the printer by altering the electrical charge wherever the beam strikes the drum. The charges produce tiny magnetic fields (dots) on the drum, forming characters. As the drum rotates, it picks up an

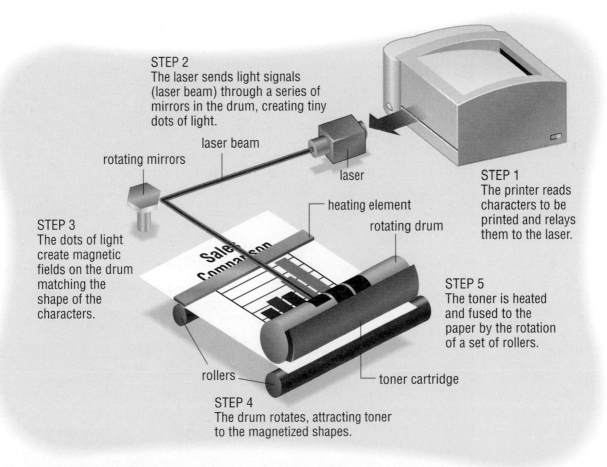

Figure 3-8 How a Laser Printer Works
A laser printer produces output in a manner similar to that of a copy machine.

Laser printers produce output of exceptional quality and are among the most popular printers.

ink-like powder called **toner**, similar to copy machine toner. The sensitive dots on the drum are then deposited onto the paper. Using heat and pressure, a set of rollers fuses the toner onto the paper, forming the printed image. The circumference of the drum is approximately the same as the length of a standard sheet of paper. With one revolution of the drum an entire page is printed.

Thermal Printers

A **thermal printer** is an inexpensive printer that uses heat to transfer an impression onto paper. Thermal printers are widely used in calculators and fax machines. There are three types of thermal printers: direct thermal, thermal wax transfer, and thermal dye transfer.

- A **direct thermal printer** prints an image by burning dots onto coated paper when the paper passes over a line of heating elements. Early fax machines used direct thermal printing.
- A **thermal wax transfer printer** adheres a wax-based ink onto paper. During the printing process a thermal printhead melts wax-based ink from the transfer ribbon onto the paper. When cool, the wax is permanent. Images are printed as dots, meaning the images must be dithered. Dithering creates the illusion of new colors and shades by varying the pattern of black and white dots. As a result, images are not quite photorealistic, although they are very good. Newspaper photographs, for example, are dithered. If you look closely, you can see that different shades of gray are produced by varying the

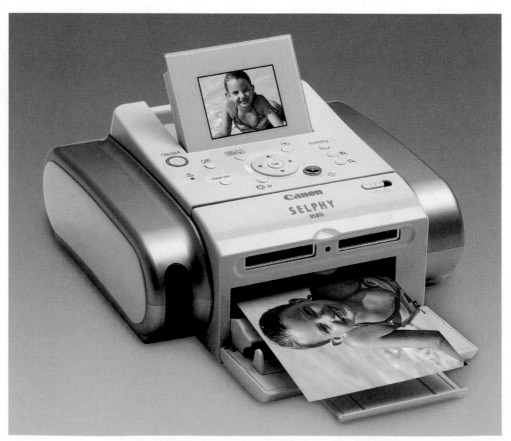

This thermal dye sublimation printer provides soft copy and hard copy output.

patterns of black and white dots. The more dither patterns that a device or program supports, the more shades of gray it can represent.

- A **thermal dye transfer printer**, also called a thermal dye sublimation printer, produces images by heating ribbons containing dye and then diffusing the dyes onto specially coated paper or transparencies. These printers are the most expensive and slowest type of thermal printer, but they produce exceptional high-quality, continuous-tone images similar to actual photographs. They require a special paper, which is quite expensive. A new breed of thermal dye transfer printers, called snapshot printers, produce small photographic snapshots and are much less expensive than other full-size thermal printers.

Plotters

A **plotter** is a type of printer used to produce specialized kinds of large-sized high-quality documents, including architectural drawings, charts, maps, diagrams, and other images. Plotters are also used to create engineering drawings for machinery parts and equipment.

Depending on the type, plotters use a variety of technologies. For example, electrostatic plotters use a series of tiny dots tightly packed to produce a high-quality printed image. The printing mechanism consists of a row of tiny electrically charged wires. When the wires come into contact with the specially coated paper, an electrostatic pattern is produced that causes the toner to be fused onto the paper. When large, color images are needed, an ink-jet plotter—also called a wide-format ink-jet printer—may be used for printing a variety of materials. Most plotters are expensive, ranging in cost from hundreds to thousands of dollars.

Special-Purpose Printers

There are several printers on the market that are made for specialized types of printing. These printers use ink-jet, laser, or thermal technology but are not general-purpose printers for everyday text and graphics. Photo printers, label printers, postage printers, and portable printers are examples of special-purpose printers.

Engineers often use plotters for producing high-quality, detailed prints of building, process, and machine designs.

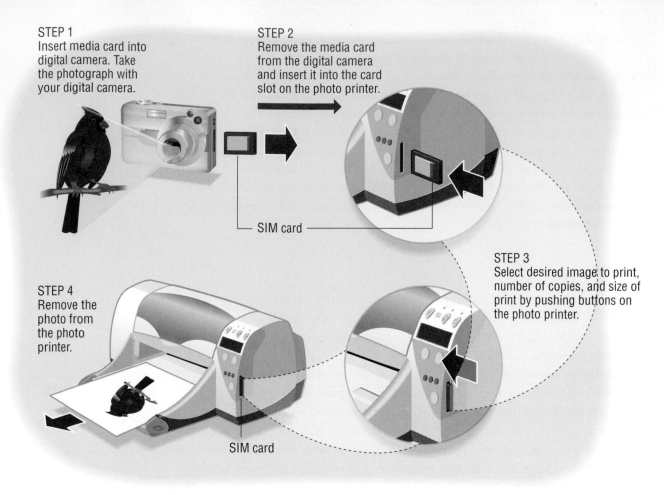

STEP 1
Insert media card into digital camera. Take the photograph with your digital camera.

STEP 2
Remove the media card from the digital camera and insert it into the card slot on the photo printer.

— SIM card

STEP 3
Select desired image to print, number of copies, and size of print by pushing buttons on the photo printer.

STEP 4
Remove the photo from the photo printer.

SIM card

Figure 3-9 Procedure for Using a Photo Printer
A photo printer is a unique type of ink-jet printer used for printing high-quality photographs and other image printing needs.

Photo Printers   A **photo printer** is a unique high-quality ink-jet printer designed to print high-quality color photographs in addition to other types of print output. Most photograph printers can print photographs after they have been loaded (entered) from a digital camera into the computer and displayed on the screen. Some contain a slot for inserting a medium containing photographs, such as a **SIM card** used with some digital cameras. Figure 3-9 shows the steps in taking a picture and printing it on a photo printer. Once the medium is inserted, the controls on the printer can be used to select a particular photograph, change its size, and choose the number of copies to print. Sizes for printed photographs range from 3 × 3 inches to 14 × 17 inches. The versatility of photograph printers makes them suitable for home and business use as they can be used for almost every printing need.

Postage Printers   A **postage printer** is similar to a label printer but also contains a weighing scale. Postage printers typically use thermal technology. Once an item is weighed, postage stamps are printed. To use a postage printer, the user purchases an amount of postage from an authorized postal service Web site. Each time a postage stamp is printed, the user's postage account is updated.

Label Printers A **label printer** is a small printer that uses thermal technology to print information on an adhesive material that can be placed on various items including packages, envelopes, cabinet-type file folders, boxes, CDs, and other items. Most are capable of printing bar codes.

Portable Printers A **portable printer** is a battery-powered, small, light-weight printer that can easily be transported by mobile workers and used with various types of computer and communications devices, such as notebook computers, personal digital assistants (PDAs), and smart phones. Most can fit easily into a standard-size briefcase. Many portable printers can be connected to a parallel of USB port, while others are capable of using wireless connections. The majority of portable printers use ink-jet printer technology.

Multifunction Devices

A **multifunction device (MFD)**, also called an all-in-one device, is a piece of equipment that looks like a printer or copy machine, but which provides a variety of capabilities, including scanning, copying, printing, and usually faxing. The capabilities of multifunction devices vary according to the manufacturer and device model. Some print in black only, while others offer color printing. Most all-in-one devices use ink-jet or laser technology.

Multifunction devices offer several advantages over a combination of separate devices. They occupy less desktop space and they are usually less expensive than the combined cost of purchasing several devices. The main disadvantage is that all functions are lost if the device breaks down or becomes inoperable.

A **facsimile machine**, also called a fax machine, is an electronic device that can send and receive copies (a **fax**, or a facsimile) of documents through a telephone line. A fax device may be a stand-alone machine or a circuit board inserted into a slot inside a computer. The technology of faxing involves

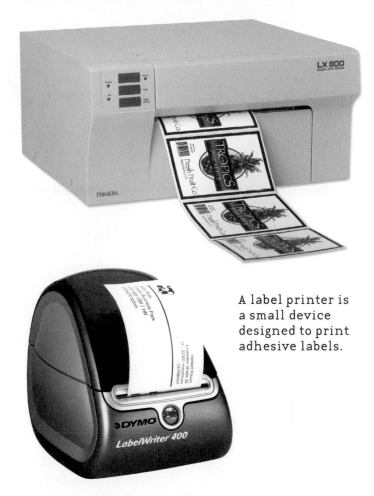

A label printer is a small device designed to print adhesive labels.

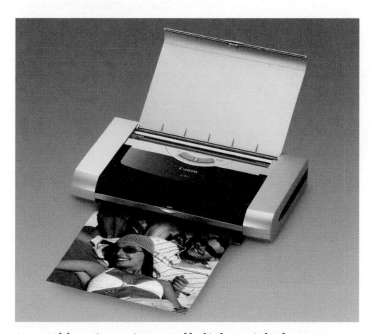

A portable printer is a small, lightweight battery-powered printer that mobile workers can easily transport and use with various types of computer and communication devices, such as notebook computers, PDAs, and smartphones.

A multifunction device is a device that provides multiple capabilities, such as scanning, copying, printing, and faxing.

scanning the page(s), converting the text and images into digitized data, and transmitting them. A fax device at the receiving end converts the digitized data into the document's original form that can be printed or stored.

Many personal computers come equipped with a **fax/modem card** that fits into an expansion slot. In addition to serving as a modem, the board provides many of the features of a stand-alone fax machine at a lower cost. A type of software called a **fax program** is needed to send and receive a fax. With fax programs, users can

Fax machines can send and receive copies of documents sent over communications media, such as telephone lines.

The fax/modem card allows communications with other fax machines.

compose, send, receive, print, and store faxes. Some of the better fax programs use optical character recognition (OCR) technology to convert a faxed transmission back into text so the document can be edited using any of the popular word processing programs.

Audio Output

Computer users want to be able to hear the sounds included in Web sites, videos, and computer games. With audio output capabilities, it is now possible to listen to Web pages or watch television over the Internet. Certain software applications can read e-mail or Web pages out loud, which is of particular benefit to people who are visually impaired. The importance of audio capability is growing rapidly, and it is increasingly being seen as a required feature for personal computer systems.

Speakers and Sound Systems

Most personal computers have built-in **speakers** that produce warning sounds to alert users to errors or other matters that require attention. A computer equipped with a powerful sound card like Creative Labs' Sound Blaster Pro can produce high-quality sound through attached speakers using CD-ROMs, MIDI (Musical Instrument Digital Interface) keyboards, or the Internet. Applications for which speakers are particularly important include computer games, multimedia distance learning programs, audio e-mail, and videoconferencing.

A **speaker headset** is a miniature version of larger speakers. Speaker headsets are already quite popular because they are frequently used with portable devices, including music CD players. As the name suggests, a speaker headset consists of two or more small speakers mounted at the tips of a flexible wire band that fits comfortably on the head, with the speakers positioned over the ears. Some computer users working in close proximity to other workers often use a speaker headset to minimize sound distractions.

Computer speakers allow users to hear sound effects from a computer game or an instructor's voice in a multimedia educational course.

Techno Eyes

A LOT HAS CHANGED since the days when Grandma wore wire-rims. The new thing in eyewear is wireless. Some specs provide privacy and convenience while others offer the opportunity to spy discreetly.

The new eyewear for those who are tired of squinting at the screen on their Palm Pilot or irritated at the guy sitting nearby stealing glances at their computer screen is the Icuiti DVD920. Donning a pair of the digital video glasses provides the wearer with the illusion of seeing what appears to be a 42-inch screen from 11 feet away. They will work with any laptop, DVD player, Video iPod, or PC.

This "virtual movie theater" consists of a pair of LCD panels offering 640 x 480 resolution, a 26-degree field of view, and 15 degrees of vertical tilt. Each panel focuses independently. The glasses; including the integrated, removable headphones, weigh a mere 3.5 ounces. A separate controller handles brightness, volume, 3D settings and power. Both run on AA batteries.

There is also new wireless eyewear for those who have more covert operations in mind. The EyeglassTek Covert Eyeglass Video Camera sees exactly what you see and relays it wirelessly to the included receiver. The glass frames have a camera mounted in the middle offering a 1000-foot line of sight. Optional sunglass lenses allows the wearer to alternate between indoor and outdoor use.

Sources: "EyeglassTek Covert Eyeglass Video Camera," *PI Mall.* December 2006 <http://www.pimall.com/nais/sunglasscam.html>; "The DV920," *ICUITI Intelligent Display Solutions.* December 2006 <http://www.icuiti.com/index.php?pageid=10>; "Icuiti Debuts Video Eyewear for iPods, Other Devices," *The iPod Observer,* January 24, 2006. December 2006 <http://www.ipodobserver.com/story/24972>.

Voice Output Systems

Modern hardware and software technologies make it possible to produce synthesized human speech in the digital form a computer can understand and use. Most people have already experienced this technology when they have dialed a telephone number and heard a computerized voice say, "The number you have dialed is no longer in service," or, "The number you dialed has been changed." This same technology (**voice output**) is now available for use with all computers, and is becoming increasingly popular. Voice output can be used to listen to talk shows, news reports, athletic events, political speeches, interviews, and more.

Storage Devices and Media

Go to this title's Internet Resource Center and read the article titled "Storage Resource Management." www.emcp.net/CUT3e

Information created and output on the devices discussed above can be stored for future use. Storage is the final phase of the information processing cycle. Earlier you learned that RAM memory provides temporary storage of programs and data during processing, and that this temporary storage is lost when the computer is turned off. To avoid losing programs and data every time the computer is turned off, all computers provide for permanent storage. **Permanent storage**, also known as secondary storage, auxiliary storage, or external storage, consists of devices and media used for permanent recording. Stored information can later be retrieved, edited, modified, displayed, imported, exported, copied, or printed. Some secondary storage systems also allow users to make changes to the stored information and to permanently save the altered information.

File Types

Almost all information stored in a computer must be in a **file**. There are many different types of files, including data, text, program, and graphics files. To distinguish among various files, the user gives each one a unique file name. A computer's operating system (operating systems are explained in Chapter 4) may impose restrictions on the format of file names. For example, earlier versions of Windows restricted the length of a file name to eight characters. Newer versions allow longer file names, but there are some characters that cannot be used in a file name.

A file name is followed by a period (.) and a set of characters called a file extension, which identifies the type of file. For example, the characters Payroll.xlsx identify a file named Payroll. The "xlsx" identifies the Payroll file as an XML-ready Microsoft Excel spreadsheet file. File names and file extensions must be separated by a period.

File extensions identify specific file types. Some are automatically added to a file by the operating system or program when a file is saved. However, in some situations a user can add an extension to a file to avoid confusion between similar files. Table 3-1 shows some examples of commonly used file extensions and the type of files they identify. In the Microsoft Office 2007 suite of programs, an x was added to the file extensions to indicate XML capabilities.

Go to this title's Internet Resource Center and read the article titled "Data Protection."
www.emcp.net/CUT3e

Table 3-1 Examples of Commonly Used File Extensions

File Extension	Full Name	Type of File
.bmp	Bitmap graphic	bit-mapped format for graphics
.bak	Backup	backup file
.bat	batch file	DOS file created in batch form
.com	command	executable command file (DOS)
.exe	executable file	executable file (DOS and Windows)
.eps	Encapsulated PostScript Vector graphic	graphics file format used by the PostScript language
.jpg	Joint Photography Experts Group	compression format for graphical images
.pcx	PC Paintbrush	graphics file format
.pdf	portable document format	non-modifiable Adobe Acrobat Reader file
.pif	program information file	instructs Windows how to run non-Windows programs
.tif	tagged image format	type of bit-mapped image
.doc, .docx	document, xml	Microsoft Word (document) file
.xls, .xlsx	Excel spreadsheet, xml	Microsoft Excel spreadsheet file
.mdb, .accdb	Access database	Microsoft Access database file
.ppt, .pptx	PowerPoint, xml	Microsoft PowerPoint file
.wbm	wireless bit-mapped	wireless bit-mapped graphic format for mobile computing devices

Secondary Storage Systems

A secondary storage system consists of two main parts: A storage device and a storage medium. A **storage device** is a hardware component that houses a **storage medium** on which data are recorded (stored), similar to the way in which a VCR (the device) is used for recording a television program on the tape (the medium) inside a cassette. Some type of secondary storage device is usually built into a PC system, but is not visible unless the case housing the CPU and related components is removed. There are two main types of storage systems: magnetic and optical.

Magnetic Storage Devices and Media

A **magnetic storage device** is the most commonly used type of secondary storage. This type is broadly classified into two categories: those using a permanent storage medium and those using a removable storage medium. A **permanent storage medium**, such as a hard disk, is permanently attached to the system unit. A **removable storage medium**, such as a CD, can be removed by the user and replaced by another medium.

Magnetic storage devices are also categorized by the way the data stored in them are accessed: sequentially (in the order in which data was stored) or *directly* (in any order, randomly). **Sequential access** can be compared to the way musical selections on a cassette tape are recorded and accessed one after the other. **Direct access** is comparable to the way songs are stored and selected on a CD player. Although the songs are stored one after another, any song can be played by selecting its number.

The speed of a disk storage device is measured by **access time**, the time a storage device spends locating a particular file. Recall that information in a computer's memory can be accessed quickly, in millionths of a second. However, accessing a file stored on a disk is slower. The access times of storage devices are measured in thousandths of a second. The speed at which data are transferred from memory or from a storage device is called the **data transfer rate**. As with access time, data transfer rates of storage devices are much slower than data transfer rates from memory.

A magnetic storage device works by applying electrical charges to iron filings on the surface medium. Specific particles are either magnetized (representing a 1-bit) or not magnetized (representing a 0-bit). Recall from Chapter 1 that a combination of 0 and 1 bits represents a byte, that is, a letter, number, or special character.

Magnetic storage devices are popular because they provide an inexpensive means for recording large amounts of information. The media used by magnetic storage devices can be read, erased, or rewritten, and can therefore be used over and over. The primary types of magnetic storage media are:

- floppy disks
- hard disks
- tape cartridges
- USB flash drives

Most personal computer systems have a built-in hard drive and CD/DVD drive, and many users are opting for the convenience of a USB flash drive as their

Go to this title's Internet Resource Center and read the article titled "Network Storage." www.emcp.net/CUT3e

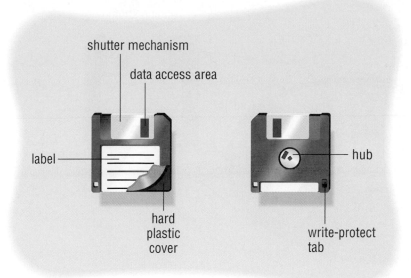

shutter mechanism

data access area

label

hub

hard
plastic
cover

write-protect
tab

Figure 3-10 Parts of a Floppy Disk

removable storage device. Due to the popularity and capacity of these storage devices, floppy disk drives are no longer common in new computer systems.

Floppy Disks and Disk Drives

A **floppy disk**, also called a diskette or simply a disk, is a thin, circular Mylar (polyester film) wafer now sandwiched between two sheets of special cleaning tissue inside a rigid plastic case (see Figure 3-10). Floppy disks must be handled carefully, as the hard plastic cases do not totally protect the circular wafers inside. Improper handling of disks can damage stored data (see Table 3.2). Floppy disks were widely used for saving (backing up) copies of files and programs as well as sharing files with other users. In recent years, PC manufacturers have begun moving customers away from the floppy disk because of the extensive range of alternative storage options.

Table 3-2 Floppy Disk Handling and Storage Guidelines

Do
Insert the disk into the drive carefully.
Store the disk in a safe place when not in use.
Do Not
Open the disk's shutter or touch the recording surface on the disk.
Eat, drink, or smoke near a disk.
Expose the disk to heat, sunlight, or cold.
Place the disk near magnetic fields such as TVs, radios, monitors, or calulators

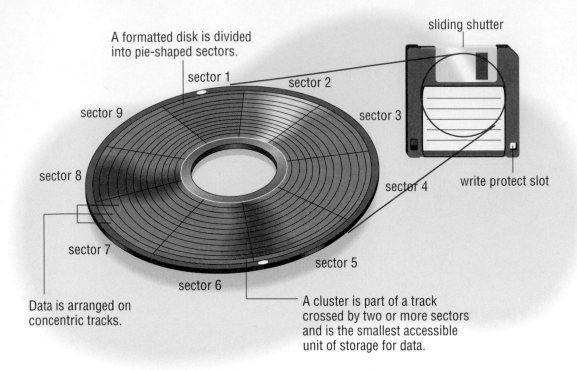

A formatted disk is divided into pie-shaped sectors.

sector 1

sector 2

sector 9

sector 3

sector 8

sector 7

sector 4

sliding shutter

write protect slot

sector 5

sector 6

Data is arranged on concentric tracks.

A cluster is part of a track crossed by two or more sectors and is the smallest accessible unit of storage for data.

Figure 3-11 Formatting a Floppy Disk
The process of formatting a floppy disk results in the disk being arranged into tracks and sectors. Data are stored in sectors along the tracks.

Before data can be stored on a disk, the manufacturer or the user must format the disk to conform to the type of disk drive and operating system with which it is intended to be used. During the formatting process, the disk surface is arranged into tracks, sectors, and clusters ready for the storage of data (see Figure 3-11). During formatting, concentric tracks are arranged on the disk. When users write data and store programs to the disk, the tracks are encoded with 0 and 1 bits.

Hard Disks and Hard Drives

Hard disks provide permanent storage for system software, application programs, and user files. A **hard drive** system consists of one or more rigid metal platters (disks) mounted on a metal shaft in a container that contains an access mechanism. The container is sealed to prevent contamination from dust, moisture, and other airborne particles, allowing the system to operate more efficiently. Hard drives range in size from 1 to 5.25 inches in diameter. Storage capacity ranges from less than 10 GB to more than 300 GB. Figure 3-12 shows the steps for formatting or reading a hard disk. Manufacturers usually format hard disks, but preformatted hard disks can be reformatted by users. Inexperienced users should never attempt to reformat a hard disk, since a PC's operating system is installed on the hard disk and reformatting destroys all of the previous contents.

People frequently use the terms *hard disk* and *hard drive* to mean the same thing, even though in technical terms the hard drive is the storage device and the **hard disk** is the magnetic storage medium. A hard drive unit may be either nonremovable (fixed) or removable (interchangeable). Most personal computers arrive from the factory with a fixed hard drive installed within the system unit housing.

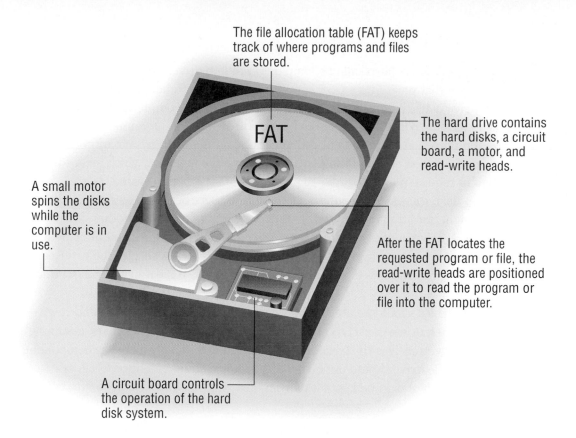

The file allocation table (FAT) keeps track of where programs and files are stored.

The hard drive contains the hard disks, a circuit board, a motor, and read-write heads.

A small motor spins the disks while the computer is in use.

After the FAT locates the requested program or file, the read-write heads are positioned over it to read the program or file into the computer.

A circuit board controls the operation of the hard disk system.

Figure 3-12 Inner Workings of a Hard Drive
A hard drive contains one or more hard disks on which data are stored. When activated, read/write heads move in and out between the disks to record and/or read data.

External hard drives can be added to a computer system as well.

Data are stored along the tracks and sectors of both hard and floppy disks. A **track** is a numbered concentric circle. A **sector** is a numbered section or portion of a disk similar to a slice of pie. A group of sectors is called a **cluster**, which is the smallest unit of storage space that is assigned a memory address. As programs or data are stored along the tracks on the disk, some computers automatically maintain a file directory, called a **file allocation table (FAT) file**, although some computers use other file allocation formats. FAT files on the disk keep track of the disk's contents. This directory shows the name of each file stored on the disk, its size, and the sector in which the file begins.

When in use, the disk spins and exposes its recording surfaces to the disk drive's read/write heads. As the disk rotates, the read/write heads move back and forth across the disk surface. When the user wants to access a particular file, the computer searches the file allocation table to find the requested file and its location on the disk. After learning the requested file's location, the computer locates and retrieves the requested file.

A hard disk rotates faster than a floppy disk. It continues spinning while the computer is in operation, whereas a floppy disk spins only when data is being stored or accessed. Continuous spinning of a hard disk provides faster access because it enables the disk surface(s) to move past the read/write heads faster. This speeds up the computer's operation because important system commands and functions are accessed and executed more quickly.

USB Flash Drives

A **USB flash drive** (also called a jump drive, thumb drive, and pen drive) is a storage device that plugs into a USB port on a computer or other mobile device. A flash drive is like a portable hard drive, except that it is completely electronic and has no moving parts. When the computer is turned on, it can immediately recognize the presence of the flash drive and store data in the drive's circuitry or retrieve previously stored data. A flash drive has nonvolatile memory, which means that it does not require power in order to maintain the information stored on it.

USB flash drives are popular among mobile users because they are small, lightweight, and transportable from one computing device to another. With a USB flash drive, a user can store large amounts of various kinds of information, including text, pictures, graphics, and spreadsheets. Once stored, the drive can be removed and transported to another device. New USB flash drives can store up to 64 GB.

Flash drives should be able to handle millions of cycles of writing and rewriting. The current life expectancy of most flash drives is about ten years, assuming that the drive receives the basic care and handling that any electronic component requires. The drive should not be dropped, subjected to weight or force, or opened, and it should be kept away from dust, and liquids.

A flash drive can be about the size of a key and hold more data than one hundred floppy disks.

Tape Cartridges and Tape Drives

One of the first types of secondary storage media for computers was magnetic tape. A **tape cartridge** is a small plastic housing containing a magnetically coated ribbon of thin plastic. Similar to a pocket-size tape recorder, a **tape drive** is used to read and write data to and from the tape.

Personal computer users do not usually use tape drives and tape cartridges since other forms of storage are available and inexpensive. Personal computer users will usually use optical storage (discussed later in this chapter) or USB flash drives. Tape storage is appropriate for storing large amounts of data that are no longer actively used but need to be saved for historical purposes. For example, an administrator of a local area network might use magnetic tape cartridges to back up company data on a daily basis. Tape cartridges provide a relatively inexpensive, sequential-access type of storage.

 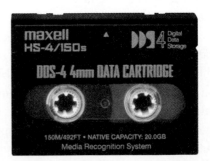

Tape cartridges are used with personal computers mainly for backing up the contents of a hard drive. The tape is housed in a small plastic container that also contains a tape reel and a take-up reel.

Optical Storage Devices

An **optical disc** is a plastic disk 4.75 inches in diameter and about 1/20th of an inch thick. Both a **compact disc (CD)** and a **digital versatile (or video) disc (DVD)** are types of optical discs that are available in a variety of formats. Optical disc systems are widely used on computer systems of all sizes, and almost every new PC comes equipped with a **CD drive** or **DVD drive** (see Figure 3-13). The drive can read nearly any kind of data recorded on an optical disc, including text, graphics, video clips, and sound.

Laser technologies are used to store information and data on compact discs. A high-intensity laser records data by burning tiny indentations, each called a **pit**, onto the disc surface. A flat, unburned area on the disc is called a **land**. A low-intensity laser reads stored data from the disc into the computer by reflecting light through the bottom of the disc. Each pit absorbs the light, causing the computer to read the pit as a binary digit 0. Each land reflects the light, causing the computer to read the land as a binary digit 1. The arrangement of 0s and 1s can thus represent data (see Figure 3-14).

Unlike floppy disks and hard disks, which store data in concentric circles, optical disc data are typically stored along a single track that spirals outward from the center of the disc to the outer edge. As illustrated in Figure 3-15, data are stored on the disc in sectors, similar to the sectors on a hard disk or floppy disk.

Optical disc technologies are not necessarily compatible with one another, and some require a different type of disc drive and disc. Within each category there

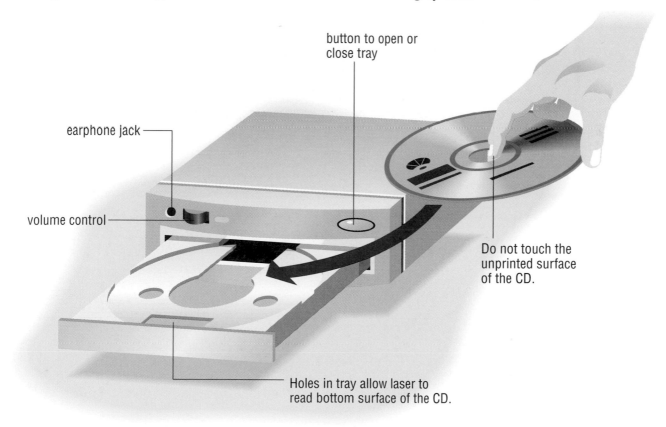

button to open or close tray

earphone jack

volume control

Do not touch the unprinted surface of the CD.

Holes in tray allow laser to read bottom surface of the CD.

Figure 3-13 Parts of a CD Drive
The CD is loaded printed side up, and the holes in the tray allow the laser to read the bottom surface of the disc once the tray is closed.

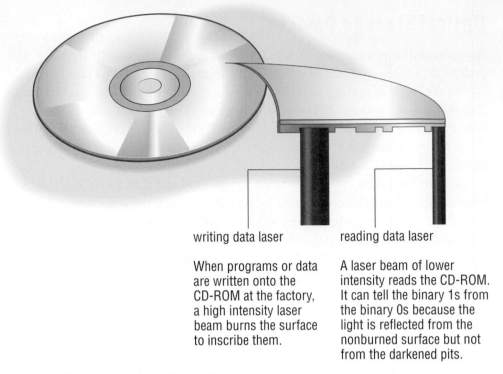

writing data laser

When programs or data are written onto the CD-ROM at the factory, a high intensity laser beam burns the surface to inscribe them.

reading data laser

A laser beam of lower intensity reads the CD-ROM. It can tell the binary 1s from the binary 0s because the light is reflected from the nonburned surface but not from the darkened pits.

Figure 3-14 Data Pattern on an Optical Disc
An optical disc drive reads binary data stored on an optical disc.

are varying storage formats, although the **CD-ROM** is relatively standard for computer data storage. Table 3-3 compares the storage capacities of various optical discs. Bit for bit, optical disc systems offer less expensive storage and greater durability than floppy disks, hard disks, and tape cartridges.

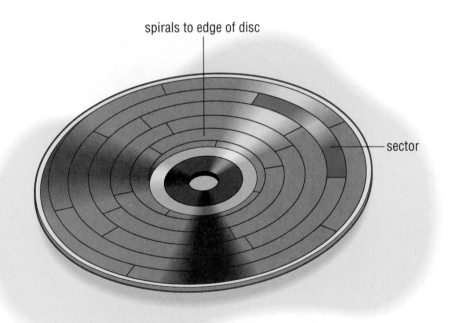

spirals to edge of disc

sector

Figure 3-15 Compact Disc Sectors
Information is stored on a series of sectors along a single track that spirals outward from the center to the outer edge of the optical disc.

Table 3-3 Types and Storage Capacities of Optical Discs

Optical Disc	Storage Capacity	Features
Compact Disc	650 MB to 700 MB	
CD-ROM		can be written to only once; used for distributing digital data such as computer software and for storing large data and graphics files
CD-R		used mainly in small businesses for creating one-of-a-kind CDs
CD-RW		allows rewriting; used mainly for backing up important files
Digital Versatile Disc	4.7 GB to 17 GB	
DVD-ROM		can be written to only once; typically used to create master copies of movies
DVD-R		can be written to only once
DVD-RW		recordable and rewritable
DVD+R		recordable one time only
DVD+RW		recordable, rewritable up to 1,000 times; cannot be read by set-top players and many computer DVD drives
DVD-RAM		recordable and rewritable up to 100,000 times
DVD-Video		used in the entertainment industry for recording movies that are sold or rented
Blu-ray		high-definition video and data

CD-ROMs

Most optical disc systems are of the CD-ROM type. Like an audio CD found in the home or automobile, a CD-ROM comes with data already encoded. The data are permanent and can be read many times, but they cannot be changed. A CD-ROM drive is needed to access the stored data. Since CD-ROMs conform to a standard size and format, any CD-ROM can be used with any CD-ROM drive. Computer CD-ROM drives are also capable of playing audio CDs. CD-ROMs are well suited for storing large computer applications containing graphics, sound, and video. A typical CD-ROM can hold about 650–700 MB of information, or about 450 times as much as a high-density floppy disk. An example of this capacity in real terms is the fact that the entire 32-volume set of the *Encyclopaedia Britannica 2004* plus the *Merriam-Webster's Collegiate Dictionary and Thesaurus,* an atlas, and timelines can be stored on just two CD-ROMs.

Data transfer rates vary among different CD-ROM drives—a factor that can be very important depending on the application being used. For example, a slow

Keeping It Personal

SOL LIPMAN NOTICED THAT KIDS TODAY take a completely different approach to using computers than do their elders. Old geezers are loyal to one or two computers. They use either a laptop to tote all their data or a USB flash drive to synchronize their files to the home PC. Students and young professionals, however, easily bounce between three and five computers a day—at school, at the library, at a café, at a friend's house, at home. They don't have an emotional need to personalize each one of them, but they do want immediate access to all their personal data—music, photos, videos and files.

Lipman's Sticky Inc. came up with the StickyDrive, a free, downloadable software that breathes new life into the old USB flash drive. Aimed at the college market, the StickyDrive is a flash desktop that makes it a breeze to manage documents and media files, and to run any flash-capable programs such as Skype and Firefox on any removable storage drive.

The next version of StickyDrive will be a "look ma, no hands!" version that allows any application to run directly from external storage. No installation, no need to touch the host's registry.

StickyDrive, what Lipman loftily deems "the one interface for humanity" may well become a must-have for young computer users obsessed with sharing and using their personal data wherever they go.

Source: Needleman, Rafe, "Data Management for College Students," April 18, 2006. <http://www.release1-0.com/freshproduce/article.php?serialnum=FPR200604180000>.

---

transfer rate can result in poor image quality or garbled sounds. CD-ROM speeds are expressed as a multiple of the speed of the first CD-ROM drives (150 KB per second). For example, the data transfer rate of a 20X CD-ROM drive is 3,000 KB per second (150 KB × 20 = 3,000 KB) and a 40X CD-ROM drive is 6,000 KB per second (150 KB × 40 = 6,000 KB). The higher the number, the faster the data transfer rate of the CD-ROM drive. Faster speeds result in clearer images and better sounds. Newer CD-ROM drives have data transfer rates ranging from 40X to 75X.

CD-Rs

A **CD-R drive** allows a PC user to record, or "burn," information on a **CD-R**. A CD-R drive is also referred to as a CD burner. This device writes once to the disc, and the resulting CD or CD-ROM can be read by a standard CD-ROM drive.

Most CD-R drives can read and write data at speeds up to 52X. In describing the speed of a CD-R, the device's writing speed is listed first. For example, a speed of 8 X 24 means the drive writes at a speed of 8X and reads at a speed of 24X. The main disadvantage of a CD-R is that it can be written on only one time. CD-RW technology overcomes this limitation.

CD-RWs

A **CD-RW** (compact disc–rewritable) uses an erasable disc that can be rewritten multiple times, similar to a floppy disk or hard disk. To use a CD-RW system, a CD-RW drive and special software are required. CD-RW discs are often used in the movie industry for making original copies of movies. Once perfected, the movie is copied to other optical discs that cannot be changed.

A typical CD-RW drive can read and write at speeds up to 32X. These speeds are usually shown on a CD-RW drive package as 12X/4X/32X. Rewrite speeds are typically slower than write speeds because the drive must first locate the file containing the information to be rewritten and then make the required changes.

With storage capacities of up to 700 MB or more, CD-RW discs are ideal for storing and backing up large or important files, such as the contents of a hard disk. In addition, they allow the creation of large files, such as those containing music, that can be shared with other users who have CD-ROM drives. Newer CD-RW burners can write an entire CD in 4 minutes and copy a 3-minute song to the user's hard drive in 5 seconds. Because of their flexibility, CD-RWs are rapidly replacing the more limited CD-Rs.

DVD-ROMs

Many of today's complex applications demand huge amounts of storage capacity, often requiring several standard CD-ROMs. DVD-ROM technology was developed to overcome this limitation. A **DVD-ROM** is an extremely high-capacity disc capable of holding many gigabytes of data, currently ranging from 4.7 gigabytes (GB) to 17 gigabytes. In appearance, a DVD looks just like a CD. The basic technology for storing data on these two types of optical discs also is the same, although minor differences in DVD technology allow for higher storage capacities. For one, packing the pits more closely means a denser disc. Manufacturers can also create two layers of pits, approximately doubling the storage capacity, and they can create double-sided discs. These variations in techniques account for the range of storage capacities from 4.7 GB for a single-sided, single-layered disc to 17 GB for a double-sided, double-layered disc. A 17 GB disc can hold the entire contents (text and color images) of a large retailer's catalog.

CD-R discs offer an inexpensive way for individuals and businesses to create their own CDs.

A DVD disc looks like its relative, the compact disc, but can store five times more data.

DVD-ROM technology was initially developed to store full-size movies. However, a DVD can also store text, graphics, images, and sound. This technology requires the use of a DVD-ROM drive or player. Because DVD-ROM drives and DVD players are backward-compatible, most can also read CD-ROMs, CD-Rs, CD-RWs, and audio CDs. Newer DVD-ROM drives are capable of reading from the disc at speeds up to 40X. DVD-ROMs are available in a variety of versions, including versions that are both recordable and rewritable. Two of the more widely used formats are DVD-R and DVD-RW.

DVD-Rs   As with CD-R discs, a **DVD-R**, can be recorded on only one time. Once data, video, or sound is recorded on the disc, the information is permanently stored. DVD-R discs created by a DVD-R device can be read by most commercial DVD-ROM players.

DVD-R discs are used extensively by the music and movie industries for creating commercial copies of music and movies. Several thousand or even millions of copies can be made from the original DVD-R.

A typical DVD-R disc can hold up to 4.7 GB of data, enough capacity to hold a full-length movie or hundreds of music pieces. Using a two-layer standard, manufacturers can increase the storage volume to 8.5 GB, and adding a second side means boosting the total capacity to 17 GB. A new format called the Blu-ray Disc will store 27 GB, which represents more than 13 hours of movies compared to the standard DVD capacity of 133 minutes. Nine electronics companies, including Sony, have collaborated in developing the Blu-ray Disc, and industry observers predict that this disc may soon become the standard recording format. Manufacturers are continually researching new techniques for creating discs with even greater storage capacities.

DVD-RWs   Another type of digital versatile disc, called a **DVD-RW**, allows recorded data to be erased and recorded over numerous times without damaging the disc. The rewriting capability makes DVD-RW discs more versatile and therefore more popular among users needing inexpensive, reusable storage media with large storage capacities. A single-layered, single-sided DVD-RW disc can store up to 4.7 gigabytes of data.

DVD-RW players and discs are becoming increasing popular. They can be used for routine storage of programs, files, and data, for making a back-up copy of the contents of a hard disk, and for archiving important files. Like DVD-Rs, data recorded on a DVD-RW disc by a DVD-RW device can be read by most commercial DVD-ROM players.

Caring for Optical Discs

Table 3-4 lists guidelines for the handling and care of compact discs and DVDs. Dirt or other foreign substances on optical discs can cause read errors and/or cause a disc to not work at all. However, an optical disc does not require routine cleaning and should be cleaned only when necessary. Using a commercially available cleaning kit is recommended, but other methods can be used, such as the procedure outlined in Table 3-5. Figure 3-16 shows the proper technique for wiping the data side of an optical disc.

Go to this title's Internet Resource Center and read the article titled "DVD Technology." www.emcp.net/CUT3e

Table 3-4 Care Instructions for Optical Discs

Do
Store each disc in a jewel case or disc sleeve when not in use.
Use felt-tip, permanent marker to write on the nonshiny side of the disc.
Hold the disc only by its edges.
Use the recommended disc cleaning method to remove dirt or other substances.

Do Not
Allow anything to touch the shiny (data) side of the disc.
Stack disks that are not in a jewel case or disc sleeve.
Place objects on the disc.
Expose disc to direct sunlight or excessive heat.
Place food or beverages near a disc.

Large Computer System Storage Devices

Large computer systems, such as mainframe and server systems, typically use storage devices and media similar to those used with smaller computers. However, large computer storage devices provide much higher capacities than smaller computers because of the huge amounts of data they deal with. For example, a large business would need multiple hard disks for storing thousands of employee records. Similarly, imagine the capacities needed for storing all domestic airline flight schedules for a year.

Magnetic Storage Devices for Large Computer Systems

Large computer systems typically use magnetic disk and magnetic tape secondary storage devices and media. For large computers, **magnetic disk storage** consists of a disk drive housing multiple hard disks contained in a rigid plastic container

Table 3-5 Steps for Cleaning an Optical Disc

1. Blow on the shiny side of the disc to try to remove dirt or dust without touching the disc.
2. If further cleaning is needed, wipe the disc from the center to the edges with a clean, lint-free, cotton cloth.
3. If further cleaning is necessary, rinse the disc in plain water. Allow the disc to air dry or wipe the disc dry according to Step 2.
4. If further cleaning is necessary, use a commercially available optical disc cleaning solution or use isopropyl (rubbing) alcohol. Apply the cleaning solution from the center to the edges of the disc. Allow the disc to air dry or wipe the disc dry according to Step 2.

Figure 3-16 Cleaning an Optical Disc
Do not wipe a disc in a circular motion because wiping with the tracks may put scratches on the disc.

called a **disk pack**. A disk pack is mounted inside a disk drive. A metal shaft extends through the center of the vertically-aligned disks (Figure 3.17). When activated, electromagnetic read/write heads record information and/or read stored data by moving inward and outward between the disks.

Disk storage provides users with direct, or random, access to stored data. Disk storage is preferred when users need to access stored information quickly. For example, disk storage allows bank and utility company employees to quickly access and update thousands of customer accounts.

Another type of secondary storage for large computer systems is **magnetic tape**

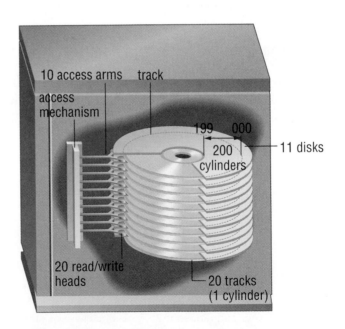

Figure 3-17 Parts of a Disk Pack
A disk pack houses multiple vertically aligned disks in a rigid plastic container placed inside a disk drive. When activated, read/write heads read or record on the disks by moving inward and outward between them.

storage, which uses removable reels of magnetic tape. The tape contains tracks that extend the full length of the tape. Each track contains metallic particles representing potential 0 and 1 bits. As is true of magnetic disks, combinations of bits are magnetized, or not magnetized, to represent bytes of data. The data is stored and accessed sequentially along the full length of the tape. Figure 3-18 shows how a tape drive reads and writes data.

Because magnetic tape is a sequential storage technology, information is accessed or updated in sequential order, that is, in numerical order. For example, if the user wants to access the twentieth record on the tape, the previous 19 records must first move past the read/write heads before the twentieth record can be accessed. Magnetic tape storage is typically used in situations where large amounts of information, such as all employee payroll records, are to be updated. In this case, all records are to be updated and the order in which individual records are processed is not important.

Magnetic tape storage may be used for other kinds of applications. Information stored on magnetic disk is often backed up onto tape and stored in a safe place in case it is needed. For example, a serious fire could damage or destroy a company's disk drives, tape drives, and other equipment. Having a backup copy of the data can eliminate the need to reconstruct important information.

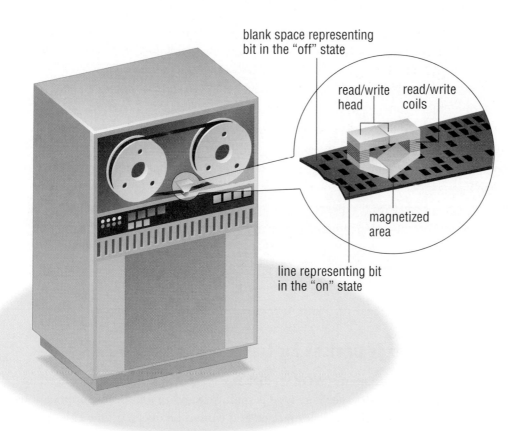

Figure 3-18 How a Tape Drive Reads and Writes Data
A magnetic tape contains tracks that extend the full length of the tape. Each track contains metallic particles representing potential 0 and 1 bits.

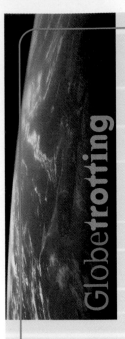

Globetrotting

Freedom in the Desert

FOR ALL THE MIRACLES COMPUTERS PERFORM, THE GREATEST FEAT of the new technology may be liberating people enslaved by truly horrible jobs.

Take camel racing. It's a sport of royals in a number of Arab lands. The animals may cost hundreds of thousands of dollars, but the riders needed to goad them forward are dirt poor. Children, some as young as four, are recruited or virtually stolen from other countries such as Sudan or Pakistan.

The lives of the camel jockeys are bleak—they receive no schooling, they're kept on starvation diets to keep their weight down, and their injuries often go untreated. Their lives consist of obeying orders barked at them from walkie-talkies strapped to their chests while hurling down a racetrack on an enormous camel.

Qatar happens to be a superbly rich Arab country that, while still tied to past traditions, leans closer to the West than many of its neighbors. When the United Nations and the U.S. State Department started pressuring Qatar about this form of slavery, the current emir, Hamad Bin Khalifa Al-Thani, responded. There would be no more child jockeys in his country, he declared.

K-team, a Swiss company, was assigned the job of creating a replacement that could perform as well as a four-year-old and yet deal with the extreme temperature, dust, and shocks that camel racing entails. The K-team came up with a 2-foot, 35-pound robotic structure. The right "hand" bears the whip and the left manipulates the reins. Inside the jacket is a box containing microcontrollers, processor, soundboard, and GPS.

The trainers race alongside the track in SUVs, using joysticks to control the jockey and a remote screen to monitor camel heart rate and speed as well as the jockey's battery life.

The camels balked at being ridden by mere boxes, so a head was added to the jockey. The childlike head is empty and exists only to keep the skittish camel under the pretense that a human is on board. But after training, the faces are removed in deference to Islamic law forbidding human likenesses.

The Qatar government pays $10,000 per computer jockey, which is then leased to camel racers. For the camel jockeys who have been returned to their homelands, the value must be far more.

Source: Lewis, Jim. "Robots of Arabia," *Wired*, November 2005, pp. 188–195.

Optical Storage Devices for Large Computer Systems

A **write once, read many (WORM) disk** is a type of optical laser disk used for very high-capacity storage. This type is mainly found in mainframe applications. WORM disks can only be written once and cannot be overwritten. This safety feature, combined with their high capacity, makes them ideal for storing archival-type material such as records or images. One of the drawbacks to WORM disks is that they are usually readable only by the drive on which they were written. The rapid advances in optical disk technology mean that newer optical disk formats such as CD-R are gradually supplanting WORM disks.

OnThe**Horizon**

SCIENTISTS, COMPUTER ENGINEERS, AND ENTREPRENEURS OF ALL KINDS are working feverishly to develop new and improved hardware devices that will make information access faster and easier. After all, much is at stake—the millions and billions of dollars in revenue to be shared by successful individuals and companies. Inventors are also motivated by the great satisfaction that comes with creating something new and better. Several trends are worth watching.

Increased Optical Disc Storage Capacity

Computer users needing huge storage capacities may be pleased with a new type of optical disc storage called High Definition Digital Multilayer Disc (HD-DMD). Manufactured by D Data Inc., an HD-DMD disc currently holds up to 32 gigabytes (GB) of data, a capacity to increase up to 100 GB. This amount is currently 45 times greater than a CD-ROM and 5 times greater than a DVD-ROM.

HD-DMD discs contain fluorescent materials embedded in the pits and grooves of all 10 or more layers. The fluorescent materials are stimulated to produce coherent and incoherent light when in contact with a laser. Data are stored in the incoherent light. Because the technology is not based on reflection, multiple layers are read at the same time.

Current plans are for HD-DMD discs to be used in a read-only format, which will require an HD-DMD drive. HD-DMD drives will likely be backward-compatible with DVD disc formats.

Solid State Drives

Lower production and raw material costs are making solid state drives an increasingly attractive option for notebook computers and other mobile computing devices. Non-volatile flash memory forms the core of these drives. Because they contain no moving parts the drives are less vulnerable to damage from shock and impact than hard disk drives. Additional benefits include improved read access times, reduced power requirements of up to 50%, and quieter operation.

Holographic Storage

IBM's Almaden Research Center has conducted pioneering research in computer storage since its founding in 1986, and has been responsible for a number of advances in hard disk drive technology. Anticipating future storage needs, researchers at Almaden are currently working on making holographic storage practical. The use of multidimensional holographic images will allow the layering of digitized information, vastly exceeding the storage capacity of today's magnetic and optical discs. IBM estimates that by 2010 we will see CD-size holographic storage media with a storage capacity of a terabyte of data (1,000 GB), the equivalent of 1,600 of today's CDs.

Holographic storage media may provide huge storage capacity for text and images, which would be displayed using a plastic-like material. Shown here is Plastic Logic's flexible display using E Ink Imaging Film.

Wireless Power Supply

While wireless technologies can be used to communicate with output devices, supplying those devices with the electrical power they require involves dealing with a variety of different electrical sources and an often unruly tangle of power cords. Those headaches may soon be a thing of the past as MIT researchers are now working on a power delivery system that will wirelessly transmit electrical energy from one object to another. The basic principle employed is resonance, a phenomenon which causes objects to vibrate when subject to certain energy frequencies. Power would be transmitted through electromagnetic waves and absorbed by receiving devices. Once this technology is perfected, wireless equipment will be truly wireless in all respects, eliminating the need for power adaptors and rechargers and resulting in a much-simplified connection process.

Chapter**Summary**

 For an interactive version of this summary, go to this text's Internet Resource Center at www.emcp.net/CUT3e. A Spanish version is also available.

What is output?

Output is processed data, usually text, graphics, or sound that may be produced as hard copy or soft copy. An **output device** is a hardware device that makes information available to a user. An **output medium** is material on which information is recorded. Computer systems can produce four types of output: **text**, **graphics**, **audio**, and **video**.

How do display devices work?

A **monitor** is the most common soft-copy output device. **Cathode ray tube (CRT) monitors** are being replaced by **flat-panel displays**. **Screen projectors** display the output from the monitor onto a much larger screen. Factors in monitor performance and quality include the **video card**, the monitor's **resolution**, and the **refresh rate**.

What types of printers are available?

Considered the most common hard-copy output devices, **printers** are classified as **impact printers** that print by physically striking an inked ribbon against the paper or **nonimpact printers** that form characters and images using electricity, heat, laser technology, or photographic techniques to produce output. **Dot-matrix printers** and **line printers** are examples of impact printers. **Ink-jet printers**, **laser printers**, **thermal printers**, and **plotters** are examples of nonimpact printers. **Postage printers**, **label printers**, and **photo printers** are special-purpose nonimpact printers.

A **multifunction device** is a single piece of equipment that provides multiple capabilities, including scanning, copying, printing, and sometimes faxing. A **facsimile (fax) machine** is a device that can send and receive copies or duplicates of documents through a telephone line.

What is audio output?

Computer users want to be able to hear speech and music related to their computer activities. Most personal computers have built-in **speakers**, and newer models often include a **speaker headset**. **Voice output** is available with all new computers and is becoming increasingly popular.

What are storage devices and storage media?

Also called auxiliary storage or secondary storage, permanent storage devices and media provide the capability of reentering and reusing stored information. A **storage device** is a component that houses a **storage medium** on which data are recorded (stored). Two main types of storage systems are magnetic and optical.

A **magnetic storage device** works by applying electrical charges to iron filings on revolving media, orienting each filing in one direction or another to represent a "0" or a "1." Data are stored and retrieved, or accessed, either sequentially (in linear order) or directly (in any order, randomly). Three main types of magnetic storage media are floppy disks, hard disks, and tape cartridges. A **floppy disk** (or diskette) is a thin, circular Mylar wafer, sandwiched between two sheets of special cleaning tissue inside a rigid plastic case. Data are stored along the **tracks** and in the **sectors** of a floppy disk. A **hard disk** system consists of one or more rigid metal platters (disks) mounted on a metal shaft and sealed in a container that contains an access mechanism. **Tape cartridges**, consisting of a small plastic housing containing a magnetically coated ribbon of thin plastic, are used mainly for backing up the contents of a hard drive and for archiving large amounts of data.

Data or information created and saved using a computer is called a **file**. A file name is typically followed by a period (.) and a set of characters called a **file extension**, which identifies the type of file. Similar files are often stored in a directory, a special kind of file that allows other files to be grouped together logically. A file's extension is usually created by the software program.

How do optical storage devices store data?

Optical disc systems are widely used on computer systems of all sizes. Most new PCs come equipped with an **optical disc drive** that can read data recorded on an **optical disc**, which is a flat, round, plastic disk. Data are stored as tiny indentations, called **pits**, and flat areas, called **lands**. Two lasers record and read the data. The main optical disc formats are **CD (compact disc)** and **DVD (digital versatile disc)**. Each disc type has various versions, including recordable one time only and both recordable and rewritable.

What storage devices are used in large computer systems?

Mainframe systems typically use storage devices and media similar to those used with smaller computers. For large computers **magnetic disk storage** consists of a disk drive housing multiple hard disks contained in a rigid plastic container called a **disk pack**. Another type of secondary storage for large computer systems is **magnetic tape storage** using removable reels of magnetic tape. **WORM (write once, read many) disks** are a type of optical laser disc used for very high-capacity storage such as images.

KeyTerms

Numbers indicate the pages where terms are first cited in the chapter. An alphabetized list of key terms with definitions (in English and Spanish) can be found on the Encore CD that accompanies this book. In addition, these terms and definitions are included in the end-of-book glossary.

What Is Output?
output, 101
hard copy, 101
soft copy, 101
text, 101
graphics, 101
audio, 102
video, 102
output device, 102
output medium, 102

Display Devices
monitor, 103
cathode ray tube (CRT) monitor, 105
video card (graphics card or video adapter), 105
flat-panel display, 105
liquid crystal display (LCD), 105
active-matrix display (thin-film transistor [TFT]) display, 105
bit depth (also called color depth), 107

true color (color depth), 107
resolution, 107
pixel, 107
dot pitch, 109
refresh rate, 109
ergonomics, 110
wearable computer, 110
high-definition television (HDTV), 111
screen projector, 112

Printers
printer, 113
portrait format, 113
landscape format, 113
impact printer, 113
nonimpact printer, 113
dot-matrix printer, 114
draft quality, 115
letter quality, 115
line printer, 115
ink-jet printer, 115
laser printer, 117
toner, 118
thermal printer, 118
direct thermal printer, 118
thermal wax transfer printer, 118
thermal dye transfer printer (thermal dye sublimation printer), 119
plotter, 119
photo printer, 120

SIM card, 120
postage printer, 120
label printer, 121
portable printer, 121
multifunction device (MFD), 121
facsimile machine (fax machine), 121
fax, 121
fax/modem card, 122
fax program, 123

Audio Output
speakers, 123
speaker headset, 123
voice output, 123

Storage Devices and Media
permanent storage (secondary storage, auxiliary storage,
    or external storage), 124
file, 125
file extension, 125
storage device, 126
storage medium, 126

Magnetic Storage Devices and Media
magnetic storage device, 126
permanent storage medium, 126
removable storage medium, 126
sequential access, 126
direct access, 126
access time, 126
data transfer rate, 126
floppy disk (also called diskette or disk), 127

hard drive, 128
hard disk, 128
track, 129
sector, 129
cluster, 129
file allocation table (FAT) file, 129
USB flash drive (jump drive, thumb drive,
    and pen drive), 130
tape cartridge, 130
tape drive, 130

Optical Storage Devices
optical disc, 131
compact disc (CD), 131
digital versatile (or video) disc (DVD), 131
CD drive, 131
DVD drive, 131
pit, 131
land, 131
CD-ROM, 132
CD-R drive (CD burner), 134
CD-R, 134
CD-RW, 135
DVD-ROM, 135
DVD-R, 136
DVD-RW, 136

Large Computer System Storage Devices
magnetic disk storage, 137
disk pack, 138
magnetic tape storage, 139
write once, read many (WORM) disk, 140

Chapter**Exercises**

 The following chapter exercises, along with new activities and information, are also offered in the Internet Resource Center for this title at www.emcp.net/CUT3e.

Tutorial > **Exploring Windows**

Tutorial 3 teaches the four methods for running an application: from the Start menu, using the desktop icons, using the Run command, and from a file management window. You will learn to choose a method based on the situation.

Expanding Your Knowledge > Articles and Activities

 Visit the Internet Resource Center for this title at www.emcp.net/CUT3e, read the articles related to this chapter, and complete the corresponding activities. The article titles are as follows:

- Topic 3-1: Storage Resource Management
- Topic 3-2: Data Protection
- Topic 3-3: Network Storage
- Topic 3-4: DVD Technology

Terms Check > Matching

 For additional practice, go to the Internet Resource Center for this title at www.emcp.net/CUT3e for a chapter crossword puzzle.

Write the letter of the correct answer on the line before each numbered item.

a. plotter	f. sector
b. pixel	g. diskette
c. optical disc	h. monitor
d. ergonomics	i. facsimile machine
e. laser printer	j. dot-matrix printer

_____ 1. A type of printer used for large-sized high-quality printing, including architectural drawings, charts, maps, diagrams, and other images.

_____ 2. A hard-copy output device that produces characters in a manner similar to the way in which numbers appear on a football scoreboard.

_____ 3. An electronic device that can send and receive documents through a telephone line.

_____ 4. A tiny single point in an alphabetic letter, number, graphic, or picture displayed on the screen.

_____ 5. A numbered section of a disk similar to a slice of pie.

_____ 6. A flat, round, plastic disc measuring approximately 4.75 inches in diameter on which data are stored in the form of pits and lands.

_____ 7. The study of the interaction between humans and the equipment they use.

_____ 8. The most common soft-copy output device.

_____ 9. A hardware device that produces high-quality hard-copy output using a technology similar to that of photocopy machines.

_____ 10. Another name for a floppy disk.

Technology Illustrated > **Identify the Process**

What process is this? Identify the process illustrated in the drawing below and write a paragraph explaining it.

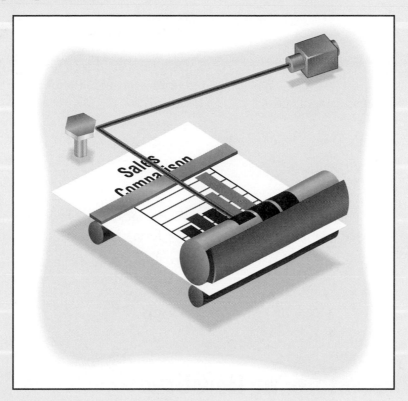

Knowledge Check > **Multiple Choice**

Circle the letter of the best answer from those provided.

1. Processed data that can be used immediately or stored in computer-usable form for later use are called
   a. input.
   b. output.
   c. data retrieval.
   d. manipulated data.

2. A term that describes the number of pixels in the display, or the quality of the text and graphics being displayed, is
   a. resolution.
   b. density.
   c. coordination.
   d. element filtering.

3. The most common type of device for producing hard-copy output is the
   a. monitor.
   b. printer.
   c. plotter.
   d. speaker.

4. A type of printer that produces output of exceptional quality using a technology similar to that of a photocopy machine is the
   a. ink-jet printer.
   b. dot-matrix printer.
   c. impact printer.
   d. laser printer.

5. A piece of equipment that looks like a printer or copy machine, but which provides a variety of capabilities, including scanning and copying, is known as a

a. scanner.
b. duplicator.
c. multifunction device.
d. special-purpose device.

6. Permanent storage is also known as all of the following except

a. secondary storage.
b. auxiliary storage.
c. primary storage.
d. external storage.

7. The time a disk storage device spends locating a particular file is called

a. data transfer rate.
b. access time.
c. file search time.
d. disk spin rate.

8. The most common removable magnetic storage device is the

a. CD-RW drive.
b. DVD-ROM drive.
c. tape drive.
d. USB flash drive.

9. On a compact disc, a laser records data by burning tiny indentations onto the disc surface called

a. lands.
b. pits.
c. tracks.
d. sectors.

10. Which one of the following is not an optical disc format?

a. hard disk
b. CD-ROM
c. CD-RW
d. DVD

Things That Think > Brainstorming New Uses

In groups or individually, contemplate the following questions and develop as many answers as you can.

1. Car washes and parking garages currently use digital license plate readers to identify customers' vehicles and to ensure that correct fees are paid for the companies' services. A camera in the license plate reader takes a picture of the front or rear of the vehicle. Optical character recognition software then converts the number in the photo to text, which is sent to a database of license numbers for verification. Although the digital license plate readers have some limitations, including problems reading curvy letters or unusual typefaces, security experts think this technology could be valuable in tracking the movement of vehicles around airports or other high-security areas. What other uses can you think of for digital license plate readers?

What kinds of problems might be associated with the technology?

2. Smart cards are plastic cards the size of credit cards with tiny chips embedded in them. They are growing in popularity with major U.S. corporations because of their ability to protect personal information, such as account numbers, during Internet business transactions. With a Web-enabled cell phone, a user could access a company Web site, order a product, and then pay for it by inserting a smart card into a slot in the phone. Can you think of other ways in which this intelligent plastic could be used? Brainstorm applications in business and beyond.

Key Principles > Completion

Fill in the blanks with the appropriate words or phrases.

1. A(n) _____ is a computer-generated picture produced on a computer screen, paper, or film.

2. A(n) _____ display is used for portable computers and other applications where weight and space considerations are critical.

3. The distance between pixels on a display is called _____.

4. Processed data that can be used immediately or stored in computer-usable form for later use are called_____.

5. _____ is a term that refers to the permanent storage of computer programs, files, and data.

6. A(n) _____ system consists of one or more rigid metal platters (disks) mounted on a metal shaft and sealed in a container containing an access mechanism.

7. A(n) _____ is a secondary storage medium on which data are typically recorded by means of a high-intensity laser.

8. Printers that form characters and images using electricity, heat, laser technology, or photographic techniques to produce output are called _____ printers.

9. A file name is typically followed by a(n) _____, which identifies the type of file.

10. On a floppy disk, data are stored along the _____ and in the _____.

Tech Architecture > Label the Drawing

In this illustration of a floppy disk, identify the pie-shaped sections and the two types of data storage areas.

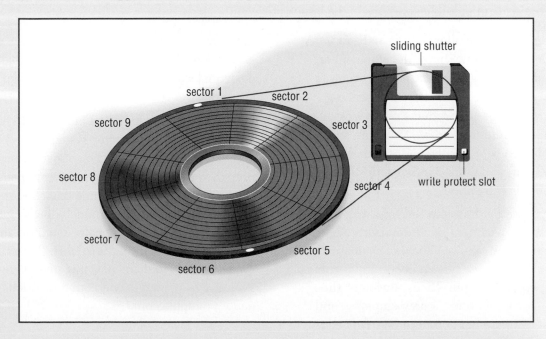

sliding shutter

sector 1

sector 2

sector 9

sector 3

sector 8

sector 4

write protect slot

sector 7

sector 5

sector 6

Techno Literacy > **Research and Writing**

Develop appropriate written responses based on your research for each item.

1. What is inside the printer?

   Ask your instructor to allow you to open up a printer in the computer lab and look at the components inside. Using paper and pen, draw the components that you recognize and label each of them. At a minimum, include the printing mechanism, the ribbon, ink or toner container, and paper tray or container. Ask your instructor to explain other components you do not recognize. Write a brief summary of each component's function.

2. How many ways can a user output data?

   Page through a computer magazine such as *PC World*, or visit a computer store and select a personal computer that interests you. Research and describe all the different output devices that could be used with that particular computer system.

3. Which features should be considered when you purchase a printer?

   Hewlett-Packard is a major manufacturer of printers for personal computers. Visit the company's Web site at www.hp.com to learn about the various kinds of printers HP produces. Select one printer and write a brief report describing the following features of the printer:

   a. type of printer (ink-jet, laser, etc.)
   b. model number
   c. printing speed
   d. color printing capability
   e. amount (if any) of storage capacity inside the printer
   f. graphics printing capability

4. Which storage device meets my needs?

   Numerous secondary storage devices are available for personal computers. Research the major brands and models. Create a table that compares the various storage devices and media. Identify the one that would best meet your needs, and explain why. How would you use it?

Technology Issues > **Team Problem-Solving**

In groups, brainstorm possible solutions to the issues presented.

1. Computers currently offer both visual and audio communication. Under development are devices and technologies that will incorporate olfactory communication, allowing users to smell various types of products while looking at them on the computer screen. What are some new applications of this technology for the food industry? Can you think of other industries that could use this capability?

2. Picture yourself working in the Information Technology department of a mid-sized company. Your responsibilities include evaluating employees' computer system needs and recommending equipment purchases. Recently, the company president hired a new employee and you must evaluate her computer system needs.

   The new employee is Marsha Wellington, a graphics designer, who will be responsible for designing sales and promotional pieces for the company.

   Considering you have a budget of $8,500 for equipping the computer system (or systems) she needs, research possible configurations and prepare a report outlining your recommendations, including costs. Assume that she needs a complete computer system, including graphics software, high-resolution color monitor, and high-resolution printing capability. *(Hint: Check computer magazines, retail stores, and Internet sites such as* www.gateway.com*,* www.dell.com*, and* www.apple.com*.)*

Mining Data > Internet Research and Reporting

Conduct Internet searches to find the information described in the activities below. Write a brief report that summarizes your research results. Be sure to document your sources, using the MLA format (see Chapter 1, page 42, to review MLA style guidelines).

1. Renting data storage is becoming widely used among large companies that generate huge amounts of data. Using the Internet, locate information that explains data storage hosting and discusses the benefits, costs, and potential growth rate for this service.

2. Using an Internet search engine, find out how "geographic information systems" (also called GIS) are used. Find three companies or government agencies that use GIS and summarize how they use this technology.

Technology Timeline > Predicting Next Steps

Look at the timeline below that outlines the major milestones in the development of storage devices and media. Research this topic and think of what the next steps will be. Complete the timeline through the year 2010 or later, if the research warrants it.

1956 IBM unveils the 350 Disk Storage Unit, the first random access (direct access) hard disk.

1973 IBM releases the 3340, the first Winchester hard disk with a capacity of 70 megabytes (MB) spread over four disk platters.

1985 The first CD-ROM drives make their debut on personal computers.

1998 The DVD-ROM drive debuts with 5.2 gigabytes (GB) of rewritable capacity on a double-sided cartridge—enough to hold a two-hour movie.

2001 Constellation 3D Inc. introduces a new type of optical disc storage called FMD-ROM, which holds up to 140 GB of data.

2003 USB flash drives (also called keychain drives because they are about the size of a key fob) hit the consumer market.

2003 D Data, Inc., acquires FMD-ROM patents and begins manufacturing multi-layer optical disk storage technology called HD-DMD.

Ethical Dilemmas > Group Discussion and Debate

As a class or within an assigned group, discuss the following ethical dilemma.

Many companies today have the ability to monitor employees' Internet usage as well as their inbound and outbound e-mail messages. Employees may consider this an invasion of privacy, but employers contend that they have the right to track usage of company property and ensure employees are doing their jobs efficiently. Is it legal for companies to monitor employee Internet and e-mail usage? Is it ethical for them to do so? Should employers be required to tell employees when they are being monitored? How much personal use of workplace computers should employees be allowed?

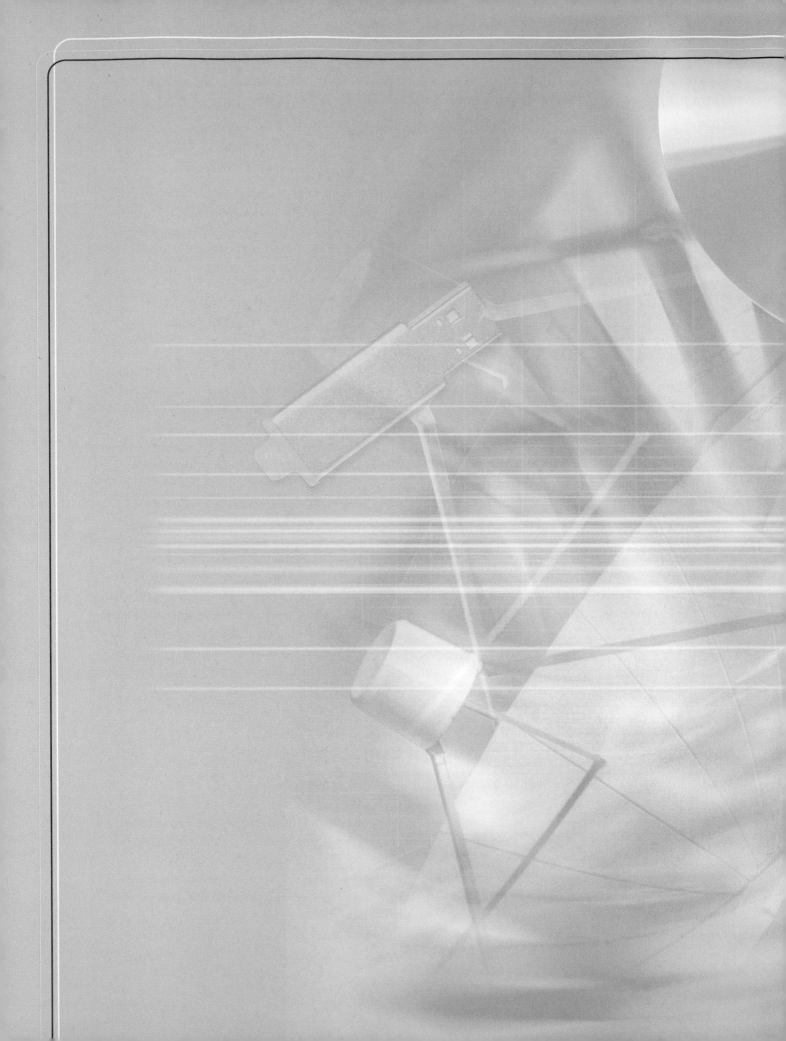

Telecommunications and Networks

COMPUTERS WERE ORIGINALLY STAND-ALONE DEVICES, incapable of communicating with other computers. This situation changed with the development of special telecommunications hardware and software in the 1970s and 1980s that allowed computers to be linked together to form networks, which in turn linked to larger networks and to the Internet. As a result, people around the world can communicate, access information, and share data almost instantly.

Telecommunications originally referred to the sending and receiving of information over telephone lines. As telecommunications systems evolved, the term was broadened to include other types of media used to transmit data, including satellite systems, microwave towers, and wireless devices such as cell phones. Figure 1 illustrates the basic concept of telecommunications.

A network consists of two or more computers, devices, and software connected by means of one or more communications media, such as wires, telephone lines, or wireless signals. These media form the fundamental part of a network—the channel or medium through which data bits and bytes are transmitted. The Internet is a worldwide network of networks that enables users to communicate and work together efficiently and effectively. A major part of the Internet is the World Wide Web (usually shortened to the Web) that allows individuals, businesses, and organizations to establish Web sites offering information that can be viewed by anyone having access to a computer and the Internet.

Because communications media are basic to networking, it is helpful to begin the study of networks by exploring the process of data transmission and the different types of media used to send data across networks.

Data Transmission Characteristics

The transmission of data over computer networks is characterized by the rate of transmission (bandwidth), type of signal (analog or digital), and order of bits (parallel or serial).

Bandwidth

Data is transferred from one computer to another in digital form (1s and 0s), known as bits. In a network, the number of bits that can be transferred per second

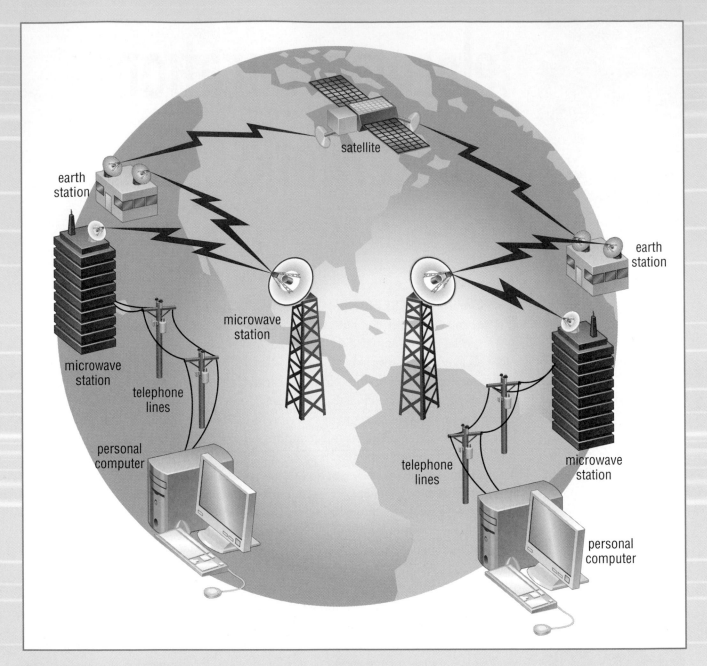

Figure 1 Telecommunications

Telecommunications, the combined use of computer hardware and communications software for sending and receiving information over communications media, make it possible for computer users throughout the world to communicate.

over a given medium is known as bandwidth. The basic measurement of bandwidth is bits per second (bps). Bandwidth varies among different types of communications media. A communications medium capable of carrying a large amount of data at faster speeds is referred to as a broadband medium, whereas one carrying a smaller amount of data at slower speeds is referred to as a narrowband medium. Fiber-optic cable is an example of a broadband medium; twisted-pair cable, commonly used in telephone lines, is an example of a narrowband medium.

Bandwidth can be an important factor in choosing a communications medium. Broadband media are more suitable when large amounts of data need to be transmitted quickly, such as with high-quality sound and video transmission. When only small amounts of data need to be transmitted and transmission time is less important, such as for simple text transmission, narrowband media may be suitable.

Analog and Digital Transmission

Telephone systems were established to carry voice transmissions using analog signals. An analog signal is composed of continuous waves transmitted over a medium at a certain frequency range, which is the number of complete fluctuations in energy per sound wave. Changes in the wave transmissions reflect changes in voice and sound pitch, or tone. In addition to using telephone lines, some cellular networks, cable television systems, and satellite dishes use analog communications media for carrying voice and sound transmissions.

Computers cannot understand data in analog form. Instead, computers use the binary number system to transform data into digital signals. Newer communications technologies generally employ digital signals.

A modem converts digital signals into analog form so an analog communications medium can send those signals. Modems also convert incoming analog signals back to their digital equivalents so computers can receive those signals. Some newer modems are able to transmit and receive digital data without analog conversion, provided they are connected to the right communications media.

Notebook and other portable computers use a Personal Computer Memory Card International Association (PCMCIA) modem that inserts into a PCMCIA slot. The modem is connected to a telephone outlet using a standard telephone line. Mobile users without access to standard telephone outlets can use a special cable to connect the PCMCIA modem to a cellular phone.

Parallel and Serial Transmission

Peripheral devices typically are connected to the system unit of a personal computer by means of a cable, one end of which is plugged into the device and the other end plugged into a port, or interface, on the system unit. Most computers are equipped with two types of ports: parallel and serial. A parallel cable is needed to connect a device to a parallel port, whereas a serial cable is needed to connect a device to a serial port. Many peripheral devices, including printers and mice, may be either parallel or serial.

Data travels within a computer system and over long distances in either parallel or serial form. In serial transmission, 8 bits are transmitted one bit after another in a continuous line. In parallel trans-

mission, 8 bits are transmitted at the same time over separate paths. Thus, parallel transmission is generally faster than serial transmission. A modem that connects the system unit to a telephone line contains a serial port because the telephone line expects the data being transmitted to be in serial form.

Communications Media

A communications medium is a link (a connection) that allows computers in different locations to be connected. When communications take place between distant computers, a combination of media may be used, some of which the user may never see. Communications media are broadly classified as either wired or wireless.

Wired Communications Media

While many computers, devices, and networks now use wireless technologies, traditional wired technologies are still a common a means of communicating. The method chosen depends mainly on user requirements relating to availability, cost, speed, and other factors.

Twisted-Pair Cable Twisted-pair cable, one of the older types of communications media, was originally developed for telephone networks. Early versions consisted of wires wrapped (twisted) around one another to reduce noise. Twisted-pair cable can be used to connect computers in networks for transmitting data over relatively short distances. Millions of home computer owners use this medium with a modem because the cable is already in place. The advantages of twisted-pair cable are its availability and low price.

Coaxial Cable Coaxial cable is commonly used for cable television connections, in telephone networks, and in some computer networks. The cable consists of an insulated center wire grounded by a shield of braided wire.

Millions of cable television subscribers already have cable installed in their homes and offices. By adding a cable modem, television subscribers can take advantage of this communications medium to receive much faster data transmission speeds than twisted-pair cable can offer.

Fiber-Optic Cable A twisted-pair cable and a coaxial cable both contain copper conductors and transmit electrical signals—streams of electrons. Instead of copper, a fiber-optic cable uses a string of glass to transmit photons—beams of light. A fiber-optic cable typically consists of hundreds of clear fiberglass or plastic fibers (threads), each approximately the same thickness as a human hair. Data is converted into beams of light by a laser device and transmitted as light pulses. Billions of bits can be transmitted per second.

Integrated Services Digital Network (ISDN) Lines In some locations a special digital telephone line, called Integrated Services Digital Network (ISDN) line, is available. This type of line can be used to dial into the Internet and transmit and receive information at very high speeds, ranging from 64 Kbps to 128 Kbps. Using an ISDN line requires a special ISDN modem. Monthly fees for ISDN lines are higher than for regular phone lines, adding to a user's communications costs.

Digital Subscriber Line (DSL) Digital Subscriber Line (DSL) technology uses existing copper phone lines and new optimized switched connections to achieve faster telecommunications speeds than traditional dial-up phone access. DSL separates voice and data into discrete channels so that users can still make phone calls while connected to the Internet via a DSL modem. DSL is considered a broadband technology, as connection speeds range from 144 Kbps to 1.56 Mbps. DSL technology is not available in all locations because there is a physical limitation on how far away from a telephone company office a DSL line can reach.

T Lines A T line is any of several types of digital high-speed long-distance telephone lines. Developed by Bell Labs, T lines are capable of carrying multiple types of signals, including both voice and data. T lines can carry data at very high speeds, but they are expensive. Unlike a standard dial-up telephone line that can carry only a single signal, T lines use multiplexing, thereby making it possible for multiple signals to share a single telephone line. Two popular types of digital T lines are T1 lines and T3 lines, both of which can carry voice and data. There are no T2 lines.

A fiber-optic cable typically consists of hundreds or thousands of clear glass or plastic fibers, each about the same thickness as a human hair.

Wireless Communications Media

Wireless media transmit information as electromagnetic signals through the air in much the same way as a battery-operated radio sends radio waves. Individual users, businesses, and organizations are rapidly embracing wireless technologies as workers become more mobile and wireless devices become more powerful. Wireless technologies include microwave systems, satellite systems, infrared technology, cellular technology, Wi-Fi technology, and Bluetooth technology.

Microwave Systems Microwave transmission involves the sending and receiving of information in the form of high-frequency radio signals. A microwave system transmits data through the atmosphere from one microwave station to another, or from a microwave station to a satellite and then back to earth to another microwave station.

Satellite Systems A communications satellite is a solar-powered electronic device containing several small, specialized radios called transponders. A transponder receives signals from a transmission station on the ground, called an earth station. Communications satellites are positioned thousands of miles above the earth. A satellite receives transmitted signals, amplifies them, and then retransmits them to the appropriate locations on earth. Communications satellites are capable of transmitting billions of bits per second, making them ideal for transmitting very large amounts of data.

Infrared Technology In recent years infrared technology has become increasingly popular for providing wireless communication links between computers and peripheral devices. Infrared technology transmits data as light waves instead of radio waves. Television remote control units use the same technology. Wireless keyboards, also called cordless keyboards, are a recent application of infrared technology. The battery-powered keyboards communicate with computers by transmitting data to a receiver connected to a port on the computer's system unit.

Cellular Technology People can communicate wirelessly to and from nearly anywhere in the world using cellular technology. Cellular phones and devices work by maintaining contact with cellular

antennae that resemble metal telephone poles positioned throughout a cellular calling area. Each area, called a cell, has its own antenna encompassing an area approximately 10 to 12 square miles in diameter. As users move from cell to cell, the closest antenna picks up the signal and relays it to the appropriate destination.

Communications networks that support cellular communications also work well for handling business data. Using a portable computer with a cellular modem, a person can access both Internet resources and information stored on a company's intranet databases.

Wi-Fi Technology The most commonly used wireless technology today is Wi-Fi. Wi-Fi is a wireless local area network (WLAN) technology. A Wi-Fi device, such as a PDA or a notebook computer with a Wi-Fi card, must be in close proximity (usually within 150 feet indoors or 300 feet outdoors) to a device called a wireless access point. The wireless access point is a hardware device that transmits a wireless network signal to Wi-Fi–enabled devices. A Wi-Fi hotspot is a location that has one or more wireless access points.

Bluetooth Technology Bluetooth wireless connectivity is becoming increasingly common. Most PDAs, cell phones, and notebook computers have

A wireless access point is a device that connects Wi-Fi-enabled devices to a local area network.

Cell phone users can talk on a hands-free Bluetooth headset while their phone is in a bag or jacket pocket.

built-in Bluetooth capabilities. This technology offers short-range (usually 15 to 20 feet) connectivity with other Bluetooth devices. Devices connected with Bluetooth essentially form their own small, temporary network that can transmit both voice and data. Common uses of Bluetooth include connecting mobile headsets to cell phones and synchronizing PDA information with notebook computer or cell phone information.

Network Classifications

Networks vary enormously, from simple interoffice systems connecting a few personal computers and a printer, to complex global systems connecting thousands of computers and computer devices. Networks can be classified by their architecture, by the relative distances they cover, and by the users they are designed to support.

Networks Classified by Architecture

The term network architecture refers to the way a network is designed and built. Client/server and peer-to-peer are the two major architectural designs for networks.

Client/Server Architecture In client/server architecture, a client (such as a networked personal computer, workstation, or terminal) can send requests to, and receive services from, another typically more powerful computer called a server (see Figure 2). The server can store programs, files, and data that are available to authorized users. A major advantage of the client/server model is that application programs, such as Microsoft Office, can be stored on the server and accessed by multiple users.

Peer-to-Peer Architecture Peer-to-peer architecture is a network design in which computers composing the network have equivalent capabilities and responsibilities, each acting as both client and server (see Figure 3). Peer-to-peer networks are usually simpler to install and maintain and are less expensive.

Networks Classified by Coverage

Small networks confined to a limited geographical area are called local area networks (LANs), while wide area networks (WANs) are extensive and may span hundreds of miles.

Local Area Networks A local area network (LAN) is a private network serving the needs of a business, organization, or school with computers located in the same building or area. LANs make it convenient for multiple users to share programs, data, information, hardware, software, and other computing resources. LANs use a special computer, called a file server, to house all of the network resources. A print server allows multiple users to share the same printer. Using networks to share resources such as applications programs, hard disk capacity, and high-quality printers saves companies money in hardware, software, and related costs. Figure 4 shows the arrangement of a LAN.

Wide Area Networks A wide area network (WAN) spans a large geographical area, connecting two or more LANs (see Figure 5). A business might use a WAN to communicate between a manufacturing facility in one state and corporate headquarters in

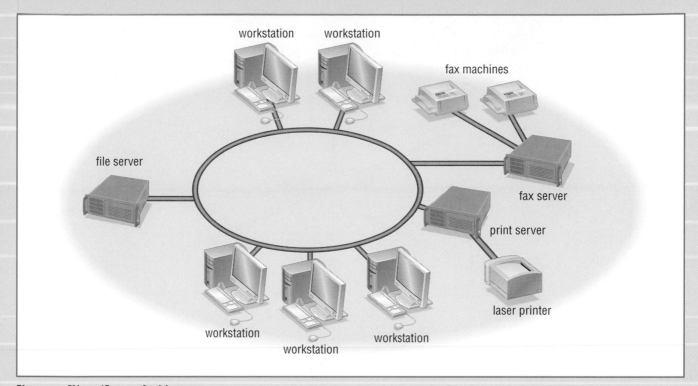

Figure 2 Client/Server Architecture

In this type of network architecture structure, the networking paths allow a networked client computer to send information to a server, which then can relay the information back to the client computer, or to another client on the same network. In this network, the two fax machines and the laser printer are shared resources, available through their respective servers. In addition, the file server provides access to a shared hard disk.

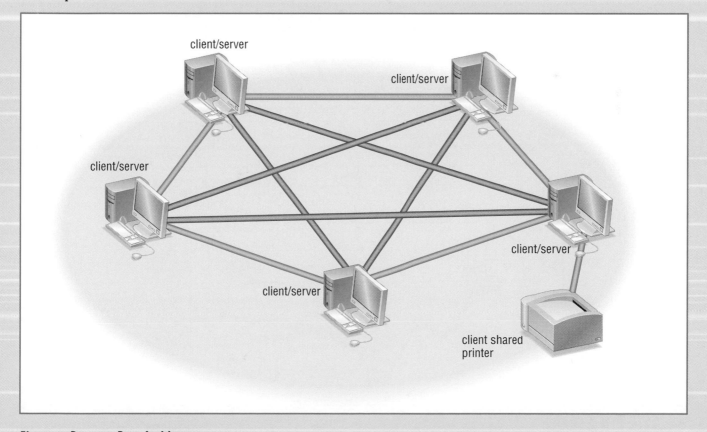

Figure 3 Peer-to-Peer Architecture

In this network architecture, computers act as both client and server.

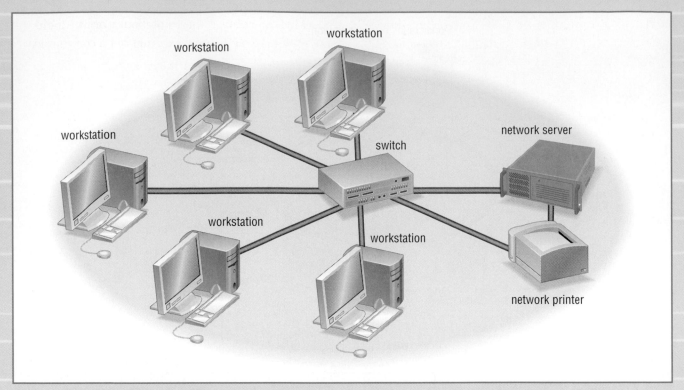

Figure 4 A Local Area Network (LAN)
In a LAN, workstations are connected to network resources such as printers and servers via a switch.

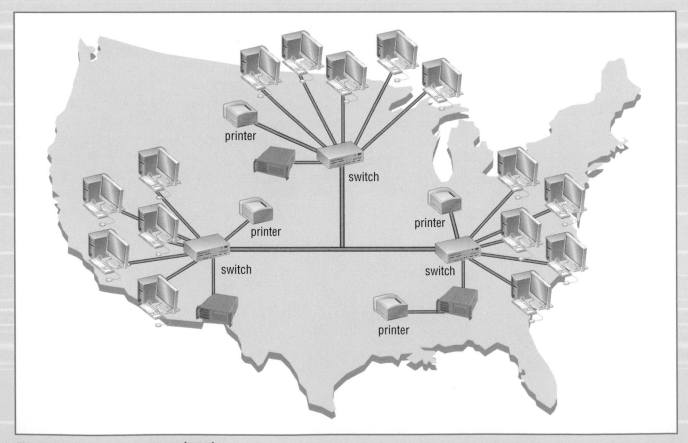

Figure 5 A Wide Area Network (WAN)
In this WAN, three offices, each with an individual LAN, are able to share resources through the network connection.

another. Governments, universities, and large corporations use WANs to share data among separate networks. WANs typically make use of high-speed leased telephone lines, wireless satellite connections, or both.

There are several types of wide area networks. A metropolitan area network (MAN) is a wide area network limited to a specific site, such as a city or town. A public access network (PAN) is a wide area network operated and maintained by a large company, such as AT&T, MCI, or Sprint, which provides voice and data communications capabilities to customers for a fee. Businesses that use the facilities of large communications companies to provide subscribers with additional services are called a value added network (VAN). Typical services offered include access to various network databases, electronic mail, and online advertising and shopping. America Online is a well known VAN.

Networks Classified by Users

Networks can also be classified by the groups of users they were designed to accommodate. This classification includes intranets and extranets.

Intranets A network that is housed within an organization to serve internal users is called an intranet. Access to an intranet is typically protected by a firewall, which consists of special hardware and/or software that prevents or restricts access to and from the network. All inquiries and messages entering or leaving the intranet pass through the firewall, which examines them and blocks those that do not meet the firewall's specified security criteria.

An intranet functions in the same way as a LAN that is not connected to other networks outside the organization. Stored information is available only to authorized users, and certain kinds of information may be available only to specific persons, groups, or departments within the organization.

Extranets An extranet is an extension of an intranet that allows specified external users, including customers and business partners, access to internal applications and data via the Internet. An extranet allows external users with a valid user ID and password to pass through the firewall and access certain resources in the organization's network. Mobile workers can connect their notebooks or handheld computers to a company extranet via a communications medium such as a telephone line.

Like intranets, extranets can be used for a variety of business activities. For example, an automobile manufacturer can post a request for bids for raw materials, such as engine parts, seat covers, and tires. An accompanying electronic bid form allows potential suppliers to submit a bid to supply these materials.

Network Topologies

Network topology, or layout, is the pattern by which the network is organized. One way to think of topology is to picture a map showing roads, rivers, railroads, cities, mountains, and other features. The relationship between the various locations can be understood by looking at the map. A diagram of a network's topology functions in much the same way, allowing a viewer to locate each network component, or node. The common network topologies are bus, star, and ring.

Bus Topologies

In a bus topology, all computers (nodes) are linked by means of a single line of cable with two endpoints. The cable connection is called a bus. All communications travel the length of the bus. As the communication passes, each computer's network card checks to see if it is the assigned destination point. If the computer finds its address in the message, it then reads the data, checks for errors in the transmission, and sends a message to the sender of the data acknowledging that the data was received. If the computer's network card does not find its address, it ignores the message. To prevent transmitted data from bouncing back and forth, a bus topology may include a terminator at both ends of the line. A terminator is a device that absorbs signals so they do not reflect back down the line. Figure 6 shows the layout of a bus topology.

Star Topologies

In a star topology, multiple computers and peripheral devices are linked to a central hub, in a point-to-point configuration resembling a star (Figure 7). The hub acts as a switching station, reading message addresses

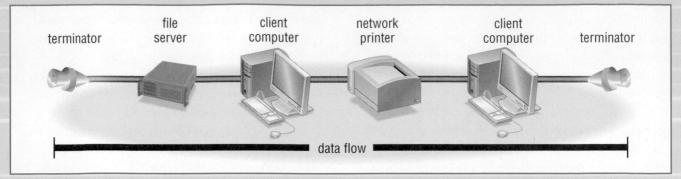

Figure 6 Bus Topology
In a bus topology, all communications travel the full length of the bus, with each computer's networking transceiver checking the message for its intended destination.

the nodes send and routing the messages accordingly. The chief disadvantage of star topology is its dependence on the host computer. Because all communications must go through the hub, the network becomes inoperable if it fails to function properly.

Ring Topologies

In a ring topology there is no hub, and each computer is connected to two other computers in a cir-

cular path (Figure 8). A type of ring technology called token ring uses a single electronic signal, or token, to pass information from the source computer to the destination.

Hybrid Topologies

Some businesses prefer using one kind of topology throughout the organization, but the more common practice is for companies to combine network lay-

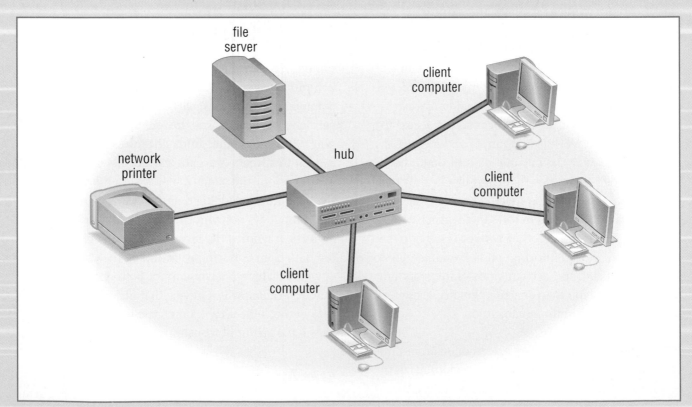

Figure 7 A Star Topology
In a star topology, all computers are linked to a central host computer, through which all communications travel.

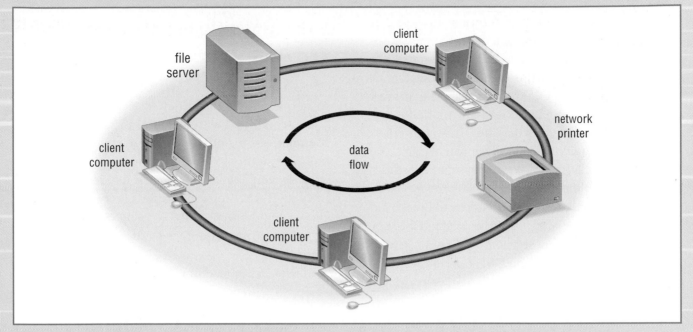

Figure 8 Ring Topology

In a ring topology, each computer is connected to two other computers in a circular path.

Network Hardware

A computer network generally requires special hardware to link all of the computers and to facilitate communication. LANs and WANs may require different hardware devices. Among the various kinds of devices used to establish networks are network interface cards, modems, hubs, repeaters, routers, gateways, and bridges.

A computer must be connected to a network in order to communicate with a network server of another computer. One element of the connection is a network interface card (NIC), which is located on the motherboard of each client computer. Most NICs are designed for a particular kind of network, protocol, and media, although some can work with more than one type of network. Additionally, the sending and receiving of information from one computer to another computer across an analog communications medium, such as a standard telephone line, requires both computers to be equipped with a modem.

A hub is an electronic device used in older LAN topologies to link computers and allow them to com-municate with one another. The hub is usually a separate hardware device, but it can also be a server that can function as a hub. The hub coordinates the message traffic computers connected to the network send and receive.

A switch is a hardware device that joins multiple computers together within one LAN. Physically, network switches appear to be nearly identical to network hubs but, unlike hubs, are capable of inspecting data packets as they are received, determining the source and destination device of that packet, and forwarding it to the appropriate destination. In general, this capability renders a network switch a higher-performance alternative to a hub.

Information often travels long distances. However, the wires and cables used may not be designed to carry messages the full distance. A repeater, also called an amplifier, is a specially designed electronic device that receives signals along a network, increases the strength of the signals, and then sends the amplified signals along the network's communications path. Thus, a repeater helps rectify the problem of information not being able to go the full distance of that path. It functions much like an amplifier in a home stereo system. A network spread over wide distances may use several repeaters along the way.

A router is an electronic device usually found in

large networks, including the Internet. Routers connect different networks to each other to carry messages to their intended destinations. When a router receives a message, it sends (routes) it along the path to the next router, and so on, until the message reaches its final destination. Routers are designed and programmed to work together. If a part of the network is not working properly, a router can choose an alternate path so the message will still arrive at its final destination.

With the growth of home networks and broadband Internet access, special devices called cable/DSL routers are used to connect a home network to a cable Internet service provider or a DSL Internet service provider. These devices act as both a modem and a router.

A gateway is hardware and/or software that allows communication between dissimilar networks. For example, a gateway is needed if an investment broker using a ring topology network wants to retrieve information stored on a star topology network.

A bridge consists of hardware and/or software allowing communication between two similar networks. If the investment broker in the previous example wants to retrieve information stored on the same kind of network another broker is using, a bridge between the two networks allows mutual communication.

Network Software

Many different kinds of software are required to make a network operational. A network's architecture determines the kind of software needed. For example, a client/server network requires a different kind of software than a peer-to-peer network.

The most important type of networking software is a network operating system. A network operating system (NOS) controls the flow of messages from client computers and also provides services such as file access and printing. Some network operating systems, such as UNIX and the Mac OS, have networking functions built in. Popular network operating systems for Windows systems include Novell's NetWare, and Microsoft's Windows 2000 Server, Windows Server 2003, and Windows Server 200X (Longhorn), each of which is designed to enhance a system's basic operating system by adding networking features.

Communications Software and Protocols

Communications software is a type of utility software that allows computers to "talk" with each other. Combined with the appropriate hardware, communications utilities allow users to connect their computers to other computers, such as network servers, and to access and use resources on a LAN or WAN. Communications software also allows modem dial-up for sending e-mail messages, accessing the Internet, surfing the Web, and more.

Newer PCs containing a modem often come equipped with communications software. If not, it can be purchased from a variety of sources. Users who subscribe to an Internet service provider are typically provided with communications software that can be installed.

Network communications software must adhere to a particular network protocol for network communications. A protocol is a set of rules and procedures for exchanging information among computers on a network. Numerous protocols have been developed over the years to indicate the beginning and end of characters; to communicate on LANs, WANs, and over the Web; and to send e-mail.

Almost all communications use directional protocols to determine the flow of transmissions among devices. The three possible directions are simplex, half-duplex, and full-duplex transmissions. Simplex transmission means the data flows in one direction only: the computer can either send or receive data, but it cannot do both. With half-duplex transmission communications can flow in both directions, but not at the same time. Full-duplex transmission allows simultaneous sending and receiving.

Protocols that govern data transmissions vary among LANs using different topologies or different PCs and workstations. Local area network protocols specify how the network is to be set up, how network devices communicate with each other, how problems are identified and corrected, and how components are connected. Ethernet provides for fast and efficient communications.

Wide-area network protocols have been developed for use with WANs. These standards facilitate communications among computers and networks extending over a large area, such as an area covering several states.

The Internet and the Web require specific protocols to communicate with computers around the world. A popular Internet protocol called Transmission Control Protocol/Internet Protocol (TCP/IP) governs how packets are constructed and sent to their destinations.

A World Wide Web protocol called Hypertext Transfer Protocol (HTTP) allows for the transfer of Web pages to computers. Most Web addresses, or URLs, begin with the letters "http" to indicate the protocol is being used. Millions of files are available to Web users through HTTP.

Most Internet service providers and online services provide an electronic mail service to facilitate the sending and receiving of e-mail messages. Messages are transmitted according to a communications protocol called Simple Mail Transfer Protocol (SMTP). SMTP, installed on the ISP's or online service's mail server, determines how each message will be routed through the Internet, and then sends the message. Upon arrival at a receiving mail server, messages are transferred to another server, called a Post Office Protocol (POP) server. POP allows the recipient to retrieve the message.

Wireless technology is available worldwide. Every day, millions of users exchange information using a variety of devices, including notebook computers, cellular telephones, pagers, messaging services, and other wireless communications products. The Wireless Application Protocol (WAP) enables wireless devices to access and use the Internet using a client/server network. In 1997 the Institute of Electrical and Electronic Engineers (IEEE), an organization that develops standards for computers and the electronics industry, approved the 802.11 protocol for wireless LAN technology. Commonly called Wi-Fi, the 802.11 protocol specifies an over-the-air interface between a wireless client device and a server, or between two wireless client devices. The protocol includes specifications that provide for the transmission of data and graphics, and that allow information to be downloaded from Web sites to wireless devices, such as Web-enabled notebook computers and cell phones.

Three variations of the 802.11 protocol are widely used. The first major revision, the 802.11b protocol, offers a relatively low cost and a faster transfer rate of 5.5 Mbps to 11 Mbps at a range of up to 250 feet (76 meters). This protocol is popular in home and small office wireless networks. The 802.11a protocol standard offers transfer rates of up to 54 Mbps when devices are at a range within 60 feet of the primary access point, or hub. Transfer rates are approximately 22 Mbps at longer distances. The 802.11a standard operates in a different frequency range, which results in less interference from other devices. One potential drawback is that 802.11a networks are costly to implement in comparison with 802.11b networks. The 802.11g protocol standard operates in the same frequency range as 802.11b but offers transfer rates similar to 802.11a—up to 54 Mbps. 3G is a third-generation cellular technology offering exceptional transfer speeds for both voice and nonvoice data. The bandwidth for devices using 3G ranges from 384 Kbps for mobile device users up to 2 Mbps for stationary users.

The future holds tremendous promise for computer network users. New developments in fiber-optic technology, including the use of lasers to send optical signals through the air, could make high-speed data transmission available to more users. Researchers are also working to develop faster infrared transmission technologies over networks. The wireless industry will continue to see improvements both in the amount of data that can be transmitted and in transmission speed.

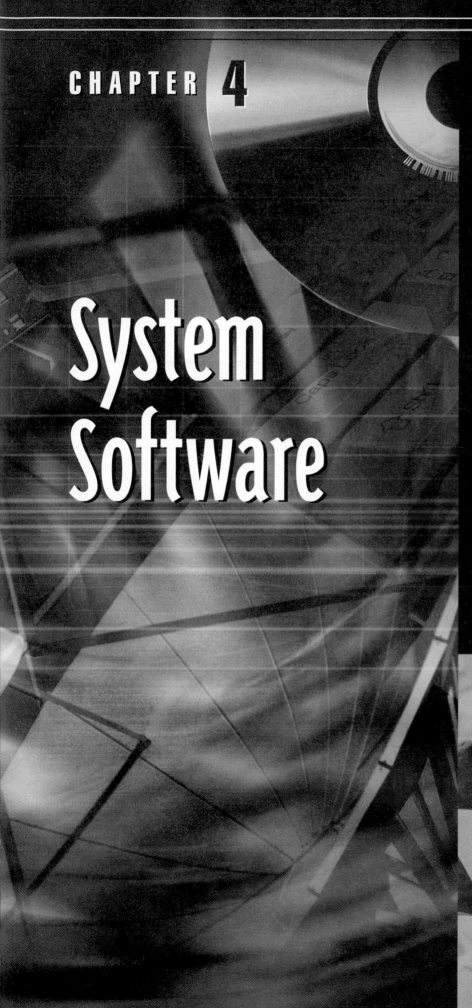

CHAPTER 4

System Software

Learning Objectives

> Define software and identify the three principal types of system software

> Explain the concept of an operating system and identify its main functions

> Identify the differences between command-line interfaces and graphical user interfaces (GUIs)

> Differentiate PC, server, and handheld device operating systems

> Describe the different types of utility programs and their functions

> Explain language translators and describe the primary difference between compilers and interpreters

Cyber**Scenario**

SHORTLY AFTER SUNRISE, Vincente Chamarro boards the high-speed train that will take him to his biweekly staff meeting at InterMed. The company designs and manufactures pacemakers and other medical devices that can be monitored over the Internet. Vincente is a product manager for InterMed's Cardiac Devices division. For more than three years he has worked from his mountain home and communicated with the InterMed office by computer and telephone (telecommuting), but he meets face to face with the marketing team every two weeks to maintain personal contact and to resolve any issues that cannot be handled well through remote communication.

Arriving in the city at 7:30 a.m., Vincente gets off the train and heads for the company headquarters two blocks away. As he walks to work he pulls a cell phone from his pocket and says a Web address, "www.ananova.com," into the mouthpiece. In a few seconds the face of a virtual newsreader named Ananova appears on the high-resolution screen of the cell phone. Vincente says, "Latest business news," and Ananova begins reading the latest business headlines from around the world.

As he walks into his office on the ninth floor of the InterMed building, Vincente remembers that he needs to check his bank balance. He issues a command to his computer with the words, "Turn on and go to the Web site for Fidelity National Bank." He continues with, "This is Vincente Chamarro. What's the balance in my checking account?" The bank's automated teller system recognizes his voice and promptly reports that he has $1,956 in his account. "Good," he thinks, "no need to transfer any funds from savings."

The marketing team will meet to discuss plans for

exhibiting at an upcoming international trade show for cardiac surgeons to be held in Zurich, Switzerland. Reflecting on his communication needs for the show, Vincente decides to buy a new handheld device that will let him track all the materials his company ships to Zurich. A handheld would also provide access to current cultural events as well as maps and directions for Zurich and other European cities.

Vincente accesses a Web site where he can purchase the most powerful handheld on the market. A webcam enabled with advanced pattern recognition software captures his image and quickly compares it with others in a database of images. "Hello, Vincente," says a human-sounding voice. "What can I help you with today?" Vincente tells the automated system that he is looking for a new handheld device. The voice asks whether he is interested in upgrading his smartphone at the same time. Vincente agrees with the system's recommendation and is presented with two options. He tells the automated ordering system which one he wants. The order is repeated for confirmation and the purchase is deducted from his bank account. He can expect to receive his new "toy" in two days.

Vincente's meeting with his marketing manager and team members proceeds without a hitch. They approve his plan to use the company's Ananova-like synthetic character, Jillian, to pitch their new devices over computer monitors at the international trade show. Vincente stays late to finish a rough draft of the script for Jillian, dictating to his computer until 8 p.m. He sets the presentation up to be multilingual, rotating between English, German, and French to appeal to the international audience. He then directs the computer to send copies to team members and leaves to catch the 8:50 train home.

Vincente Chamarro's job is made easier through advances in speech recognition, natural language processing, language translation, and artificial intelligence technologies. Driving these changes is an intricate interaction among computer hardware manufacturers, scientists, and software developers.

The Function of System Software

Software is the term for the programs that tell a computer what to do and how to do it. Software manages the computer's resources, including all hardware devices. Software programs work by issuing instructions to computers to perform actions in a certain order, allowing them to process data into information. **Hardware** is the term for the physical components of any computer system, such as the motherboard, circuitry, and peripheral devices. A popular expression in computer circles is that "software drives hardware," meaning that without software a computer can do little more than search for essential program files that direct the computer to load additional software. It is the software that launches information processing and puts the hardware to work.

Software is divided into two main categories: application software and system software. **Application software** includes programs that perform a single task such as word processing, spreadsheet analysis, or database management. (Application software will be discussed in Chapter 5.) **System software** includes those programs that control the operations of a computer system, meaning the system unit as well as all components and devices that make up the computer system.

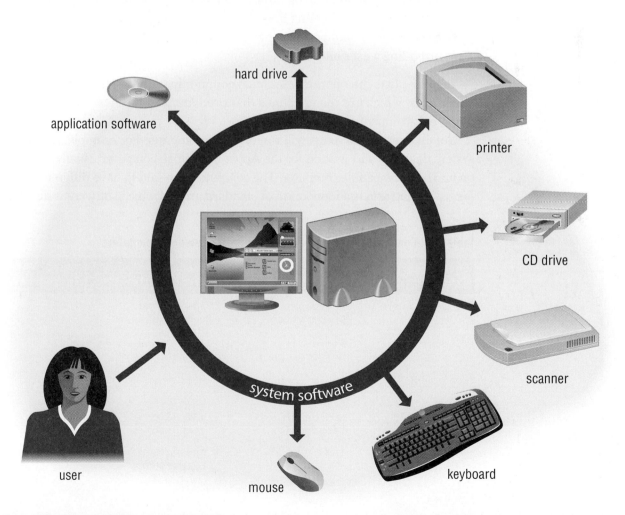

Figure 4-1 The System Software as a Gateway
System software serves as the gateway (interface) between the user, the user's application software, and the computer's hardware.

System software performs a number of essential functions, including starting the computer, formatting disks, copying files, and enabling applications to work smoothly with a computer. It thus serves as the gateway between the user, the user's application software, and the user's computer hardware (see Figure 4-1). The three major categories of system software are operating systems, utility programs, and language translators.

The Function of the Operating System

An **operating system (OS)** is the most important piece of software on a personal computer. The location of the operating system identifies the **boot drive** for the personal computer. Typically, this is the hard drive. When the computer is started (or booted), the operating system is loaded into random access memory (RAM) from the boot drive. Once started, the operating system manages the computer system and performs a variety of interdependent functions related to the input, processing, output, and storage of information, including:

- managing main memory, or RAM
- configuring and controlling peripheral devices
- managing essential file operations, including formatting or copying disks, and renaming or deleting files
- monitoring system performance
- providing a user interface

Table 4-1 lists the operating systems commonly found on today's personal computers, which are the machines that predominate in the workplace and home environments.

Not all operating systems will run on every computer. For example, an operating system designed and written for the Apple Macintosh computer usually will not run on an IBM-compatible computer. The computers are said to have different platforms. A **platform** is a foundation or standard around which software is developed.

Table 4-1 Commonly Used Operating Systems for Personal Computers

Operating System	Developer	Computer Designed for	Year Introduced
Windows Vista	Microsoft Corporation	IBM PC and compatibles	2007
Windows XP	Microsoft Corporation	IBM PC and compatibles	2001
Macintosh OS X	Apple Computer	Macintosh	2001
Windows 2000	Microsoft Corporation	IBM PC and compatibles	2000
OS/2 Warp	IBM	IBM PC and compatibles	1994
Linux	various, including Red Hat, Novell, SUSE, and Ubuntu	various	various

Globetrotting

Booting Up Bhutan

BHUTAN IS A TINY BUDDHIST NATION nestled in the snow-capped mountains between India and China. The Himalayan kingdom has managed to stay isolated by virtue of both geography and choice.

Aversion to contact with the outside world stemmed from the King's philosophy that happiness takes precedence over prosperity, and that happiness is rooted in a strong national identity. Television and the Internet were kept out until 1999, and recent laws enforce the use of Dzongkha, Bhutan's national language.

The gap between Western modernity and traditional Bhutanese culture was bridged in 2006, when Bhutan's Department of Information Technology completed a computer system that operates in Dzongkha. Among other benefits, Buddhist monks in Bhutan's monasteries will now be able to work on their sacred texts on computers instead of copying them by hand.

Credit for the Bhutan-customized software goes to Debian, a collaboration of global volunteers who work together to develop and distribute free software in local languages. The moniker Debian is a mix from the names of the founder, Ian Murdock, and his wife, Debra.

Debian has a long history of "localizing" computers. The first Debian installation program produced in 2002 supported 16 languages. The current version supports 63.

Debian hopes to get software in native languages to more Asian countries, with Malaysia next on its list.

Sources: McConnachie, Dahna. "Debian Gives Linux a Bhutanese Touch," *LinuxWorld*, June 22, 2006. December 2006 <http://www.linuxworld.com.au/index.php/id;1239885333;fp;2;fpid;1>; Noronha, Frederick. "Computers Can Now Speak Bhutan's Dzongkha," *NewKerala.com*, June 21, 2006. <http://www.newkerala.com/news3.php?action=fullnews&id=11689>.

The two determinants of a platform are the operating system and the processor type. For example, early versions of Windows were called 16-bit operating systems because they supported microprocessors that could process 16 bits of data at a time. Later Windows versions, including Windows 95 and 98, supported 32-bit processors, and Windows XP and Vista have both 32- and 64-bit versions.

Operating systems and other software that run on a specific personal computer platform are referred to as native to that platform. Thus there is software native to the PC platform and to the Macintosh platform. Recently, Microsoft and Apple have released their operating systems for use on alternate platforms.

Booting (Starting) the Computer

The procedure for starting or restarting a computer is called **booting**, because the operating system is housed in the boot drive. Starting a computer after power has been turned off is referred to as a **cold boot**. Restarting a computer while the power is still on is called a **warm boot**. Most computer systems allow users to perform a warm boot by pressing a combination of keyboard keys.

When a computer is booted, an electrical current from the power supply sends signals to the motherboard and its components, including the processor chip. The electrical current resets the processor, which then looks for the read-only memory (ROM) chip containing the basic input/output system (BIOS).

The BIOS chip contains instructions that start the computer. The BIOS chip(s) also performs a series of tests, called power-on self test (POST). POST instructions check the computer's components and peripheral devices, including RAM, the system clock, keyboard, mouse, and disk drives. The POST checks determine whether the components and devices are connected and functioning properly. If problems are identified, many operating systems will notify the user to take corrective action. If components and devices are working properly, the BIOS searches the boot drive for operating system files.

The operating system then takes control of the computer and loads the system configuration and other necessary operating system files into memory. Portions of the operating system are automatically loaded from the hard disk into the computer's main memory, including the kernel and frequently used operating system instructions. The **kernel** is an operating system program that manages computer components, peripheral devices, and memory. It also maintains the system clock and loads other operating system and application programs as they are required. The kernel is **memory resident**, remaining in memory while the computer is in operation. Other operating system parts are **nonresident** and remain on the hard disk until they are needed. The loaded portion (memory resident) contains the most essential instructions for operating the computer, controlling the monitor display, and managing RAM efficiently to increase the computer's overall performance.

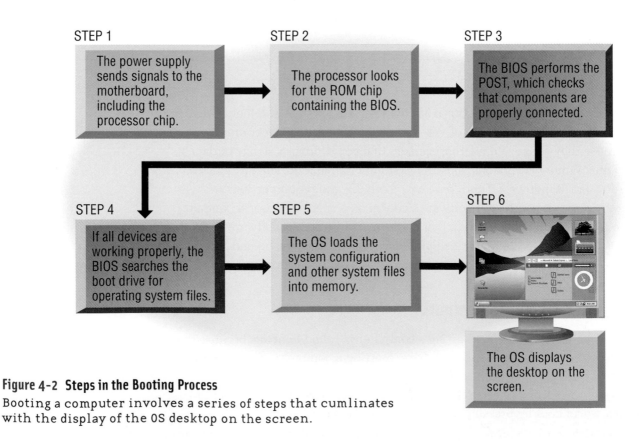

STEP 1
The power supply sends signals to the motherboard, including the processor chip.

STEP 2
The processor looks for the ROM chip containing the BIOS.

STEP 3
The BIOS performs the POST, which checks that components are properly connected.

STEP 4
If all devices are working properly, the BIOS searches the boot drive for operating system files.

STEP 5
The OS loads the system configuration and other system files into memory.

STEP 6

The OS displays the desktop on the screen.

Figure 4-2 Steps in the Booting Process
Booting a computer involves a series of steps that cumlinates with the display of the OS desktop on the screen.

Coming Soon— Transistors on Steroids!

WHAT'S IN A CHIP? Millions of microscopic transistors, those tiny pieces of semiconductor material, usually silicon, that amplify a signal or open and close a circuit. So what happens when you lace silicon with the chemical element geranium and plunge it to a temperature of absolute zero? You get a supersonic transistor, the building blocks of supersonic chips. That's what IBM has done, creating a super-fast transistor that will lead to ever-faster computers and wireless networks.

IBM's super-speedy transistors run 100 times faster than those currently available, reaching speeds of 500 gigahertz (GHz). For comparison, cell phone chips dawdle along at a mere 2 GHz, digital music players around 5 GHz.

In initial tests, the IBM transistor attained its highest speed at a temperature near absolute zero (that's minus 451 degrees Fahrenheit), but was still running at 300 GHz at room temperature. While mass-produced prototypes would probably not match the racecar speed of the prototypes, mere much-faster-than-today transistors would be economical to produce.

Super-fast transistors may soon lead to wireless networks that can download a DVD in five seconds, buildings outfitted with 60 GHz wireless connections, and cars equipped with radar that would automatically adjust speed according to traffic or swerve to avoid an oncoming car.

Sources: "IBM Builds Super-fast Transistor," *CNN.com*, June 20, 2006. <http://www.cnn.com/2006/TECH/ptech/06/20/ibm.chip.reut/index.html>; Needle, David. "IBM has world's Coolest Chip," *InternetNewsBureau.com*, June 20, 2006. December 2006 <http://www.internetnews.com/dev-news/article.php/3614586>.

With Microsoft Windows Vista, the operating system displays the Windows desktop and executes programs in the StartUp folder once loading is complete. Users can then click on the Office Start button, point to *Programs*, point to *Microsoft Office*, and then activate an application program such as Microsoft Word or Excel. The process of booting a computer is illustrated in Figure 4-2.

Managing Memory

An important operating system function is optimizing RAM so that processing occurs more quickly, an activity referred to as throughput. **Throughput** is a measure of the computer's overall performance. Loading programs and data from secondary storage into RAM speeds up processing because it takes significantly less time for the processor to access the programs from RAM than from secondary storage. Processing cannot occur until the programs and data are moved from RAM to the processor. Users can add RAM chips or upgrade the processor if programs, such as downloads from e-mail or Web pages, execute slowly.

To speed up the transfer of programs and data to the processor even further, some computers contain cache memory. Recall from Chapter 2 that cache memory may be contained on the CPU in the form of memory chips hardwired onto the motherboard or as reserved space on a storage device such as a hard disk. Some operating systems also allow users to set aside a portion of RAM to be used as cache memory.

As information is being processed, the operating system assigns application programs and data to selected areas of RAM called buffers. A **buffer** holds information and data waiting to be transferred to or from an input or output device. When the information or data residing in the buffers is no longer needed, it is erased (cleared) by the operating system. When a document is placed in a buffer, the CPU is free to begin executing the next computer instruction or carry out the user's next command.

Some output devices, such as printers, may contain their own buffer memory chips. A computer typically sends a document to a printer much faster than the printer can print it. With **print spooling**, a document is held in a buffer until the printer is ready. Once printed, the buffer is cleared and ready to accept other printing jobs.

An important part of managing RAM is allowing an individual user to work on two or more applications at the same time. This capability is called **multitasking**. When using a multitasking operating system, such as Microsoft Windows, it is not necessary to quit one application before working in another. For example, if a Microsoft Word document and a Microsoft Excel spreadsheet are both loaded into RAM, users can switch back and forth between the two applications as often as they wish.

Configuring and Controlling Devices

Configuring and controlling computer components and attached devices is a major function of the operating system. Included with a computer's operating sys-

A user can access Windows Explorer in Microsoft Windows Vista through the Programs/Accessories submenu. Windows Explorer allows users to view, copy, delete, and move files.

tem are small programs called drivers. A **driver** enables the operating system to communicate with peripheral devices, including the keyboard, monitor, mouse, modem, printer, and disk drives. A keyboard driver recognizes input, while a monitor driver directs the display of text and images. If a user decides to add other devices, a driver will need to be installed for each new device. A driver program usually accompanies the device, and is contained on a disk with easy-to-follow instructions to guide users through the installation process. Many driver programs are also available on the device manufacturer's Web site.

Tech Demo 4-1
Device Driver
Path

Managing Essential File Operations

An operating system contains a program called a **file manager** to maintain a record of all stored files and their locations, allowing users to quickly locate and retrieve files. File managers also perform basic file management functions, such as keeping track of disk storage space; formatting and copying disks; and renaming, deleting, sorting, or viewing stored files. For example, users can copy, delete, and move files using Windows Explorer.

Monitoring System Performance

An operating system typically includes a **performance monitor** for checking the computer system's speed and efficiency, as well as the performance of the CPU, memory, and storage disks. In Microsoft Windows Vista, clicking the command sequence of Office Start button, Control Panel, System, and Performance opens a window from which system performance can be evaluated and improved.

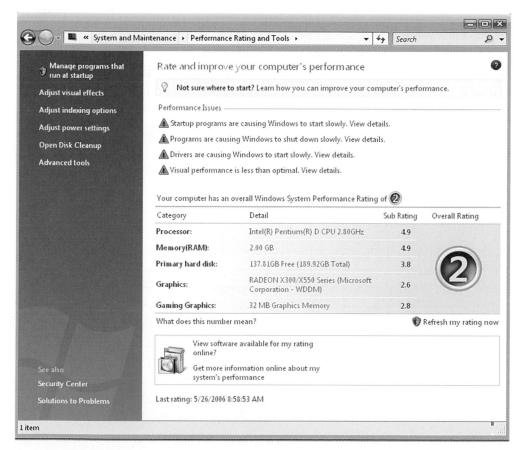

The *Performance Information and Tools* window allows a user to evaluate the computer's performance and make improvements if needed.

A system's performance rating depends not only on the installed hardware but also on settings configured in the operating system such as video display mode and drivers set to load automatically at system startup.

Providing Basic Security Functions

An operating system can protect against unauthorized users gaining access to the computer and stored information. Many operating systems require users to enter a valid name and password before they can access a computer or network. A **user name**, also called a user ID, is a unique combination of characters (letters and numbers) identifying an individual user.

A **password** is a unique combination of characters that allows a user to gain access to computer resources, such as data and files. When a password is typed, most operating systems display a series of characters (such as asterisks) that differ from those entered. This is to prevent other people from seeing the entered characters. The user ID and password combinations are compared with a list of authorized users. If the combination of user ID and password is on the list, the operating system allows access. The operating system denies access if the user ID and password combination does not match any of those on the list.

Computer network operating systems provide additional security measures, such as maintaining a record of attempts to access the network and its resources. The network administrator can determine which computer made the attempt and the time the attempt was made, allowing suspicious activity to be traced.

Software User Interfaces

All software, including operating systems, contains a **user interface** that allows communication between the software and the user. The interface controls the manner in which data and commands are entered, as well as the way information and processing options are presented on the screen. Application programs are written for use with specific operating systems. The operating system and application software user interfaces must be able to work together (be compatible). Two types of user interfaces have been developed for personal computers:

- command-line interfaces
- graphical user interfaces (GUIs)

Command-Line Interfaces

Early personal computer operating systems, including CP/M (Control Program for Microcomputers) and DOS (Disk Operating System), used what is known as a **command-line interface**. This interface presents the user with a symbol called a **prompt** (for example, C:\>), indicating the computer is ready to receive a command. Users would respond by typing in a line of code telling the computer what to do. For example, the command COPY A:\INCOME.STM C:\ instructs the computer to copy the file named INCOME.STM, located on drive A, to drive C. Command-line interfaces were ideal for early personal computers, which had limited graphical display capabilities. They could also be complicated and difficult to learn, because the commands often involved long sequences of

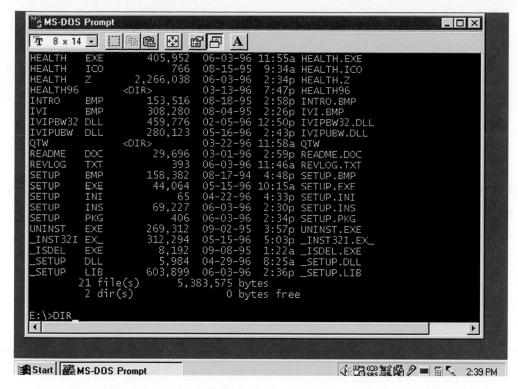

```
MS-DOS Prompt                                          _ □ ×

T  8 x 14 ▼    [:]  🗎  🗎  ⊞    🗎  🖨  A

HEALTH   EXE       405,952   06-03-96  11:55a  HEALTH.EXE
HEALTH   ICO           766   08-15-95   9:34a  HEALTH.ICO
HEALTH   Z       2,266,038   06-03-96   2:34p  HEALTH.Z
HEALTH96         <DIR>       03-13-96   7:47p  HEALTH96
INTRO    BMP       153,516   08-18-95   2:58p  INTRO.BMP
IVI      BMP       308,280   08-04-95   2:26p  IVI.BMP
IVIPBW32 DLL       459,776   02-05-96  12:50p  IVIPBW32.DLL
IVIPUBW  DLL       280,123   05-16-96   2:43p  IVIPUBW.DLL
QTW              <DIR>       03-22-96  11:58a  QTW
README   DOC        29,696   03-01-96   2:59p  README.DOC
REVLOG   TXT           393   06-03-96  11:46a  REVLOG.TXT
SETUP    BMP       158,382   08-17-94   4:48p  SETUP.BMP
SETUP    EXE        44,064   05-15-96  10:15a  SETUP.EXE
SETUP    INI            65   04-22-96   4:33p  SETUP.INI
SETUP    INS        69,227   06-03-96   2:30p  SETUP.INS
SETUP    PKG           406   06-03-96   2:34p  SETUP.PKG
UNINST   EXE       269,312   09-02-95   3:57p  UNINST.EXE
_INST32I EX_       312,294   05-15-96   5:03p  _INST32I.EX_
_ISDEL   EXE         8,192   09-08-95   1:22a  _ISDEL.EXE
_SETUP   DLL         5,984   04-29-96   8:25a  _SETUP.DLL
_SETUP   LIB       603,899   06-03-96   2:36p  _SETUP.LIB
         21 file(s)      5,383,575 bytes
          2 dir(s)               0 bytes free

E:\>DIR_
◄                                                          ►

Start   MS-DOS Prompt                  ◁🔊📻SRS🎙️🖊️▪️📋🗔  2:39 PM
```

This DOS command DIR shows a directory, or list of files, stored on a medium such as a hard disk.

code. A mistyped letter would lead to an error message, forcing the user to type the command again.

Graphical User Interfaces

In 1983, Apple Computer introduced its Lisa computer. Lisa featured an entirely new kind of operating system with a screen display known as a **graphical user interface (GUI)**. Based on the Alto computer operating system developed at the Xerox Corporation's Palo Alto Research Center, this new type of interface was graphics-based rather than command-based, making it more intuitive and user-friendly. Unfortunately, the Apple Lisa was a commercial failure because of its high price and the limited availability of software applications. The following year Apple introduced the Macintosh, another computer incorporating a GUI. This time Apple scored a success. The Macintosh operating system revolutionized personal computing.

GUIs are now the most popular type of personal computer interface. They are easier to use than command-line interfaces because they enable users to interact with on-screen simulations of familiar objects. Remembering long strings of commands is no longer necessary, since the screen itself becomes a virtual desktop on which the user's work (programs and documents) is spread out. An **icon**, or thumbnail picture, appears on the screen and represents such familiar items as a trash can or recycle bin (for deleting or throwing away files) and file folders (for storing groups of files).

In addition to representing common commands, icons are used to symbolize programs and files. For example, a calculating program may be represented by a tiny calculator on the screen, or a time management program might be represented by a

Apple's Macintosh, introduced in 1984, quickly became popular because of its innovative operating system.

clock. To use an analogy, GUIs are to operating systems what special keyboards are to cash registers in fast-food restaurants. Both use pictures or text symbols to stand for complex commands, simplifying and streamlining actions for the user.

GUIs were made possible with the development of mouse technology and the introduction of more powerful computers and high-resolution monitors. Almost all PCs arrive from the factory with a GUI operating system preinstalled, and most application software is designed to work with them smoothly. Once a user knows the features of a GUI such as Windows, the fundamental operations of any Windows-based application are easy to execute because both the operating system and the application use the same icons and commands. A typical GUI offers many features to make tasks easier, including:

- on-screen desktop
- display windows
- key feature option menus
- common command icons
- dialog boxes
- online help

On-Screen Desktop   GUIs for personal computers incorporate the concept of an on-screen **desktop**. A desktop is a screen on which graphical elements such as icons, buttons, windows, links, and dialog boxes are displayed, much as manila folders, pens, scissors, and paper might be arranged on a desk. Using a desktop containing these elements is easier for many users because it allows them to interact quickly and accurately with the computer. During the installation of a software application, an icon representing the program may be automatically added to the desktop.

A **button** is a graphical element that causes a particular action to occur when selected. For example, clicking the Office Start button in the lower left corner of the screen displays a list of options related to starting and operating the computer.

The Windows Vista GUI desktop is a work area displaying graphical elements such as icons, windows, and buttons. Graphical elements allow faster, easier access to programs and commands.

Clicking the Office button in Windows Vista displays a menu of options, including programs to run such as Internet Explorer, folders to display such as Documents and Pictures, and utilities to use such as Search.

In many GUIs, when a button is selected, the button changes color or appears in depressed form, as though a user's finger has pressed it.

Display Windows   The main feature of a graphical user interface is the **display window**. A display window is a rectangular area of the screen used to display a program or various kinds of data, such as text and numbers. At the top of each

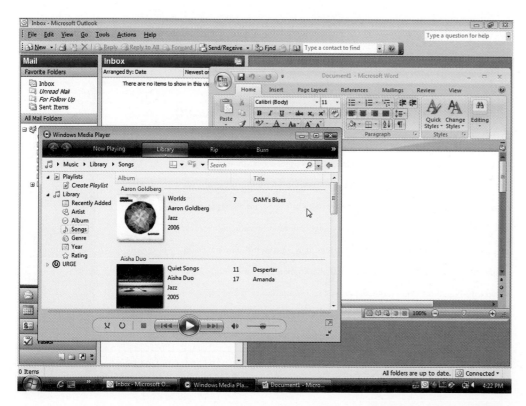

Most GUIs allow users to work with multiple applications at the same time. Each application appears in its own window. A user can switch back and forth among applications by clicking on a window's title bar.

window is a horizontal bar called the **title bar**, displaying the name of the item and the program in the display window. Windows are useful in multitasking environments, which allow multiple programs and applications to be open at the same time (concurrently). By dividing the screen into different windows, users can see and work with the output produced by each program. To work within a particular program—to enter data, for example—clicking on the program's window brings it to the forefront.

Documents are sometimes too large to be displayed in their entirety in a window. To overcome this problem, a **scroll bar** at a window's side or bottom enables users to see and work with the portions of a document that are beyond the edge of the screen. Small arrows at the tips of a scroll bar can be used to move documents horizontally or vertically. A small box between the two arrows can also be used to scroll through a document page by page.

Key Feature Option Menus   A **menu** provides a set of options. Users can select options they want by highlighting the option and clicking on it with the mouse, or by typing one or more keystrokes. Making a selection launches an action, such as saving a document.

When activated, many software programs display a horizontal or vertical bar at the top or side of the screen. This **menu bar** (also called a main menu) lists the highest-level command options by name, usually composed of one or two words. Each high-level option may be accompanied by another menu, called a **drop-down menu** (or pull-down menu), containing various lower-level options. These menus may in turn include submenus offering more precise choices.

In Microsoft Office 2007 programs, sets of commands on a tabbed **ribbon** are used instead of a menu bar. The tabs are like menu names, and the commands on the tabs are like menu commands.

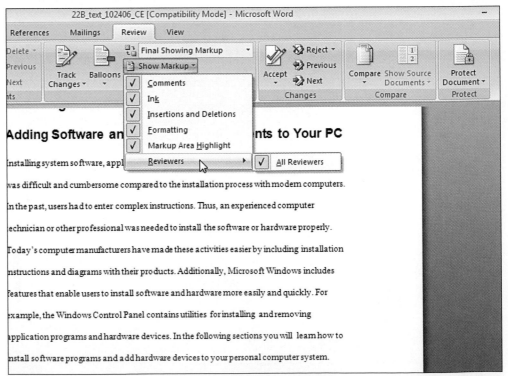

Most programs provide a menu bar. For example, when users select a menu item, a drop-down menu is displayed, providing additional choices.

The ribbon is integral to the Microsoft Office 2007 programs. The design is intended to reduce the use of menus, allowing users quicker access to basic features and options.

Software programs usually contain predetermined default options. A **default option** is a setting that the software publisher has preprogrammed under the assumption that this option is the choice favored by most users. For example, WordPad (the word processor that comes with Windows) uses 10-point Arial as the default font. Users can choose a different font by clicking the *Format* option on the menu bar, and then the *Font* option from the drop-down menu that appears.

Depending on the action being taken, some drop-down menu options may be unavailable to users at certain times. Options that are available typically appear in darker type. Unavailable options usually appear grayed out, or dimmed, letting the user know the option cannot be chosen. Figure 4-3 shows a drop-down menu containing choices that are available and some that are not.

On some menus, a small triangular pointer to the right of an option indicates that additional options are available. Clicking on the pointer displays the associated menu. A check mark at the left of an option indicates the option has been

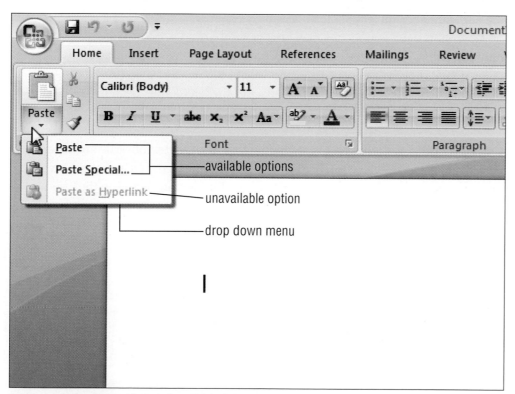

Figure 4-3 Available Choices in a Drop-Down Menu
Options available on a menu appear in darker print. Options that are unavailable appear in grayed-out print.

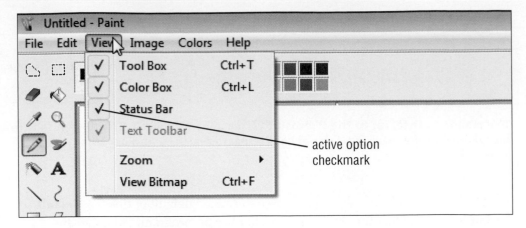

Figure 4-4 Active Check Mark
A check mark to the left of an option such as the Tool Box option on the View drop-down menu in Microsoft Paint indicates that the option has been selected and is therefore active.

selected and is therefore active. Figure 4-4 shows a drop-down menu associated with the *View* option in Microsoft Paint.

Common Command Icons   Because clicking on an icon is easier than having to remember and enter a series of keystrokes, GUIs use icons to represent common actions such as opening, saving, or printing files. These icons may be displayed in a row near the top of the screen, called a **toolbar**. To reinforce the meaning of the icons, when the mouse pointer is positioned on an icon, a one- or two-word identification label (often called a Screen Tip) displays immediately below it. Clicking the icon launches the associated action.

As with menus, some icons may be unavailable and appear in grayed-out or dimmed form. These icons usually represent actions that depend on a related, previous action. For example, users cannot select the scissors icon (for "cutting" or removing text) until some text or an object to be deleted has been highlighted (selected) with the mouse.

Dialog Boxes   A **dialog box** is a window that displays temporarily and disappears once the user has entered requested information. GUIs use dialog boxes to provide information and to prompt responses. Interactions between the user and the software are carried out through various elements that allow choices. Some of the more common elements are tabs, option buttons, check boxes, and text boxes.

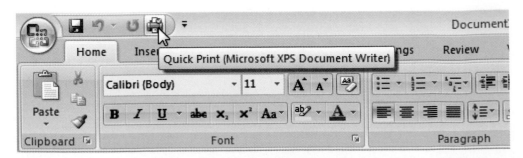

Screen Tips are used in a limited basis in Microsoft Word 2007.

- **Tabs** Many dialog boxes offer several option subsets, each labeled as if it were a manila folder within a file drawer. The name of a subset of options is displayed in a **tab** at the top of the folder. Clicking the tab brings the selected group of options to the front of the dialog box (the file drawer).

- **Option Buttons** Another standard dialog box element is an outlined box containing a set of buttons, each one called an **option button** (or a radio button). Named for their resemblance to old-fashioned push buttons on car radios, these buttons offer different choices. Only one button can be activated at a time. For example, in the Microsoft Word Print dialog box there are option buttons in the *Page Range* section directing Word to print *All, Current Page,* or specific pages. Only one of these options can be selected at a time.

- **Check Boxes** A **check box** allows users to select an option that can be turned on or off. An option in the box can be turned on by clicking it. When an option is activated, a check mark appears in the check box. Unlike option buttons that limit users to selecting a single option, check boxes allow users to choose multiple options at one time.

- **Text Boxes** Information is entered into a **text box** to allow the computer to continue or complete a task. For example, to save a document in Microsoft Word, users must click on the *Save* button to display the Save As dialog box. Once the dialog box appears, a drive where the document will be saved needs to be indicated, and a file name for the document keyed in a text box . Most dialog boxes also contain command buttons such as Save (or OK) and Cancel that enable users to submit or re-enter the information entered into a text box or a check box.

Online Help Computer users will occasionally encounter problems or think of questions while they are working with an operating system or application. Answers can be found by clicking the Help option or by pressing a designated key. Clicking the Help option causes a dialog box to appear that offers topics to browse

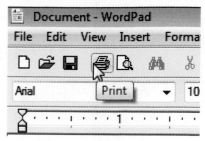

Picture icons are reinforced with Screen Tips to explain the function of the icon, such as this *Print* button in WordPad.

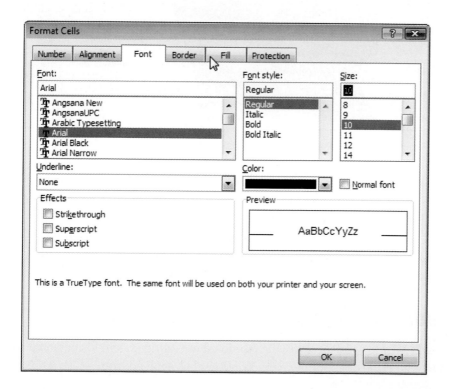

Dialog boxes provide information to a user and also offer choices or prompt responses so commands can be executed. The Format Cells dialog box in Excel 2007 is an example of such an interface.

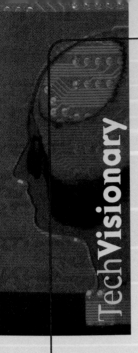

CHAIRMAN, MICROSOFT CORPORATION
Bill Gates

WILLIAM H. (BILL) GATES III is a cofounder and, at present, chairman of the board of directors of Microsoft Corporation, the world's leading provider of software for personal computers. Born on October 28, 1955, Gates grew up in Seattle, Washington, where he attended public elementary school before moving on to the private Lakeside School in North Seattle. He began programming computers at the early age of 13.

In 1973, Gates entered Harvard University. While at Harvard, he developed a version of the BASIC programming language for the first microcomputer, called the MITS Altair. He dropped out of Harvard in his junior year to devote his full time to building Microsoft Corporation, a company he had started in 1975 with his boyhood friend Paul Allen. Guided by a belief that the personal computer would be a valuable tool on every office desktop and in every home, Gates and Allen began developing software for personal computers.

Twenty-five years later, Microsoft and Bill Gates (along with Allen and other early players) are worth billions. Under Gates's leadership, Microsoft has forged a mission to advance and improve software technology to make it easier, more cost-effective, and more enjoyable for people to use computers. The company is committed to a long-term view, which is reflected in its annual investments of millions of dollars for research and development. Gates and his wife, Melinda, have endowed a foundation with more than $21 billion to support philanthropic causes dedicated to worldwide health and education, such as providing vaccines for children in developing countries and scholarship programs for low-income high-achievers.

Microsoft has been quick to take advantage of opportunities created by the Internet. Gates has a substantial investment, along with cellular telephone pioneer Craig McCaw, in the Teledesic project, an ambitious plan to launch low-orbit satellites around the earth to provide a worldwide two-way broadband telecommunications service.

Source: "William H. Gates," Microsoft. December 2006 <http://www.microsoft.com/billgates/bio.asp>.

and a Search box in which to type keywords. When you enter a keyword and press *Enter* or click on one of the topics, the program searches its online documentation and displays articles that match that specification.

Some programs display a **context-sensitive Help message** based on either the user's location in the program or the activity the user is performing. This kind of Help system can suggest Help topics that are relevant to what the user is doing.

Personal Computer Operating Systems

Microsoft Windows is currently the dominant operating system for personal computers. Over a period of about 15 years, Windows has evolved from a GUI/DOS combi-

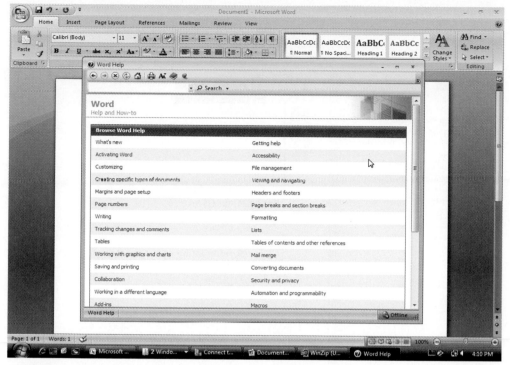

Clicking on the *Help* option displays a list of topics from which a selection can be made.

nation (Windows 3.0 through 3.11) to a true GUI with versions for all types of personal computers (Windows Vista). The newer versions of Windows provide numerous useful features users prefer. According to some estimates, Windows is used on about 90 percent of all PCs. The remaining 10 percent are primarily Apple Macintosh personal computers using the Apple Mac OS operating system. The following sections explain some versions that have been developed during more recent years.

Windows

Microsoft embraced the term "windows" to describe the graphical user interface it developed for use on PCs. The first versions of Windows, referred to as Windows 3.x, were not actually operating systems. Each was an **operating environment**, meaning they were graphical user interfaces on top of an underlying DOS kernel. Windows 95 offered Internet access, and it still included some DOS programs and could run DOS-based applications. Windows 95 enjoyed immediate acceptance by users with its improved GUI, increased speed, and ease of use.

Tech Demo 4-2
History of
Windows

Upgraded from earlier versions of Windows, Windows 98 contained several new and improved features. Windows 98 offered improved access to the Internet and World Wide Web through its Web browser, Internet Explorer. Equally important, Windows 98 provided support for multimedia peripherals, including DVD-ROM drives and USB devices. Windows NT Workstation was a powerful GUI operating system designed for executing large applications in networked environments. This idea was reinforced by abbreviating "new technology" as NT in the operating system name.

Windows 2000   **Windows 2000**, which was introduced in late 1999, was designed for use with business computers and was the successor to Windows 98

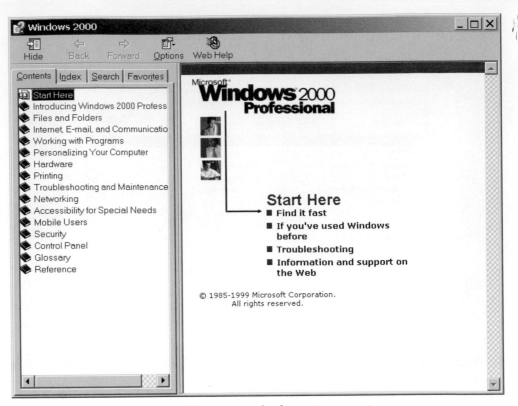

Windows 2000 was intended for networked environments.

for office environments. Incorporating the power of Windows NT, Windows 2000 was used to link computers in a network environment. Its more-advanced operating system was particularly well suited for newer, faster, and more powerful PCs. Because it required more disk space for storage, it ran better on computers equipped with newer microprocessors. Minimum system requirements for Windows 2000 were:

- 133 MHz or higher Pentium-compatible processor
- 64 MB of RAM
- 2 GB hard disk with a minimum of 650 MB of available space
- CD-ROM, CD-R, CD-RW, or DVD-ROM drive
- VGA or higher-resolution monitor
- Microsoft mouse or compatible pointing device

Windows XP   Microsoft's **Windows XP** was designed for computers that were fast, powerful, and had lots of memory and hard disk space. It required two gigabytes of hard drive space to install. The XP operating system combined the more powerful features of Windows 2000 and Windows NT. Microsoft Corporation touted XP as virtually crash-proof, offering greater stability and reduced computer downtimes for large corporate users.

New features built into Windows XP were impressive. Unlike earlier Windows versions that were incompatible with many hardware and software add-ons, XP was designed to work smoothly with more than 12,000 hardware devices. This system was designed to keep files and settings separate for every PC user. Users logged on with a name and password so the operating system would know which desktop to bring up. This made XP ideal for school computer labs and for businesses where multiple users shared the same PC.

The Windows XP desktop sported a refreshingly clean look.

Users of earlier Windows versions quickly noticed the many cosmetic changes in Windows XP. The XP taskbar and window borders appeared as shimmering light blue, and icons had a three-dimensional look. Design changes were evident throughout the XP's GUI. A click on the Start button displayed two columns—one to the left that listed recently used programs, and one to the right that listed everything else, including My Documents, My Computer, and the Control Panel. The desktop sported a refreshingly clean look filled with a photo of a gentle hill-side. Users who did not like the cosmetic changes could turn them off to make the desktop look like an older version of Windows.

Windows XP was extremely user-friendly. For example, a new CD could be burned simply by dragging folders and files onto the CD burner icon. A new "E-mail this file" button shrank digital photos to a usable size as they were sent, to avoid tying up a recipient's phone line for long periods. Built-in automatic firewall software helped block hacker invasions from the Internet. A new Windows Messenger program allowed the exchange of instant messages over the Internet with other users on MSN, Hotmail, or Windows Messenger "Buddy Lists."

Many older PCs did not support Windows XP's increased needs. Minimum system requirements for installing and effectively using Windows XP included:

- 300 MIIz or faster Pentium-compatible or Celeron-compatible processor
- 2 GB of hard disk space for installation
- minimum of 64 MB of memory (128 MB is recommended)
- CD-ROM or DVD drive
- Microsoft mouse or compatible pointing device

Young enthusiastic users found Windows XP especially useful, as it provided impressive features for managing photo and music files. Just plugging a digital camera into the computer displayed a dialog box that enabled photos to be copied to the computer, printed, or displayed as a slide show. Music files could be downloaded easily and the user could enjoy a concert right from the desktop using Windows Media Player.

Many other new and improved features that users found useful were built into Windows XP. Its impressive design was a welcome departure from older Windows versions. However, some users did not appreciate all the new XP features. For example, it was the first Windows version to be copy-protected. Users wanting to reinstall XP or install it on a newly purchased computer found they were locked out, requiring the purchase of another copy.

Windows Vista   Windows Vista, released in 2007, improves and expands upon Windows XP's capabilities in several key areas. Because of the increasing threat of viruses and other attacks from the Internet, Windows Vista includes much more robust security features than any earlier version. The centerpiece of this security system is **User Access Control (UAC)**, a protection system that prompts the user for administrator-level credentials whenever an operation is attempted that might affect system stability or security in some way, such as moving or deleting an important system file. Other security features include **Windows Defender**, which monitors for and defends against spyware and adware, and **Windows Firewall**, which blocks other computers from gathering information or communicating with the system via unused network ports.

Windows Vista provides new features that help users diagnose and repair common system problems. It enables users to report crashes and other problems to Microsoft's Web servers, which in turn send back messages recommending fixes and patches to correct the errors. For problems caused by older hardware or incompatible drivers, users can often find solutions via a Performance Rating and Tools utility.

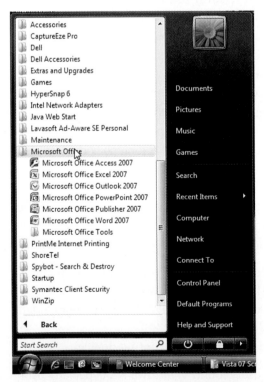

The Windows Vista menu system provides a new way to present files and programs.

Home networking is easier than ever with Windows Vista. When a computer is connected to a local network, it immediately acquires a network address and begins participating automatically; setup is not normally required. Network security is also improved; users can participate in a network, using resources from a file server, for example, without any risk of others discovering and using their own local files. For wireless networking users, Windows Vista makes it easy to configure wireless security between the PCs and the access point or router.

The Start menu in Windows Vista has a new look. Rather than opening fly-out submenus for each menu level, it collapses and expands folders within the main pane of the menu system. This keeps the Start menu at a manageable size no matter how much it contains and makes it easier to access commonly used shortcuts and locations.

Windows Vista also comes with new and improved versions of its most popular utilities and productivity applications, including Internet Explorer and Windows Media Player. The aging Outlook Express from earlier Windows versions is replaced by a new, more powerful e-mail client called Windows Mail. Windows Vista also provides some new tools for easier folder navigation.

Across the top of each Windows Explorer window is a navigation bar containing **breadcrumbs** that show the path of the current location. For example, when displaying C:\Windows\System32\config, the following appears in the navigation bar: Computer > Local Disk (C:) > Windows > System32 > config. Each of those words can be clicked to return to that location. So, for example, to return to the root level of the C: drive, users click Local Disk (C:).

Macintosh Operating System

The **Macintosh OS** was the first commercial GUI, released in 1984 and updated many times since the initial release. It included a virtual desktop, drop-down menus, dialog boxes, and icons representing common commands and programs. With its impressive graphics and ease of use, it quickly became the model for other GUIs. Soon after its introduction, manufacturers and users of IBM-PCs and compatibles wanted a comparable GUI for their computers. Within a short time Microsoft introduced its first Windows product for IBM-PCs and compatibles.

Until recently, the Mac OS ran only on Apple Macintosh computers. The Tiger release of Mac OS X can also be installed on Intel-based personal computers. The Mac OS contains many impressive and useful features, including both the Netscape Navigator and Internet Explorer Web browsers. Its extraordinary graphics capabilities help make the Apple Macintosh the computer of choice among graphic designers, desktop production specialists, printing companies, and publishers.

Mac OS 9, the version widely available in 2000, contained several new and improved features. It offered better speech recognition, supported files up to 2 terabytes (2 trillion bytes), provided for multiple users, allowed for file encryption, and supported voice-entered passwords.

Mac OS X was introduced in spring 2001. Particularly noteworthy was the new interface, called Aqua, and its UNIX operating system foundation, widely considered a stable and powerful system. With the debut of Mac OS X, more than 200 developers, including Microsoft, Adobe, IBM, Sun Microsystems, and Hewlett-

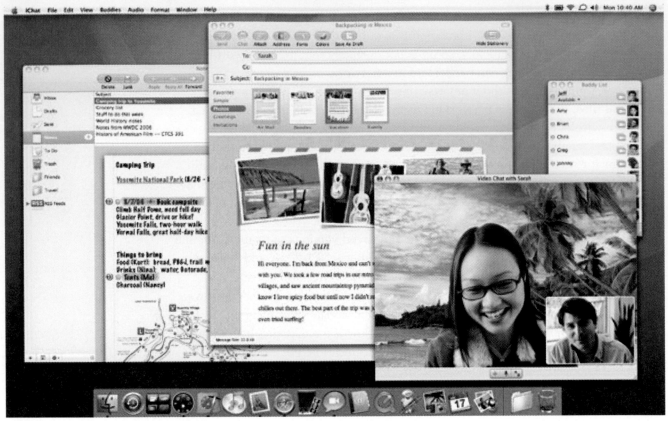

The Mac OS X Interface, called Aqua, is interactive and easy to use.

Packard, agreed to create software for the new system. Mac OS X provided greater stability and true multitasking capability.

The bottom of the startup screen is similar to the Windows taskbar. MAC OS X also provides a terminal window that reveals the file system tree, enabling users to quickly locate programs and files. MAC OS X includes versions of popular programs, including the QuickTime player and Stuffit, a file compression program. It comes with Apple's Safari web browser and FTP capability, allowing users to easily send and receive large files. Its backward compatibility supports applications from previous versions, such as OS 9.

OS/2

IBM's **OS/2** GUI operating system was the company's response to the popularity of Microsoft Windows and the Apple Mac OS. The latest version of OS/2 is called OS/2 Warp. In addition to running native application programs, OS/2 can run programs written for DOS and Windows systems. The OS/2 operating system is designed mainly for business PC users running business applications. IBM announced that they are ending support for OS/2 on December 31, 2006, but there are still several companies that have applications running on this platform.

Linux

Tech Demo 4-3
Linux Timeline

Linux (pronounced LIN-UKS) is a UNIX-based operating system that runs on a number of computer platforms, including PCs, servers, and handheld devices. The Linux kernel (the central module or basic part) was developed mainly by Linus

Torvalds. Torvalds designed Linux as an **open-source software program**, which means that the developer retains ownership of the original programming code but makes the programming code available free to the general public, who is encouraged to experiment with the software, make improvements, and share the improvements with the entire user community.

Open-source software contrasts with another category called proprietary software, which includes the majority of programs in widespread use. **Proprietary software** is software that does not adhere to open standards but instead uses algorithms, protocols, file formats, and so on that were exclusively for this software by its developers to fulfill a certain purpose. A company or an individual owns proprietary software programs and requires a fee for using the software.

Fans of Linux praise its stability, flexibility, security, and generally low cost (vendors usually package it with various tools; hence there is a charge). Red Hat Linux, Novell Linux Desktop, SUSE Linux, and Ubuntu Linux are commercially available Linux software packages for personal and business computers.

The popularity of Linux on personal computers is growing, especially as the number of software programs available on the Linux platform increases. Word processing, spreadsheet, and presentation programs are available in an open source format called Open Office. Software companies are also developing software programs that will allow Windows-based programs to run on Linux-based computers.

Go to this title's Internet Resource Center and read the article titled "Open Source Software." www.emcp.net/CUT3e

Server Operating Systems

Some operating systems are designed specifically for use with local area networks, allowing multiple users to connect to the server and to share network resources

Linux is one of the fastest-growing server operating systems. Red Hat produces a version of Linux, called Red Hat Linux, that is gaining popularity among businesses and government agencies including the Federal Aviation Administration.

CREATOR OF THE LINUX OPERATING SYSTEM

Linus Torvalds

LINUS TORVALDS IS THE CULT HERO of computer nerds worldwide. This is because, as a student, he challenged Big Business by writing the Linux operating system. He was upset with how many flaws there were in MS-DOS, the software he was using, so he wrote a new program and stuck his penguin mascot named Tux to it. By putting his new software on the Web for other computer users to retool and refine, he created a movement of support for his new, independent program. That program would eventually become a viable substitute for the industry standard.

Born December 28, 1969, in Helsinki, Finland, he was named after Linus Pauling, the American Nobel Prize–winning chemist. Torvalds's first experience with a computer was at the age of 10, using his grandfather's Commodore VIC-20. Once enrolled in college, he already felt capable of writing his own operating system. His goal was to write a PC-based version of UNIX, a different operating system. When he finished, he 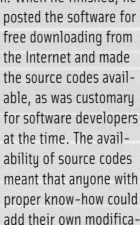 posted the software for free downloading from the Internet and made the source codes available, as was customary for software developers at the time. The availability of source codes meant that anyone with proper know-how could add their own modifications to Linux and warp it to their personal needs. Over the years, Linux has been changed constantly by its adoring fans, while Torvalds chose which alterations to include in the newest versions.

He wrote a master's thesis titled *Linux: A Portable Operating System*, and graduated in 1996 from the University of Helsinki with a master's degree in computer science.

Linux and Torvalds shot into stardom when the competitors of Microsoft Corporation began taking the free operating system seriously. Netscape Communications Corp., Corel Corp., Oracle Corp., Intel Corp., and other companies announced their plans to support the Microsoft Windows alternative.

While roughly 2 percent of the Linux program can be credited to Torvalds directly, he still has the right to monitor the use of it through the nonprofit organization Linux International. About 7 million computers operated on Linux in 1999, and his wide fan base makes it difficult for people to abuse the program because it is nearly constantly checked by other users.

Throughout the years Torvalds has kept a relatively low profile. He remains neutral in most debates among program writers, unless the subject is open-source and free software, which he staunchly defends.

In 1997 he began working with Transmeta Corporation, a company spearheaded by Paul Allen, who codeveloped Microsoft Corporation with Bill Gates. He received some criticism for allegedly joining the enemy, but he didn't seem to mind. Torvalds left Transmeta in 2003 and now works at Open Source Development Labs, a software corporation based in Beaverton, Oregon.

His status as a cult-hero has caused people to praise him, both formally and informally. In 1996 "Asteroid 9793 Torvalds" was named after him. In 1998 he received the EFF Pioneer Award. In the 2001 film *Swordfish*, a character named Axl Torvalds is the number one computer hacker in the world. In 1999 he was voted to number 17 in *TIME* magazine's Person of the Century poll, and in 2004 he was named one of the most influential people in the world by *TIME* magazine.

Sources: <http://www.dataworks.biz/Linux/LinusBio.htm>; "About Linus Torvalds," *Linux Online!* December 2006 <http://www.linux.org/info/linus.html>.

such as files and peripheral devices such as printers. The kind of operating system selected for use with a network depends on network architecture and processing requirements. Some server operating systems that became widely used are explained in the following sections.

Novell NetWare

NetWare, developed by Novell, Inc. during the 1980s, is a popular and widely used operating system for microcomputer-based local area networks. Network users have the option of working with or without network resources. When a user logs on to a NetWare-equipped network, NetWare provides a shell around the user's personal desktop operating system (such as Windows), allowing the retrieval or saving of files on the server's shared hard disk. Users can also print using the network's shared printer. The NetWare operating system resides on the network's shared hard disk, allowing network users to communicate with the operating system.

Those who prefer not to work on the network do not have to log in. Instead, they work just as they would with their own stand-alone personal computer. However, users must log on to the network if they wish to use the network's resources. See Chapter 6 for more information on network operating systems.

Go to this title's Internet Resource Center and read the articles titled "Network Operating Systems" and "Setting Up a Home Network."
www.emcp.net/CUT3e

Windows

Microsoft's **Windows NT Server** was one of Microsoft's earlier entries into the client/server market. It supported the connection of various peripheral devices (including hard drives and printers) and multitasking operations in which networked computers could process applications at the same time. It was quickly adopted for many local area networks immediately after it was introduced. Windows NT Server was replaced by Windows 2000 Server.

Windows 2000 Server   Microsoft's **Windows 2000 Server** was designed for network servers. It supported multitasking operations and allowed for the connection of various peripheral devices. Installed on a properly equipped server computer, Windows 2000 Server provided for Internet access and the development of Web pages. Windows 2000 Advanced Server and Datacenter Server were editions created for the largest network environments. Advanced Server supported up to nine processors and could handle up to 8 gigabytes of data, while Datacenter Server could support up to 32 processors and 64 gigabytes of data.

Windows Server 2003   Microsoft offered **Windows Server 2003** in four editions: Standard Edition, Enterprise Edition, Datacenter Edition, and Web Edition. The Standard Edition was intended to support small-to-medium sized businesses. The Enterprise Edition supported large businesses that clustered multiple servers together for increased power. The Datacenter Edition was also meant for large organizations, as it offered the ability to cluster even more servers together for mission-critical application support. The Web Edition was a scaled-down version of the software that allowed companies to choose a more economical solution for servers that hosted only Web applications.

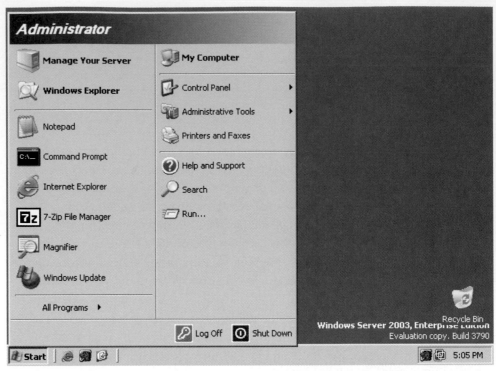

Windows Server 2003 is designed for small and medium-size LANs. Many small and medium-size businesses found this server software ideally suited for their needs.

Windows Server 200X (Longhorn) **Windows Server 200X** is the server version released following Windows Vista. This new server was referred to by its code name, Longhorn, during development. It shares the many benefits described earlier of the Windows Vista platform over earlier versions, and also offers server-specific tools, protocols, and utilities for network management. For example, Windows Server 200X (Longhorn) contains a Network Access Protection tool that enables an IT administrator to define health requirements for the network, such as the presence of updated antivirus software, and to restrict computers that do not meet these requirements from using the network. Windows Server 200X (Longhorn) also makes it easier for administrators to deploy installations and patches remotely and to use and configure services. It has a new and greatly improved version of Internet Information Services (IIS), Microsoft's Web server technology, and Windows SharePoint Services, used for team collaboration and document sharing.

UNIX

Developed in the early 1970s by programmers at Bell Laboratories, the **UNIX** (pronounced YOO-NIKS) operating system was originally designed for servers and large computer systems. It uses a complex command-line interface and offers some superb capabilities, including simultaneous access by many users to a single powerful computer. There are several variations of UNIX, including Linux and Solaris.

From its inception, UNIX has been a **multi-user operating system**, an operating system that allows many people to use one CPU from remote stations. It is also a **cross-platform operating system**, one that runs on computers of all kinds, from PCs to supercomputers. UNIX was the first language of the Internet because of its dominance in universities and laboratories, and many Internet service providers continue to use it to maintain their networks.

Sharing Code through Krugle

OPEN SOURCE MEANS SHARING CODE— using software that others have created before to develop new and improved software. It's a nice idea, but in actuality the majority of programmers just write their own code from scratch. It's just too darn hard to find the relevant bits of code they need.

Krugle is a new search engine designed to make it easier for programmers to find and share code. Its creators hope that by creating an orderly, accessible library of freely available code, Krugle will increase the efficiency of programmers and breath new life into software development.

Krugle's index of programming code and documentation—what the company dubs "the technical Web"—is 100 million pages long. It stands out from other source-code search engines because it lets programmers search for code by programming language. It also offers programmers the ability to annotate code and documentation, create bookmarks, and save collections of search results in a tabbed workspace. Each saved workspace can have a unique URL, enabling a developer to forward it to a collaborator by e-mailing a link.

As a free search engine, Krugle will support itself with advertising. A new edition called Enterprise is planned for 2007 and will focus on code sharing within companies.

Sources: Tweney, Dylan. "Here Comes a Google for Coders," *Wired News*, February 17, 2006. December 2006 <http://www.wired.com/news/technology/0,70219-0.html>; "Demo—The Premier Launchpad for Emerging Technologies," <http://www.demo.com/demonstrators/demo 2006/63003.html>.

Linux Linux is one of the fastest-growing server operating systems. As discussed in the previous section on personal computer operating systems, Linux is an open-source software program based on the UNIX operating system.

Like UNIX, Linux was originally designed for use with servers and large computer systems, including midrange servers and mainframes. Linux can be downloaded via the Internet for free, and numerous utilities are also available. In addition to downloading Linux from the Internet, there are other ways Linux can be obtained. Some vendors will install Linux on new computers, or provide a CD-ROM containing the software. Some books about the software include a CD-ROM that can be used to install it. A copy of the software may also be obtained from other users. Various versions of Linux are available, including command-line versions and GUI versions. Two popular GUI versions are called GNOME and KDE.

Linux software has quickly gained widespread acceptance and usage because of its low cost (in many cases, free) and its cross-platform nature. Most UNIX software programs can run on the Linux platform. Some companies market their own versions of the software, such as Red Hat and Novell. Many computer professionals believe Linux is a strong competitor with other, more established operating systems. IBM and Hewlett-Packard have created internal Linux business units to support their customers' ventures into the Linux environment.

The future for Linux is promising. Its popularity as a general-purpose operating system is growing, and several companies are testing and refining Linux for use with the embedded chips found in a variety of mobile devices, including Internet appliances and handheld devices.

Solaris Solaris is a UNIX-based operating environment developed by Sun Microsystems. It was originally developed to run on Sun's SPARC workstations, but, the software now runs on many workstations from other manufacturers.

Solaris includes the SunOS operating system and a windowing system. It currently supports multithreading, multiprocessing, networking, and centralized network management. An add-on program, called Wabi emulator, is available that allows Solaris to run numerous Windows applications.

Operating Systems for Handheld Devices

In recent years, two operating systems have solidified their place in the handheld device market. Palm OS and Windows Mobile have become standard choices for the multitude of PDAs, smartphones, and other handheld computing devices.

The Palm Tungsten E2 handheld computer uses the Palm OS.

Palm OS

Palm Inc., manufacturer of one of the earliest calendar and time management devices on the market, has developed its own operating system for its handheld personal digital assistants (PDAs). Called **Palm OS**, this system provides a simple graphical user interface that is used in the various versions of the Palm PDAs, Sony PDAs, and several smartphones, including the Treo. The Palm OS is the most common operating system for handheld PDAs in the corporate environment.

Windows Mobile

The **Windows Mobile** operating system is used in wireless devices and other systems with embedded processors, such as smartphones, PocketPC PDAs, and other handheld devices. Replacing a previous operating system called Windows CE, Windows Mobile is a 32-bit, multitasking, GUI operating system with special built-in power management, Internet, and e-mail capabilities. A user can easily set up a Wi-Fi (wireless) connection for connecting to the Internet. On handheld LCD screens, data and images appear clearly. Windows Mobile allows the interchange of information with desktop and networked Windows-based PCs.

Windows Mobile enables a user to check Outlook e-mail and attachments, schedule meetings, browse the Internet, and even listen to music. For a business user, Windows Mobile allows the user to access e-mail and the Internet and to perform various business tasks.

Utility Programs and Translators

System software may contain other special software, or allow for the use of specialized programs. Two important examples of this kind of system software are utility programs and translators.

Windows Mobile is used in a variety of handheld devices, including PocketPC PDAs and smartphones.

Utility Programs

A **utility program** performs a single maintenance or repair task, such as checking for viruses, uninstalling programs, or deleting data no longer needed. An operating system typically includes several utility programs that are preinstalled at the factory. Several companies, including Symantec and McAfee, produce software suites containing a variety of utility programs. Symantec's Norton SystemWorks includes programs that allow users to check for and erase viruses, diagnose and

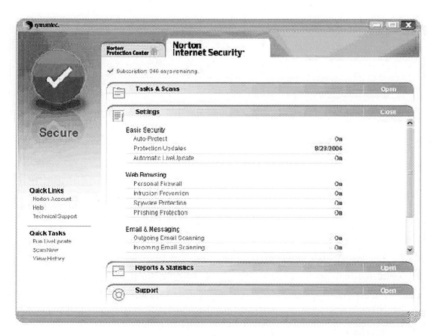

Symantec's Norton SystemWorks can perform a variety of maintenance and repair tasks, including defragmenting a disk and checking for viruses and quarantining them.

Table 4-2 Utility Programs and Their Functions

Utility Program	Function
antivirus software	protects the computer system from a virus attack
anti-spyware	protects the computer system from software that tracks the activity of Internet users
backup utility	makes a backup copy of files on a separate disk
device driver	allows hardware devices, such as disk drives and printers, to work with the computer system
diagnostic utility	examines the computer system and corrects problems that are identified
disk optimizer	identifies disk problems, such as separated files, and rearranges files so they run faster (includes disk scanners and disk defragmenters)
disk toolkit	recovers lost files and repairs any that may be damaged
extender utility	adds new programs and fonts to the computer system
file compression utility	reduces the size of files so they take up less disk space
file viewer	displays quickly the contents of a file
firewall	protects a personal computer or network from access by unauthorized users such as hackers
screen capture program	captures as a file the contents shown on the monitor
spam blocker	filters incoming spam messages
uninstaller utility	removes programs, along with related system files

Go to this title's Internet Resource Center and read the article titled "Utility Software." www.emcp.net/CUT3e

Tech Demo 4-4 Antivirus Software

repair hard disk problems, optimize hard drive performance, restore deleted files, erase deleted files permanently, perform file management, and rescue and restore files from a crashed hard drive. Users can also purchase and install additional utility programs of their choice. Table 4-2 lists some popular kinds of utility programs. Utility programs are usually stored on a hard disk along with the basic operating system and activated when needed by the user.

Utility programs are useful for correcting many of the problems that computer users are likely to encounter. Some of the most popular kinds of utility software are antivirus software, firewalls, diagnostic utilities, uninstallers, disk scanners, disk defragmenters, file compression utilities, backup utilities, disk toolkits, spam blockers, and anti-spyware.

Antivirus Software **Antivirus software** (also called a virus checker) is one of the most important types of utility programs. Examples include Norton AntiVirus and McAfee VirusScan. A virus is programming code buried within a computer program, data, or e-mail message and transferred to a computer system without the user's knowledge. Virus contamination of a computer system can have consequences varying in severity from the mildly annoying to the disastrous. Antivirus utilities perform many functions to keep a computer's software healthy. They scan new disks or downloaded material for known viruses, and diagnose storage media for viral infection. They can also monitor system operations for suspicious activities, such as the rewriting of system resource files, and alert users when such activities are occurring. Most businesses use antivirus utilities as a daily startup routine. Home users find them valuable as well, as their computer systems are no less vulnerable to damaging viruses. The spread of viruses across the Internet represents the major source of virus transmission, principally through attachments to e-mail messages.

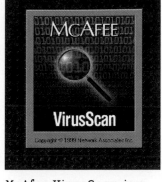

McAfee VirusScan is a popular virus-checking utility.

Firewalls   A **firewall** is a security system that acts as a boundary to protect a computer or network from unauthorized access. Firewalls may consist of hardware, software, or a combination of both. A main use is to prevent unauthorized Internet users from accessing a personal computer or a network connected to the Internet. Incoming and outgoing messages pass through the firewall, which examines each message and blocks those that do not meet specified security criteria. Firewalls are designed to work in a manner similar to the way firewalls between individual housing units in an apartment building are designed to prevent fire from spreading from one apartment to other apartments.

A **personal firewall** such as McAfee Personal Firewall Plus or Norton Personal Firewall is a software-based system designed to protect a personal computer from unauthorized users, called hackers, attempting to access other computers through an Internet connection. Hackers who gain access to other PCs can access the information on them, such as passwords, personal data, and possibly use those computers for a variety of illegal activities. Windows XP Service Pack 2 and Windows Vista also include a personal firewall called Windows Firewall that is enabled by default and is adequate for most PCs.

A **network firewall** typically consists of a combination of hardware and software. In addition to installing firewall software, a company may add a hardware device, such as a dedicated firewall device or proxy server, that screens all communications entering and leaving networked computers to prevent unauthorized access (see Figure 4-5). For example, the device or server may check an incoming message to determine whether the message is from an authorized user. If not, the message is blocked from entering the network.

Firewalls provide a first line of defense against unauthorized access and intrusion. Although most firewall systems are effective, users should practice other security measures, such as safeguarding passwords.

Diagnostic Utilities   A **diagnostic utility** diagnoses a computer's components and system software programs and creates a report identifying problems. The utility provides suggestions to correct any problems encountered, and in some situations can repair problems automatically. The Windows operating system contains a diagnostic utility. More advanced diagnostic utility software can be purchased separately from software vendors.

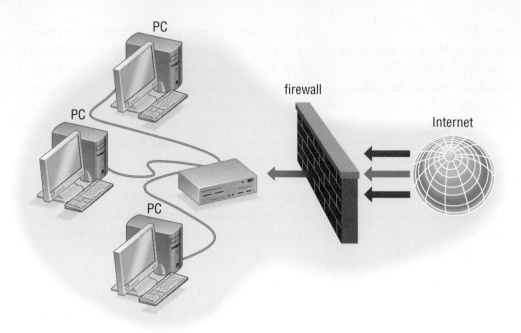

PC

PC

PC

firewall

Internet

Figure 4-5 A Firewall
Firewalls are designed to prevent unauthorized Internet users from accessing a personal computer or a network connected to the Internet.

Uninstallers   An **uninstaller** is a utility program for removing (deleting) software programs and any associated entries in the system files. When an application program is installed, the operating system stores additional files related to the program. Associated files may remain on the hard disk and waste valuable space if a user attempts to remove a program without using an uninstaller utility. An uninstaller utility solves this problem and frees up disk space by automatically removing both programs and related files.

Disk Scanners   A **disk scanner** examines hard or floppy disks and their contents to identify potential problems, such as bad sectors. During the scanning process a disk scanner program checks for both physical and logical problems. For example, it detects and notifies users if a disk contains clusters or sectors that are damaged and therefore unusable. Scan Disk is the disk scanner utility included with the Microsoft Windows operating system.

Disk Defragmenters   A **disk defragmenter** utility scans hard or floppy disks and reorganizes files and unused space, allowing operating systems to locate and access files and data more quickly. Operating systems store a file in the first available sector on a disk. However, there may not be enough space in one sector to store the entire file. If a portion of the sector already contains data, the remaining portions of the file are stored in other available sectors. This may result in files stored in noncontiguous (separated) sectors, known as fragmented files. This causes operating systems to take more time locating and retrieving all segments of a particular file.

This problem can be solved by **defragmenting** the disk so files are stored in contiguous sectors. Microsoft's Windows operating system includes a disk defrag-

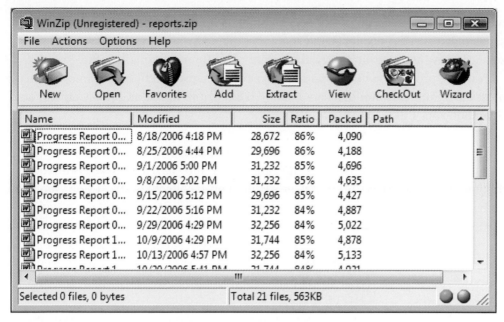

WinZip allows users to compress and decompress files for sharing and storage.

menting utility called Disk Defragmenter. If a system does not come equipped with a disk defragmenter, utilities packages containing one can be purchased.

File Compression Utilities   A **file compression** utility compresses (shrinks) the size of a file so it occupies less disk space. Examples of compression utilities are WinZip, PKZIP, and StuffIt. Files are compressed by reducing redundancies, such as the binary descriptions of rows of identically colored pixels in graphics files. The ability to compress and decompress files is especially helpful when sending or receiving large files on network systems or over the Internet.

Compressed files, often called zipped files, typically have a .zip file extension. Users must compress (zip) the file. When a compressed (zipped) file is received, it must be uncompressed (unzipped) to restore its original form. Both senders and recipients of compressed files must have compression software installed on their computers.

Backup Utilities   A **backup utility** allows users to make copies of the contents of disks or tapes. The utility can be directed to back up the entire contents or only selected files. Some backup utilities will compress files so they take up less space than the original files. Because compressed files are unusable until they are uncompressed, many backup utilities include a restore program for uncompressing files.

Disk Toolkits   A **disk toolkit**, such as Norton Utilities Disk Doctor, contains utility programs that let users identify and correct a variety of problems they may have with a hard or floppy disk. Disk toolkits can diagnose and repair problems with files on the disk as well as physical damage to the disk.

Spam Blockers   The proliferation of unwanted e-mail messages, called spam, is a serious concern among Internet users. According to Brightmail, a company that blocks spam for some of the nation's top Internet service providers, spam messages that advertise products and services ranging from automobiles to dating services now account for nearly 40 percent of all Internet e-mail traffic.

A utility program called a **spam blocker** is often used to filter incoming spam messages. Popular spam blockers include iHateSpam, Matador, SpamCatcher, and SpamSubtract PRO.

Anti-Spyware   **Spyware** is a form of **malware** (malicious software) that tracks the activities of Internet users for the benefit of a third party. Spyware is unknowingly downloaded to an Internet user's computer to collect keystrokes or Web site activity for malicious purposes such as password interception, fraudulent credit card usage, or identity theft. One particular type of spyware, called **adware**, is more annoying than harmful. Adware tracks the Web sites that a user visits in order to collect information for marketing or advertising. Some adware presents users with pop-up advertisements that contain contests, games, or links to unrelated Web sites.

Not all antivirus software protects Internet users from spyware, but separate anti-spyware and adware protection software is available. Windows Vista contains anti-spyware software called Windows Defender. Other popular anti-spyware software includes Webroot Spy Sweeper, Lavasoft's Ad Aware, and Bayden Systems' Popup Blocker.

Translators

A computer cannot understand programming code written in a human language, such as English or Spanish. Instead, it can only understand machine language: binary code written in zeros (0s) and ones (1s). (The concept of machine language was explained in Chapter 2.) Operating systems and other programs may be written using machine language, which enables them to execute very quickly.

Machine language is difficult to learn and programmers find that writing machine language programs is time-consuming. To avoid this, application programs are usually written using an English-like programming language, called a **high-level language**. Examples of high-level languages are COBOL, Java, and BASIC, which has several versions. Figure 4-6 shows a sample of programming code in DOS BASIC.

High-level languages must be translated into machine-language format before the CPU can execute them. To accomplish this task, a special program called a **language translator** is used to translate (convert) high-level language into machine language so it can be run by the computer. Microsoft Windows includes a version of BASIC.

The two major types of language-translating software are interpreters and compilers. Each programming language generates code that needs to be either compiled or interpreted for execution. A **compiler** translates an entire program into machine language before the program will run. Each language has its own unique compiler. After reading and translating the program, the compiler displays a list of program errors that may be present. Once the errors are corrected, a compiled program will usually execute more quickly than an interpreted program.

```
10 REM ***SIMPLIFIED PAYROLL PROGRAM***
20 PRINT "ENTER HOURS WORKED";
30 INPUT H
40 PRINT "ENTER HOURLY PAY RATE";
50 INPUT R
60 REM *** COMPUTE WAGE***
70 LET W=H*R
80 PRINT "WEEKLY WAGE IS $";W
90 END
RUN


OUTPUT


ENTER HOURS WORKED? 40
ENTER HOURLY PAY RATE? 8
WEEKLY WAGE IS $ 320
```

By typing the RUN command, the program executes and these messages appear on screen.

User enters the hours worked and the hourly pay rate.

When the program is executed (RUN), the computer multiplies the hours worked (40) by the hourly pay rate (6) and automatically displays the weekly wage (240) on the screen.

Program Explanation

Every instruction begins with a line (instruction) number. A **REM** (short for remark) is a statement that describes what the program does but has no effect on the program itself. A PRINT statement displays on the screen the text within quotes. An **INPUT** instruction requires the programmer to enter specific data when prompted. A **LET** statement processes the data according to the formula identified. An **END** statement indicates the end of the program.

Figure 4-6 DOS BASIC Payroll Program
Shown is a simple payroll program written in DOS BASIC.

An **interpreter** differs from a compiler by reading, translating, and executing one instruction at a time. Since an interpreter acts on just one line of instruction at a time, it identifies errors as they are encountered, including the line containing the error, making it somewhat more user-friendly.

OnThe**Horizon**

INSPIRED BY BREAKTHROUGHS IN PROCESSING TECHNOLOGY as well as changing market needs, developers of system and utilities software are continually brainstorming new programs and improvements to existing software. Although trying to divine the path of software development is risky, some of today's leading-edge technologies provide clues to the future.

Linux Gets a Boost

The open source Linux operating system will get a big push if the One Laptop per Child project succeeds as planned. The project aims to produce laptops for every child in developing nations, at a price of around $100 per machine once production is in full swing. Project engineers needed a scaled-down operating system that used little power, and decided that Linux was the best match for those requirements. Production is planned in the tens of millions, and Project Head Nicholas Negroponte feels that this choice will one day make Linux as popular on desktop computers as it is currently on servers.

Software Streaming

Software streaming is a promising alternative to installed software, involving the distribution of operating system and applications software to networked computers from centrally managed servers. When networked computers are switched on they send a request for operating system and applications software. The advantages of this type of software platform include lower maintenance costs, ease of software upgrades, and improved security because no software remains on individual machines when they are switched off. Results of this method of software distribution are promising, and some think it may one day become a leading method of software distribution.

Web-Based Operating Systems

YouOS is an innovative new operating system that lets users run applications located on a desktop resident on a remote Web server. YouOS uses a combination of scripting and markup languages known as Ajax (Asynchronous JavaScript and XML) to create a remote desktop with speed and interactivity comparable to that offered by desktop programs. Currently available in beta version, YouOS and other similar projects may develop into popular alternatives to computer-based operating systems.

Chapter**Summary**

 For an interactive version of this summary, go to this text's Internet Resource Center at www.emcp.net/CUT3e. A Spanish version is also available.

What is the function of system software?

Software is the broad term for the programs that tell a computer what to do and how to do it. Programs are sets of instructions telling computers to perform actions in a certain order. The two main categories of software are **application software** and **system software**. Application software includes programs that perform a single task such as spreadsheet analysis. System software includes programs that manage the basic operations of a computer such as starting up and saving and printing files.

What is the function of the operating system?

The **operating system** is the most important piece of software on a personal computer. It manages main memory, or RAM; controls and configures peripheral devices; formats and copies disks; manages essential file operations; monitors system performance; and provides a user interface. Operating systems are designed for a particular **platform**, which is determined by the type of computer and processor.

What are the two types of software user interfaces and how do they work?

All software, including operating systems, must have a **user interface** to allow communication between the software and the user. The interface controls the manner in which data and commands are entered and the way information and processing options are presented on the screen. Two types of user interfaces have been developed for personal computers: command-line interfaces and graphical user interfaces (GUIs). **Command-line interfaces** are, as the name sug-

gests, designed to accept commands from the user in the form of lines of text code. The DOS operating system has a command-line interface. **Graphical user interfaces (GUIs)** accept user commands in the form of mouse clicks on icons or menu items. Windows is the most commonly used GUI for personal computers, and it uses the same icons and basic file commands as Windows-based applications, which makes learning the new applications much easier. The major GUI features with which users interact include an on-screen desktop, display windows, key feature menus, common command **icons**, **dialog boxes**, and **context-sensitive help**.

What are the popular operating systems in use on personal computers?

Since its development in 1985, the Windows operating system has dominated the PC market, from Windows 3.1 through **Windows 2000**, **Windows XP**, and **Windows Vista**. Besides adding features with each version, the Windows releases have required increasingly more powerful microprocessors and more disk space for installation. The **Mac OS** was the first commercial GUI, serving as a model for the Windows GUI that followed. Long a favorite of graphic artists and designers, the Mac OS now runs on both Apple Macintosh and Intel-based personal computers. Its newest version, Mac OS X, includes a new interface called Aqua and is based on the UNIX operating system. IBM's **OS/2** GUI operating system was developed to compete with Microsoft Windows and the Apple Mac OS. The latest version, OS/2 Warp, can run programs written for both DOS and Windows systems. **Linux**, an open-source operating system based on UNIX, is emerging as the next competitor in the personal computer operating system market.

What are the popular operating systems used on servers?

Server operating systems are designed for local area networks, allowing multiple users to connect to the server computer and to share data files, programs, and peripheral devices. **Novell NetWare** is a popular and widely used operating system for microcomputer-based local area networks. Other major server operating systems include Windows (including **Windows Server 2003** and **Windows Server 200X [Longhorn]**) and **UNIX** (including Linux and Solaris).

What are the operating systems used for handheld devices?

The development of handheld devices has created a need for operating systems designed exclusively for these mobile computers with smaller screens. The two operating systems for handheld devices are **Palm OS** and **Windows Mobile**.

How are the functions of utility programs different from translators?

A **utility program** performs a single maintenance or repair task. Common utility programs include **antivirus software**, **firewalls**, **diagnostic utilities**, **uninstallers**, **disk scanners**, **disk defragmenter**s, **file compression** utilities, **backup utilities**, **disk toolkits**, **spam blockers**, and anti-spyware.

A **language translator** is a special program that converts a high-level program language into machine language so the computer can run the program. Two major types of language translators are **compilers** and **interpreters**. Compilers translate an entire program at once, whereas interpreters act on just one line of instruction at a time.

KeyTerms

Numbers indicate the pages where terms are first cited in the chapter. An alphabetized list of key terms with definitions (in English and Spanish) can be found on the Encore CD that accompanies this book. In addition, these terms and definitions are included in the end-of-book glossary.

The Function of System Software
software, 155
hardware, 155
application software, 155
system software, 155

The Function of the Operating System
operating system (OS), 156
boot drive, 156
platform, 156
booting, 157
cold boot, 157
warm boot, 157
kernel, 158
memory resident, 158
nonresident, 158

throughput, 159
buffer, 160
print spooling, 160
multitasking, 160
driver, 161
file manager, 161
performance monitor, 162
user name (user ID), 162
password, 162

Software User Interfaces
user interface, 162
command-line interface, 162
prompt, 162
graphical user interface (GUI), 163
icon, 163
desktop, 164
button, 164
display window, 165
title bar, 166
scroll bar, 166
menu, 166
menu bar (main menu), 166
drop-down menu (pull-down menu), 166
ribbon, 166
default option, 167

toolbar, 168
dialog box, 169
tab, 169
option button (radio button), 169
check box, 169
text box, 169
context-sensitive Help message, 170

Personal Computer Operating Systems
operating environment, 171
Windows 2000, 171
Windows XP, 172
Windows Vista, 174
User Access Control (UAC), 174
Windows Defender, 174
Windows Firewall, 174
breadcrumbs, 175
Macintosh OS, 175
OS/2, 176
Linux, 176
open-source software program, 177
proprietary software, 177

Server Operating Systems
NetWare, 179
Windows NT Server, 179
Windows 2000 Server, 179
Windows Server 2003, 179
Windows Server 200X (Longhorn), 180
UNIX, 180

multi-user operating system, 180
cross-platform operating system, 180
Solaris, 182

Operating Systems for Handheld Devices
Palm OS, 182
Windows Mobile, 182

Utility Programs and Translators
utility program, 183
antivirus software (virus checker), 184
firewall, 185
personal firewall, 185
network firewall, 185
diagnostic utility, 185
uninstaller, 186
disk scanner, 186
disk defragmenter, 186
defragmenting, 186
file compression, 187
backup utility, 187
disk toolkit, 187
spam blocker, 188
spyware, 188
malware, 188
adware, 188
high-level language, 188
language translator, 188
compiler, 188
interpreter, 189

Chapter**Exercises**

 The following chapter exercises, along with new activities and information, are also offered in the Internet Resource Center for this title at www.emcp.net/CUT3e.

Tutorial > **Exploring Windows**

Tutorial 4 focuses on maximizing, minimizing, and restoring application and file management windows. You also will learn how to move and resize a window.

Expanding Your Knowledge > Articles and Activities

 Visit the Internet Resource Center for this title at www.emcp.net/CUT3e, read the articles related to this chapter, and complete the corresponding activities. The article titles include:

- Topic 4-1: Open Source Software
- Topic 4-2: Network Operating Systems
- Topic 4-3: Setting Up a Home Network
- Topic 4-4: Utility Software

Terms Check > Matching

 For additional practice, go to the Internet Resource Center for this title at www.emcp.net/CUT3e for a chapter crossword puzzle.

Write the letter of the correct answer on the line before each numbered item.

a. on-screen desktop	f. system software
b. window	g. graphical user interface (GUI)
c. interpreter	h. icon
d. utility	i. menu bar
e. software	j. platform

_____ 1. Programs that tell a computer what to do and how to do it.

_____ 2. An interface that uses menus, buttons, and symbols, making it easier to work with text, graphics, and other elements.

_____ 3. A horizontal or vertical row display that shows the highest-level command options.

_____ 4. An on-screen work area displaying graphical elements such as icons, buttons, windows, links, and dialog boxes.

_____ 5. A picture or symbol representing an action such as opening, saving, or printing a file.

_____ 6. A rectangular area of the screen used to display a program, data, or information.

_____ 7. Translation software that reads and executes one program line at a time.

_____ 8. A type of program that performs a maintenance or repair task, such as formatting a disk.

_____ 9. The foundation or standard around which software is developed.

_____ 10. A set of programs controlling the operation of a computer system, including all components and devices connected to it.

Technology Illustrated > **Identify the Process**

What features are illustrated in this drawing? Identify the features and write a paragraph describing them.

Knowledge Check > **Multiple Choice**

  Additional quiz questions are available on the Encore CD that accompanies this book as well as on the Internet Resource Center for this title at www.emcp.net/CUT3e.

Circle the letter of the best answer from those provided.

1. An option that has been built into a software program under the assumption that it is the one most likely to be chosen is called a(n)

   a. default.
   b. driver.
   c. buffer.
   d. algorithm.

2. A rectangular area of the screen used to display a program, data, or information is a

   a. pane.
   b. menu.
   c. toolbar.
   d. window.

3. A box that provides information or requests a response is called a(n)

   a. query box.
   b. dialog box.
   c. answer box.
   d. data box.

4. A small program that enables a computer to communicate with devices such as printers and monitors is a

   a. driver.
   b. graphical user interface (GUI).
   c. speaker.
   d. compiler.

5. A program that converts a high-level programming language into machine language is called a(n)

a. coprocessor.
b. binary operator.
c. utility program.
d. language translator.

6. Which of the following is not a function of an operating system?

a. providing a user interface
b. processing data
c. managing RAM
d. configuring and controlling peripheral devices

7. A foundation or standard around which software is developed is called a(n)

a. system program.
b. platform.
c. utility.
d. PC model.

8. A screen on which graphical elements such as icons, buttons, windows, links, and dialog boxes are displayed is called the

a. desktop.
b. menu bar.
c. icon interface.
d. title bar.

9. A program that performs a single maintenance or repair task, such as checking for viruses, is called a(n)

a. repair program.
b. maintenance program.
c. utility program.
d. operating system.

10. The most important piece of software on a personal computer is the

a. operating system.
b. utility program.
c. application program.
d. defragmenting program.

Things That Think > **Brainstorming New Uses**

In groups or individually, contemplate the following questions and develop as many answers as you can.

1. One of the features introduced in Windows XP is the "remote assistance" feature. This allows someone with Windows XP to access (via the Internet) another user's Windows XP computer as if he/she were there in person. The primary intent is for software vendors or ISPs to provide technical support to their customers from distant locations. What other uses of this remote assistance technology can you imagine? What problems can you see this technology causing?

2. One of the features introduced in Windows XP is a copy-protection feature called "product activation" that Microsoft included to reduce software piracy. When Windows XP is installed on a PC, the installer must use an activation wizard to register the product key. This product key is then permanently tied to the internal address of that computer. If someone tries to install the same copy of Windows XP on another computer, the activation process will not work. Can you

think of legitimate needs that consumers might have to reinstall or copy the software that would not be considered piracy? Can you think of any nonsoftware industries that might have a use for this copy-protection technology?

3. Many antivirus utility programs use "heuristics" to discover new viruses. The use of heuristics means that the antivirus program assesses programming code against a set of rules to determine if the programming code exhibits any suspicious behavior. For example, if the programming logic appears to modify system files, send out hundreds of e-mails at a time, or performs an action that could be dangerous to a computer system, the file (or e-mail) message will be quarantined for the user's protection. This behavior-based approach to identifying viruses has proved to be more effective than traditional virus discovery techniques. Can you think of other uses for behavior-based problem-solving software?

Key Principles > Completion

Fill in the blanks with the appropriate words or phrases.

1. A collection of programs that manage basic operations such as starting and shutting down the computer and saving and printing files is known as _____.

2. A foundation or standard around which software is developed is called a(n) _____.

3. An operating system program that manages computer components, peripheral devices, and memory is the _____.

4. A _____ is a unique combination of characters that allows a user to gain access to computer resources such as programs, data, and files.

5. A _____ is a graphical element that causes a particular action to occur when selected.

6. GUIs use _____ boxes to provide information and prompt responses to the user.

7. The _____ was the first commercial GUI, released in 1984 and updated many times since the initial release.

8. One of the fastest growing operating systems, called _____, was developed by Linus Torvalds, and is based on the UNIX operating system.

9. A _____ is programming code buried within a computer program or an electronic mail message and transferred to a computer system without the user's knowledge.

10. A utility program that scans hard or floppy disks and reorganizes files and unused space, allowing operating systems to locate and access files and data more quickly is called a disk _____.

Tech Architecture > Label the Drawing

In this illustration of an application window, label the four graphical elements called out with arrows.

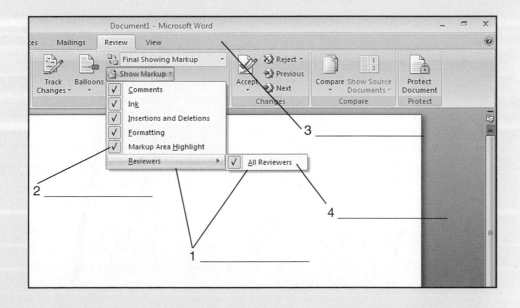

Techno Literacy > **Research and Writing**

Develop appropriate written responses based on your research for each item.

1. How does open-source productivity software stack up against Microsoft Office? Research Linux-based Open Office productivity software and compare it with that found in Microsoft Office. Are the same types of applications in Microsoft Office available in Open Office? Are there any unique features of Open Office that are not available in Microsoft Office? Can files created in one product be viewed and edited in the other product? How do the prices compare? Are the same support resources available for both products (e.g., manuals, books, online help)? Which would you prefer, and why?

2. Is there a vaccine for this virus? With team members assigned by your instructor, investigate a computer virus that has infected large numbers of computers in recent years. Discuss and answer these questions:

   - What does the virus do?
   - Where did it originate, and how does it spread?
   - What were the costs of the damage?
   - How widespread was the outbreak?
   - How was the virus stopped?

Technology Issues > **Team Problem-Solving**

In groups, brainstorm possible solutions to the issues presented.

1. User expectations for operating systems are complex. Some users want more robust technical features and programming utilities, and others want them to become more user-friendly and "intelligent," so the OS can predict what the user wants or needs to do. Brainstorm ways developers of operating systems can resolve, address, or reconcile these conflicting expectations.

2. Researchers and developers claim that one of the most important goals for operating systems is to become self-healing. Discuss what this characteristic means and list the types of problems "self-healing" computers will be designed to solve.

3. Microsoft claims it will soon break the mold and create a new generation OS interface that is touch- and voice-driven. If the company is right, what adaptors or utilities will be required to accommodate physically disabled customers and others with special needs?

Mining Data > **Internet Research and Reporting**

Conduct Internet searches to find the information described in the activities below. Write a brief report summarizing your research results. Be sure to document your sources, using the MLA format (See Chapter 1, page 42, to review MLA style guidelines).

1. Research the advantages and disadvantages of open-source software programs such as Linux. Is there evidence to suggest that providing source code to developers results in better programs over a shorter development time?

2. Several companies are dreaming up designs for the PC of the future. Research the design ideas of companies such as Lenovo, Microsoft, Asus Design, Personal Computer Environments, and Dell. Discuss these questions as you study their computer designs for the future:

   - What design objectives are guiding the design decisions?
   - What markets are being targeted?

- How might the market respond?
- Will these products win acceptance?
- What advice could you offer designers to ensure a positive market response?

3. A variety of utility programs are currently available, and new ones are being developed on an ongoing basis. Research the topic of utility programs to answer the following questions:

   - What are the most popular utilities? (Which are used most often, according to industry research?)

- What utilities are included in Windows XP and Windows Vista?
- What are some new utilities now under development?
- What is the most effective way to "package" utilities for consumers? Individually? In groups of those most commonly used? What are other options?

Technology Timeline > Predicting Next Steps

Many improvements have been made to the Windows operating system since Microsoft first introduced it. Below is a timeline showing versions of Microsoft Windows for the personal computer and the year each was introduced. Visit Microsoft's Web site at www.microsoft.com and other sites to learn more about Windows and its features. Predict when the next version is likely to be introduced, and prepare a list of features you believe the next version will, or should, include.

1985	Windows 1.0	**2000**	Windows 2000
1992	Windows 3.1	**2000**	Windows Millennium Edition
1995	Windows 95	**2001**	Windows XP
1998	Windows 98	**2007**	Windows Vista

Ethical Dilemmas > Group Discussion and Debate

As a class or within an assigned group, discuss the following ethical dilemma.

The illegal copying of commercial software is a major concern among software publishers, including Microsoft and Corel. According to publishers, thousands of copies are made and distributed to other users in violation of copyright laws.

Software publishers may spend thousands and even millions of dollars developing new software products. Illegal copies distributed to other users rob publishers of profits they would have gained from the sale of these products. Additionally, publishers say they must charge legitimate customers higher prices to make up for lost sales.

Many users believe that purchasing a legal copy makes the buyer the product's owner, which should entitle them to make extra copies. Additionally, they point out that because software publishers have the option of making their products "copy protected," publishers must not consider copying a serious problem.

What is your position on this issue? Are there situations that justify copying copyrighted software? Why or why not? What are your ethical obligations, if any, concerning this matter?

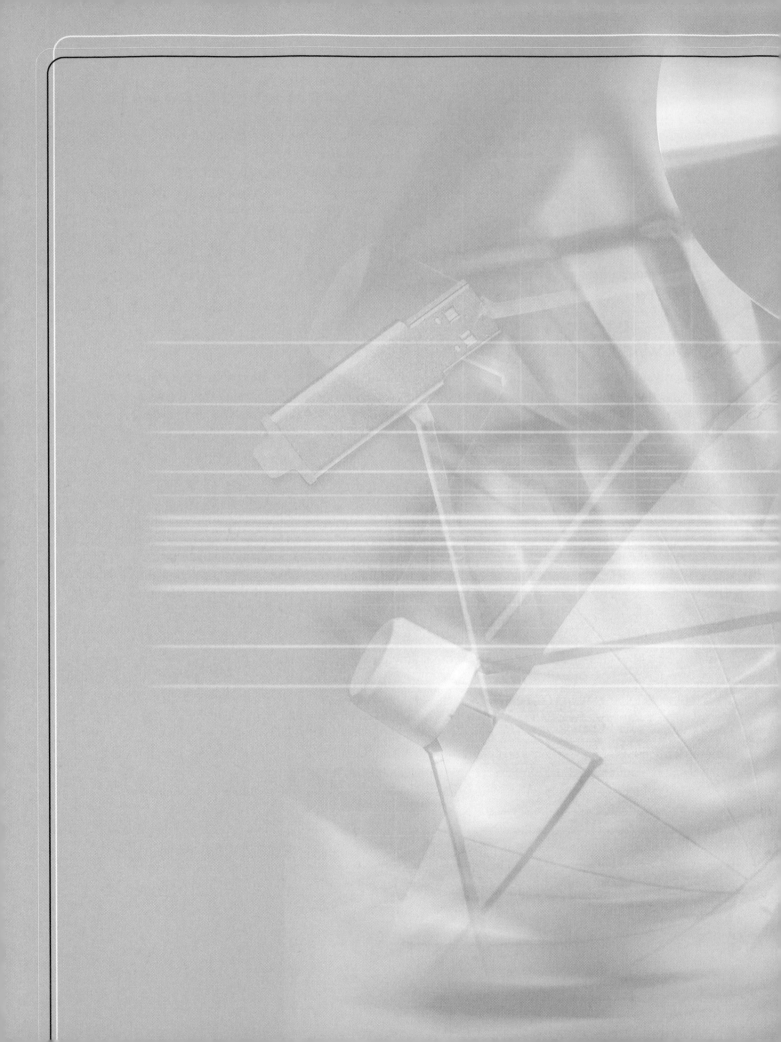

The Internet and the World Wide Web

THE INTERNET IS THE LARGEST COMPUTER NETWORK in the world. Its design closely resembles a client/server model, with network groups acting as clients and Internet service providers acting as servers. An Internet service provider (ISP) is an organization that provides user access to the Internet, usually charging a subscription fee. Since the inception of the Internet in the early 1970s, this enormous invisible structure has expanded to connect more than 1 billion users worldwide. Many knowledgeable observers consider this vast system of networked computers and telecommunications systems the most significant technical development of the twentieth century, potentially connecting every person on Earth to vast resources of information and services.

Internet Services

Individuals, organizations, businesses, and governments use the Internet to accomplish a number of different activities, which can be subdivided into categories:

- communications
- entertainment
- electronic commerce
- research
- distance learning

Communications

One of the chief functions of the Internet is its ability to allow people to quickly and easily communicate with one another. Internet users have a number of different communications applications that they can take advantage of, including e-mail, chat rooms, instant messaging, blogs, mailing lists, electronic message boards, newsgroups, telecommuting, and file transfer.

Electronic Mail   Electronic mail (e-mail) is the most widely used Internet application. It allows users to create, send, receive, save, and forward messages in electronic form. It is a fast, convenient, and inexpensive way to communicate. Computer industry research firms estimate that the number of e-mails sent on an average day now exceeds 36 billion.

Each e-mail user has a unique electronic address, that is supplied by the user's ISP. Sending an e-mail message is simple. A message writer only has to specify the recipient's e-mail address, type a subject in the subject bar, create a message, and click the *Send* button.

In addition to sending messages, users can attach files to their e-mail messages. In Microsoft Outlook and Outlook Express, the attachment feature is called Insert File, and this button is marked with a paper clip. Virtually any kind of electronic document can be attached and sent with an e-mail message, including reports, spreadsheets, photos, and video files. Recipients can then open the attached files for viewing or storing on their computer.

Large file attachments are often compressed as ZIP files. A zipped file is usually half the size of the original file, meaning that it takes half the time to download (copy from the host computer). Before a zipped file can be viewed it must be unzipped, a process that reverses the compression process and creates a new file that is full-sized again.

Chat Rooms   A chat room is an application that allows users to engage in real-time dialogue, or live, instantaneous conversations with one or more participants. Most online services provide chat rooms. Users can sign up to participate in a chat room on almost any topic. For example, an environmentally conscious user can participate in a chat room discussing global warming. User comments and opinions can be exchanged freely and anonymously with other online participants, and are often frank and uncensored.

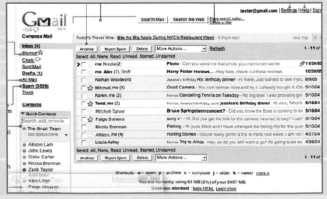

Google's Gmail is a free e-mail service that includes several valuable features.

Instant Messaging   Instant messaging (IM) works like a chat room, but usually with only two participants in a connection. IM also allows for conversations to take place in real time, using a chat-room-like environment. The process is similar to a telephone conversation, but all the communication is done via typing. People who know one another's handle (user name) can open connections and engage in one-on-one conversations. What makes this system different from normal chatting is that it constantly runs in the background while users are working on their PCs. The program notifies users automatically when someone wants to contact them for a chat. Because of this feature, IM systems demand a person's attention, making them more interruptive than e-mail.

Blogs   Originally called a weblog (a combination of the words *Web* and *log*), a blog is a frequently updated journal or log containing chronological entries of personal thoughts and Web links posted on a Web page. The content and style of blogs vary as widely as the people who maintain them (called "bloggers"), but in general they function as a personal diary or guide to others with similar interests. Myspace.com and Blogger.com are Web sites specifically dedicated to supporting thousands of blogs. Collectively, the world of blogs is known as the blogosphere.

In the corporate world, blogs provide a unique opportunity for businesses to communicate with their employees, customers, and partners. Bloggers add a personal, informal tone to company communications, achieving a realism that sometimes is absent from the traditional glossy marketing brochures. This growing trend is under the careful watch of company attorneys, who are responsible for the company's image and disclosure of sensitive information.

Entertainment

Using computers for entertainment purposes is a common activity among Internet users of all ages. Computers are capable of emulating almost all entertainment devices, and they can be used to play games, listen to music, or even to watch movies or video programs.

Online Games   An enormous number of free games is available online, including traditional

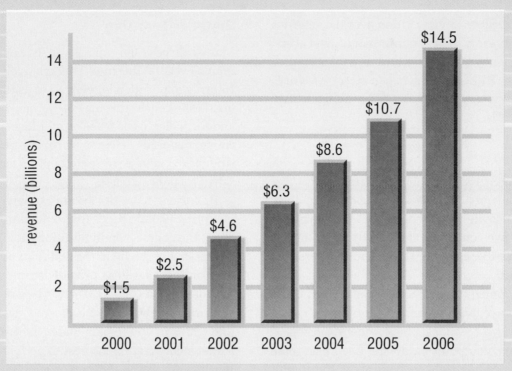

Figure 1 Internet Gaming Revenue Growth

games such as backgammon, checkers, and bridge. Figure 1 illustrates the dramatic increase in Internet gaming revenue growth since 2000. Some retail games, for example, *EVE Online* and *World of Warcraft*, require users to buy the software. Users can play by themselves or compete with other players. More than 6 million players pay monthly fees of approximately $15 to play *World of Warcraft*, the most popular online game in the world. Games attempt to create a virtual reality by giving people a virtual body, called an avatar, which serves as their point of view in the game world. Virtual reality (VR) involves a computer simulation of an environment or set of surroundings that does not exist, but is reasonably convincing to the user.

Music and Video Music from various Internet sources can be downloaded and played on computers. The most popular of the music download services is iTtunes from Apple. Most music download Web sites charge service fees. Copyright considerations have put some companies into lawsuits and criminal liability, and downloading free music is not as easy as it once was.

Moving Pictures Expert Group Layer III (MP3) is the most widely used music file format. MP3 is a compression format capable of reducing the size of CD music files by a factor of 10 to 14. This is done by removing recorded sound that the human ear cannot perceive. Because the MP3 format results in much smaller files, they are easily downloaded. Once a file is on a computer's hard disk, it can be transferred to a portable MP3 player, where it resides on the player's hard drive.

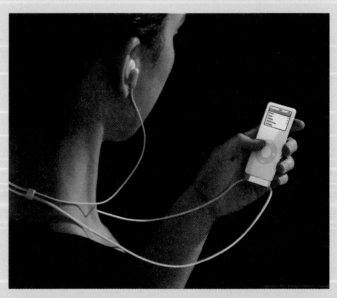

An iPod, a portable MP3 player, offers a convenient way to listen to music downloaded from the Internet.

It is also possible to view video over the Internet, including television shows, music videos, and even movies. Many news networks and newspapers offer video on their Web sites. Users can click on a story and then view a short video newscast filling them in on all the details.

Electronic Commerce

Electronic commerce (e-commerce) refers to the Internet exchange of business information, products, services, and payments. E-commerce is commonly divided into two categories defined by target audience: business-to-consumer (B2C) and business-to-business (B2B).

Online shopping expenditures make up the bulk of B2C e-commerce, with the top category being apparel, followed by books, music, videos, auction items, toys, and computer hardware. Each year, retail e-commerce sales continue to grow about 15 percent per year as a segment of overall spending. According to the U.S. Commerce Department, for example, retail e-commerce sales for the year 2005 were $172 billion and will grow to $329 billion by 2010.

Research

The Web has opened up thousands of opportunities for people interested in research. Aided by increasingly sophisticated software, users can explore any topic, from anacondas to Zen Buddhism. Information retrieval has become an important application for students, writers, historians, scientists, and the curious.

In addition to the information available on millions of Web sites, material from libraries and databases around the world also is available for viewing at the touch of a keyboard. Researchers can access books, periodicals, photos, videos, and sound files from the comfort of their own homes. Information can be read online or downloaded for later use.

A search engine is a good starting place to find practically anything on the Internet. Search engines are software programs available at Web sites that store searchable snapshots of the information found on millions of other Web sites. Most college research projects today begin on the Web rather than in the library, and the first tool used is the student's favorite search engine.

Distance Learning

Many colleges offer online courses and study programs over the Internet. This relatively new Internet application is referred to as distance learning. Distance learning may be defined as the back and forth electronic transfer of information and course materials between learning institutions and students. A course presented in this manner is called an online course.

Preformatted platforms are available, and these platforms include pages to provide information about the course, communication tools such as online chat and e-mail, the ability to post and grade tests online, as well as provide learning resources to support course content. The top two online course platforms, WebCT and Blackboard, merged in 2006. The platform will remain under the Blackboard name, incorporating the best of both products. With Blackboard, instructors can provide their own content or take advantage of Blackboard-ready course content developed by textbook publishers.

Distance learning is becoming increasingly popular with students of all ages, and with people whose interests may not be included in a standard college curriculum or at a nearby school. It has also proved an attractive learning alternative for students whose schedules or careers make it difficult for them to attend regular classes. Distance learning offers them an opportunity to pursue or continue their education while maintaining their jobs.

Connecting to the Internet

Millions of people throughout the world are able to connect to the Internet. Although the United States has the largest number of Internet users, some areas in Asia and Europe are showing strong growth. Figure 2 shows the top 15 countries in Internet usage as of the end of 2005, according to Computer Industry Almanac.

Hardware and Software Requirements

The following equipment and software are required to connect to the Internet:
- computer, personal digital assistant (PDA), or smartphone
- wireless network card, local area network card, digital subscriber line (DSL) modem,

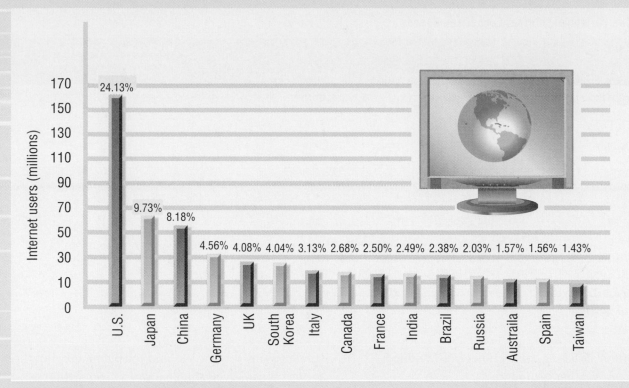

Figure 2 Top 15 Countries in Internet Use in 2005

The percentages indicate the percentage of total Internet use for each country.

Source: Computer Industry Almanac, Inc.

cable modem, or dial-up modem
- wireless network, local area network, telephone line, or cable connection
- Web browser
- an account with an Internet service provider (ISP) or value added network (VAN)

An ISP is a company that provides Internet access for a fee, or sometimes for free. Firms that provide free access usually require subscribers to view advertisements when viewing Web pages. A value added network (VAN) is a large ISP company that provides a connection to the Internet as well as additional content such as online news, weather forecasts, financial reports, and sports news. Some popular VANs are America Online (AOL) and the Microsoft Network (MSN). It should be noted that all ISPs and online services are equal in terms of the number of e-mail users and Web sites they can reach.

ISPs are available on the local, regional, and national level. In the United States, local ISPs typically operate within a state, regional ISPs serve one or more states, and national ISPs provide connections from anywhere in the country. Larger ISPs provide local telephone numbers in several cities so that

connections can be made without paying for long-distance calls. National ISPs are convenient for people who travel a great deal, but their monthly charges are usually considerably higher than local ISPs.

Types of Internet Connections

There are several different ways for users to connect to the Internet: dial-up, local area network (LAN), cable modem, digital subscriber line (DSL), wireless network, and satellite. Table 1 compares the connection speeds for each. Forrester Research reported in 2005 that approximately one-third of all connected households in the United States had DSL, digital cable, or satellite service.

Dial-up Access Dial-up access allows access to the Internet over a standard telephone line by using a computer and a modem to dial into an ISP or VAN connection. Dial-up access is a feature typically included with the software an ISP or VAN provides. Once the software is installed, a dial-up access icon can be placed on the user's computer desktop. Clicking on the ISP or VAN icon initiates a connection to the Internet. Advanced computer users can

Table 1 Comparison of Internet Connection Speeds

Hardware	Download Speed*	Upload Speed*	Millions of Users in the United States in 2005
56 Kbps dial-up modem	28 Kbps	28 Kbps	102
LAN connection	1 Mbps	1 Mbps	55
Cable modem	1 Mbps	500 Kbps	25
DSL	1 Mbps	500 Kbps	14
wireless	varies widely	varies widely	2
satellite	500 Kbps	56 Kbps	3

*Upload speed means how fast you can send a file from your computer to another computer out on the Internet. Download speed measures how fast you can receive a file from another computer. In most cases, download speed is more important.

Note: The speeds actually attained may vary greatly depending on quality of service and equipment.

also configure dial-up connections from within a Windows operating system.

Local Area Network (LAN) Connection   A local area network (LAN) Internet connection provides faster and more direct Internet access by connecting users to an ISP on a direct wire at speeds 20 or more times faster than can be achieved through a dial-up modem. Because they are more expensive than dial-up access, LAN connections are more commonly found in the workplace. Despite the increased cost ($20 to $50 per month), by the end of 2005 more than 42 million (up from 6 million in 2003) LAN users in the United States were using cable and DSL connections to connect from their homes.

Cable Modem   The same coaxial cable that provides cable television service can also provide Internet access to a household. Cable TV companies provide a special modem and software for broadband (high-speed) Internet access. This method allows simultaneous television viewing and Internet usage, but the service is not available everywhere. Nationwide, as of 2005, there were more subscribers to cable modem service (23 million) than DSL (17 million). The cost is about $30 to $60 monthly, plus a possible installation fee.

Digital Subscriber Line   Digital subscriber line (DSL) Internet service is also broadband Internet access. It is as fast as a cable modem and provides

simultaneous Web access and telephone use, but the service is usually available only to users within three miles of the telephone carrier's central switching office. The line is dedicated to one household, and is not shared with neighbors. A DSL provides access to the Internet through the user's existing phone lines, with the phone carrier or Internet service provider providing the DSL modem and the network card. DSL service costs about $20 to $50 monthly, plus an installation fee. Some carriers include the Internet service account in the monthly fee for the line.

Wireless   The fastest growing segment of Internet service involves wireless connections to the Internet. Thousands of wireless or Wi-Fi hot-spots are springing up, allowing access in public places and even aboard airplanes with a wireless network card. Wi-Fi supports the IEEE standard for radio-wave connections to the Internet. Wireless connections to the Internet are often slower than wired connections, but they provide a great deal of portability. Many Wi-Fi hot-spots are free for users, and wireless service providers also provide broader access for a fee.

Satellite   Downloading Web files is quick via satellite, but uploading is not as fast. To use a satellite connection, a person needs a satellite dish, a modem built into the PC or handheld, and an Internet account. Costs are about $50 per month for

Web Browsers

A Web browser is an application that finds Web pages and displays them on the computer screen. The two most popular browsers are Microsoft's Internet Explorer and Mozilla's Firefox. Internet Explorer currently holds about 90 percent of the browser market.

Internet Protocol Addresses and Universal Resource Locators

Web browsers locate material on the Internet using Internet Protocol (IP) addresses. An IP address works like an Internet phone number. It is a four-group series of numbers separated by periods, such as 207.171.181.16, representing a server on the Internet. Every server connected to the Web can be located using its IP address.

Since remembering IP numbers would be difficult, every computer also has a corresponding Web address called a Uniform (or Universal) Resource Locator (URL). For example, the IP address above is represented by the URL http://www.amazon.com, home page of the pioneering online bookseller Amazon.com.

Viewing Web Pages

A Web page is the term for a single document viewable on the World Wide Web. A Web site comprises all of the Web pages composing the site. The first Web page displayed when a Web site is accessed is usually the site's home page. Like the table of contents in a book, the home page is an overview of the site's information and features.

A special type of Web site is called a portal, or a site that acts as a gateway to access a variety of information. A portal serves as a "launching pad" for users to navigate through categorized Web pages within the same Web site or across multiple Web sites. The U.S. government's FirstGov Web site (http://www.firstgov.gov) is an example of a portal. The majority of the material on the FirstGov site is located on the FirstGov servers, but there are also links to individual federal, state, and local government agency Web sites. The home page for FirstGov contains an overview of the information contained within the site.

Users can access the Internet if they have a wireless network card in their computer and there is a wireless router in range.

the service, plus about $350 for the dish, modem, and installation charges.

Navigating the Internet

Once they are connected and online, the next step for users is to start up a Web browser to begin surfing the Web. To access and move about the Web they need to know how to navigate using a browser, an activity called surfing. It is also helpful to know something about Internet protocol (IP) addresses and Uniform (or Universal) Resource Locators (URLs), and to know how these are used to identify and locate all the resources available on the Internet.

Accessing Information on the Internet

One of the most useful capacities of the Internet is its ability to act like a global library of limitless data on practically any topic. Better still, it doesn't even require a library card or a trip to a university to use it. At present, more than a billion pages of information are available on the Web. In addition, the Internet is opening up different ways to share infromation.

Figure 3 Search Engine Text Boxes and Search Command Buttons

Searching

Users can search for and retrieve information from Web pages by using a search engine. A search engine is a software program that can find and retrieve information located on the World Wide Web. Unlike a browser, in which an address is entered to access a Web site, a search engine allows users to locate information by entering search criteria in the engine's search box. For example, suppose a student wants to find information about the Battle of Vicksburg for a history class report. Typing the search criteria—in this case the words "Battle of Vicksburg"—in the search box, and clicking the *Search* button causes a list of articles, hyperlinked to their respective Web sites, to appear on the student's screen. They can be selected and read by clicking the article title. Figure 3 shows the basic search pages for some of the most frequently used search engines. Each of these pages contains a search text box as well as a search command button.

Search Techniques

One of the primary considerations in any Internet search is placing the right keywords (also called search terms) in a search engine's search text box. Using too many keywords will result in users having to wade through hundreds or even thousands of search results to find what they are looking for. Using vague, obsolete, or incorrectly spelled terms

further reduces the chances of a successful search. Users need to think of what combinations of words are likely to be found in the material they are looking for. To get the most out of a search, a user needs to know how a search engine's advanced search options work.

Peer-to-Peer File Sharing

Peer-to-peer (P2P) file sharing is a relatively recent player among popular ways to use the Internet. P2P allows people to download material directly from other users' hard drives, rather than from files located on Web servers. Napster, the famous pioneer of peer-to-peer file sharing, functioned by maintaining a list of files made available for sharing by subscribers to the system. For example, someone would let Napster know that he had 50 music files on his hard disk that he would be willing to share. Other users could then use Napster to locate these files and request that they be sent to their computers. Newer systems remove the central server entirely and allow user computers with the fastest connections to provide the search function and keep track of which computers have shared a file. Peer-to-peer is a powerful idea that allows every computer to function as a server as well as a client. Figure 4 shows the process of downloading a single file using a peer-to-peer system.

Today's peer-to-peer technologies allow the sharing of any type of file, including games, movies, and software programs. Since Napster, the biggest file-sharing technology has been BitTorrent. Industry research firms estimate that BitTorrent usage accounts for 35 percent of all Internet traffic. Although illegal files may be found and downloaded using BitTorrent, software companies and media companies such as TimeWarner are also embracing the distribution technology as another sales channel.

Using peer-to-peer technologies to harness the individual efforts of millions of computers around the world represents a vast potential for communications. However, with additional access comes increases in security risks.

Internet Telephony

Internet telephony is another increasingly popular way to use the Internet. Through this technology, also called Voice over IP (VoIP), two or more people with sufficiently good connections can use the Internet to make telephone-style calls around the world.

The primary benefit of VoIP service is the elimination of long-distance telephone charges, and some customers are eliminating traditional telephone lines from their homes and making all calls using their VoIP service. In early 2006, there were more than 1,000 providers of VoIP services in the United States. The market leaders include pioneer Vonage as well as high-speed Internet service providers TimeWarner Cable and SBC Communications. The Yankee Group reported that the number of VoIP users will likely reach 28.5 million by 2009, up from 150,000 users in 2003.

Streaming Audio and Video

An alternative to downloading a piece of music or a video is to access it using a technique called streaming (also known as webcasting). Streaming sends a continuous stream of data to the receiving computer where it is immediately played as audio or video. Old data is erased as new data arrives. This protects the owner of copyrighted material to some degree,

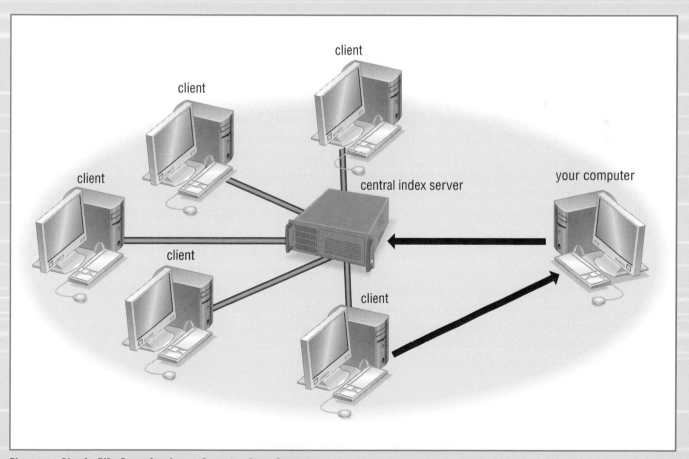

Figure 4 Single File Download on a Peer-to-Peer System

An Internet connection is an important way to stay connected wherever you may be.

as a complete copy of the material is not downloaded, and therefore cannot be copied and shared. High-quality video streaming normally requires a broadband connection such as a cable modem, DSL, or LAN.

Internet2

Internet2 is a research platform for the development of advanced high-speed Internet applications and technologies. A consortium of more than 200 universities working in partnership with industry and government, Internet2 enables large research universities in the United States to collaborate and share huge amounts of complex scientific information at amazing speeds, with the goal of some day transferring those capabilities to the boarder Internet community.

Internet2 provides a testing ground for universities to work together and develop advanced Internet technologies such as telemedicine, digital libraries, and virtual laboratories. An example of such collaboration is the Informedia Digial Video Library (IDVL) project. Once implemented, IDVL will offer a combination of speech recognition, image understanding, and natural language processing technology to automatically transcribe, partition, and index video segments, enabling intelligent searching and navigation, along with selective retrieval of information.

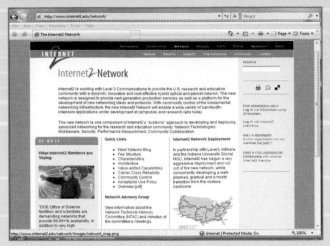

The Internet2 home page at www.internet2.edu is a link to a revolutionary type of Internet that will connect people quicker and more effectively through an ultra-high-speed network.

The Internet2 consortium is currently transitioning from the Abilene backbone to a hybrid optical and packet network provided by Level 3 Communications, capable of supporting speeds of more than 40 Gbps. More can be learned about Internet2 by visiting the project's Web site at www.internet2.edu.

Broadband over Powerline

A new technology that transmits broadband Internet over powerlines has overcome several hurdles and is now being readied for wider use. Broadband over Powerline (BPL) lets an electrical outlet in a BPL-equipped electrical grid serve as a broadband Internet connection using low-cost plug-in adaptors. BPL offers speeds comparable to cable Internet, but differs from cable in offering equal upload and download speeds. Since very electrical outlet is a potential Internet connection, computers in the same home or office can be networked without requiring a router. BPL benefits utility companies as well, letting them monitor line usage as well as allowing remote meter reading.

CHAPTER 5

Application Software

Learning Objectives

> Define application software and provide examples of the different kinds of tasks it can be used for

> Differentiate between the four major types of application software

> Describe the activities that productivity software supports

> Identify examples of software that are used in the household

> Describe the different types of graphics and multimedia software

> Explain how communications software is used

CyberScenario

ERIK TOWNSEND LIVES IN WASHINGTON, North Carolina, and grooms dogs and cats for a living. He has always wanted to complete his college degree, but his work schedule and family obligations made it difficult to enroll in local colleges or universities. After researching online degree programs, Erik decided to enroll at the University of Phoenix to complete a B.S. in Business Management.

Using his high-speed Internet connection, Erik walks through the tutorial for succeeding in University of Phoenix's online programs. He learns that an important task in his first class will be to share an autobiography so other class members can get to know him. Erik opens up his word processing software program and begins typing his student profile, which includes facts and goals about his work, family, and personal experiences. Thinking that he should include a photo, he digs through his online photo album. After finding a good picture, he adjusts the size in his image-editing software, pastes it into his profile, and saves the document.

Erik clicks on a link in his registration e-mail and logs into the school's Web site to enter his first class, Introduction to Management. Just as he expects, there is an assignment from his instructor asking everyone to upload their profile with a picture so that the students in the class can get to know each other. He also sees the breakout of groups for the course and notes that his group is having a webconference the next evening to discuss how to tackle their first project.

After checking the first week's assignments for the course, Erik starts the research for his first paper on teambuilding exercises. He knows he will need to use research databases and other reference sources in the school's online library as well as Internet search engines to find the information he needs.

After additional research and planning, Erik is ready to write a draft of his paper. He uses a word processing program for the text and creates supporting illustrations and charts using presentation graphics software and spreadsheet software. After this week's lecture and discussions, Erik will need only to edit the text and lay out the diagrams and figures using a desktop publishing program.

Different software programs help Erik Townsend make effective use of his most valuable resource—time. He is able to schedule his class work at his convenience, work with members of a group online, edit digital photos, access the resources of a full business school library from his home computer, and prepare documents that look as though a commercial publisher created them. Erik is using software programs to greatly improve his productivity, which is the major purpose of application software for individual use.

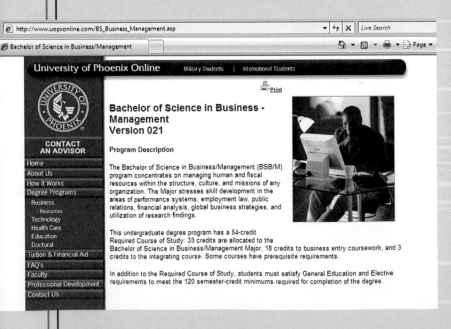

Millions of individuals use application software programs in their daily activities, as do companies, organizations, and government agencies.

Types of Application Software

Application software enables users to perform the types of activities and work that computers were designed for. The specific type of application used depends on the intended purpose, and there are application programs available for almost every need.

Three broad types of application software are available for business users: individual, collaboration, and vertical programs. Table 5-1 displays the different application software categories and their uses.

Individual application software refers to programs individuals use at work or at home. Examples include word processing, spreadsheet, database management, and desktop publishing programs.

Table 5-1 Types of Application Software for Business Users

Business Software Type	Uses
individual application software	create letters, spreadsheets, slide shows, and database reports design and develop publications design Web pages
collaboration software (also called groupware)	collaborate on the development of documents communicate online through instant messaging and e-mail conduct virtual meetings share calendars, image banks, and databases of information track and manage projects generate Web pages
vertical application software	perform core business processes for a particular type of industry software is typically custom-designed

Collaboration software (also called groupware) enables people at separate PC workstations to work together on a single document or project, such as designing a new automobile engine.

Vertical application software is a complete package of programs that work together to perform core business functions for a large organization. For example, a bank might have a mainframe computer at its corporate headquarters connected to conventional terminals in branch offices, where they are used by managers, tellers, loan officers, and other employees. All financial transactions are fed to the central computer for processing. The system then generates managers' reports, account statements, and other essential documents. This type of software is usually custom-built and is frequently found in the banking, insurance, and retailing industries.

Commercial Application Software

Application software is also categorized by its market availability. **Commercial software** is intended for businesses or other organizations with multiple users. Packaged application software is available in the mass market for purchase or lease, whereas customized software is usually developed to meet the special needs of a single company. Because packaged programs have a huge market, they cost much less than a custom program built for one customer.

Packaged Software   **Packaged software** includes programs created and sold to the public on a retail basis by software development companies such as Microsoft, Adobe, and Corel. Both individuals and companies buy commercial software, although businesses typically purchase network versions that can be installed on servers for access by more than one employee.

Many packaged software programs are available from software developers such as Adobe and Peachtree.

Warning: This computer program is protected by copyright law and international treaties. Unauthorized reproduction or distribution of this program, or any portion of it, may result in severe civil and criminal penalties, and will be prosecuted to the maximum extent possible under the law.

OK

System Info...

Tech Support...

Disabled Items...

Software manufacturers usually obtain a copyright that prohibits the illegal copying and distribution of software. Warnings such as this one are designed to remind users of the copyright law.

These products are considered **proprietary software**, meaning that a company or an individual owns the copyright. A license packaged with the software grants the customer or user permission to make a backup copy, but prohibits the distributing of copies to other people. The illegal copying or unauthorized use of copyrighted software is called **software piracy**. By completing and submitting the product registration information, purchasers receive a license from the manufacturer granting them the right to use, but not own, the software. In a network environment, a **site license** provides multiple-user rights. Registering the software provides the benefits of technical assistance and notification of software upgrades.

Packaged software can be obtained from many sources, including manufacturers, computer stores, bookstores, mail-order houses, and the Internet. Programs purchased through a retail source are usually contained on one or more CD-ROMs and come in a box with documentation and a registration card. Programs purchased and downloaded from a Web site typically include online documentation and an electronic registration form that can be e-mailed to the vendor. Many application programs are commercially successful and are periodically upgraded, while others enjoy only brief marketplace popularity and soon disappear.

Customized Software Businesses often have needs that commercial software cannot meet. For example, since payroll data and processing requirements vary among companies, commercial payroll programs may lack certain specialized features. The alternative to purchasing commercial software is to hire programmers to develop software to meet the company's requirements. The resulting software is called **customized software** or a custom program, and is usually owned by the customer. Because of their unique processing requirements, large businesses often maintain a substantial inventory of customized application software programs.

Other Application Software Models

Relatively few software programs were available for purchase when PCs were still in their infancy in the early 1980s. Some programmers began writing software to meet their own needs and made the programs available for free, or for a small fee, usually over the Internet. Others wanted computer users to test their programs and offer suggestions for improvement. This type of software program distribution can be divided into two categories: shareware and freeware.

Tech Demo 5-1
Applications on the Web

Go to this title's Internet Resource Center and read the article titled "Software Licensing Arrangements." www.emcp.net/CUT3e

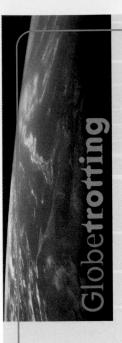

To Stop a Moving Target

HEART SURGERY IS ALWAYS RISKY BUSINESS. It involves opening the chest, stopping the heart, and using an artificial pump to keep the blood flowing throughout the body while the operation proceeds. Another option is to slow down the heart by cooling it, but even the movements of a slowly beating heart can be a steep challenge for a surgeon. Either route is traumatic for the body.

An Englishman has found a way to let the heart keep beating while making it look like it is perfectly still. George Mylonas of Imperial College London has developed motion compensation software that enables a surgeon to operate on a beating heart without even opening the chest cavity.

The software is designed for use with a miniature surgical robot inserted into the patient's chest. The robot's endoscope records real-time images of the heart with its two infrared cameras. The software calculates the changes in focal point as the heart beats, and then synchronizes the endoscope to move exactly with the heartbeats. This creates a 3-D image that appears stationary for the surgeon. The software also moves the robot's instruments back and forth in exact time with the heartbeats to make the needed incisions.

So far the software has been tested only on an artificial heart using a robotic arm, but the future for a heart procedure that is less invasive and easier on the patient looks bright.

Source: Graham-Rowe, Duncan. "Operate on a Heart Without Missing a Beat," *New Scientist*, February 27, 2006. December 2006 <http://www.newscientist.com/article.ns?id=mg18925406.800&print=true>.

Shareware   **Shareware** is software developed by an individual or software publisher who retains ownership of the product and makes it available for a small "contribution" fee. The fee is typically $5 to $50, and is payable only after a user has tried the product and decided to continue using it. The voluntary fee normally entitles users to receive online or written product documentation, new software updates, and technical help. Most shareware developers even encourage users to share the product with others in the hope that they will end up paying for product support, which is how the developers make their money.

Tech Demo 5-2
Shareware and
Freeware

Freeware   **Freeware** is software that is provided free of charge to anyone wanting to use it. Hundreds of freeware programs are available, many written by college students and professors who create programs as class projects or as part of their research. Their motive is altruistic—they want to share their creation with others and are not interested in making a profit. Some freeware programs have become quite widely used, including 123 Free Solitaire, a popular entertainment site, and Ad-Aware, a popular spyware prevention program. Some freeware programs—for example, WebCT—begin as free software but eventually become viable commercial products. WebCT has recently been acquired by Blackboard, another educational and communications software program.

Freeware does have some drawbacks compared with commercial software. Because freeware developers do not charge for their products, they are not obligated to guarantee that the products are error-free. They also may not provide users with documentation or technical help.

Early freeware programs were distributed over electronic bulletin boards and at computer users' club meetings. Now, the Internet provides an almost unlimited market for both shareware and freeware.

Tech Demo 5-3 Installing Applications

Open-Source Software   As discussed in Chapter 4, an open-source software program is software whose programming code is owned by the original developer but made available free to the general public, who is encouraged to experiment with the software, make improvements, and share the improvements with the user community. A software company or individuals may develop open-source software. Other programmers can copy, modify, and redistribute the programming code without paying license fees to the developers. Often, developers and users work together in a cooperative manner to improve the software. Linux, Eclipse, Apache, and Mozilla are some examples of open-source initiatives.

Application Software for Individual Use

The thousands of application programs that individuals use to perform computing tasks at work and at home can be grouped into four types:

- productivity software
- software for household use
- graphics and multimedia software
- communications software

The rest of this chapter will focus on each of these types of application software in more depth.

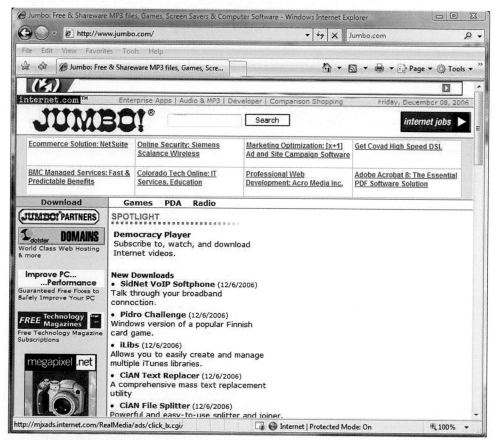

The Jumbo! Web site is one of several Web sites with freeware programs for downloading.

Productivity Software

Productivity software is designed to improve efficiency and performance on the job and at home, and is the largest category of application software for individual use. Employment notices appearing in newspapers and magazines often identify required computer skills, such as word processing or spreadsheet expertise. Some employment notices even specify that an applicant must be certified in a particular application, such as Word, Excel, or WordPerfect. Certified applicants often receive priority consideration over those without such qualifications.

In-depth knowledge and skill in using productivity software applications can make a potential employee more valuable to a business, organization, or agency. Table 5-2 lists productivity software categories and examples and common uses of each group.

Word Processing

A **word processing software** can be used to create almost any kind of printed document. Word processors are the most widely used of all software applications because they are central to communication. Communicating is a skill essential to nearly every business endeavor. At one time computers appealed only to scientists and programmers. Their utility for everyone became evident when they advanced enough to allow the easy creation, editing, saving, and printing of documents. Computers would not play the central role that they do in our society today without their word processing capabilities.

Almost all computers can run word processing software applications, and word processing is probably the easiest application to learn and use. Word processing programs are often available for more than one platform. For example,

Table 5-2 Examples of Productivity Software

Category	Software Example	Common Uses
word processing	Microsoft Word, Corel WordPerfect	write, format, and print letters, memos, reports, and other documents
desktop publishing	PageMaker, QuarkXPress, InDesign	produce newsletters, advertisements, and other high-quality documents
spreadsheet	Microsoft Excel, Lotus 1-2-3, Corel Quattro Pro	produce spreadsheets and manipulate financial and other numerical data
database management	Microsoft Access, Corel Paradox, Lotus Approach	organize and manipulate textual, financial, and statistical records and data
presentation graphics	Microsoft PowerPoint, Corel Presentations, Lotus Freelance	create and display slide shows
software suite	Microsoft Office	link data or share information between individual programs
personal information manager (PIM)	Microsoft Outlook, Palm Desktop	organize calendar, address book, task lists, and notes
project management	Microsoft Project	schedule and manage projects

Microsoft Word and Corel WordPerfect are available for DOS, Windows, and Macintosh computers. Another popular word processor is Lotus Software's Word Pro.

Whatever the type of document created with a word processing program, the essential parts of the procedure remain the same:

- create (enter) text
- edit the text
- format the document
- save and print the file

Creating Text   Creating text refers to the development of a document by entering text, numbers, and graphics using one or more input devices, such as a keyboard or mouse. Documents can be created starting from a blank page, or by using a previously created and stored form called a **template**. A feature called a **wizard** guides a user through a series of steps that allow the user to select content, format, and layout options. For example, with a wizard a user creates template-type documents incorporating specific information about the user, such as company name and address. Both templates and wizards are used extensively in the Microsoft Office and Corel WordPerfect suites.

Word processing is a popular and widely used productivity software application.

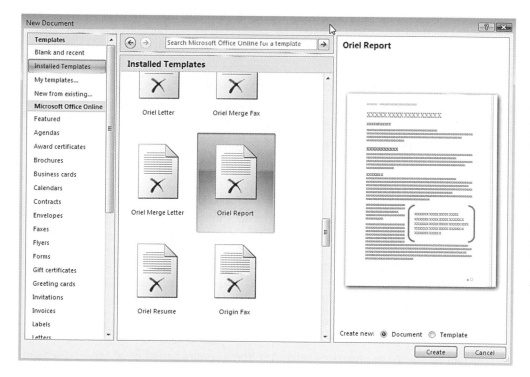

Microsoft Word 2007 contains preformatted templates with specialized formatting that can be adapted to help create professional-looking documents. These templates are accessible through the New Document dialog box. With an active Internet connection, a user can access additional templates through the *Microsoft Office Online* section of this dialog box.

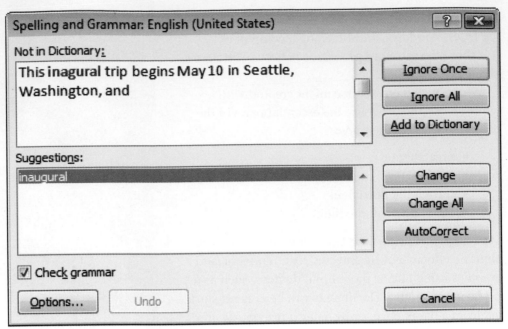

Spelling and Grammar: English (United States)

Not in Dictionary:

This inagural trip begins May 10 in Seattle, Washington, and

Ignore Once
Ignore All
Add to Dictionary

Suggestions:

inaugural

Change
Change All
AutoCorrect

☑ Check grammar

Options...   Undo

Cancel

Microsoft Word 2007, like many word processors, includes a proofing feature that helps to catch misspelled words. Proofreading is still important bcause the spelling checker is not context-sensitive.

Editing Text   The process of altering the content of an existing document is called editing. Editing occurs anytime something is inserted, deleted, or modified within a document. Editing features allow users to make changes until they are satisfied with the content. Perhaps the most valued word processor editing feature is a **spelling checker**, which matches each word in a document to a word list or dictionary. A spelling checker is not context-sensitive. It will not flag words that have been spelled correctly, but used incorrectly—for example, "their" when "there" would have been correct. A **grammar checker** checks a document for common errors in grammar, usage, and mechanics. Grammar checkers are no substitute for careful review by a knowledgeable editor, but they can be useful for identifying such problems as run-on sentences, sentence fragments, double negatives, and misused apostrophes.

Formatting Text   Word processing software allows many different types of formatting, or the manipulation of text to change its appearance at the word, paragraph, or document level. The following features are found in many word processors:

- **Text formatting.** Text formatting features include the ability to change font type, size, color, and style (such as bold, italic, or underlined). Users can also adjust leading (the space between lines) and kerning (the amount of space that appears between letters).
- **Paragraph formatting.** Paragraph formatting changes the way a body of text flows on the page. Features related to the appearance of a paragraph include placing the text in columns or tables; aligning the text left, right, center, or justified within the margins; and double- or single-spacing lines.

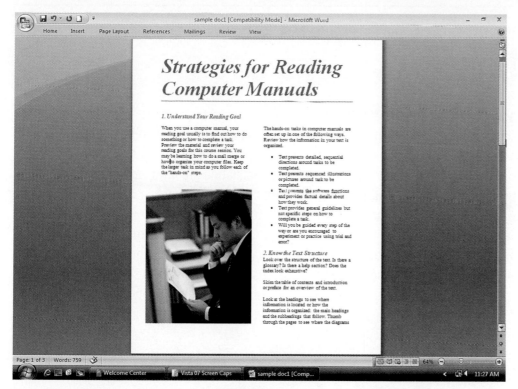

Word processing software include several formatting features that can be applied to words, lines, paragraphs, pages, or entire documents.

- **Document formatting.** Document formatting lets users specify the form of a document as a whole, defining page numbers, headers, footers, paper size, and margin width. A **style** is a special shortcut feature that allows text to be formatted in a single step. Styles allow users to apply text and paragraph formatting to a page, and then automatically apply those same attributes to other sections of text.

Saving and Printing   Storing a copy of the displayed document to a secondary storage medium such as a flash drive or CD is called saving. A saved document (or portion of a document) can be retrieved and reused. Saving a document requires specifying the drive and assigning a file name to the document. The application generally automatically adds the an extension following the file name. The extension identifies the type of file.

Printing means producing a hard copy of a document on another physical medium, such as paper or transparency film. Although most documents are eventually printed, a document may first be sent electronically over a network to another computer, where the receiver may choose to print the document.

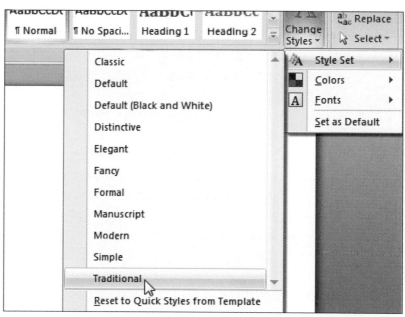

The Microsoft Word 2007 documents contain style sets called Quick Styles. Using this feature, it is possible to apply paragraph and character styles to specific text.

MACPAINT AND HYPERCARD
Bill Atkinson

RARELY DOES A COMPUTER PROGRAMMER achieve the status of a hero, but many computer users have reason to grant heroic status to Bill Atkinson, the legendary programmer who created the first painting program for personal computers, MacPaint. Atkinson's concept for the program, which helped to popularize the first personal computer graphical user interface, was simple and clever: The user was presented with a white screen (a sketchpad) and a set of painting tools, including a paintbrush and a paint bucket. Selecting the paintbrush with the mouse cursor changed the cursor into a brush tip. When the brush tip was moved across the white screen with the mouse button depressed, it turned the pixels beneath it from white to black. By this means, shapes were formed on the screen. Selecting the paint bucket enabled the user to fill an area with a predefined pattern. Later, Atkinson and others developed color versions of painting programs based on the same concept.

Not content to rest with this significant accomplishment, Atkinson initiated a second software revolution by creating Hypercard, a program that enabled users to build customized programs, called stacks, without learning a complex programming language. To develop a program in Hypercard, a user first created a stack of cards, like the cards in an old-fashioned library card catalog, employing painting and text tools to design these cards. The user could then add buttons, icons, and text fields to the cards. The user could apply simple scripts in the HyperTalk scripting language to these objects. These scripts caused the buttons, icons, and text fields to perform such tasks as moving to another card, making mathematical calculations, importing text, animating graphics, and bringing up dialog boxes. Using Hypercard, nonprogrammers were able to create their own programs. Hundreds of thousands of Hypercard programs were created, including tutorials, grade books, statistical analysis applications, and slide shows.

Hypercard is not widely used today, but it was the program that first introduced many personal computer users to the concept of hypertext—pages containing text and graphics that are linked to one another in an associative rather than linear fashion. The same concept is today the basis of the World Wide Web. Hypercard was also ahead of its time because it gave ordinary computer users—people who were not programmers—the ability to assemble their own programs using object-oriented programming, in which user-definable objects, containing both instructions and data, were combined in erector set fashion to produce full-scale applications. In the future, it is likely that successors to Hypercard—programs that enable users to create individualized applications—will be widely used on corporate intranets, on the Internet, and on the network user interfaces that will replace older operating systems. For these reasons, many people consider Atkinson a visionary, one of those rare programmers whose work takes a quantum leap into the future.

Source: Shepherd, Robert D. *Introduction to Computers and Technology*, Paradigm Publishing: October 1997.

Desktop publishing software is used to produce visually appealing newsletters, magazines, and other print products.

Desktop Publishing

Desktop publishing (DTP) software allows users to create impressive documents that include text, drawings, photographs, and various graphics elements in full color. Professional-quality publications can be produced with DTP software. Textbooks such as this one may be designed and laid out with a desktop publishing application such as PageMaker, QuarkXPress, or Adobe InDesign. The completed files are sent to a commercial printer for printing on high-quality paper. The pages are then collated and bound into finished books. Using a page layout program requires extensive training and a background in graphics design.

Major word processors such as Microsoft Word offer a growing selection of desktop publishing features, including the capability of drawing graphics, importing images, formatting text in special fonts and sizes, and laying out text in columns and tables. These features are sufficient for creating simple newsletters, fliers, and brochures. Microsoft Publisher, included in some editions of the Microsoft Office suite, provides more sophisticated desktop publishing elements, including predefined layouts, pull quotes, picture captions, and picture frames.

PageMaker, a feature-rich program from Adobe Systems, Inc., allows users to create a master page that establishes the format of repeating elements on all pages of a publication, such as page numbers and the chapter number and title. The program includes page description features that allow users to determine how each page will look. Graphics can be cropped and placed precisely where they are wanted. When an image is inserted into a publication, PageMaker inserts tiny rectangles at the edges, allowing it to be resized by dragging the rectangles to the desired position.

High-quality color documents like these can be produced using desktop publishing software.

Spreadsheets

Spreadsheet software is an electronic version of the ruled worksheets accountants used in the past. Spreadsheet software provides a means of organizing, calculating, and presenting financial, statistical, and other numerical information. For example, an instructor may use Microsoft Excel to calculate student grades. Other well-known spreadsheet programs include Lotus 1-2-3 and Corel Quattro Pro.

Businesses find spreadsheets particularly useful for evaluating alternative scenarios when making financial decisions. The spreadsheet uses "what if" calculations to evaluate possibilities. For example, company management might ask, "What happens to our profit if our sales increase by 50 percent, or our labor costs decrease by 10 percent?" These types of questions can be answered quickly and accurately by entering a **value** (such as a number) and a mathematical **formula** into a spreadsheet. Calculations are made immediately.

"What if" calculations are used in school and home scenarios as well. A college instructor could show a worried student the test score needed in order to achieve a certain grade. Or, a young couple could determine the effects of various income and savings strategies on their retirement plans. Since the computer does all of the tedious calculations, users can experiment with many different data combinations.

Other common business uses of the spreadsheet include calculating the present value of future assets, analyzing market trends, making projections, and manipulating customer and company statistics.

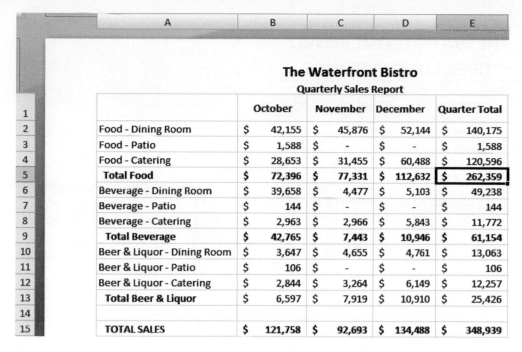

The Waterfront Bistro
Quarterly Sales Report

	October	November	December	Quarter Total
Food – Dining Room	$ 42,155	$ 45,876	$ 52,144	$ 140,175
Food – Patio	$ 1,588	$ -	$ -	$ 1,588
Food – Catering	$ 28,653	$ 31,455	$ 60,488	$ 120,596
Total Food	$ 72,396	$ 77,331	$ 112,632	$ 262,359
Beverage – Dining Room	$ 39,658	$ 4,477	$ 5,103	$ 49,238
Beverage – Patio	$ 144	$ -	$ -	$ 144
Beverage – Catering	$ 2,963	$ 2,966	$ 5,843	$ 11,772
Total Beverage	$ 42,765	$ 7,443	$ 10,946	$ 61,154
Beer & Liquor – Dining Room	$ 3,647	$ 4,655	$ 4,761	$ 13,063
Beer & Liquor – Patio	$ 106	$ -	$ -	$ 106
Beer & Liquor – Catering	$ 2,844	$ 3,264	$ 6,149	$ 12,257
Total Beer & Liquor	$ 6,597	$ 7,919	$ 10,910	$ 25,426
TOTAL SALES	$ 121,758	$ 92,693	$ 134,488	$ 348,939

Many businesses use spreadsheets such as Excel 2007 to record and calculate financial reports.

For the individual user, spreadsheets fulfill many purposes, including:

- preparing and analyzing personal or business budgets
- reconciling checkbooks
- analyzing financial situations
- tracking and analyzing investments
- preparing personal financial statements
- estimating taxes

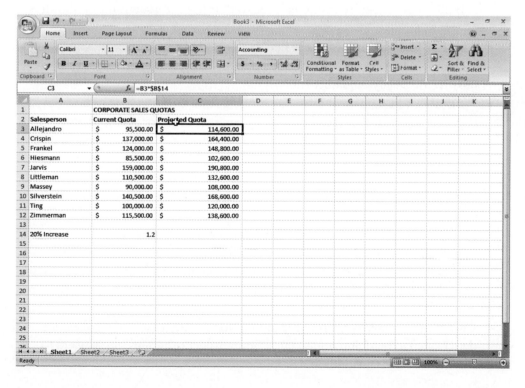

"What if" calculations can be used to evaluate different possibilities. For example, if salesperson Allejandro increases sales by 20 percent, the new quota becomes $114,600. To calculate what happens if Allejandro increases sales by 40 percent, one could simply change the value of field B14 to 1.4.

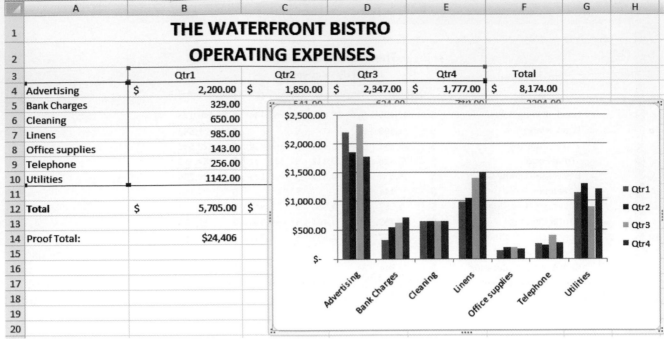

	A	B	C	D	E	F	G	H
1		THE WATERFRONT BISTRO						
2		OPERATING EXPENSES						
3		Qtr1	Qtr2	Qtr3	Qtr4	Total		
4	Advertising	$ 2,200.00	$ 1,850.00	$ 2,347.00	$ 1,777.00	$ 8,174.00		
5	Bank Charges	329.00						
6	Cleaning	650.00						
7	Linens	985.00						
8	Office supplies	143.00						
9	Telephone	256.00						
10	Utilities	1142.00						
11								
12	Total	$ 5,705.00	$					
13								
14	Proof Total:	$24,406						
15								
16								
17								
18								
19								
20								

Microsoft Excel 2007 includes several charting options. These features allow users to present numerical values visually. This 3-D column chart is just one of the chart types Excel supports.

Although spreadsheet programs differ, most offer the following features:

- **Grid.** Spreadshects display numbers and text in a matrix, or **grid**, formed of columns and rows. Each intersection, or **cell**, has a unique address consisting of the column and row designations. Columns are usually identified alphabetically, while rows are numbered. For example, cell address A1 refers to the cell located at the intersection of column A and row number 1.

- **Number formatting.** Numbers may be formatted in a variety of ways, including decimal point placement (1.00, 0.001), currency value ($, £, ¥), or positive or negative quanity (1.00, -1.00).

- **Formulas.** Mathematical formulas ranging from addition to standard deviation can be entered into cells, and they can process information derived from other cells. Formulas use cell addresses, not their contents. For example, a formula might direct a program to multiply cell F1 by cell A4. The formula would then multiply the numerical contents of the two cells. The use of cell addresses means that a spreadsheet can automatically update the result if the value in a cell changes.

- **Macros.** Most spreadsheets allow users to create a **macro**, a set of commands that automates complex or repetitive actions. For example, a macro could check sales figures to see if they meet quotas, and then compile a separate chart for those figures that do not. The macro would automatically perform all the steps required.

- **Charting.** A **chart** is a visual representation of data that often makes the data easier to read and understand. Spreadsheet programs allow users to display selected data in line, bar, pie, or other chart forms.

Database Management

Prior to computers, employee, voter, or customer records were typically placed in file folders and stored in metal cabinets, along with thousands of other folders. Locating a particular folder could prove time-consuming and frustrating, even if the records were stored in an organized manner.

Electronic databases that use appropriate software to manage data more efficiently have replaced many of these manual systems. Although the first electronic databases were developed for large computer systems, today's database software is also available for PCs. Microsoft's Access, Lotus Development's Approach, and Corel's Paradox are among the more popular and best-selling database programs for personal computers.

In a computerized database system, data are stored in electronic form on a storage medium, such as flash drives or CDs. A **database** is a collection of data organized in one or more tables consisting of individual pieces of information, each located in a **field**, and a collection of related fields, each collection making up one **record**. Figure 5-1 shows an example of a table created in a database program. A commercial database program typically allows users to create a form for entering data. A user can design an electronic form to make entering information into the database easier. The information entered using such a form will become a record in a table. Users can add, remove, or change the stored data.

A **database management system (DBMS)** allows users to create and manage a computerized database and to produce reports from stored data. Almost all businesses and organizations use database management systems to manage inventory

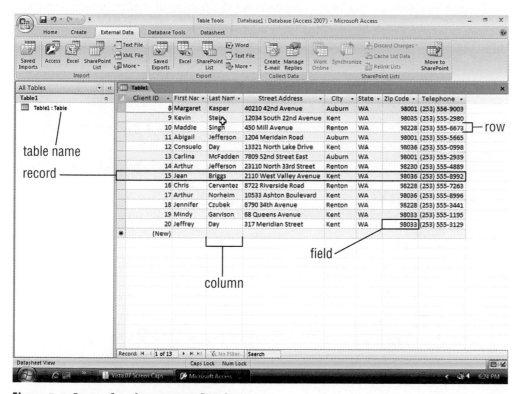

Figure 5-1 Parts of an Access 2007 Database

Within a database program, data are organized into one or more tables, each with its own name. A table consists of columns and rows. A complete row of information is called a record.

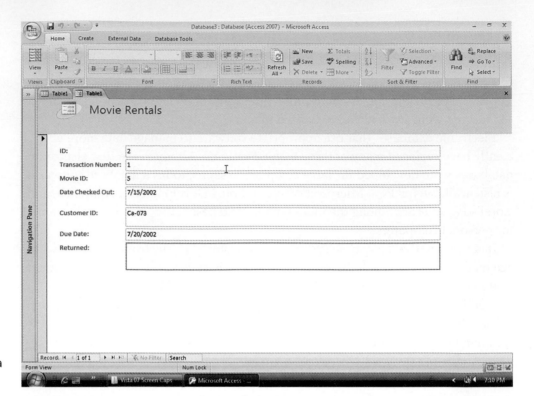

Forms such as this one created in Access 2007 provide an efficient way to enter data into a table.

records, scientific or marketing research data, and customer information. For example, a university collects the data students supply during the course registration process and stores those data in a database. To produce a roll for each class, the DBMS is instructed to locate and retrieve the names of students registered for each course and to insert (in a specified order) the names in a report. The printed report is sent to the instructor.

A report is a selection of data in a database. The user chooses which types of information should be included in the report, and the database automatically finds and organizes the corresponding data.

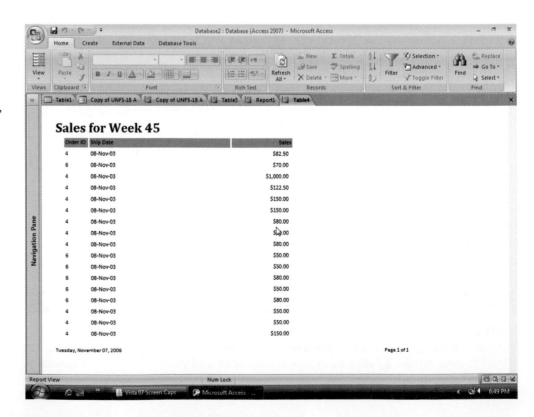

Businesses use database software in much the same way. For example, a business storing customer data in a database can use a DBMS to create and print reports containing the names of customers in specific areas or territories. Sales representatives can use the reports to contact the listed customers.

Although various DBMS programs are available, the most popular type is the **relational database** model. In a relational database, tables can be linked (or related) in a way that allows data to be retrieved from more than one table. Tables are linked through a common data field, such as a product number. Accessing a product number lets users retrieve different kinds of information associated with that number, even though the information may be stored in several different tables in the database.

For example, suppose a potential customer visits an automobile dealer and expresses an interest in buying a blue Chevrolet Corsica. The dealer may have several Chevrolets in stock, but may not know if there is a blue Corsica among them. Using a computerized relational database, the dealer can quickly find the answer by querying (asking) the database, which would then search all linked tables for blue Corsicas. Figure 5-2 illustrates the manner in which separate tables are linked to provide a response to a query.

Database programs typically include the following features:

- **Sort.** Records can be sorted (arranged) in many different ways by using a **sort** feature. For example, records included in a table consisting of cities and ZIP codes for each customer can be sorted alphabetically by record's city name or numerically by the ZIP code.
- **Find.** Information in a table can be located by using **Find** to look up a number or a particular type of text, such as a name or an address.
- **Query.** Searches too advanced for the Find command to handle can be made by using a **query**, or method of asking the database for results. The database

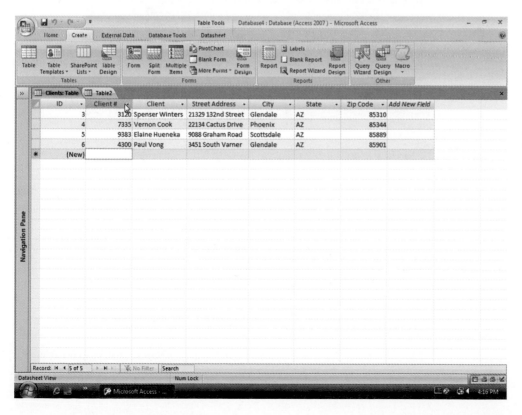

Records in a Clients table created in Microsoft Access 2007 can be sorted in different ways and used to create a report that answers a specific query, or question.

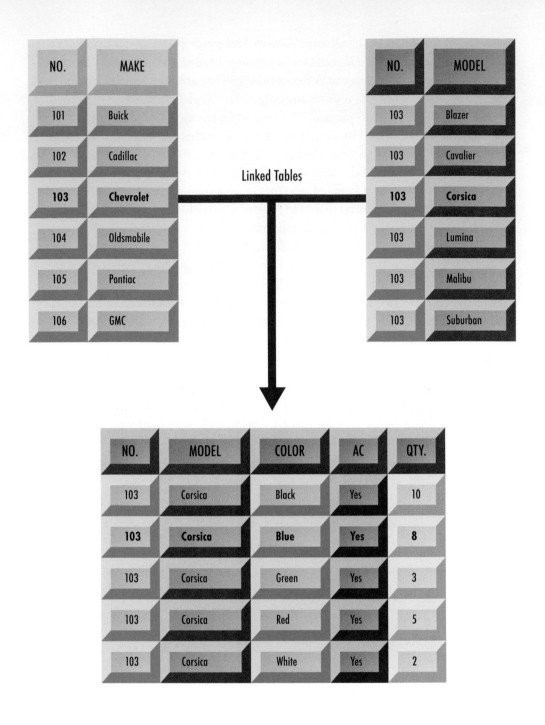

Figure 5-2 Results of a Query to Linked Tables
A relational database allows multiple tables to be linked so that users can retrieve related data from more than one table.

can be queried using **Structured Query Language (SQL)** or **Query by Example (QBE)**. For example, in a table containing many customers in several ZIP codes, a query can be to locate all of the contacts with a specific ZIP code. One of these query methods could be used to search a table for contacts in ZIP code 85889.

- **Links.** Tables can be linked in meaningful ways that make sense for a particular business. For example, for an insurance company, the Clients table could be linked to Claims and Policy List tables.
- **Reports.** Tables can be linked in order to create a **report** of combined information from the linked tables. For example, Client and Policy List tables could be combined to produce invoices for clients.

Presentation Graphics

Anyone who has attended group lectures or presentations knows how boring they can be. One way to make a presentation more interesting is to use presentation graphics software. **Presentation graphics software** allows users to create computerized slide shows that combine text, numbers, animation, graphics, sounds, and videos. A **slide** is an individual document that is created in presentation graphics software. A **slide show** may consist of any number of individual slides. For example, a sales representative may use a slide show to promote products to customers, using the electronic format to feature key components of the product. An instructor may use a slide show to accompany a lecture to make it more engaging and informative. A businessperson may use a slide show to deliver information and present strategies at a meeting. Microsoft PowerPoint and Corel Presentations are two popular presentation software programs.

With presentation graphics software, you can create dramatic slide shows that combine text, graphics, sounds, and videos.

Another advantage of presentation software is that it allows users to easily repurpose information, meaning that the information can be modified to suit different audiences. Other capabilities include being able to import files created in other programs, such as word processors or spreadsheets. This material can then be incorporated within one presentation.

In addition to presenting a slide show via computer, users can also output the presentation as 35 mm slides, transparencies, or hard-copy handouts. A presentation run on a portable computer can be projected onto a screen using a multimedia projector (a self-contained projection unit with a plug-in for a computer) or an LCD panel (a semitransparent projection device that attaches to the computer and sits on top of an overhead projector).

Presentation applications typically include the following features:

- **Wizards.** Most presentation programs offer users a choice of presentation types. After a particular type is chosen, the program provides a wizard to guide the user step by step through the creation of the slide show.
- **Templates.** A predesigned style format, called a template, saves time because the file contains background colors, patterns, and other elements that work well together. Users can also create their own personalized templates.
- **Handouts.** Creating handouts with Microsoft PowerPoint is as easy as selecting an option from the Print dialog box. Handouts can be in outline or note format. It is also possible to create handouts containing graphic reproductions of the slides.

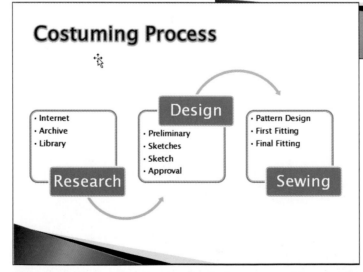

Microsoft PowerPoint 2007 includes many clip art images and charting features that can be integrated into presentations to help make them more interesting.

- **Clip art.** Powerful, attention-grabbing graphics enliven presentations and can sometimes convey messages more effectively than text alone. Presentation programs generally include collections of **clip art** (simple line drawings) that can be inserted into slides. Additional images can be located and imported from other sources, including the Internet and clip art software packages.

Software Suites

Some software vendors bundle and sell a group of software programs as a single package called a **software suite**. Software suites consist of **integrated software programs**. In other words, the individual programs are designed to work well together, with similar interface design and features. Software suites typically include the four most widely used applications: word processing, database management, spreadsheet, and presentation programs. Some, such as Microsoft Office, also include Web page authoring programs since the development of personal Web sites is becoming increasingly important to consumers. Suites are popular because buying one is cheaper than purchasing the component programs separately.

Software suites offer other advantages. Because the programs were developed using the same user interface, all programs in the suite work in a similar manner. Once someone has become familiar with one program, learning to use the others is easier because of the similarity of screen layouts, menus, buttons, icons, and toolbars.

Another strong feature of suites is their ability to seamlessly integrate files from other programs. For example, information produced using a spreadsheet can be placed into a word processing document, or a database table can be imported into a slide show presentation.

One method of moving information from one suite program to another is by copying and pasting. Although quite easy, this method has some disadvantages. For example, if a user created a PowerPoint slide show containing a copied Excel spreadsheet file, the Excel file would need to be recopied each time it is updated with new calculations.

A second method called **object linking and embedding (OLE)** addresses the problem of changing or updating information. It involves creating an object (a table, chart, picture, or text) in one program and then sharing it with another program. Two types of sharing are possible: embedding and linking. Embedding is a type of copying, allowing the embedded file to be changed using the original program's editing features. However, the changes are not reflected in the original file. Using the example in the previous paragraph, a spreadsheet file embedded in the PowerPoint presentation could be edited, but the changes would appear only in the PowerPoint presentation. However, linking the file ensures that any changes made in the original spreadsheet will also be reflected in the PowerPoint presentation.

Personal Information Manager (PIM)

Many PDAs have application software called a **personal information manager (PIM)**. This software helps organize contact information, appointments, tasks, and notes. An increasing number of smartphones also have a PIM. Typically, the PIM also allows this organized information to be synchronized with similar software on a desktop or laptop. This allows users to view and modify the information on a full-size screen. The most common PIMs are Microsoft Outlook and Palm Desktop.

Go to this title's Internet Resource Center and read the article titled "Project Management Software." www.emcp.net/CUT3e

Project management software is widely used to plan construction projects and to track schedules and budgets.

Project Management

Many businesses regularly engage in planning and designing projects, as well as scheduling and controlling the various activities that occur throughout the life of the project. For example, before a construction firm begins erecting a building, it needs to develop a comprehensive plan for completing the structure. During planning, an architect prepares a detailed building design, or set of blueprints. Schedules are then prepared so that workers, building materials, and other resources are available when needed. Once construction begins, all activities are monitored and controlled to ensure that they are initiated and completed on schedule.

Prior to computers, projects like this were planned, designed, scheduled, and controlled manually. Today these tasks are performed using **project management software**. This type of software facilitates the effective and efficient management of complex projects. It can be used for just about any project, including those involving construction, software development, and manufacturing. Microsoft Project is the most prevalent project management software today, helping to optimize the planning of projects and to track schedules and budgets.

Software for Household Use

When browsing computer stores, shoppers are likely to see numerous software applications designed for use in the household. Among the many products available are applications for writing letters, making out wills, designing a new home, landscaping a lawn, preparing and filing tax returns, and managing finances. Software suites are also available for home and personal use, although sometimes the suites available for home use do not contain all the features found in business versions.

More than one-half of U.S. homes now include a personal computer on which a variety of software applications has been installed. Most application software programs are relatively inexpensive. Some vendors advertise popular word processing software for as little as $99, and more organizations are offering open source software versions of popular software titles.

Personal Finance

Personal finance software assists users with paying bills, balancing checkbooks, keeping track of income and expenses, maintaining investment records, and other financial activities. The software also enables users to readily view how their money is being spent.

Some personal finance software provides online services available over the Internet and Web. These services allow users to go online to learn the status of their investments and insurance coverage. They can also conduct normal banking transactions, including accessing and printing bank statements showing monthly transaction summaries. These programs can perform most of the financial activities previously requiring mail or telephone contact.

Personal finance software enables users to manage their money by helping them pay bills, balance checkbooks, keep track of income and expenses, maintain investment records, and other financial activities.

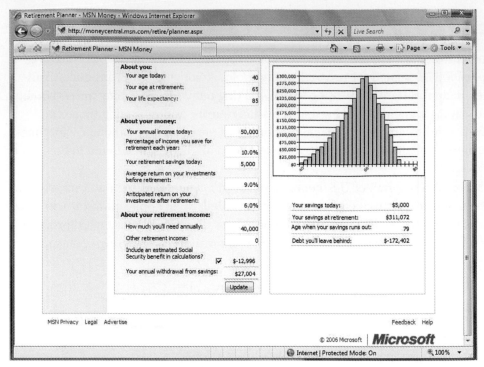

Many personal finance Web sites offer retirement calculators to help individuals determine how much to save to meet their retirement goals.

Tax Preparation

Tax preparation software is designed to aid in analyzing federal and state tax status, as well as to prepare and transmit tax returns. Most of the programs provide tips for preparing tax documents that can help identify deductions, possibly

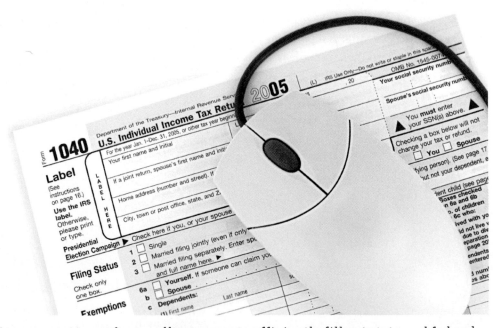

Tax preparation software allows users to efficiently fill out state and federal tax forms and submit them electronically.

resulting in great savings. Some programs include actual state and federal tax forms for entering tax data. Programs that do not include forms provide instructions for downloading them from the software publisher's Web site. Finished tax returns can be printed for mailing or filed electronically. Because federal and state tax laws change frequently, as do tax forms, users will probably need to obtain the software version for the appropriate taxable years or period.

Legal Documents

Legal software is designed to help analyze, plan, and prepare a variety of legal documents, including wills and trusts. It can also be used to prepare other legal documents, such as the forms required for real estate purchases or sales, rental contracts, and estate planning. Included in most packages are standard templates for various legal documents, along with suggestions for preparing them.

The program begins by asking users to select the type of document they want to prepare. In order to complete a document, users may need to answer a series of questions or enter needed information on a form. Once this activity is complete, the software adapts the final document to meet individual needs.

After a document is prepared, it can be sent to the appropriate department, agency, or court for processing and registration. It is always a good

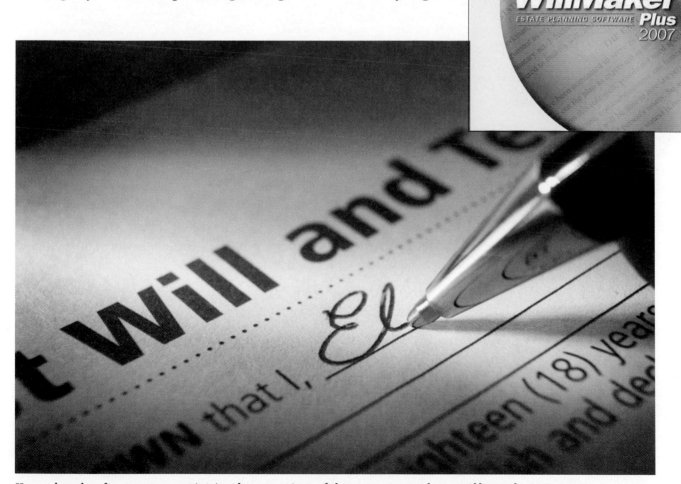

Home legal software can assist in the creation of documents such as wills and contracts.

Entertainment software allows users to enjoy a variety of entertainment experiences, including music and games.

idea to have an attorney review documents to make certain they are correct and legal in the intended state or local jurisdiction.

Games and Entertainment

Entertainment software refers to programs that provide fun as well as challenges. Included in this group are interactive computer games, videos, and music. Versions of Microsoft's Windows operating system come with several popular entertainment programs, including Hearts, Pinball, Solitaire, and Minesweeper.

If a PC is equipped with a CD-ROM drive, users can play music CDs just as they would on a stereo CD player. Music can also be downloaded from commercial and personal Web sites. If a PC is equipped with a DVD drive, users can purchase or rent movies and play them on their computers.

Reference software such as Microsoft Encarta provides information on a huge range of topics.

Educational and Reference Software

The widespread use of home computers has brought about an increase in the availability of educational and reference software, making computers a popular learning and reference tool. Examples of **educational and reference software** include encyclopedias, dictionaries, and tutorials.

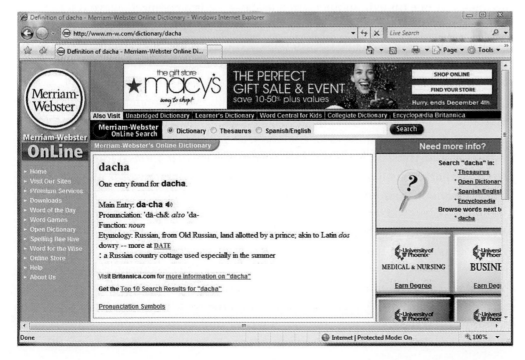

The Merriam-Webster's Collegiate Dictionary in CD form gives users access to terms and definitions in an easy-to-access format.

To Catch a Plagiarist

WARNING TO COLLEGE KIDS: Think twice about using the essay-writing Web sites and online databases for term papers. Antiplagiarism software can fish you out in a nanosecond.

Plagiarism has become an epidemic on college campuses. According to one study, 36 percent of students admit to having plagiarized a written paper at some point in their college career. The causes for this growth of copycat behavior may be varied. Some college students left high school without getting a proper education in using citation for research papers. Today's kids, who file-swap music without a care, have a foggier definition of property ownership. And the Internet, of course, makes finding information and patching it together all too easy.

To combat the misappropriation of the written word, more colleges are turning to software such as Turnitin and MyDropBox.com. These antiplagiarism software programs gen-

erate a "digital fingerprint" of a document that has been electronically submitted. The paper's verbal patterns are cross-checked against a huge database of Internet, newspaper, and encyclopedia archives, as well as previously submitted student work. Suspicious sentences or paragraphs are highlighted, and source matches annotated. The thieving writer is—in seconds—busted.

Students can also use the software as a self-screening tool. And even for classes whose professors do not use this plagiarism-detection software, its very existence acts as a deterrent to students prone to copycat writing.

Antiplagiarism software is also catching the attention of newspaper editors and publishing houses alarmed by recent scandals.

Source: Pilon, Mary. "Anti-plagiarism Programs Look Over Students' Work," *USA Today*, May 22, 2006. December 2006 <http://www.usatoday.com/tech/news/2006-05-22-plagiarism-digital_x.html>.

Go to this title's Internet Resource Center and read the article titled "Computer-Based Learning." www.emcp.net/CUT3e

Encyclopedias and Dictionaries Almost everyone has used an encyclopedia or dictionary at one time or another. An encyclopedia is a comprehensive reference work containing detailed articles on a broad range of subjects. Before computers, encyclopedias were available only in book form. They are now available electronically, usually in CD-ROM format. Many new PCs include a CD-ROM–based encyclopedia, such as *Encyclopaedia Britannica* or Microsoft Encarta.

A variety of dictionaries are available on CD-ROM. A standard dictionary is a reference work containing an alphabetical listing of words, with definitions that provide the word's meaning, pronunciation, and usage. Examples include *Webster's Dictionary* and *Webster's New World Dictionary of Computer Terms*. Other specialized dictionaries, such as multilanguage dictionaries, contain words along with their equivalent in another language for use in translation.

Tutorials Many people learn new skills by using CD- or Internet-based tutorials. A **tutorial** is a form of instruction in which students are guided step by step through the learning process. Tutorials are sometimes referred to as computer-based training or Web-based training. Tutorials are available for almost any subject, including learning how to assemble a bicycle, use a word processor, or write a letter. Once an electronic tutorial is accessed, students need only follow the instructions displayed on the screen. Many tutorials include graphics to help guide students during the

Tutorials guide users step by step through the learning process using graphics, text, and audio media, such as the online tutorials that provide instructions on using an iPod.

learning process. Software manufacturers often provide tutorials for training users in the application of software products, such as their word processors, spreadsheets, and databases. The goal is to help users acquire skill in using the manufacturer's product, in the hope that this will entice users to make a purchase.

Graphics and Multimedia Software

Graphics and multimedia software allows both professional and home users to work with graphics, video, and audio. A variety of application software is focused in this area, including painting and drawing software, image-editing software, video and audio editing software, Web authoring software, and computer-aided design (CAD) software.

Painting and Drawing Software

Painting and drawing programs are available for both professional and home users. The more expensive professional versions typically include more features and greater capabilities than do the less expensive personal versions.

With a **painting program**, a user can create images in bit-map form and also color and edit an image one bit at a time. Microsoft Paint is an example of a popular painting program. A **drawing program** enables a user to create images that

CODEVELOPER OF VISICALC
Dan Bricklin

HAVING WORKED ON PROGRAMMING for an online calculator and a word processing program for DEC, Bricklin understood how useful computers could be in business, but his classroom experience also showed him their limitations and inefficiencies. Students had to learn to perform calculations for business spreadsheets manually, inserting new figures for everything from labor costs to shipping, then recalculating the effect of each change on the bottom line. The process was tedious and every new calculation was an opportunity for mistakes that could lead to serious business errors.

Out of his frustration with the tasks and his certainty that there must be a better way to do it, Bricklin began to develop a software program that would do for numbers what word processing did for words—enable the user to insert and delete data and to see an immediate change in the results.

Bricklin joined up with Bob Frankston, his friend from MIT, and together they began to turn Bricklin's basic ideas into a commercially viable product. Founding a company called Software Arts in 1978, Bricklin worked on the functional design and documentation of the new software while Frankston wrote the programming. By the fall of 1979 a version of their program was ready. The program was called VisiCalc, short for Visual Calculation. Almost immediately, VisiCalc became a huge commercial success and the foundation for the development of a long line of spreadsheet programs that followed.

VisiCalc had a major impact in two ways. First, it allowed businesses to redistribute costs and revenues on a trial basis to see immediately how the changes would affect the bottom line. The second impact was on the computer industry itself. For the fledgling Apple Computer Company, VisiCalc was a tremendous boost because the first version was written to run on the Apple II, and people bought the computer just so they could run VisiCalc. The reputation of VisiCalc as a serious business application did much to establish the PC as a legitimate business computer. In 1985, Lotus Software purchased Software Arts.

Bricklin continues making contributions in the computing field. With his present venture, called Trelix, Bricklin helps individuals and businesses create and edit Internet projects.

can be easily modified. The size of a drawn image can be decreased without a reduction in image resolution. However, increasing the size may result in a loss of resolution quality. Popular drawing programs used in professional environments include CorelDRAW, Adobe Illustrator, and Macromedia FreeHand.

Both painting programs and drawing programs provide an intuitive interface through which users can draw pictures, make sketches, create various shapes, and edit images. Programs typically include a variety of templates that simplify painting or drawing procedures. Once finished, a painting or drawing can be imported into other documents, such as personal letters, signs, business cards, greeting cards, and calendars.

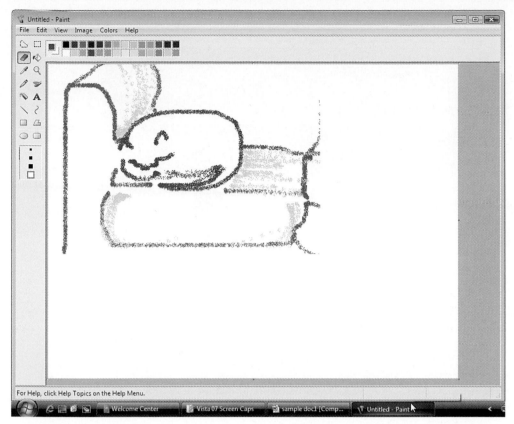

A painting program allows a user to create images and to color and edit an image one bit at a time. Once finished, a painting or drawing can be imported into other documents.

Image-Editing Software

The market demand for image-editing programs has increased concurrently with the popularity of digital cameras. An **image-editing program** allows a user to touch up, modify, and enhance image quality. Editing features include changing color, cropping, resizing, applying special features, and eliminating red-eye effects from photographs. Once edited, images can be stored in a variety of formats and inserted into other files, such as letters, advertisements, and electronic scrapbooks. Microsoft Digital Image Suite is reasonably priced software for home users, while Adobe Photoshop is more expensive software that professionals use more often.

Video and Audio Editing Software

As digital video cameras and other portable technologies have become more common, users have desired the ability to create and modify recorded video and audio clips using **video and audio editing software**. To create DVDs, CDs, or digital video or audio files, home users can often use basic video and audio editing software contained within their computer's operating system. Some users prefer the additional features of an application software package such as Pinnacle Studio MovieBox. Professionals use more expensive, feature-rich software such as Sony's Vegas or Sound Forge for editing audio and video.

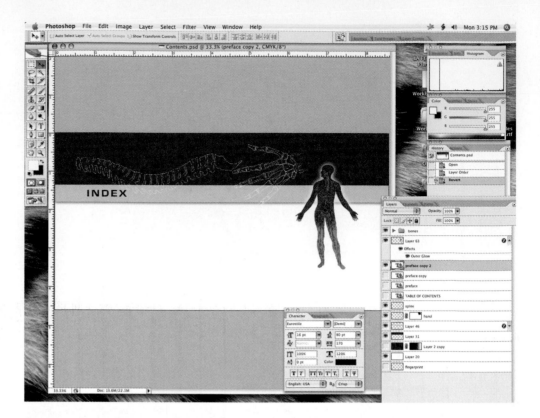

Adobe Photoshop is a popular image-editing program that provides numerous tools for editing an image.

Web Authoring Software

Web authoring software helps users develop Web pages without learning Web programming. Software packages such as Macromedia DreamWeaver and Microsoft Expression Web use a **WYSIWYG** (what you see is what you get) approach to Web page development. This means that during the development process, the layout and content of the actual Web page can be seen within the Web authoring software. Software such as Macromedia Flash and Macromedia Fireworks allows users to add interactive graphics and animation to Web pages.

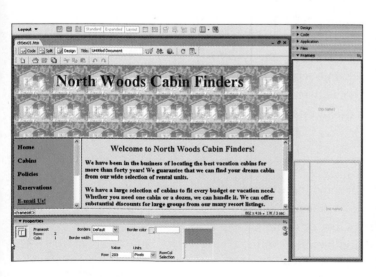

Web authoring software allows a user to create Web pages without learning Web programming. A user can add and edit text, photographs, sound and video for Web pages.

Computer-aided Design Software

Computer-aided design (CAD) software is a sophisticated kind of drawing software, providing tools that enable professionals to create architectural, engineering, product, and scientific designs. Engineers can use the software to design buildings or bridges, and scientists can create graphical designs of plant, animal, and chemical structures. Some software programs display designs in three-dimensional form so they can be viewed from various angles. Once a design has been created, changes can easily be made until it is finalized.

An aircraft engineer designing a new type of aircraft can use CAD software to test many design versions before the first prototype is built. This process can save companies considerable time and money by eliminating defective designs before beginning production.

Full-feature CAD programs are very expensive. Some producers of CAD software offer scaled-down versions of their more expensive software for use by small businesses, and for individual and home use.

Computer-aided design software is used to create designs for buildings, bridges, and commercial products.

Communications Software

One of the major reasons people use computers is to communicate with others and to share information. Software that enables communication over the Internet and the Web is available for individual, home, and business use. This software allows users to send and receive e-mail, browse and search the Web, engage in group communications and discussions, and participate in webconferencing activities.

Electronic Mail

Electronic mail (e-mail) is rapidly becoming the main method of communication for many individual, home, and business users. **E-mail** is the transmission and receipt of electronic messages over a worldwide system of communications networks. The real value of e-mail lies in its speed and low cost. Messages can be sent and received within seconds or minutes, and transmission costs are minimal.

Sending and receiving e-mail requires the use of special software called an e-mail client or simply a Web browser. Some of the more common e-mail clients are Microsoft Outlook Express, Mozilla Thunderbird, and Eudora. Web-based e-mail services such as Yahoo! Mail, MSN Hotmail, and GMail require a Web browser pointed at a Web address (or URL).

Preparing an e-mail message is similar to preparing a word processing document. Users can create, edit, spell-check, print, and store messages. In addition, the software allows users to send, receive, and delete messages and maintain contact address information within the program. Most e-mail software will notify users when a message has been received.

Go to this title's Internet Resource Center and read the article titled "Collaboration Software Trends." www.emcp.net/CUT3e

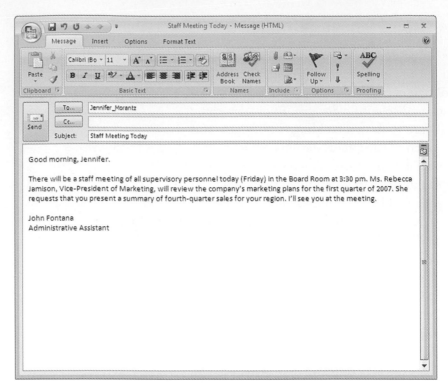

E-mail is a fast and efficient way of communicating with other computer users.

Web Browsers and Search Engines

Recall that Web browsers, also called browsers, allow users to move from one location to another on the Web, and to access and retrieve Web pages. Web browsers use a GUI that can retrieve and display Web pages containing graphics, pictures, and other high-resolution text and images.

Text messaging allows people to send quick, short messages via cell phones.

Most browsers provide for sending and receiving e-mail messages, participating in chat groups, and maintaining a listing of favorite Web sites and pages. The two most popular browsers are Microsoft's Internet Explorer and Mozilla's Firefox.

A **search engine** is used to search, locate, and retrieve information from various Web sites. Among the more popular search engines are Yahoo!, WebCrawler, Google, and AltaVista. Users can access these programs by typing the search engine Internet address in the browser address box.

Instant Messaging Software

Instant messaging (IM) software is a technology that enables people to communicate with other users over the Internet in real time. Several IM services are available, including AIM, MSN, Yahoo!, and Jabber. Although the industry is working on IM standards, not all IM software is compatible with other IM services. Instant messaging can be used on all types of devices, including PCs, handheld

A Web browser allows users to move from one location to another on the Web, and to locate and retrieve information.

computers, notebook computers, and Web-enabled cell phones or smartphones. PCs, handheld computers, and notebook computers require the instant messaging software to be installed, whereas cell phones and smartphones typically have built-in messaging capabilities. Subscribers to instant messaging services must have instant messaging software installed on their computers.

Tech Demo 5-4
PDA Applications

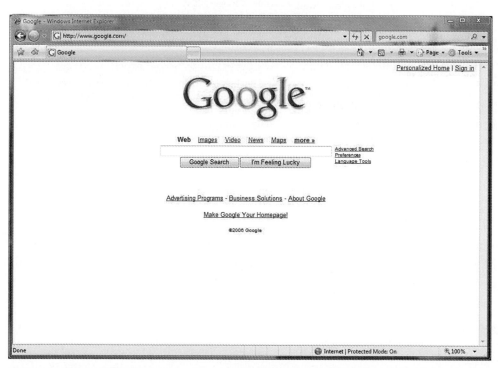

The Google search engine (www.google. com) is a popular tool for finding information on a specific topic on the Internet.

Can You Meet Me Now?

FOR THE COLLEGE KID WHO IS HUNGRY— right here, right now—and doesn't want to eat alone, MoSoSo can make it happen.

MoSoSo stands for Mobile Social Software, and it's the logical extension of social networking services on the Web. Accessible from either a mobile phone or a laptop, MoSoSo weaves time and location into digital networking. MoSoSos typically cater to the tech-savvy, in-the-moment youth market.

For example, the MoSoSo software at Dodgeball.com combines 15,000 users in 22 cities with a database of hundreds of bars and nightclubs. Users will get a message notifying them of any other users within ten blocks. It also provides a "crush" feature, where users can be notified of the proximity of a member whose profile has piqued their interest. Similarly, Playtxt is a cell-phone service using MoSoSo that connects users with similar music and sports interests within their ZIP code.

The hitch with MoSoSo applications is that they require critical mass to catch on. If users log on repeatedly without getting any results, they'll quickly lose interest. That's where Roger Desai is ahead of the game. His start-up, Rave Wireless, has made the campus connection. He's found the perfect market—thousands of students condensed in one area, all with cell phones and computers, all needing to know the location of tonight's kegger.

Students can get updates on what's happening through both text messaging and mobile Internet browsing combined with a GPS system. They simply type in "moods" such as *hungry*, *bored*, or *studying*, and will immediately connect with other like-minded students.

Rave Wireless features also allow students to track in real time more pragmatic college-life information such as bus schedules, library resources, or schedule changes. The service also can act as a personal alarm, alerting 911 to the location of a student in distress. In fact, the software is so appealing to administrators on campuses that one in five universities using Rave Wireless actually require students to have the software on their cell phones.

Sources: "MoSoSo," *Wikipedia*, <http://en.Wikipedia.org/wiki/MoSoSo>; "Campus Wireless Rave," *Red Herring*, June 5, 2006. December 2006 <http://www.redherring.com/Article.aspx?a=17123&hed=Campus+Wireless+Rave>; Terdiman, Daniel. "MoSoSos Not So So-So," Wired, March 8, 2005. December 2006 <http://www.wired.com/news/culture/0,1284,66813,00.html>; Kharif, Olga, and Peter Elstrom. "Connections, the Wireless Way," *Business Week*, June 29, 2005. December 2006 <http://www.businessweek.com/technology/content/jun2005/tc20050629_3438_tc024.htm>; Home page, *Rave Wireless*. December 2006 <http://www.ravewireless.com>.

Once members are signed up with an instant messaging service, they can exchange messages or files and use the service to participate in chat groups. Some IM services will notify members of an incoming message and also provide financial news, stock quotes, appointments, weather updates, and other practical information.

Groupware

Groupware, also called collaboration software, allows people to share information and collaborate on various projects, such as designing a new product or preparing employee manuals. Groupware can be used over a local area network (LAN), wide

Groupware, also called collaboration software, allows people to share information and collaborate on various projects, such as designing a new product or preparing employee manuals.

area network (WAN), or the Internet. All group members must be using the same groupware programs to collaborate on projects.

Most groupware includes an address book of members' contact information and an appointment calendar. One of the most desirable features of groupware is a scheduling calendar that allows each member to track the schedules of the other members. This makes it possible to coordinate activities and to arrange meetings to discuss project activities and other matters.

Webconferencing

A **webconference** is an online meeting between two or more participants at different locations using computer networks and **webconferencing software** to transmit electronic information. Participants share presentations, diagrams, documents, and spreadsheets within webconferencing software. They may also use special features in the software such as an electronic whiteboard and marker, highlighting, and instant messaging. For audio, participants will use either Internet voice capabilities or a phone line.

Because it saves time and travel expenses, many businesses are promoting the use of webconferencing software over face-to-face meetings. Most webconferenc-

Webconferencing software enables meeting participants to communicate and share information over long distances as though the participants are in the same room.

ing software is Web-based and just requires a browser on each participant's computer. WebEx, Centra, MeetingPlace, and Microsoft Office Live Meeting are some examples of webconferencing software currently in use.

OnThe**Horizon**

INSPIRED BY BREAKTHROUGHS in processing technology and changing market needs, software developers are continually brainstorming new programs or improvements to existing software. Some of today's leading-edge technologies allow us to make educated guesses about digital applications that soon may be standard-issue.

Automatic Multimedia Tagging Software

Tags are keyword descriptions that can be attached to multimedia files in order to assist in identifying and retrieving the files at a later date. For example, an image of a lakeside cabin with people standing in front of it might be tagged with "cabin," "people," and "lake." Tag creation is currently a time-consuming manual process, but an EU-supported project is working on automating this task. The proposed system would use a combination of imaging technology and analytical tools to scan through files in order to identify content and automatically create the appropriate tags, and will work with both still and moving images. The concept has proved viable, and efforts to expand system capabilities are ongoing.

Advances in Speech Recognition Software

Several hardware devices and productivity applications currently incorporate speech recognition software. Although much improved compared with earlier attempts, the present speech recognition technologies have yet to meet the high accuracy transcription demanded by industries such as medicine. The proliferation of Web-enabled handheld computers indicates a trend of continuing improvements in speech recognition, simply because of rising market demand.

IBM has pioneered a technology called speech biometrics, which may provide one of the significant advances. The goal of IBM's Super Human Speech Recognition Initiative is to perform better than a human in transcribing speech in memos, customer service calls, and meeting minutes.

This type of technology is also suited for identification and verification needs, such as those required during Internet purchases. The technology works by comparing voices with a database of voices of known speakers. The software is able to recognize voices even though the database may not include the exact words spoken.

A related technology called natural-language processing (NLP) has advanced to the stage where systems can understand the conversations of a five-year-old child. A number of challenges remain, but if NLP software can live up to its potential and accurately recognize adult speech, it will revolutionize personal and business communications.

Pattern Recognition Software

Pattern recognition is a branch of artificial intelligence (AI) that compares data with previous information or extracts statistical data to form a new model for information. The security implications of pattern recognition have focused interest on this technology in the wake of 9/11, and it is employed in a number of different fingerprint and facial identification systems currently in use. Pattern recognition also forms the basis for spam filters used to differentiate legitimate e-mail messages from spam.

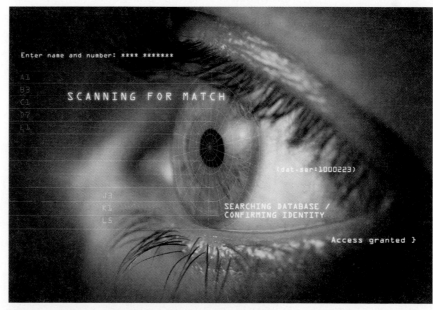

Retinal scanning can be used with pattern recognition software to confirm a person's identity.

Distributed Computing

Software designers are picturing a future in which software programs consist of groups of services available through the Internet, rather than from CD-ROMs. The first generation of companies offering these programs were called application service providers (ASPs), and though their vision held great promise, market enthusiasm for the idea cooled in 2000.

The next generation of software as services will be offered in the distributed computing model; computer industry giants IBM, Microsoft, and Sun Microsystems are leading the quest. Based on an open set of standards and protocols, the distributed computing model combines the power of an almost limitless number of computers over the Internet. Distributed computing is often called grid computing, as well, particularly in reference to some of the huge, scientific research projects that have been launched in recent years. SETI@Home, for example, is a project in which home computer users donate overnight usage of their systems to search for signs of intelligent life beyond our planet. Special software recognizes times when the computer is idle and uses that time toward the project. Industry experts estimate that the SETI@Home project has amassed the effect of thousands of years of computing power, simply by harnessing idle PC processing time.

Recently, computer industry leaders have adapted the distributed computing technology for the business world by developing distributed computing software that allows the pooling and sharing of resources over the Net. Possible applications are limitless, but the more pragmatic ones include actuarial analysis, processing of financial market trades, generation of extremely detailed engineering drawings, and scientific simulations. In effect, companies create virtual organizations to share data and computing, as well as human brainpower and resources. The end result is enormous cost savings and skyrocketing productivity.

Chapter**Summary**

 For an interactive version of this summary, go to this text's Internet Resource Center at www.emcp.net/CUT3e. A Spanish version is also available.

What is application software?

Application software performs the types of activities and work that computers were designed for. **Individual application software** refers to programs used by individuals. **Collaboration software** enables people at separate PC workstations to work together. **Vertical application software** is a complete package of programs for performing core business functions.

Commercial software refers to programs intended for businesses or other organizations with multiple users. **Packaged software** includes programs created and sold to the public on a retail basis by software development companies. **Proprietary software** is copyrighted software owned by a company or an individual. Software developed to meet special business needs is called **customized software**. **Software piracy** involves the illegal copying or unauthorized use of copyrighted software. **Shareware** is software available for a small "contribution" fee. **Freeware** is software provided for free. Open source software is software whose programming code is owned by the original developer but made available free to the general public, who is encouraged to experiment with the software, make improvements, and share the improvements with the user community.

How is productivity software used?

Productivity software is designed to improve efficiency and performance on the job. **Word processing software** can be used to create almost any kind of printed document. **Desktop publishing (DTP) software** allows the creation of professional-looking printed documents. **Spreadsheet software** provides a means of organizing, calculating, and presenting financial, statistical, and other numeric information. A **database** is a collection of data organized in one or more tables containing **records**.

A commercial database program usually allows users to create forms for entering data into a database. A **database management system (DBMS)** allows users to create and manage a computerized database and to create reports. A **relational database** allows tables to be linked in a way that allows data to be retrieved from more than one table. **Presentation graphics software** lets users create computerized **slide shows**. **Software suites** are software programs bundled and sold as a single package. A personal information manager (PIM) is software that helps users organize contact information, appointments, tasks, and notes. **Project management software** assists with the management of various kinds of complex projects.

What types of application software are used in the household?

Many of the productivity programs used on the job are also used by individuals on their home computers. **Personal finance software** can help users manage their money. **Tax preparation software** helps users prepare and transmit tax returns. **Legal software** is designed to analyze, plan, and prepare a variety of legal documents. **Entertainment software** refers to a large group of software programs that provide fun and often challenge users' thinking abilities as well. The widespread use of home computers has brought about an increase in the availability of **educational and reference software** such as encyclopedias, dictionaries, and tutorials. A **tutorial** is a form of computerized instruction in which the student is guided step by step through the learning process.

What are examples of graphics and multimedia software?

Graphics and multimedia software allows users to work with graphics, video, and audio files. **Painting programs** allow users to create images in bit-map form and also to color and edit an image one bit at a time. **Image-editing programs** allow a user to touch up, modify, and enhance image quality. **Video and audio editing software** allows users to create and modify recorded video and audio clips. **Web authoring software** helps users develop

Web pages without learning Web programming. **Computer-aided design (CAD) software** provides tools that enable professionals to create architectural, engineering, product, and scientific designs.

How can application software make communicating easier?

One of the main purposes for which people use computers is to communicate with others and to retrieve and share information. **E-mail** is the transmission and receipt of messages over a worldwide system of communications networks. Web browsers allow users to move from one location to another on the Web, and to access and retrieve Web pages. **Search engines** find information located on Web sites. **Instant messaging (IM) software** allows users to communicate with each other in real time. **Groupware** allows people to share information and collaborate on various projects. A **webconference** is an online conference between two or more participants at different sites, using computer networks and **webconferencing software**.

KeyTerms

Numbers indicate the pages where terms are first cited in the chapter. An alphabetized list of key terms with definitions (in English and Spanish) can be found on the Encore CD that accompanies this book. In addition, these terms and definitions are included in the end-of-book glossary.

Types of Application Software
application software, 203
individual application softw are, 203
collaboration software (groupware), 204
vertical application software, 204
commercial software, 204
packaged software, 204
proprietary software, 205
software piracy, 205
site license, 205
customized software (custom program), 205
shareware, 206
freeware, 206

Productivity Software
productivity software, 208
word processing software, 208
template, 209
wizard, 209
spelling checker, 210
grammar checker, 210
style, 211
desktop publishing (DTP) software, 213

value, 214
formula, 214
spreadsheet software, 216
grid, 216
cell, 216
macro, 216
chart, 216
database, 217
field, 217
record, 217
database management system (DBMS), 217
relational database, 219
sort, 219
find, 219
query, 219
Structured Query Language (SQL), 221
Query by Example (QBE), 221
report, 221
presentation graphics software, 221
slide, 221
slide show, 221
clip art, 223
software suite, 223
integrated software program, 223
object linking and embedding (OLE), 223
personal information manager (PIM), 223
project management software, 224

Software for Household Use
personal finance software, 225
tax preparation software, 226
legal software, 227
entertainment software, 228

educational and reference software, 229

tutorial, 230

Graphics and Multimedia Software

graphics and multimedia software, 231

painting program, 231

drawing program, 231

image-editing program, 233

video and audio editing software, 233

Web authoring software, 234

WYSIWYG, 234

computer-aided design (CAD) software, 235

Communications Software

e-mail, 235

search engine, 236

instant messaging (IM) software, 236

groupware (collaboration software), 238

webconference, 239

webconferencing software, 239

Chapter**Exercises**

 The following chapter exercises, along with new activities and information, are also offered in the Internet Resource Center for this title at www.emcp.net/CUT3e.

Tutorial > **Exploring Windows**

In Tutorial 5, you will learn to use the computer window to browse the contents of your computer's hard drive.

Expanding Your Knowledge > **Articles and Activities**

 Visit the Internet Resource Center for this title at www.emcp.net/CUT3e, read the articles related to this chapter, and complete the corresponding activities. The article titles include:

- Topic 5-1: Software Licensing Arrangements
- Topic 5-2: Project Management Software
- Topic 5-3: Computer-Based Learning
- Topic 5-4: Collaboration Software Trends

Terms Check > **Matching**

 For additional quiz practice, go to the Internet Resource Center for this title at www.emcp.net/CUT3e for a chapter crossword puzzle.

On the next page, write the letter of the correct answer on the line before each numbered item.

a. software piracy

b. database

c. software suite

d. legal software

e. word processing software

f. proprietary software

g. presentation graphics software

h. productivity software

i. tutorial

j. application software

____ 1. A collection of data organized in one or more tables consisting of fields and records.

____ 2. Software produced and owned by a business and offered for purchase or lease.

____ 3. A form of instruction in which students are guided step by step through the learning process.

____ 4. Software designed to enhance efficiency and performance in the workplace.

____ 5. The illegal copying or unauthorized use of copyrighted software.

____ 6. Software used to create documents such as wills, trusts, or rental contracts.

____ 7. A software program used to create slide shows.

____ 8. A broad category of software that allows users to perform tasks such as creating documents or preparing income tax returns.

____ 9. The most widely used of all software applications.

____ 10. A group of productivity programs bundled and sold as a single package.

Technology Illustrated > Identify the Process

What process is illustrated in this drawing? Identify the process and write a paragraph describing it.

No.	Make	No.	Model	No.	Color
101	Chevrolet	102	Taurus	102	Beige
102	Ford	102	Mustang	102	Red
103	Buick	102	Thunderbird	102	Green
104	Chrysler	102	F-150	102	Silver

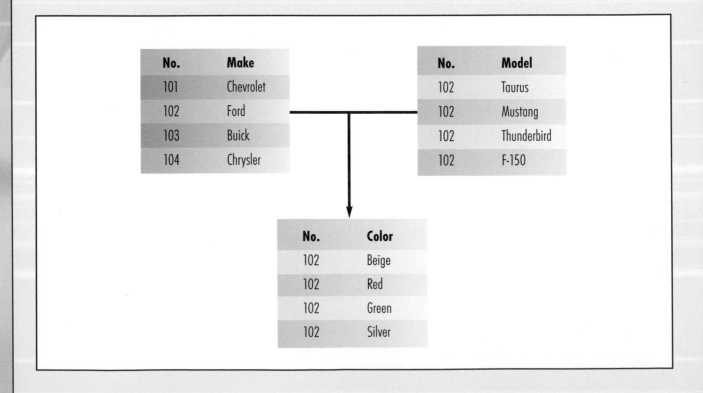

Knowledge Check > Multiple Choice

 Additional quiz questions are available on the Encore CD that accompanies this book as well as on the Internet Resource Center for this title at www.emcp.net/CUT3e.

Circle the letter of the best answer from those provided.

1. Software that enables users to perform the types of activities and work computers were designed for is called
   a. working software.
   b. tutorial.
   c. system software.
   d. application software.

2. Software used to create professional-quality publications is called
   a. a desktop publishing (DTP) software.
   b. a word processor.
   c. application software.
   d. print software.

3. A previously created and stored form is called a(n)
   a. user form.
   b. program form.
   c. electronic form.
   d. template.

4. A word processor editing feature that checks a document for common errors in grammar, usage, and mechanics is called a(n)
   a. spelling checker.
   b. grammar checker.
   c. English checker.
   d. syntax checker.

5. The transmission and receipt of messages over a worldwide system of communications networks is called
   a. e-mail (electronic mail).
   b. file transfer.
   c. telnet.
   d. electronic communication.

6. Software versions of the ruled worksheets accountants used in the past are called
   a. accounting software.
   b. worksheet software.
   c. electronic spreadsheets.
   d. financial software.

7. A collection of data organized in one or more tables consisting of fields and records is known as a(n)
   a. electronic spreadsheet.
   b. raw data.
   c. composite information.
   d. database.

8. A group of software programs bundled into a single package is called
   a. combination software.
   b. a software suite.
   c. a special package.
   d. a software collection.

9. A communication method that enables people to communicate over the Internet with other users in real time is called
   a. real-time processing.
   b. electronic telephoning.
   c. instant messaging.
   d. electronic messaging.

10. Software that allows people to share information and collaborate on various projects, such as developing a new product, is called
    a. collaboration software.
    b. groupware.
    c. shareware.
    d. developmental software.

Things That Think > **Brainstorming New Uses**

In groups or individually, contemplate the following questions and develop as many answers as you can.

1. Many application software programs feature wizards. Wizards assist with tasks by prompting users to enter data and then automatically performing the needed functions. Microsoft PowerPoint is one example of a program featuring wizards that guide users through the process of creating a slide show. Discuss some of the software programs you are familiar with and come up with ideas for wizards that might make the software even more user-friendly. Are there any types of situations where you would not want a wizard to assist you? If so, describe them.

2. Encyclopedias have moved from the printed page to the electronic age in the space of less than 10 years. Electronic encyclopedias offer extra features that the printed versions could not. Users can learn about subjects by watching videos, by viewing three-dimensional images, or by listening to sound or music. Another convenience is the ability to instantly view related material using hyperlinks. The same features can and are being used to develop electronic textbooks, and some industry observers predict that these features could someday make textbooks such as the one you are reading obsolete. Do you agree, or do you feel that textbooks still offer advantages that an electronic version might not? Support your answer with examples.

Key Principles > **Completion**

Fill in the blanks with the appropriate words or phrases.

1. The process of altering content of an existing document is called _____.

2. A set of commands that automates complex or repetitive actions is known as a(n) _____.

3. A program that allows the user to create and manage a computerized database, and to produce reports from stored data is a(n) _____.

4. _____ software makes it possible to create slide shows that combine text, numbers, graphics, sounds, and video.

5. _____ software is a sophisticated kind of software providing tools that enable professionals to create architectural, engineering, product, and scientific designs.

6. A _____ is a form of instruction in which students are guided step by step through the learning process.

7. Spreadsheets display numbers and text in columns and rows known as a matrix or _____.

8. _____ software enables users to readily view how their money is being spent.

9. A _____ database allows tables to be linked in a way that allows data to be retrieved from more than one table.

10. Software provided without charge to anyone wanting to use it is called _____.

Tech Architecture > **Label the Drawing**

The figure below is a spreadsheet into which text and numerical data can be entered and calculations performed. Label each of the spreadsheet components as indicated.

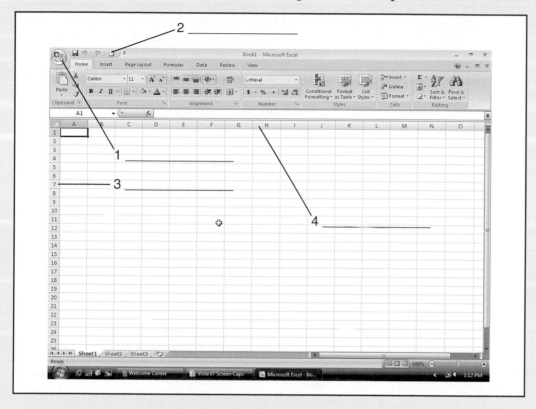

Techno Literacy > **Research and Writing**

Develop appropriate written responses based on your research for each item.

1. Which program can improve my productivity? Visit a computer store in your area. Select a particular productivity program on display and read the product description on the package. What platform is the program written for? What is the price? Will the program run on your computer? For what purpose(s) might you be able to use the program?

2. What's hot in application software? Visit your school library and look through computer magazines to find an article describing a new and innovative productivity software program. Write a summary describing the program's purpose, main features, and specifications. Include information about the user interface, the amount of internal memory needed to run the program, and the amount of disk space required to store the program. Why do you think this program is innovative? What needs does this product fulfill? Are there competing products on the market? Do you think the product will be a commercial success? Why or why not?

3. Is a picture worth a thousand words? Ask your instructor (or another person) for the name of a business or organization in your area that regularly uses presentation graphics software to train sales representatives or to provide information. Find out if you can obtain a copy of a presentation. Watch the slide show and then write an evaluation of its effectiveness. List the technologies used (hardware and software), and describe the features that impressed you most.

Technology Issues > Team Problem-Solving

In groups, brainstorm possible solutions to the issues presented.

1. Instant messaging (IM) has become a popular communication tool in social situations and in the workplace. However, the IM software AOL, Yahoo!, and MSN offerings are not fully compatible with each other. For example, AOL IM users can only communicate with other AOL IM users. What would be the benefits to each of these companies if they opened up their software to allow communication with anyone using instant messaging? How might this change come about?

2. Thinking about the different types of application software discussed in this chapter, determine how you might use some of these programs to organize activities in your life. Identify three software programs you might use if you were planning a vacation. Why did you pick these programs? What aspects of vacation planning do each of the three application software programs support?

Mining Data > Internet Research and Reporting

Conduct Internet searches to find the information described in the activities below. Write a brief report summarizing your research results. Be sure to document your sources using the MLA format (see Chapter 1, page 42, to review MLA style guidelines).

1. The first "killer app" in the history of software development was Visicalc, an early calculation program that is credited with founding the electronic spreadsheet software industry and launching widespread sales of the personal computer. Research the meaning of the term "killer app" and propose some possibilities for the next

one. Explain the reasons for your choice.

2. Explore the topic of grid computing. What kinds of applications are IBM, Microsoft, and Sun Microsystems planning? Are some types of industries better suited than others for using grid computing? Does the size of a company make a difference?

Technology Timeline > Predicting Next Steps

Look at the timeline below outlining the key milestones in the evolution of encyclopedias from printed books to digital content. Thinking about the increase in information available and the rapid growth in computing technologies, predict two additional milestones in the encyclopedia marketplace that are likely to occur within the next 20 years.

1771 The first Encyclopaedia Britannica printed.

1917 The first World Book Encyclopedia was published.

1981 The first digital version of Encyclopaedia Britannica was created for the Lexis-Nexis service.

1993 Microsoft announces the availability of the first release of the Encarta, an online encyclopedia on CD-ROM.

1994 Encyclopaedia Britannica is made available on the Internet and on CD-ROM.

1998 The complete World Book Online Web site is launched.

2001 A multilingual encyclopedia called. Wikipedia is launched and supported in an "open source" model.

2006 Wikipedia announces that the one-thousandth user-written article has been published.

Ethical Dilemmas > Group Discussion and Debate

As a class or within an assigned group, discuss the following ethical dilemma.

When software is downloaded from the Internet and installed on a personal computer, there is a possibility that it contains spyware. Spyware is software that gathers information through an Internet connection without a user's knowledge. Some of the information commonly gathered includes a user's keystrokes, hardware configuration, Internet configuration, data from the user's hard drive, and data from cookies. Typically, this information is gathered and sent to the spyware author, who then uses it for advertising purposes or sells the information to another party.

Do you consider this to be an invasion of privacy? Should it be illegal to include spyware inside another software program? What if the software license agreement includes a disclaimer that says that spyware may be installed? Is it harmless if the information is just being gathered for market research? What other problems do you see with this technology? Can you think of any ways to protect Internet users from spyware?

Computer Ethics

ETHICS ARE THE RULES WE USE to determine the right and wrong things to do in our lives. Most ethical beliefs are learned during childhood and are derived from our family, society, or religious tradition. Ethics are not the same as laws or regulations. Ethics are internalized principles that influence the decisions we make. A law is an external rule that, if violated, is punishable by society.

The Source of Ethics

In many societies, ethics are based on what is thought to be God's, or a Supreme Being's, will. Another view alleges that ethics are based on eternal laws of unknown origin that do not change. Both these ethical viewpoints fall under the moral realism school of ethical thought. Moral realists believe ethical principles have objective foundations; that is, they are not based on subjective human reasoning.

Still other philosophers claim that ethics differ from society to society, from person to person, and from situation to situation. This school of ethical thought is

Ethics are not the same as laws, but ethics do inform the shaping of the laws. Laws are external rules that, if violated, are punishable by society.

Ethics come from numerous sources, including religious books and documents.

known as moral relativism, and is sometimes also referred to as situational ethics. Most ethical belief systems are based on one of these two schools of thought, or sometimes they are a mixture of these beliefs.

Normative and Applied Ethics

The study of ethics can be divided into two main categories: Normative ethics and applied ethics. Normative ethics involves determining a standard or "norm" of ethical rule that underlies ethical behavior. Applied ethics refers to the application of normative ethical beliefs to controversial real-life issues. For example, while most cultures believe it is wrong to steal, some people may believe that the stealing of food by a starving person is ethically acceptable.

Ethics and Technology

New technologies often create ethical dilemmas because they allow humans to act in new and unforeseen ways. Computer technology poses numerous ethical dilemmas. The adapting of traditional ethical thought and behavior to these issues has resulted in new interpretations of the old rules, and these new interpretations have, in turn, led to the formation of a new branch of applied ethics called computer ethics.

Early computers were large mainframe devices that a team of engineers and programmers maintained. Ethical decision-making involving computers and their capabilities was limited to the relatively small group of people involved in the design and use of these large mainframes.

Computer technology has advanced rapidly. Today, a majority of all U.S. households have at least one computer. The widespread availability of personal computers and the Internet means that millions of people are now faced with the ethical responsibilities inherent in controlling a powerful technology.

Three categories of ethical issues that have emerged with the evolution of computer technology are privacy protection issues, property protection issues, and personal and social issues. Privacy protection issues are issues involving the use and abuse of personal information. Property issues are those involving the use and abuse of property. Personal and social issues are those involving issues of personal morality or beliefs.

Privacy Protection Issues

All people have information about their personal lives that they wish to keep private. In our society, we realize that there are times when we need to reveal personal information, such as when we apply for a job, a loan, or a credit card, or visit a doctor. Most people are generally willing to reveal information if it is absolutely necessary, and they expect that this information will remain closely guarded.

Unfortunately, the privacy that many people traditionally have taken for granted is being eroded as computer technology facilitates the gathering and transfer of information. In fact, any communication over the Internet makes us increasingly vulnerable to monitoring and data-gathering activities that can compromise our privacy. The cumulative effect of many different methods of gathering, processing, and sharing personal information could be disastrous, especially if such information falls into the wrong hands.

Public Information Availability

A controversial privacy issue concerns the use of publicly available data. A wide range of personal information has always been available through public records such as birth records, drivers' licenses, and more. This information was scattered across a wide range of jurisdictions and often stored in dusty record books. Now, database companies have created electronic databases that can provide this information to anyone with access to the Web. Many people are justifiably worried this information may be misused.

Threats to Privacy from Interception of Wireless Communications

Wireless communications devices such as cell phones and PDAs are extremely vulnerable to interception by others, partly because they transmit data into the air where anyone may intercept it. Wireless security is thus an important issue, and is becoming more so as the use of wireless devices increases. Unfortunately, traditional methods of computer security don't work well for wireless devices. For one thing, wireless devices often don't require authentication to ensure the identity of the user and the device. And encryption technology, while possible for use on wireless devices, places an undue burden on their already limited battery power and memory. Creating better security for wireless communications devices is a major challenge currently facing the computer industry.

Commercial Threats to Privacy

One of the key threats to privacy comes from e-commerce activities. Since the earliest days of e-commerce, users have expressed serious concern about the potential abuse of personal data entered at Web sites. Buyers must provide certain information to pay for the goods or services purchased over the Internet. Many commercial sites also seek information about consumer preferences or buying habits. Once entered on the Internet, personal information can be used to create a consumer profile. A consumer profile contains information about the lifestyle and buying habits of an individual that marketers can use to more effectively target and sell their goods.

Cookies   New tracking technologies allow organizations to gather personal data without the permission or even knowledge of consumers. One of the most controversial of these technologies is the cookie. A cookie is a small data file, placed on a computer's hard drive by Web sites with this programming technology. Cookies can remember passwords, User IDs, and user preferences and can automatically customize a site to those preferences during repeat visits. To accomplish this, cookies record information about the user's IP address, browser, computer operating system, and URLs visited.

Global Unique Identifiers   Another tracking technology with the potential for misuse is the Global Unique Identifier (GUID), which is an identification number that can be coded into both hardware and software. The widespread use of GUIDs would eliminate any anonymity Internet users now enjoy. If GUID use becomes widespread, it will always be possible to track down the originators of unpopular or controversial messages or ideas, a severe blow to Internet privacy.

Location Tracking   A third type of tracking device currently threatening the right to privacy is the tracking of cell phones and other types of handheld computers. Most cell phones are equipped with Global Positioning System (GPS) chips that can pinpoint the location of the cell phone within a few dozen feet. Although technologies such as this could be useful as navigation aids, monitoring the location of children or teenagers, or dispatching of emergency services to the closest unit, there is a potential for abuse as well. Moreover, the use of location-based services is on the rise. Many businesses see great potential in installing wireless location systems in cars, handheld computers, and cell phones. Advertisements could thus be tailored exactly to a consumer's location. While such technology has many obvious benefits, its widespread use in society means that anyone could track you down or figure out where you are at any given time. This greatly worries privacy advocates, who are concerned that employers, creditors, and even stalkers could use the sensitive location data.

Protection from Commercial Threats to Privacy

Consumer demands for privacy protection have led to several different kinds of responses in both the public and private sectors. The three types of responses are industry self-regulation, government regulation, and consumer self-protection.

Industry Self-Regulation   Seeking to allay consumer privacy concerns, many commercial Web sites have adopted privacy statements. A privacy statement promises that an e-tailer will protect the confidentiality of any information a customer reveals.

However, some privacy advocates claim that industry self-regulation is not sufficient, and incidents such as online retailer ToySmart's attempt to sell its customer database in violation of its privacy statement demonstrate that privacy statement promises cannot always be trusted.

Government Regulation   Passing new laws that protect consumer privacy has increasingly been viewed as the answer to the alleged failure of the Internet commerce industry to safeguard users. A number of bills to protect consumer privacy have been proposed at both the local and federal levels, but only one major piece of federal legislation has yet been passed. The Children's Online Privacy Protection Act (COPPA) of 1998 became effective April 21, 2000. This act prohibits the gathering and sharing of personal data of children under the age of 13 without the permission of parents or legal guardians.

COPPA protects children by prohibiting the gathering and sharing of personal information about children without permission of the child's parent or guardian.

Much of the debate over privacy legislation concerns whether consumers should have the right to choose to opt-in to receive cookies or opt-out to not receive cookies. Industry advocates prefer the opt-out feature, while privacy advocates worry that many consumers will be unaware of the need to opt-out or will not possess the computer skills to select that option.

Consumer Self-Protection   You can take a number of steps to reduce the likelihood of your personal privacy being violated. First, make sure you conduct e-commerce transactions only on sites protected by encryption programs, such as Secure Sockets Layer (SSL), the most common protocol used for secure servers. Microsoft Windows Vista will support the newest version of SSL (version 3) and a newer protocol called Transport Layer Security (TLS).

Second, look for sites with privacy statements and read them carefully to see what protection the site offers. Sites that pledge compliance to third-party privacy programs offer an even higher level of security against potential abuse.

Third, set your browser either to warn you when cookies are going to be placed on the hard drive or to reject them altogether. You can also install software programs that allow you to accept or reject them as you see fit.

Fourth, never volunteer any more information than is absolutely necessary to complete an e-commerce transaction. Providing details about your lifestyle, habits, interests, or shopping preferences only increases the chance that this information will be passed on to third parties for marketing purposes.

Finally, Windows Vista offers an additional protection to Internet users. The Internet Explorer browser will run in a protected area so that cookies, spyware, and downloaded applications will be isolated from the main operating system.

Governmental Threats to Privacy

According to the FBI, organized crime groups routinely use the Internet to conduct their activities. The FBI believes interception of these transmissions is essential. In fact, FBI statistics show that electronic surveillance has enabled tens of thousands of felony convictions. The FBI and other law enforcement agencies contend that if they are not allowed to monitor crime organizations under certain circumstances, society as a whole will suffer. They also worry that today's increasingly sophisticated encryption technology will provide criminals with powerful tools that law enforcement cannot counter. While many people understand the FBI's concerns, some critics believe government agencies themselves need careful policing to ensure that they do not step over the line and invade the privacy of innocent citizens.

Workplace Threats to Privacy

Some employers use special software programs that monitor workers' behavior and read messages sent and received by employees. Many employees find this kind of monitoring of their work demeaning, and they question their employer's right to do it, yet there are no laws preventing electronic surveillance of employees in the workplace.

While at work, employees are using company property, and the company has the right to monitor the use of that property. Employers insist they are justified in such snooping in order to prevent employees from engaging in activities that could result in liability for the company. However, if a company has pledged to respect employee privacy, it must keep that pledge.

Property Protection Issues

The convenience provided by linking computers through the Internet also creates some drawbacks. Computer viruses can travel around the world in seconds, damaging programs and files. Hackers can enter into systems without authorization and steal or alter data. In addition, the wealth of information on the Web and the increased ease with which it can be copied have made it simple for people to plagiarize. Plagiarism is using others' ideas and creations without permission.

Intellectual Property

Intellectual property includes just about anything that can be created by the human mind. To encourage innovation and thus benefit society as a whole, our legal system grants patents to those who invent new and better ways of doing things. A patent awards ownership of an idea or invention to its creator for a fixed number of years. To encourage and

protect artistic and literary endeavors, an author or an artist is awarded copyright to created material, allowing the right to control the use of the work and charge others for its use. Patent and copyright violation is punishable by law, and prosecutions and convictions are frequent. A recent and major threat to intellectual property rights posed by the Internet is the downloading of music, which was pioneered by the Napster Web site. The Napster program allowed computer users to share MP3 files, a digital file format for musical recordings. In early 2001, Napster went on trial for distributing copyrighted songs for free, and the company's actions were ruled illegal. The issue remains alive, however, as lawmakers and the recording industry struggle to define a fair, enforceable policy.

The Internet makes it easy to access and copy written works, photos, and artwork that may be copyrighted, and wholesale copying is illegal. However, it is legal to use a limited amount of another person's written material without permission as long as the use is acknowledged (cited), is for noncommercial purposes, and involves only the use of limited excerpts no more than 300 words of prose or one line of poetry. This right is called Fair Use and is dealt with under the U.S. Copyright Act, Section 107.

Hacking, Viruses, and Phishing

Hackers (and crackers) who break into Web sites and cause them to slow down or even shut down have a direct effect on personal computer users. The greater danger associated with hacking into Web sites is identity theft, the theft of personal credit card information and other private data. Identity theft occurs when a hacker gains entry into a Web database and copies a person's social security number, address, and credit data. The hacker then uses the victim's personal data to apply for additional credit cards, a driver's license, and so on. Then comes the spending spree, and the victim ends up with a long list of unexpected bills.

Another way that individuals can loose control of their private information is by giving it away. Phishing is an activity characterized by attempts to fraudulently acquire another person's sensitive information, such as a credit card number. The term refers to the use of increasingly sophisticated lures to "fish" for users' financial information and passwords.

In a typical situation, the criminal sends an official looking e-mail or instant message in which the criminal masquerades as a trustworthy person or business. An unsuspecting individual is asked to enter a password, credit card number, or other personal data. Once the data has been submitted, the criminal uses the data to make credit card purchases, transfer funds from the victim's bank account, or engage in other activities.

Viruses create a different sort of damage, usually to the user's computer or to software running on it. A virus must enter disguised in another file (usually an e-mail attachment), which may be downloaded from the Internet. Viruses may also reside on storage media and even on legitimate copies of software programs direct from manufacturers.

Consumers can protect themselves from identity theft by dealing only with Web merchants who encrypt credit card numbers and other private data. Secure sites are indicated by an "s" following the "http" in the URL. It is important for users to protect themselves from phishing attempts by critically reading requests before responding with private information. Users should never provide sensitive, private information without confirming the legitimacy of the request.

The main precaution against viruses is to never open an e-mail attachment from an unknown source. The second strategy is to install an antivirus program, which, when activated, seeks out and destroys any known viruses found on a computer. To keep up with the proliferation of new viruses, the antivirus software needs to be continually updated. In addition, firewall software is recommended to protect any Internet-connected computer system from hackers.

Personal and Social Issues

In addition to raising privacy and property concerns, computers have had an unanticipated impact on numerous personal and social issues. The solutions to these issues are often complicated because of a lack of consensus on what, if anything, should be done to deal with them.

Gambling Online

Online gambling has proven to be a serious problem for many individuals and for society as a whole.

While gambling may be a pleasurable pastime for some individuals, it can become an addiction for others. Most gambling occurs at casinos, but the availability of online gambling is attracting growing numbers of gamblers, including both adults and teenagers who are prohibited by law from visiting brick-and-mortar casinos. Online gambling has become a $12 billion industry. The Internet gambling industry is based almost entirely outside the United States, though about half its customers live in the U.S.

Protecting Freedom of Speech

The Internet contains material that would not be allowed in many jurisdictions if it were received by more traditional means, such as paper mail or TV. Examples of these types of materials are sites featuring hate speech or pornography.

Hate Speech Sites The freedom of speech guaranteed by the Constitution of the U.S. allows great latitude in what a person can say. Consequently, a great number of Web sites contain written material that many would find offensive. This includes material inciting hatred against people of certain races, religions, or beliefs. Some hate speech sites use foul or inappropriate language, and some even post material that may be dangerous, such as information on making drugs or explosives.

Pornography Sites Pornography is material containing sexually explicit images or script deemed unacceptable or harmful by society. Because people differ in their feelings toward sexuality, no universal agreement exists as to exactly when material crosses the line from being acceptable to constituting pornography. Adult pornography on the Internet is available with few if any restrictions and is unwelcome in many homes. Even those who do not find pornography disturbing generally agree that children or certain vulnerable adults should not view it.

Protecting against Unwanted Material

The freedom of speech guaranteed by the U.S. Constitution has been interpreted as protecting both acceptable and unacceptable expressions. Unless a

One effective way to avoid exposure to unwanted Internet content is to hit the Back button if you accidentally land on an inappropriate site.

Web site contains material that overtly and directly threatens the livelihood or well-being of an individual, a group, or the government, it enjoys protection as free speech.

For computer users, the best protection against offensive or unwanted material on the Internet is just to avoid it. If you happen to stumble across material that is pornographic or disturbing in any way, merely click the Back button on your browser and leave the offending site. One way for parents and guardians to protect vulnerable persons from viewing pornographic or hate speech Web sites is through the use of a filtering program. A filtering program can prevent access to sites, keep track of sites visited, limit connection time, record keystrokes, and prevent downloading.

In 2000, Congress passed a law that was designed to protect school children and library patrons from being exposed to pornographic sites and other types of restricted material. Called the Children's Internet Protection Act (CIPA), the law requires public schools and libraries to install Internet filtering software on their computers.

Bridging the Digital Divide

Not everyone in the world enjoys such privileges made possible by modern digital technologies. Even within developed nations, access to digital technology is not evenly distributed. The gap between those who have access to computers and the Internet and those who do not has been called the digital divide.

When looked at from a global perspective, the digital divide is striking. According to the 2004 United Nations Human Development Report, only 5 percent of the population in developing countries has Internet access.

In the United States, both private sector and government initiatives have attempted to close the digi-

tal divide. In general, everyone recognizes the need for such an effort. Computer industry leaders clearly see the benefit of supplying technology to more and more Americans. Government leaders realize that citizens' lives can improve with access to computers and the Internet.

A 2005 report from the Pew Internet and American Life Project report on Digital Divisions indicated that people in the U.S. today almost all fit into one of three tiers. Twenty-two percent of American adults are truly offline and never access the Internet, 40 percent are modestly online and are able to access the Internet when they need to, and 33 percent of American adults are part of the highly wired broadband elite.

The demographic classes that are lagging behind are those age 65 or older (only 26 percent are online), African-Americans (57 percent are online, compared with 70 percent of whites), and those with less education (29 percent of those who did not finish high school are online, compared with 61 percent of high school graduates and 89 percent of college graduates). The new digital divide recognized in the United States is currently in Internet connection speeds. In the U.S., 53 percent of Internet users have broadband access.

Much more work is needed in order to eliminate the digital divide in the U.S. and abroad. While some progress has been made, the digital divide may widen worldwide in the coming years, creating a striking gap between the prosperity of some of the world's nations and the poverty of others.

Defining Software Companies' Responsibilities

Software makers are protected by copyright legislation. But what rights do software makers themselves owe to the people who use their software programs? Bad software costs U.S. businesses an estimated $100 billion in lost productivity annually. Every day computer users around the world experience problems attributed to poor software design.

In their defense, software programmers point out that their software must interact with a number of other software programs and hardware systems, any one of which may cause problems due to incompatibility. While they try to ensure that their programs work well and are compatible with connecting software and hardware, it is impossible to guarantee 100 percent reliability. Critics, however, respond that many companies simply refuse to do enough to reduce programming errors.

Protecting against Poorly Designed Software

If software does not perform according to the manufacturer's promise, a simple protection is to ask for a refund. Many stores have generous refund policies, and a consumer's right to return goods is protected by the Uniform Commercial Code. This code contains language covering buyers' rights and allowing buyers to reject any product, "if the goods or the tender of delivery fail in any respect to conform to the contract." But this protection covers only the right to return the product for a refund. In cases where actual damages are suffered due to the software, victims must pursue redress through the legal system by filing suit.

Legal measures address only the unfortunate results of poor software design. In reality, the best protection against software problems is for software manufacturers and designers to produce better software programs in the first place.

Improving Accessibility

An estimated 30 million Americans suffer from some sort of disability. As the American population ages, this number will certainly increase. People with certain disabilities may be unable to use computers and the Internet. Some accessibility problems faced by many disabled persons involve the use of computer hardware. Individuals with motor impairment or missing limbs, for example, cannot use a mouse and may also be unable to use conventional keyboards. Persons with visual impairments may experience difficulty viewing their monitors unless their screen is capable of enlarged displays.

Disabled Americans have been active in asserting their right to improved access to computer technology and efforts are under way to make computing devices and software more accessible to physically impared individuals.

People with disabilities and their supporters point out that incorporating features making computers

Developing hardware that is accessible to physically impaired individuals is important. This specially designed keyboard and mouse is one example of such technology.

and the Internet accessible to the disabled is not just a good idea from a legal point of view, but also makes sense financially. Improving access to computers and the Internet will increase the number of potential customers for these goods and services.

Developing Personal Ethical Guidelines

Computers and the Internet are very powerful tools indeed. With a few taps on a keyboard, users have the ability to do good or to create great damage. A doctor can use the Internet to diagnose a patient many miles away. Companies can use the Internet to sell products and services around the world. Every day, users benefit by being able to use e-mail to contact friends and relatives and conduct business. On the other hand, computer technology can be used to spread damaging viruses, break into computer networks in order to steal or damage material, use copyrighted material unlawfully, spread hatred and promote violence, and create numerous other problems for society.

What can be done to prevent unethical behavior on computers and the Internet? Certainly, laws can be passed to punish the most egregious violations. But legislation is never the only, or even an adequate, answer to ethical dilemmas. Rather, sound ethical principles must begin with the individual. For starters, all computer users should be aware of the power of a computer. They should understand its capacity for good or harm, and they should realize the societal and personal consequences of perpetrating illegal or harmful behaviors with computers. Moreover, they should read, think about, and consider adapting for their own use a computer code of ethics. Table 1 is an example of a code of ethics for software engineering developed jointly by the Institute of Electrical and Electronics Engineers and the Association for Computing Machinery.

In the rapidly evolving world of computer technology, it is unlikely that a consensus will ever be reached on a single ethical code for the computer industry. Still, all users should consider it a point of personal integrity to use computers and the Internet ethically at all times.

Table 1 Software Engineering Code of Ethics and Professional Practice

Relationship	Obligations
Public	Software engineers shall act consistently with the public interest.
Client and Employer	Software engineers shall act in a manner that is in the best interest of their client and employer and that is consistent with the public interest.
Product	Software engineers shall ensure that their products and related modifications meet the highest professional standards possible.
Judgment	Software engineers shall maintain integrity and independence in their professional judgment.
Management	Software engineering managers and leaders shall subscribe to and promote and ethical approach to the management of software development and maintenance.
Profession	Software engineers shall advance the integrity and reputation of the profession consistent with the public interest.
Colleagues	Software engineers shall be fair to and supportive of their colleagues.
Self	Software engineers shall participate in lifelong learning regarding the practice of their profession and promote an ethical approach to the practice of the profession.

Source: IIEE, version 5.1, excerpted from the short version, <http://www.computer.org/tab/seprof/code.htm>

MOST PEOPLE CAN USE A TELEVISION SET, operate a microwave oven, or drive an automobile, but few of us would consider attempting to repair the sophisticated electronics in each. Yet somehow we assume that computer problems are something that we should be able to repair without instruction or experience. Consider that all computers and their architectures are not alike, and that their repair methods and diagnostics are significantly different. The age of a system also impacts the repair techniques used. Indeed, for many systems produced fewer than five years ago, replacement parts exist in used markets only. Therefore, as in your TV, car, and microwave, there are many situations in which the diagnostics and work should be left to someone who has the experience and the hardware and software to accomplish the objective. There are, however, a number of items that can be checked by anyone to help ascertain if the nature of the problem requires an experienced technician. After all, in a comparable situation, it would be embarrassing to return to a store a camera that doesn't work only to find that the lens cap was not removed!

Problem: The screen is blank—nothing is happening.

The most important first step is to be certain that the power is getting to the computer. Most computers and monitors have an LED light that glows whenever the power is on. If no power is getting to the computer, check the wall socket and surge protector in an attempt to verify current flow. Switching sockets into one that is known to work could resolve this possible problem.

Problem: The start-up process is taking too long—or it can't seem to be completed.

Several actions take place between the time a computer is turned on and the appearance of the desktop and icons. A number of checks are performed during the power-on self-test (POST) on the system basic input output system (BIOS) to verify that all required parts, such as the keyboard, mouse, memory, and hard disk drive, are functioning normally. If they are not, a message will appear on the screen or a series of beeps will announce a problem. If a screen message shows the keyboard or mouse missing, it is possible that the cable has become loose from its connection or that the raw metal contact surfaces have become corroded. Repeated connection and disconnection of the device will usually correct the corrosion problem. Be very careful to examine the small contact pins that make the connection to verify that none are bent or damaged. These connectors are very delicate and force should not ever be required to plug them in.

Inexperienced users sometimes mistakenly disrupt the startup. During the starting or boot-up process, systems will sometimes send a message to press a key to enter setup, often the escape (Esc) key or the function keys F2 or F10. This is a part of the setup process that identifies the installed components in the computer. One of the best features of modern systems is the capacity for the system setup commands to be initialized by the installing software. Virtually all components now are recognized by the operating system when they are installed. This initialization process is "automatic" in the eyes of the user, but much takes place behind the scenes to keep the system setup correct and to maintain the Windows system file, called the registry, that governs all machine applications. Inexperienced users should avoid the setup location. If the system setup or registry becomes corrupted, it is again time to seek out experienced counsel.

Problem: A message displays on screen saying there is a failure of the hard drive.

If the dreaded hard disk drive failure message appears on the screen, it may be a simple problem of a loose connection, or it could be an internal corrosion problem. In either case it should be left to experienced hands. This might be a suitable time to remind users that work that is worth saving is worth saving twice! If the data is critical, multiple backups are in order.

Internal components as well as peripheral hardware have a limited life expectancy. Most hard disks and CD drives will last typically five years, but failure can happen at any time. The cables that connect these devices are also subject to failure. The corrosion problem mentioned previously regarding metal surfaces can occur at any connection.

Problem: The printer is not working.

Printer cables are particularly vulnerable to failure since they can get moved either deliberately or accidentally. If printing problems cannot be corrected by working with the cables or by reinstalling the printer driver software provided by the manufacturer, then a new printer may be in order. It comes as a surprise to many users of inkjet printers that units up to about $300 in cost are essentially disposable. Replacement often costs less than labor and repair, and a newer printer will likely have superior capabilities.

General Guidelines

An important point to consider is taking notes that describe your problem. In order to help a diagnostician locate a problem, it is helpful to be able to describe exactly what is happening. If the system "beeps" you should note how many times and identify if it is in a pattern. If system diagnostic error messages appear on the screen, write them down.

If you attempt to install new hardware or software, make changes one at a time. In this way, if a problem occurs you should be able to back up one step to bring the system back to life.

Do not be afraid to ask for assistance rather than dive into something for which you are not trained. Sometimes your attempt to fix a problem can make things worse than they were originally. As you observe the work and diagnostics of others, you will begin to develop your own experience base, increase your confidence, and be able to attack more serious problems the second time they occur. You would not be likely to tear into a problem with your microwave oven for lack of knowledge; your computer deserves at least the same amount of respect.

TUTORIAL 1

Windows

Starting Up and Shutting Down a PC

This tutorial describes how to start up and log on with a user name and password to a Windows PC with the Vista operating system installed. The tutorial also explains the shut down procedure to correctly power off the computer when you have finished your tasks.

Starting Up and Logging On

During the installation of Vista, the setup routine includes a process to create a user name and password to log on to the computer. You will need to know the user name and password created for the PC you are using before proceeding. The first screen that appears after turning on the power, or moving the mouse to re-activate a system that is in standby mode, is called the Welcome screen (see Figure 1). On this page, all of the account names that have been set up on the computer are shown with an icon.

When you click the icon for the user name that you want to use to log on to the computer, the icon enlarges and a password text box appears if the account requires a password. The remaining user names disappear from view. If you attempt to log on with an incorrect password, Vista displays the password hint if one was created with the user account.

TIP In, out, up, down—what does it all mean? Logging on means connecting to the computer; logging in is the same thing, just different wording. Logging off means disconnecting, and logging out is the same thing.

Steps

To log on at the Vista Welcome screen:
1. Click the icon for your user name.
2. Type your password if a password is required and then click the right arrow button or press Enter.

> In an environment where multiple users access the same computer, such as in a school, logging on (and off) is important for tracking purposes. On a network, logging on also connects the computer to the network using settings and permissions that are set up especially for that user. For example, there might be certain locations on a file server that become accessible through the network when a certain user logs on, but not when some other user logs on.

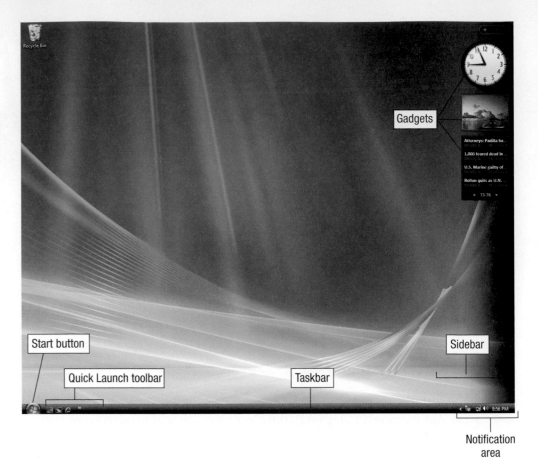

Figure 2 Vista Desktop

TIP Previous versions of Windows provided the ability to turn off the display of the Welcome screen; however, in Vista, the Welcome screen cannot be turned off.

The Vista desktop appears when you successsfully log on (see Figure 2). The desktop shown displays the default background using the Windows Vista theme. Your background may be different since other pictures are available. On the desktop, icons to launch programs are available as well as the Taskbar and the Sidebar. The Taskbar is the long horizontal bar along the bottom of the screen and is used to manage application windows. The Sidebar is a vertical bar along the right side of the screen. The Sidebar contains gadgets that are mini programs for information or frequently used tools.

Logging Off

Logging off and shutting down are two separate operations, although shutting down also logs you off. Logging off indicates the user no longer requires the computer. The user's programs and documents are closed and the Welcome screen redisplays; logging off does not shut down the PC.

Steps

To log off:
1. Click the Start button.
2. Point to the right-pointing arrow button next to the lock button in the right pane.
3. Click Log Off.

Properly end a computer session by logging off.

You can also use a feature called Fast User Switching to enable multiple users to be logged on at once to the same PC. This could be handy when one person is working on the PC and someone else comes up and wants a turn "just for a second." Instead of logging off as in Step 3 above, click *Switch User* and allow the other person to log on temporarily. Switch User leaves the original user's programs and data files open, whereas logging off closes them all.

Restarting and Shutting Down

In addition to logging off, you can also restart the PC, or you can shut it down completely. Restarting can help if you are experiencing errors or problems with Windows' operation. Shutting down completely is a good idea when you are going to be away from your PC for a while (say, 24 hours or more).

Steps

To shut down or restart:
1. Click the Start button.
2. Point to the right-pointing arrow button next to the lock button.
3. Click either Restart or Shut Down (to completely power off the computer).

Power Button

Click the Start button and then click the Power button to place the computer in Sleep mode. In Sleep mode, all of your work is automatically saved, the screen is turned off, and the computer is placed in its lowest power state. A light on the outside of the computer case blinks or turns yellow to indicate sleep mode is active. Reactivate the computer by pressing the Power button on the front of the computer case, or by moving the mouse. After logging on, the screen will be exactly as it was when you activated sleep mode.

What's New in Windows Vista?

Windows Vista brings a new experience to the desktop, which includes a simplified organizational structure, easier and faster data searching, and enhanced security to name a few of Vista's new features. In this tutorial you will read an article that explains the major changes as well as watch a demo movie on the new security features.

Steps

To read the What's new? article:

1. Click the Start button.
2. Click *Help and Support* (in the right column).
3. Click the <u>What's new?</u> hyperlink in the Find an answer section of the Windows Help and Support window.

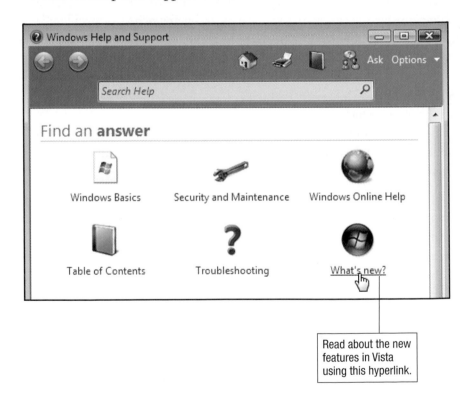

Read about the new features in Vista using this hyperlink.

4. Read the article. Click hyperlinks to topics that are of interest to you as you scroll down the page. Close the Windows Help and Support window when finished.

As you read the article, you will notice some hyperlinked text displays with a right-pointing green arrow preceding the text • → Click to open Internet Explorer. . Clicking these hyperlinked topics opens another program or window outside the Help window. You will need to close the window to return to the Help article. Click the Back button ⊖ on the Windows Help and Support window toolbar to return to the previous Help page viewed.

Security Basics Demonstration

Users must be vigilant to the risk of losing data or being the target of theft or other misuse of information stored on their computers as a result of using the Internet and e-mail. View the demonstration on Security basics to understand the features within the Security Center in Windows Vista designed to protect your PC.

Steps

To watch the Security basics movie:
1. Click the Start button.
2. Click *Help and Support* (in the right column).
3. Click the What's new? hyperlink in the *Find an answer* section of the Windows Help and Support window.
4. Scroll down and then click the Demo: Security basics hyperlink in the Security section.

Security

Features such as Windows Firewall and Windows Defender can help keep your computer more secure. Windows Security Center has links for checking your computer's firewall, antivirus software, and update status. BitLocker Drive Encryption allows you to encrypt the entire system partition, which can improve security by preventing hackers from accessing important system files. User Account Control (UAC) can help prevent unauthorized changes to your computer by requiring permission before performing actions that could potentially affect your computer's operation or that change settings that affect other users.

- • → Click to open Security Center.

- • Demo: Security basics

- • What is User Account Control?

> Click here to go to the Security basics demonstration page.

5. Click the <u>Watch the demo</u> hyperlink. Windows Media Player opens and the security movie begins playing.

Demo: Security basics

You can help protect your computer from Internet threats by taking a few simple precautions. This demo introduces you to Windows Security Center, which shows your computer's security status. You'll also learn how to automatically download the latest security updates, how to use Windows Firewall to block harmful programs, and how to use Windows Defender to keep your computer free of spyware and other potentially unwanted software.

→ Watch the demo

▸ Read   Click to watch the demo

See also

- Understanding security and safe computing
- Windows Vista demos

> Click here to open Windows Media Player and watch the Security basics demonstration movie.

6. When the movie finishes, close the Windows Media Player window.
7. Close the Windows Help and Support window.

Running Applications

A primary function of Microsoft Windows is to run applications. Without applications, there would be no reason for any of its other features, such as networking, file management, and online connectivity. There are many ways of running an application; as you work in Windows you will choose the method that is the most appropriate for a given situation.

From the Start Menu

The Start menu provides a convenient, central organizing location for shortcuts that run most of the installed applications.

Steps

To open the WordPad application from the Start menu:

1. Click the Start button.
2. Click *All Programs*. The options in the left pane are replaced with the All Programs submenu.
3. Click *Accessories* in the left pane. The Accessories option in the submenu expands to show a list of accessory programs.
4. Click *WordPad*. The WordPad application opens.

> **Prior versions of Windows opened a cascading side menu when you clicked options from the Start menu. Vista replaces the left pane or expands options in the left pane as you click menu options. Notice the Back option at the bottom of the menu that you can use to return to the previous menu.**

5. Click the Close (X) button in the top right corner of the WordPad window to close it.

TIP See Tutorial 11 to learn how to customize the Start menu.

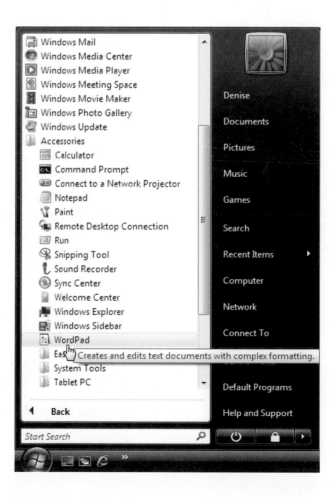

From the Desktop Icons

Depending on your system's configuration, there may be icons on the Windows desktop. The Recycle Bin will be there in all cases, and there also may be other icons for installed applications. Sometimes when a new program is installed an icon is placed on the desktop automatically.

Steps

To run an application from the desktop:
1. Double-click the application's icon on the desktop. The application opens in a new window.
2. Click the Close (X) button in the top right corner of the application's window when you are finished and want to close the program or window.

From the Run Command

The Run command enables you to run an application that has no shortcut on the Start menu or the desktop. For example, a computer technician may use the System Configuration utility program for Windows troubleshooting. The program is not available on the Start menu. Exercise caution with this utility since changes made affect your computer's performance and operation.

TIP You can place shortcuts on the desktop yourself for the applications you use most frequently. There are many ways of doing this; here's one way. On the Start menu, right-click a shortcut and click Copy. Next, close the Start menu, so that you see the desktop, and press Ctrl+V to paste the shortcut.

Steps

To run the System Configuration utility:
1. Click the Start button.
2. Click *All Programs*. The options in the left pane are replaced with the All Programs submenu.
3. Click *Accessories* in the left pane. The Accessories option in the submenu expands to show a list of accessory programs.
4. Click *Run*. The Run dialog box opens.
5. Type **msconfig** in the Open text box.
6. Click OK. The User Account Control dialog box opens. Vista requests your permission to allow the program to run. This feature prevents programs from running on your computer without your knowledge.

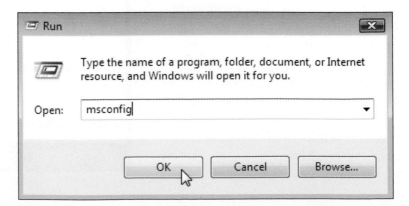

7. Click the Continue button. The System Configuration window opens.
8. Click the Close (X) button to close the application.

From a File Management Window

If you see an executable file (that is, the file that executes the application) while you are browsing a disk's contents in a Computer window, you can start the application associated with it by double-clicking the file name. You can perform file management tasks such as copying, moving, or renaming files in a Computer window.

Steps

To run the WordPad application by browsing the contents of a Computer window:
1. Click the Start button.
2. Click *Computer* in the right pane to open a Computer window.
3. Double-click the icon for the drive on which Windows is installed. (Ask your instructor which drive to use. If the instructor is not available, try drive C:.)
4. Double-click the Program Files folder.
5. Double-click the Windows NT folder. You may need to scroll down the list pane to see Windows NT.
6. Double-click the Accessories folder. An icon for WordPad appears.
7. Double-click the WordPad icon. The WordPad application opens.

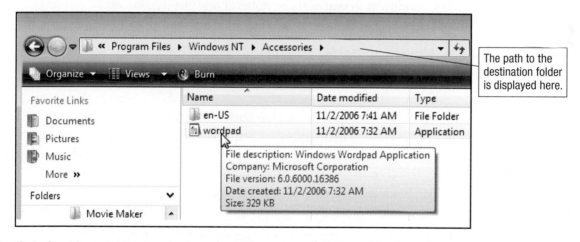

8. Click the Close (X) button in the top right corner of the WordPad window to close it.
9. Click the Close (X) button in the top right corner of the Computer window to close it.

Seem like a lot of work? Sometimes, starting an application that is on a CD or DVD that is not set to run automatically, may require you to browse the CD contents and start the program this way.

Windows

Working with a Window

Almost all content in Microsoft Windows appears in frames called windows. Each application runs in its own window, as does each file management interface such as the Computer or Documents options.

In Tutorial 3 you saw two types of windows. The window for WordPad was an application window, and the window for Computer was a file management window. In this tutorial, you will explore what you can do with windows after opening them.

Three Window States: Maximized, Minimized, and Restored

Every window is in one of three states at any given moment:

- Maximized: Fills the entire screen
- Minimized: Hidden except for its icon on the taskbar
- Restored: Open and visible, but not full-screen

You can switch among these three states with the buttons in the upper right corner of the window—not the X (that button is for closing the window)—but the other two. Why are there only two buttons, when there are three states? The Restore Down and Maximize buttons never appear simultaneously; a window has one or the other based on its current state.

When a window is restored, the buttons look like the buttons in Figure 3. When a window is maximized, the buttons look like the buttons in Figure 4.

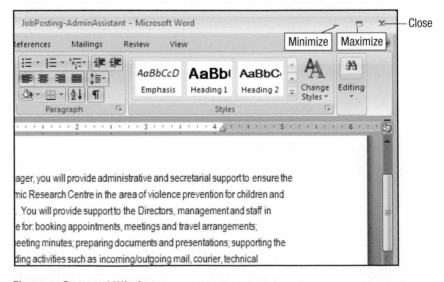

Figure 3 Restored Window

Steps

To see the action of these buttons:

1. Open a Computer window. (Recall that to do this, click Start and then click Computer in the right pane.)
2. Click the Maximize button in the Computer window. (If the Computer window is already maximized, Step 2 is not necessary; proceed to Step 3.)
3. Click the Minimize button in the Computer window. The window disappears except for the Computer button on the taskbar.
4. Click the Computer button on the taskbar. The window reappears, in maximized form.
5. Click the Restore Down button in the Computer window. The window returns to its nonmaximized size.
6. Click the Close button in the Computer window. The window closes.

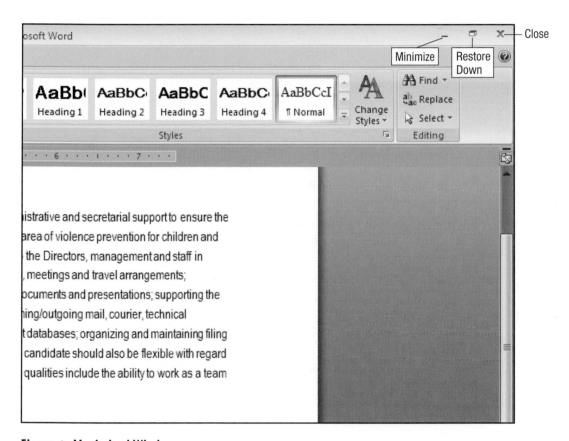

Figure 4 Maximized Window

Move and Resize a Window

When a window is restored, there's some "breathing room" around it on the desktop. You can move the window around on the desktop, and/or you can change its size.

To move a window, drag the window's title bar to the desired location. (The title bar is the horizontal bar across the top of the window, see Figure 5.)

To resize a window, drag the top, bottom, left, right, or corner border in the desired direction. Many people drag the bottom right corner of a window to resize the window's length and width simultaneously; however, you can drag any edge.

Title bar —

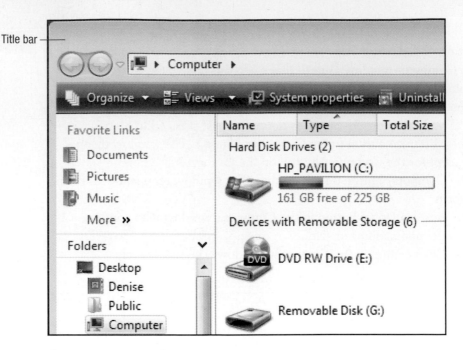

Figure 5

Steps

To move and resize a window:

1. Reopen a Computer window.
2. Point to the title bar of the window.
3. Hold down the left mouse button and drag the title bar to move the window to a different location on the desktop. Release the mouse button at the desired location.
4. Point to the bottom right corner of the window until the mouse pointer changes shape to a diagonally pointing double-headed arrow.

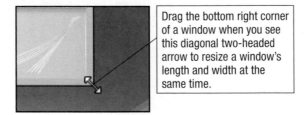

Drag the bottom right corner of a window when you see this diagonal two-headed arrow to resize a window's length and width at the same time.

5. Hold down the left mouse button and drag to change the window's size to approximately one-half the window's original length and width. Release the mouse button when finished.
6. Resize the window again, this time making it so large that it almost takes up the entire screen.
7. Close the Computer window and then reopen it. Notice that Windows remembers the Computer window's previous size and location.
8. If desired, move and/or resize the Computer window to suit your preferences.
9. Close the Computer window.

Windows

Browsing Disks and Devices Using the Computer Feature

The Computer feature is the central location in the Windows interface for browsing disk contents. The window lists all available local drives (and may also show network drives to which the computer has access).

Steps

To open a Computer window:

1. Click the Start button.
2. Click *Computer*.

By default the Computer window appears with two panes (see Figure 6). At the right is the List pane with icons depicting the drives available on the computer. The Navigation pane is at the left with the Favorite Links section and the Folders list. The Folders list can be opened or closed by clicking the up-pointing or down-pointing arrow to the right of Folders. Using the Folders list you can view the organizational structure of the disks, including all levels of folders.

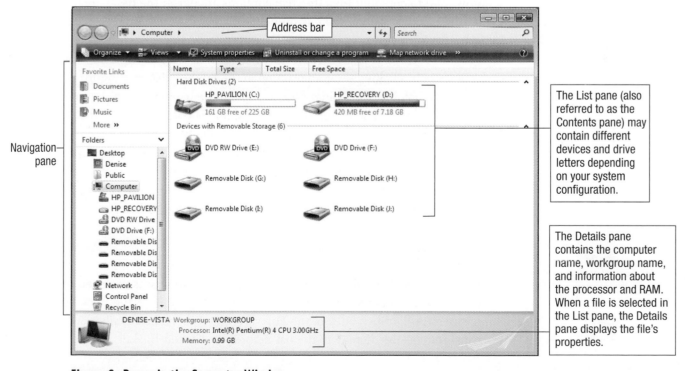

Figure 6 Panes in the Computer Window

TIP Folders are logical units that help users more easily manage the great number of files stored on a disk. In the next tutorial you will learn how to create and rename folders. Generally, you create a folder in which you will save related documents and keep them separate from other nonrelated files. For example, you could create a folder in which to place all of the documents created for a specific project. You can create folders within a folder to organize your work in a hierarchical structure.

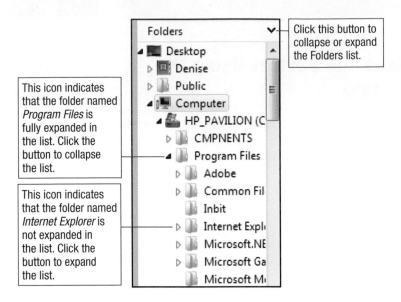

Figure 7 Folder List

Browsing Disk Content

To view the contents of a disk, double-click the desired disk icon in the Computer window. The folders and files the disk contains appear in the list pane of the Computer window. To view the contents of a specific folder, double-click the folder name in the list.

If the Folders list is expanded in the navigation pane, you can also browse the disk contents by clicking the folder name in the Folders list (see Figure 7). Double-click a folder name in the Folders list to expand the list and show the folders within that location. The list of drives and folders is commonly called a *folder tree* because the fully expanded hierarchy resembles the branches on a tree. When a "branch" of the file hierarchy is fully expanded, a black downward pointing diagonal arrow appears next to the folder name in the Folders pane; a white right-pointing arrow indicates the folder list is not expanded for that folder name. Click the white or black arrow to either expand or collapse the folder list.

Back button

Moving Back and Forward

Each time you click a different drive or folder name, the list is replaced in the list pane with the new items. To return to a previous display, click the Back button. After you click the Back button, the Forward button becomes available; clicking Forward returns the display to the list before you clicked Back.

Forward button

Moving Folder Levels

The folder structure of a drive can be many levels deep. The path to the top level of the disk is represented by a path statement that starts out with the drive letter and then lists the folders that you would travel through to arrive at that location (see Figure 8). For example:

C:\Windows\System

The above statement represents the path to the System folder, which is stored within the Windows folder, which is stored on the C: drive. The folder name to the left of another in the path—or above it in the folder tree—is called its *parent folder*. The folder names within a parent folder are its *child folders*.

When you move up one level, you move to the immediate parent folder of the current folder. For example, to go up one level from the above path, you would go to:

C:\Windows

To move to a previous level in the path and display the contents of the folder, click the folder name in the Address bar of the Computer window.

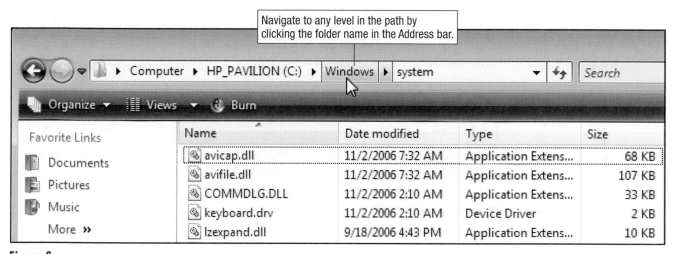

Figure 8

Windows

Creating and Renaming Folders

Have you wondered how all those folders came to exist on your disk or other storage medium? Windows itself created several of them on the computer's main disk drive, including Windows, Program Files, and Documents. Other folders are created when you install new software.

You also can create your own folder names. These can be used as organizers for storing files you create or acquire, such as digital camera pictures, word processing documents, and applications and data that you download from the Internet or receive as e-mail attachments.

Creating a New Folder

A new folder can be created only in relation to an existing folder (or a drive's root folder), so you must start the folder-making process by displaying a particular location's content in the list pane of the Computer window (refer to Tutorial 5). Whatever location is currently displayed becomes the parent folder for the new folder you will create.

TIP Each drive's top level is its root folder. An analogy: When you walk into an office building, you first go into the lobby. At that point you are not in any particular office—you are simply in the building. The root folder of a drive is like that lobby. You're not in a folder yet—you're just "in the drive."

Steps

To create a new folder:

1. Open a Computer window and display in the List pane the folder in which you want to place the new folder. (For example, display the contents list for the folder named *Documents*.)
2. *Right*-click the mouse in a blank area of the list pane, point to New, and then click *Folder*. A folder icon appears with a text box containing the text *New Folder*. The default name New Folder is automatically selected indicating you can begin typing the name you want to assign to the folder.

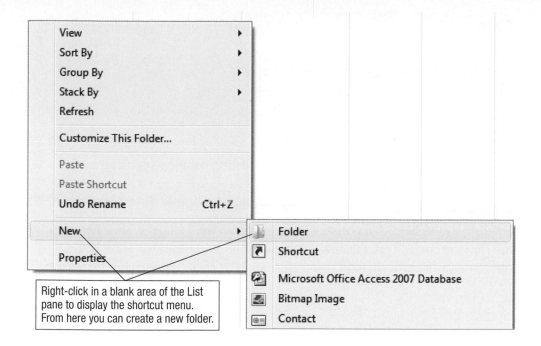

View	▶
Sort By	▶
Group By	▶
Stack By	▶
Refresh	
Customize This Folder...	
Paste	
Paste Shortcut	
Undo Rename	Ctrl+Z
New	▶
Properties	

	Folder
	Shortcut
	Microsoft Office Access 2007 Database
	Bitmap Image
	Contact

Right-click in a blank area of the List pane to display the shortcut menu. From here you can create a new folder.

3. Type the name that you want to assign to the new folder.

> **Folder names can be up to 255 characters and can include spaces and most punctuation symbols (but not reserved symbols such as *, \\, /, or ?). Windows will let you know if you have entered a prohibited character. Even though long names are possible, most people prefer to keep folder names relatively short (under 12 to 16 characters or so) to make it easier to refer to them and to make the display more tidy.**

4. Press Enter. The new folder name is accepted and appears next to the folder icon.

 TermProject

Renaming a Folder

You can rename folders any time. However, use caution when renaming folders. If you rename a folder that a certain application relies on to operate, the application might not work anymore. When evaluating whether a folder can safely be renamed, ask these questions:

- Does the folder contain only data files, such as word processing documents, spreadsheets, and so on? If so, you can rename it safely. However, if a certain application has a default Save location set up for its data files, you may need to change it to the new folder name within that application.
- Is the folder stored within the Windows or Program Files folder? If so, do not rename it, or some application will probably stop working.
- Is the folder used to store the operating files for an application, or is it stored within the Windows or Program Files folder? If so, do not rename it, or the application will probably stop working.

Steps

To rename a folder:

1. Click the folder once to select it.
2. Press F2. The name becomes editable.

> 📁 WindowsProject

3. Type a new folder name, or edit the existing name by inserting and/or deleting characters.
4. Press Enter.

You can also *right*-click an existing folder name in the List pane, click *Rename* at the shortcut menu, type the new name and press Enter to rename a folder. Using the context-sensitive shortcut menu alleviates the need to remember function keys.

Copying and Moving Files and Folders

In previous tutorials you learned how to use a Computer window to view disk content and create folders within the file system. Now that you know how the file system is organized, you are ready to start manipulating folder content.

You can move and copy files and folders to other locations—that is, to other disks or storage mediums such as a USB flash drive, or to other folders within the same disk. You might move a file to archive it on another storage medium, or copy a file to create a backup copy in another folder or storage medium.

Moving/Copying Using Drag-and-Drop

One easy way of moving or copying is to select and drag the file or folder to the desired location. The desired location must be visible (or at least an icon for it must be visible) either in a window or in the Folders list.

Steps

To move or copy a file or folder using drag-and-drop:

1. Open a Computer window.
2. If the Folders list is not expanded in the Navigation pane, click the up-pointing arrow to the right of Folders to display the list.

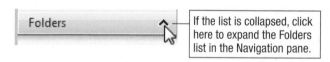

If the list is collapsed, click here to expand the Folders list in the Navigation pane.

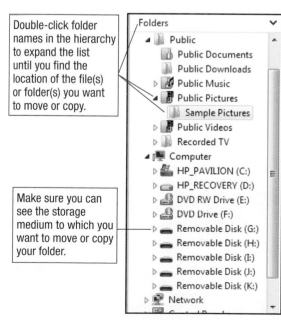

Double-click folder names in the hierarchy to expand the list until you find the location of the file(s) or folder(s) you want to move or copy.

Make sure you can see the storage medium to which you want to move or copy your folder.

3. Display in the list pane the file(s) and/or folder(s) you want to move or copy.
4. Expand the folder tree as needed (refer to Tutorial 5) so that the destination disk or folder's icon is visible on the tree. If necessary, consider resizing the window to view a larger Folders list.
5. Select the file(s) and/or folder(s) you want to move or copy.

> **To select multiple contiguous files or folders at once, click the first file or folder name and then hold down the Shift key while clicking the last file or folder name. For a non-contiguous selection, hold down the Ctrl key as you click individually on each desired file or folder name.**

6. If you are moving a file or folder, hold down the Shift key; if you are copying, hold down the Ctrl key.
7. Position the mouse pointer over any of the selected file or folders names in the List pane, drag the selected files/folders to the desired destination storage medium in the Folders list in the Navigation pane, and then release the mouse. You'll see a plus sign with the arrow pointer, as shown below, if you are copying; an absence of a plus sign means you are moving.

What happens if you do not hold down the Shift or Ctrl key while dragging? It depends on the relationship between the original location and the destination. If they are on different disk drives, the default action is copy. If they are on the same disk drive, the default action is move.

Moving/Copying Using the Clipboard

The drag-and-drop method works well if both the original location and the destination can be viewed onscreen at once. If that is not possible (or not convenient due to a lengthy or complex folder list), you can use the Clipboard feature to move and copy files or folders. This method involves the Cut, Copy, and Paste commands.

For a move operation, select the file or folder and use the Cut command. Next, display the destination location and use the Paste command. Copying uses the same routine with the exception that you use the Copy command instead of Cut at the first step. The advantage is that you do not have to paste immediately after the cut/copy operation, so both locations need not appear onscreen simultaneously.

The Clipboard is a temporary holding area accessible by all Windows applications. Items are placed in the Clipboard with Cut and Copy operations, and inserted from the Clipboard with the Paste operation.

Steps

To move or copy files or folders with the Clipboard:

1. Open a Computer window and select the file(s) and/or folder(s) you want to move or copy.
2. *Right*-click the selected object and click either *Cut* or *Copy* at the shortcut menu.

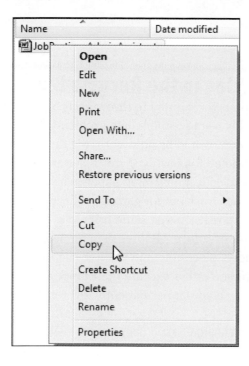

3. Navigate to the drive and/or folder to which you want the files or folders moved or copied.
4. *Right*-click in the List pane and click *Paste* at the shortcut menu.

The above steps illustrate the shortcut menu method of issuing the Cut, Copy, and Paste commands, but there are alternative methods, as listed in Table 7.1. Feel free to select the most convenient method for a given situation.

Table 7.1 Cut, Copy, and Paste Methods

	Shortcut Menu	Keyboard	Computer Window Toolbar
Cut	Right-click, Cut	Ctrl+X	Click Organize button; Cut
Copy	Right-click, Copy	Ctrl+C	Click Organize button; Copy
Paste	Right-click, Paste	Ctrl+V	Click Organize button; Paste

Deleting and Restoring Files in the Recycle Bin

Imagine what would happen if every time you wanted to throw away a piece of paper, you set it on fire. You can probably see two immediate problems: 1) It would be extremely time-consuming, and 2) there would be no way to "dig through the trash" to recover something that you deleted too hastily. A much better way—and the way that you probably practice—is to collect unwanted paper in a wastebasket, and then once a week or so, set all of your trash out for garbage collection.

In Windows, file and folder deletion works on that same principle. The Recycle Bin is like a wastebasket in your computer "office." Rather than immediately destroying files that you delete, Windows places them in the Recycle Bin, a temporary holding area. It then waits until you either execute the Empty Recycle Bin command or run low on hard disk space before it permanently deletes the items.

TIP The Recycle Bin works only on local hard disks. It does not work with removable disks or network locations.

Deleting a File or Folder

To delete a file or folder which moves it to the Recycle Bin, select the desired file(s) or folder(s) and then do any one of the following actions:

- Press the Delete key on the keyboard.
- Click the Organize button on the Computer window toolbar and then click Delete.
- *Right*-click and then click Delete at the shortcut menu.
- Drag the file to the Recycle Bin icon on the desktop.

Depending on how your PC is set up, you might see a confirmation dialog box or not. If the Delete File dialog box opens, click Yes.

TIP To bypass the Recycle Bin when deleting so that the file is immediately destroyed, press Shift+Delete. This would be useful if you want to make sure a confidential file is destroyed right away.

Restoring a Deleted File or Folder

Suppose you made a mistake in deleting a certain file. You can recover it by opening the Recycle Bin and retrieving it.

Steps

To restore a deleted file or folder:

1. Double-click the Recycle Bin icon on the desktop. The Recycle Bin window opens.
2. Locate the file to be retrieved and click the file name to select it.
3. Click the Restore this item button on the Recycle Bin toolbar. The file or folder disappears from the Recycle Bin. If you then open its original location in a Computer window, you will find the file in the folder from which it was deleted.

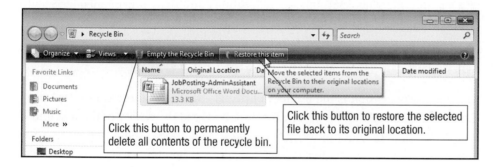

Click this button to permanently delete all contents of the recycle bin.

Click this button to restore the selected file back to its original location.

Occasionally you may run into an issue where you have multiple copies of the same file in the Recycle Bin, perhaps from different original locations or with different dates. How can you tell them apart? One way is to *right*-click one of the files and click *Properties*; a Properties dialog box appears letting you know the date it was created, the date it was deleted, its size, and the folder it was deleted from.

Emptying the Recycle Bin

If you have plenty of free hard disk space, it's okay to let files build up in the Recycle Bin indefinitely. Windows will automatically start deleting the oldest ones whenever disk space becomes an issue. However, some people like to keep things orderly by regularly emptying the Recycle Bin. Privacy is one motivator; another is that if you have only a few items in the Recycle Bin, it becomes much easier to locate and restore any files that you accidentally delete.

You can empty the Recycle Bin from the desktop without opening the Recycle Bin window. *Right*-click the Recycle Bin icon and then choose Empty Recycle Bin at the shortcut menu.

If the Recycle Bin is already open, you can empty it by clicking the Empty the Recycle Bin button on the window's toolbar.

Changing Display Settings

Customization is an important concept for each individual. Each person is unique and has different ideas of what constitutes the "perfect" settings for his or her desktop. Windows has many customization options; however, the options used most frequently relate to the display settings since each person wants his or her desktop to be a reflection of his or her personality and work habits.

TIP In some school settings, customization options are prevented unless you are logged on with a user account that has administrator privileges.

Changing Display Resolution and Color Depth

The *display resolution* is the number of pixels—that is, colored dots—that compose the display. The setting for screen resolution affects the clarity of the text and images. At high resolutions, objects on the screen appear sharp and clear. They also appear smaller, and so higher resolutions allow more items to fit on the screen. At a lower resolution setting, items are larger and easier to see; however some loss of clarity may occur and at resolutions set too low, the objects may appear to have jagged edges. Upon installation, Windows Vista sets the resolution dependent on the monitor size and video card. You can change the default setting to a higher or lower resolution if desired. A common setting for a 15-inch monitor is 1024 x 768 pixels.

Color depth is the number of colors that Windows and applications can use to generate the display. At a high color depth, photos look more realistic, but system performance may be slightly better at a lower color depth. Color depth is measured by the number of binary digits (bits) required to uniquely describe each color. Color depth can range from 1 bit (black and white) to 32-bits (over 16.7 million colors).

Steps

To change the resolution and color depth:

1. *Right*-click the desktop and click Personalize.
2. Click the <u>Display Settings</u> hyperlink in the Control Panel, Personalization window.
3. Drag the *Resolution* slider bar left or right to change the screen resolution setting.
4. Click the *Colors* button to open the list box and click a different color depth if desired.

5. Click OK. At the confirmation dialog box, click Yes or No depending on whether you like the new settings or not.

6. Close the Control Panel, Personalization window.

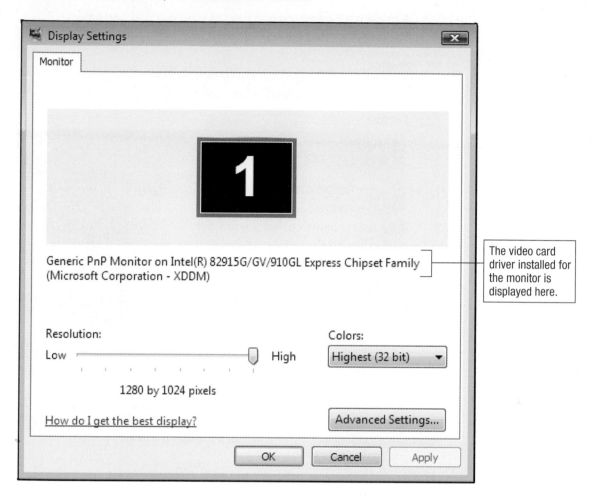

The video card driver installed for the monitor is displayed here.

Applying Appearance Themes

Appearance themes change the style of the windows, menus, dialog boxes, and buttons. By default, Windows Vista comes with two themes: Windows Vista and Windows Classic. Windows Classic makes the display look like earlier versions, which can be helpful for someone who is anxious about upgrading. You can also create your own themes or download more themes from the Internet.

Steps

To change the theme:

1. *Right*-click the desktop and click *Personalize*.

2. Click the Theme hyperlink in the Control Panel, Personalization window.

3. Click the Theme button to open the Theme drop-down list and click the desired theme.

4. Click OK to apply the theme and close the Theme Settings dialog box.

5. Close the Control Panel, Personalization window.

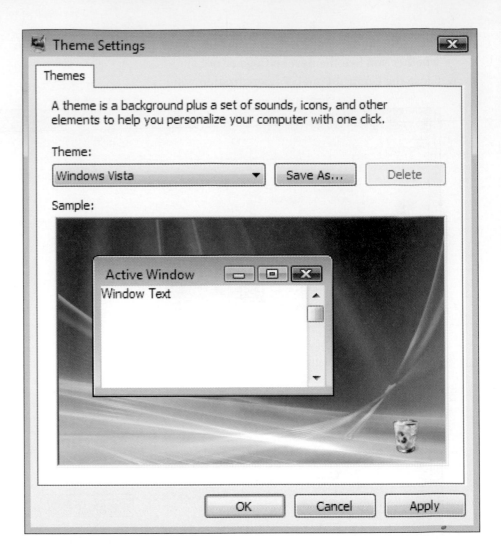

Changing the Desktop Image

In the default Windows Vista installation, a background is selected based on the Vista software edition and the hardware for your computer. A new visual theme for Vista is based upon a feature called Windows Aero. Windows Aero includes a transparent glass design and new window colors. The screens in these tutorials show the Aero interface. Some versions of Vista and some hardware cannot display the Aero interface due to its system requirements. Regardless, you can choose a different picture or turn off the picture altogether for a solid color background.

Steps

To change the desktop image:

1. *Right*-click the desktop and click *Personalize.*
2. Click the Desktop Background hyperlink in the Control Panel, Personalization window.
3. Click a picture in the list to see it applied to your desktop.
4. Click OK.
5. Close the Control Panel, Personalization, Desktop Background window.

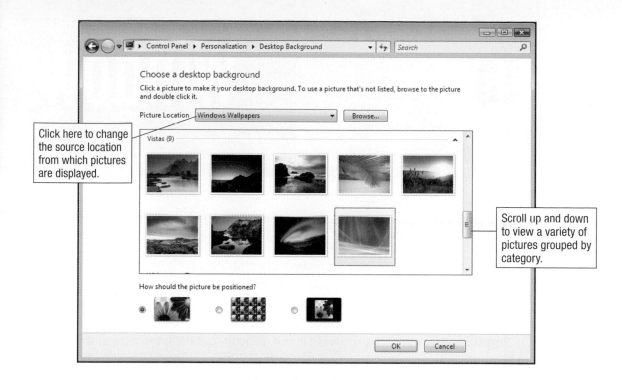

Click here to change the source location from which pictures are displayed.

Scroll up and down to view a variety of pictures grouped by category.

Changing the Color Scheme

Windows Vista Ultimate edition includes seven color schemes. You can select a different color scheme at the Appearance Settings dialog box.

Steps

To choose a different color scheme:

1. *Right*-click the desktop and click Personalize.
2. Click the Window Color and Appearance hyper-link in the Control Panel, Personalization window.
3. Click the desired color scheme option in the *Color scheme* list box in the Appearance Settings dialog box.
4. Click OK.
5. Close the Control Panel, Personalization window.

Installing and Removing Software

Although Windows does have some important utilities built in, its main purpose is to run software that you buy separately. Some of the software you can buy for Windows includes office suites (word processor, spreadsheet, database), Web site creation applications, programming tools, and games.

Installing and removing software is not difficult, but it's important that you do it the right way. You can't simply copy the files for an application to your hard disk to install it, and you can't simply delete its files to remove an application. Windows maintains a configuration database called the Registry that stores information about which applications are installed and where their files are stored. By using the proper procedures for installing and removing software, you allow Windows to update its Registry to reflect the change.

Installing Software

Most software comes on a self-running CD or DVD. To install the application, insert the CD or DVD into the appropriate drive and follow the prompts that appear. If the Setup program does not begin automatically, you can locate and run the Setup program in a Computer window.

TIP In some school settings, installation and removal of software is prohibited on shared computers.

Steps

To run a Setup program:

1. Insert the program's CD or DVD into the appropriate drive. If you are installing software that you have downloaded from the Internet, proceed to Step 3.
2. Most CD or DVD drives are set to AutoPlay meaning the Setup installation program begins on its own. Otherwise, a window opens that displays a list of files stored on the CD or DVD. If the Setup program begins automatically, follow the prompts that display within the setup dialog boxes; otherwise, proceed to Step 3.
3. At a Computer window, display in the list pane the contents of the appropriate CD or DVD drive, or, if you are installing software that was downloaded

from the Internet, display the contents of the folder in which you saved the downloaded setup file.

4. Double-click the file named Setup.exe to start installing the software. For some older software CDs (such as hardware drivers), you may need to browse the folders on the CD until you locate the correct one containing the setup file.

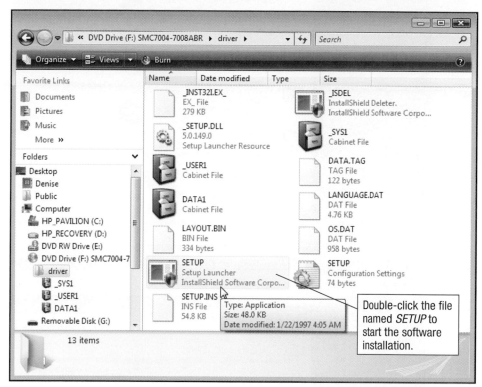

5. Follow the prompts that display within the setup dialog boxes to complete the software installation.

> **During installation, you might be asked to choose which type of installation routine you want to perform. The best choice is usually Typical.**

Removing Software

Removing software that you don't use is not essential, but it frees up space on your hard disk. In addition, if the installed software was loading some portion of itself automatically at startup, removing it will prevent that from happening and will free up some RAM.

If an application has a Remove or Uninstall option on the Start menu, you should use it to remove the software. Otherwise, use options in the Control Panel.

Steps

To remove software using the Control Panel:

1. Click the Start button and then click *Control Panel*.
2. Click the Programs hyperlink in the Control Panel window.

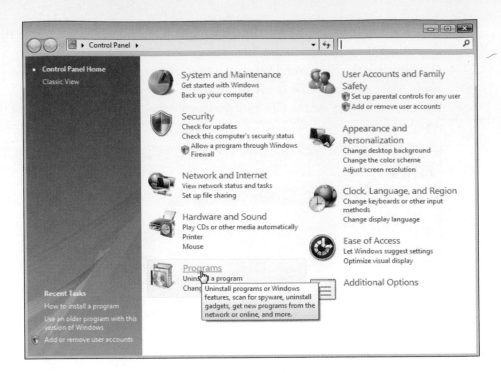

3. Click the <u>Programs and Features</u> hyperlink in the Control Panel, Programs window.

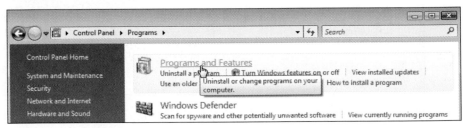

4. Click the name of the software program that you want to remove in the list of installed programs and then click the Uninstall or Uninstall/Change button on the Control Panel toolbar.

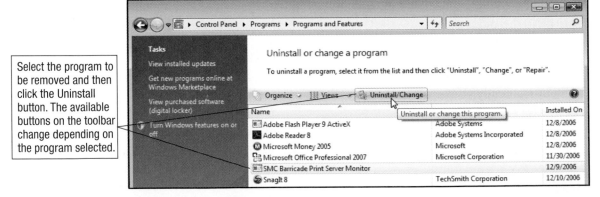

Select the program to be removed and then click the Uninstall button. The available buttons on the toolbar change depending on the program selected.

5. Follow the prompts in the dialog boxes that appear to guide you through the removal process. The procedure varies depending on the software being removed.

Some applications have separate buttons for the Uninstall and Change functions; others have a single Uninstall/Change button and still others have no Change functionality at all and have only an Uninstall button.

Customizing the Start Menu

The Start Menu can be customized by rearranging, adding, and deleting application shortcuts.

Pinning a Shortcut to the Start Menu

You might have already noticed that the applications you use most often appear in the left pane of the Start menu. The shortcuts in this area change depending on your usage (see Figure 9).

Notice also that above these changing shortcuts are two additional shortcuts, one for Internet and one for e-mail. These are shortcuts to the e-mail and Web programs you have configured as the default applications. You can place other shortcuts in this top section of the left pane as well, to make a program's shortcut a permanent part of the Start menu's top level. This feature is known as pinning the shortcut to the Start menu.

Steps

To pin a shortcut to the Start Menu:

1. *Right*-click the application's icon.
2. Click *Pin to Start Menu* at the shortcut menu.

Steps

To unpin a shortcut:

1. *Right*-click a pinned shortcut.
2. Click *Unpin from Start Menu* at the shortcut menu.

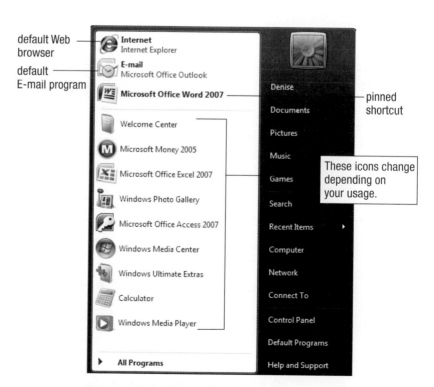

Figure 9   Start Menu

Figure 10

Reorganizing the All Programs Menu

When you click Start, *All Programs*, the left pane is replaced with a menu containing shortcuts for installed applications. Some of these have their own folders (submenus); others appear directly on the first level of the All Programs menu.

To move a shortcut or folder to another position on the All Programs menu, drag-and-drop the desired shortcut to the new location. If you need to open a submenu while dragging-and-dropping, pause on the folder name with the dragged item and the submenu will open within a second or two.

To delete a shortcut from the All Programs menu, *right*-click the shortcut, click Delete (see Figure 10), and then confirm the action at the dialog box that appears. Deleting the shortcut does not uninstall the application; it simply removes its shortcut. You can still start the application using other shortcuts (for example, on the desktop) or by browsing for the executable file in a Computer window.

For more extensive reorganization, open the All Programs menu in a Computer window. From there you can create new folders (which will be submenus) for organizing. This works because All Programs is actually just a folder on your hard disk and the shortcuts on the menu are merely shortcut icons stored within it.

TIP In some school settings, customization options are prevented unless you are logged on with a user account that has administrator privileges.

Steps

To open the All Programs menu:

1. Click the Start button.
2. *Right*-click All Programs and then click *Open All Users*. The Start Menu items open in a Computer window.
3. Double-click the *Programs* folder name. The contents of the All Programs menu appears in the list pane.

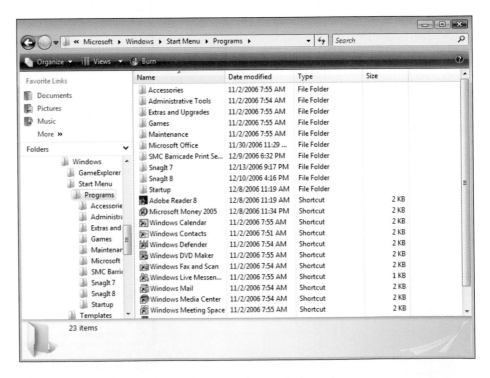

4. Add, delete, and arrange folders and shortcuts as desired. You learned in earlier tutorials how to create and delete folders and how to move and copy files.
5. Check the results of your customization by opening the Start, All Programs menu. When you are finished customizing the menu, close the Computer window.

Choosing Which Items to Show

In the right pane of the Start menu are icons for commonly used shortcuts such as Documents, Pictures, Music, Games, Computer, Control Panel, and so on. You can use the Start Menu Properties dialog box to control which of these icons appear in the right pane and whether the item appears as a submenu or a shortcut to a folder.

Steps

To define the Start Menu right pane content:

1. *Right*-click the taskbar and click *Properties* at the shortcut menu. The Taskbar and Start Menu Properties dialog box open.
2. Click the Start Menu tab.
3. Click the Customize button next to Start menu. The Customize Start Menu dialog box opens.
4. In the Start menu list box, scroll through the list of items and select the desired setting for each menu option. For example, you can make the Control Panel not appear at all, display as a link (the default setting), or display as a menu.
5. Click OK to close the Customize Start Menu dialog box.
6. Click OK to close the Taskbar and Start Menu Properties dialog box.

By default, *Computer, Control Panel,* and *Documents* display as links in the start menu.

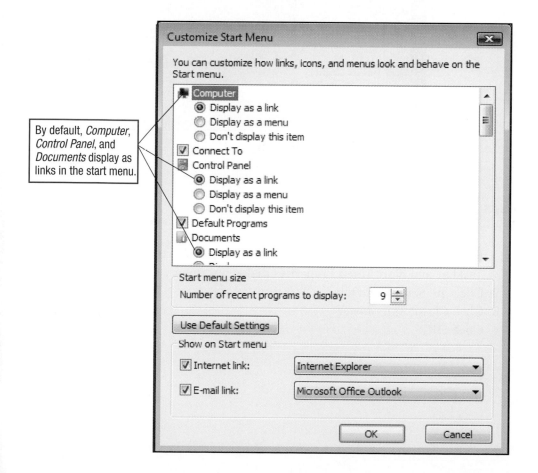

Using the Windows Classic Start Menu

If you have recently upgraded from an earlier Windows version, you might prefer to go back to the Classic Start menu style that was used in Windows XP (see Figure 11).

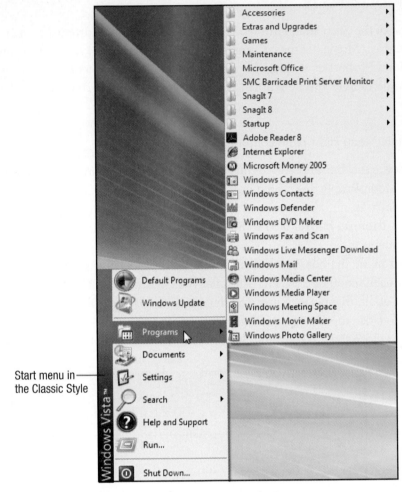

Figure 11 Classic Start Menu Style

Steps

To revert to the Classic Start menu style:

1. *Right*-click the taskbar and click *Properties* at the shortcut menu. The Taskbar and Start Menu Properties dialog box opens.
2. Click the Start Menu tab.
3. Click *Classic Start menu*.
4. Click OK.

Playing Music or Movies

Windows Media Player is a music and video player application that is provided with Windows Vista. Windows Media Player plays a wide variety of music and movies in various file formats including the popular MP3, WMA, WAV, MOV, and AVI formats.

TIP Windows Media Player does not support all audio and video compression formats in use; however you can install a codec (a piece of software that acts as a converter) that will allow Windows Media Player to play a file that is not recognized. See the Help system in Windows for information on third-party add-on applications for the player.

Playing an Audio CD

To play an audio CD, simply insert the CD in the appropriate drive. The music will start playing automatically. The first time you play a music CD you may need to set the AutoPlay option at a pop-up dialog box; however, once set the option becomes the default for all future CDs. If for some reason, the music does not begin to play, open the Windows Media Player window to start the CD.

Steps

To start or restart an audio CD with Windows Media Player:

1. Click the Start button and click *All Programs.*
2. Click *Windows Media Player.*
2. Click the down-pointing arrow on the Now Playing tab.
3. Click Play *'[title of audio CD]'* (x:) where x is the drive letter for the drive containing the CD in the drop-down list. As the CD plays, a graphic in the media player window moves in response to the music.

The Now Playing tab also displays a track list. From this screen (see Figure 12) you can:

- **Play a track out of sequence.** Double-click a track in the list to begin playing it immediately.
- **Skip a track.** Click the Next button while a song is playing to skip the track.
- **Play Next, Previous, Pause, or Stop the player.** Use the buttons at the bottom of the window. These are standard buttons for any player device.

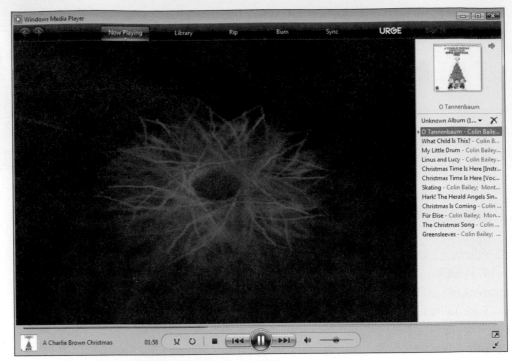

Figure 12 Windows Media Player Now Playing Tab

Playing a DVD Movie

Most computers that come with a DVD drive also come with extra software that works with that drive to play DVD movies. One popular brand is WinDVD. Such software is usually more full-featured than Windows Media Player, so you may prefer to use it if available. However, in the absence of a third-party DVD movie player utility, Windows Media Player will serve.

Figure 13 AutoPlay Dialog Box

Steps

To play a DVD movie using Windows Media Player:

1. Insert the DVD movie in the DVD drive. In most cases, the movie will begin playing automatically. If this is the first time a DVD movie has been inserted, the AutoPlay dialog box (shown in Figure 13) appears in which you choose the AutoPlay option. Once set, the selected option becomes the default for all future DVDs.
2. Click Play DVD Movie using Windows Media Player. Notice the check box *Always do this for DVD movies* is selected by default.

Windows

Burning to a CD or a DVD

Most new computers have at least one drive that can write content to either a CD or a DVD. Windows Vista has functionality built-in to use these drives for writing ("burning") a CD or DVD. You may also elect to use a third-party application such as Nero or Easy Media Creator, which include additional features and capabilities.

Nearly all writable CD/DVD drives can use either CD-recordable (CD-R), DVD-recordable (DVD-R), CD-rewritable (CD-RW), or DVD-rewriteable (DVD-RW) discs. CD-R or DVD-R discs are cheaper but can be written to only once. CD-RW or DVD-RW discs are more expensive, but the contents can be changed after the initial write.

Creating a Data CD

CD is a great medium for creating backups of important files and digital pictures. A CD can hold about 700 MB of data while a DVD can hold up to 4.7 gigabytes of data.

Steps

To copy files to a writable CD:

1. Insert a blank CD-R in the drive. Depending on whether AutoPlay defaults have been set in the Control Panel, a blank window may appear in which you specify the files to copy (see Step 5). Otherwise, proceed to Step 2.
2. At the AutoPlay dialog box, click *Burn files to disc using Windows.*

3. Type the title text you want to assign to the CD in the *Disc title* text box at the Burn a Disc dialog box and then click Next.

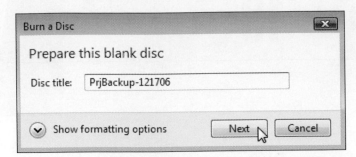

4. Windows formats the disc to prepare the disc to receive data. A progress bar indicates the format progress. When the formatting is complete, a blank Computer window will appear in which you specify the content to be burned to the disc.

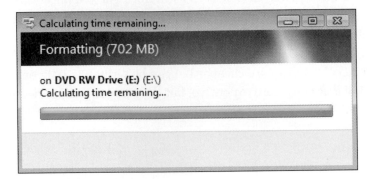

5. Do either of the following:

- Navigate to and select the file(s) and/or folder(s) using standard Windows selection techniques (Shift + click contiguous files; Ctrl + click noncontiguous files), *right*-click within the selection, point to *Send To*, and then click the appropriate drive containing the blank CD.
- To copy multiple file(s) and/or folder(s), navigate to the desired source locations in the Navigation pane, and use the Copy and Paste routines you learned in Tutorial 7 to copy the content to the CD drive. As you paste each selection, Windows copies the source files to the CD.

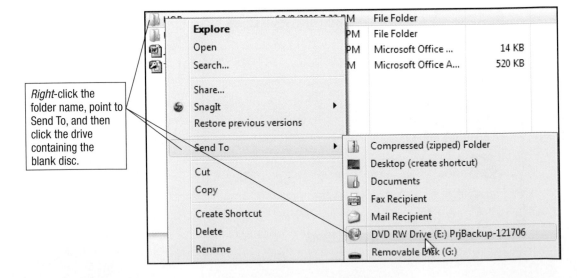

Right-click the folder name, point to Send To, and then click the drive containing the blank disc.

6. A progress bar indicates the estimated time for the copying. Wait for the files to be written to the CD. Try not to use the computer while it is writing, to minimize the possibility of write errors. When the CD is finished, the window displays the CD contents in the list pane. Close the window.

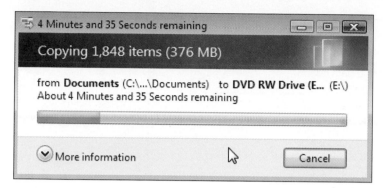

7. Eject the disc using the button on the drive. The disc session will close. This process takes a few seconds to complete since Windows has to finalize the disc preparation and close the session before the CD is ready for use. A message in the notification area of the taskbar indicates the session is being closed.

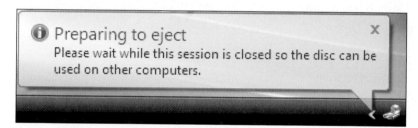

TIP By default, Windows Vista uses the Live File System to burn files, meaning you can copy files to the disc at any time rather than creating a master list and burning all of the files at once. If the CD may be used in older computers, use the Mastered format to avoid compatibility problems. See Windows Help for information on the Mastered format.

TIP What does it mean to rip a CD? You can copy tracks from an audio CD to the computer with Windows Media Player. Once ripped, the songs become files on your computer which you can play back from the library. Be careful that you do not violate copyright laws when copying music files.

Burning a DVD

Burning information to a DVD offers more options than for a CD. You can burn music and pictures to the DVD using Windows Media Player by dragging and dropping items from the library to a burn list and then burn the DVD from the media player window. Create a data DVD by following a process similar to the one described above for burning a data CD (by selecting files and/or folders and copying and pasting to the DVD in a Computer window). Finally, you can create a video DVD using the Windows DVD Maker application. Using Windows DVD Maker allows you to create a DVD that can be played back on a TV. When you insert a blank DVD into the writeable drive, the AutoPlay dialog box appears with

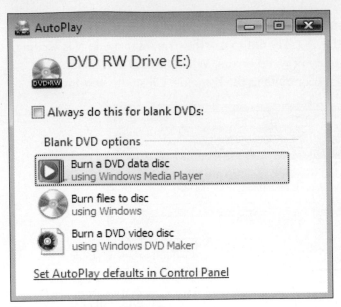

Figure 14 AutoPlay Dialog Box

the options shown in Figure 14. Click the desired method to create the DVD. Use Windows Help to learn more about Windows DVD Maker or Windows Media Player to burn DVDs.

Securing Your Computer

The Windows Security Center provides the current status of several security features in one window (see Figure 15). Windows displays alert icons in the notification area of the taskbar when a problem is detected with a security setting. For example, if the Windows firewall has been turned off, the red security alert icon ⊠ displays. A yellow alert icon 🛡 appears for other types of less serious security issues.

Steps

To open the Windows Security Center:

1. Double-click the security alert icon in the notification area; or Click the Start button, click *Control Panel*, click the <u>Security</u> hyperlink in the Control Panel window, and then click <u>Security Center</u> in the Control Panel, Security window.

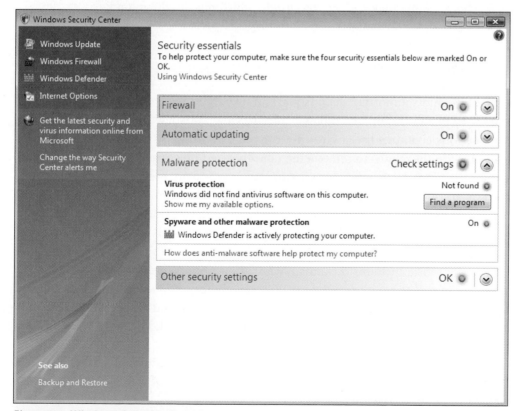

Figure 15 Windows Security Center

At the Windows Security Center, items displayed in green are deemed to be operating okay. Items displayed in yellow require attention to further harden the PC from attack, and items displayed in red are considered critical issues that require immediate correction.

Preventing Unauthorized Access with a Firewall

A firewall can include software or hardware. Firewalls prevent hackers or other malicious software from accessing your computer through the Internet or via a network. Windows includes a software firewall by default and turns the firewall on. Firewalls other than Windows may be installed on the computer you are using meaning the Windows Firewall may be turned off, but the system may still be protected. In this case, you should check the third-party firewall to make sure it is operating correctly.

If your security center displays *Firewall* in red and you do not have a third-party firewall, click the Turn on now button that displays below the red banner. A User Account Control dialog box may appear in which you need to click the Continue button to confirm the change.

Turn on now button

Automatically Updating Windows Vista

By default, Windows searches for critical and recommended updates to your computer, downloads the updates from Microsoft, and installs them each day. If you prefer you can change the update setting to:

- download updates but install only after you have reviewed the update list and discarded those you do not want.
- check for updates and let you decide which ones to download.
- never check for updates.

Protecting Your PC from Malware

One of the most important actions you can take to protect your computer and your data is to install and update reliable antivirus and antispyware software. These applications contain a list of virus and spyware definitions that identify malware and provide the means to remove the unauthorized object and fix the damage (when possible). New computer viruses and spyware are created daily. Most applications automatically check for updates and install them on a weekly basis. Antivirus and antispyware software is sold on a subscription basis which means you buy the license for a certain period of time, after which you need to pay a renewal fee to maintain the updates.

Window Vista includes the antispyware application Windows Defender that operates in real-time to protect your PC from pop-ups and security threats caused by spyware. However, an antivirus program is not included with Windows Vista. At the Security Center, if no antivirus software is detected, Windows provides a button to assist you with finding a program (see Figure 16).

Clicking the Find a program button links you to a Web site maintained by Microsoft with links to popular antivirus programs many of which offer free trials before you have to buy the application license.

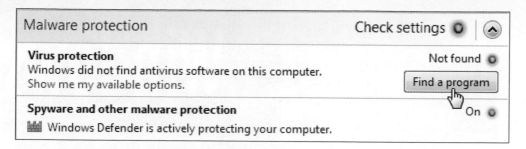

Figure 16 Windows Defender Find a Program Button

Internet and User Account Control Settings

The last option at the Windows Security Center indicates if Internet security and User Account Control settings are at the recommended levels. By default, Internet security is set to medium-high, which means you will be prompted before downloading potentially unsafe content from the Internet and unsigned Active X controls will not be downloaded. User Account Control causes a dialog box to pop up requiring your authorization to continue with a change that will affect your computer's operation or change settings that affect other users. In some cases, you may be prompted to enter an administrator password to continue the operation.

Windows

Maintaining Your Computer

Operating a computer is similar to operating a motor vehicle—after a certain period of time the vehicle requires a tune-up to optimize the vehicle's performance. In the same way, a computer requires a "tune-up" periodically to clear the hard disk of temporary files and improve performance.

Part of your regular computer maintenance should also include checking for Windows Updates and ensuring your virus and antispyware software definitions and subscriptions are up to date. Recall from Tutorial 14 the Windows Security Center provides a one-stop window to perform these checks.

Deleting Temporary Files with Disk Cleanup

As you surf the Internet and work with data files, temporary files are created on your hard disk which are not removed when you have finished your work. The Disk Cleanup utility frees up space on your hard disk by finding and removing these temporary files. As well, the utility empties the recycle bin and removes any system files that are no longer needed.

Steps

To perform a disk cleanup:

1. Click the Start button.
2. With the insertion point positioned in the *Start Search* text box, type **disk cleanup**.
3. Click *Disk Cleanup* in the results list at the top of the left pane.

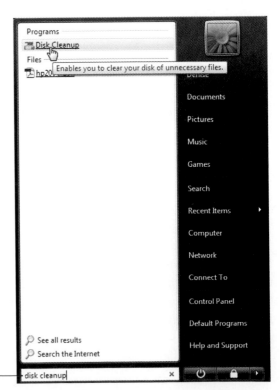

Type the name of the program you want to find in the Start Search text box to save time browsing the menu structure.

4. At the Disk Cleanup Options dialog box, click the option to clear your files only or the files from all users on this computer.

5. At the Disk Cleanup: Drive Selection dialog box, choose the drive you want the temporary files removed from and click OK. Disk Cleanup begins by calculating how much disk space can be freed. When finished, the Disk Cleanup for [computer name] appears in which you can specify which files to delete.

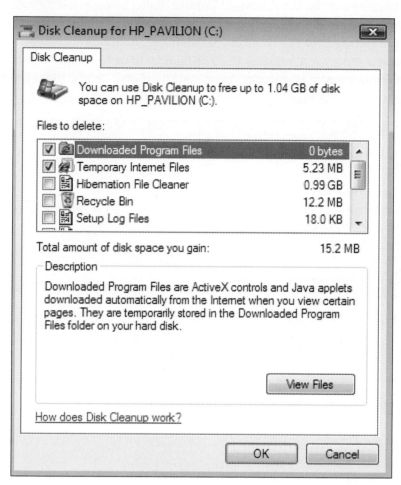

6. Click OK to proceed with the removal of files, or deselect the options that you want to retain and then click OK.

7. Click Delete Files at the next dialog box to confirm you want to permanently delete the files. A progress bar displays as the program removes the files.

Improving Performance using Disk Defragmenter

As you add and delete files to and from your computer, the hard disk becomes fragmented with gaps where files were deleted. A fragmented disk slows down the computer's performance. Defragmenting the hard disk rearranges the data so that the hard disk operates efficiently. By default, Disk Defragmenter is scheduled to run each week; however, you can defragment manually if you have been performing a large amount of file maintenance, or if you have disabled the automatic operation.

Steps

To defragment the hard disk:

1. Click the Start button.
2. With the insertion point positioned in the *Start Search* text box, type **disk defragmenter**.
3. Click *Disk Defragmenter* in the results list at the top of the left pane.
4. Click Continue at the User Account Control dialog box requesting your permission to open the program.
5. Click the Defragment now button. The defragmentation process may take anywhere from several minutes to more than an hour to complete depending on the amount of fragmentation on your hard disk. While the process is working, you can continue doing other tasks on the computer.

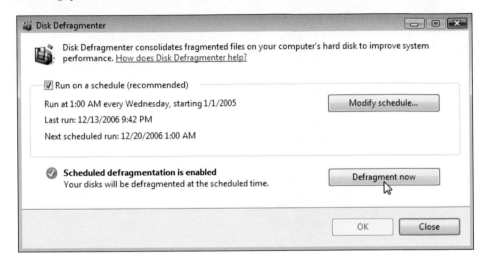

TUTORIAL 1

Internet

Browsing the Web Using Web Addresses

The Internet is a collection of computers around the world connected through telephone lines, cables, satellites, and other telecommunications media. The World Wide Web, called the Web, is a part of the Internet that contains Web pages consisting of text, sounds, video, and graphics that link to other related Web pages. These links are called hyperlinks. Many Web pages are stored in a language called HTML (Hypertext Markup Language) that can be viewed on any computer regardless of the operating system platform (Macintosh, Windows, UNIX, Linux, and so on).

To connect to the Internet and view Web pages you will need the following resources:

- A computer with Internet access.
- Browser software, such as Internet Explorer, Firefox, or Netscape, that provides the interface for viewing Web pages.

In the steps that follow, you will explore Web sites on the Internet using Web addresses in Microsoft Internet Explorer version 7.0 operating in the Windows Vista environment. If you are using another operating system, Web browser, or a different version of Internet Explorer, you may need to alter these instructions slightly.

Steps

1. Click the Launch Internet Explorer Browser icon in the Quick Launch toolbar next to the Start button, or click the Start button and choose *Internet Explorer* from the Start menu.

    If you are completing this tutorial using your computer at home, you may need to enter your user name and password and click OK to connect through a dial-up connection to your Internet service provider (ISP).

    The Internet Explorer window appears with the configured home page displayed in the window as shown in Figure T-1. (The default Web page shown when Internet Explorer first opens may vary from the U.S. Government page shown.)

Figure T-1 Internet Explorer Window with U.S. Government Web page

2. Move the mouse pointer over the current entry in the Address bar, and then click the left mouse button.

> **Clicking the left mouse button selects the entire address and changes the white arrow pointer to an I-beam which indicates you can type text and/or move the insertion point using the arrow keys on the keyboard.**

3. Type **usatoday.com** and then press Enter. The USA Today home page appears in the window. Watch the Status bar for messages displaying the status of loading the page. When the page has finished displaying all of its text, graphics, and other components, the Status bar displays the word "Done."

> **The entry in the Address bar is called a URL (Uniform Resource Locator). URLs are the addressing method used to identify Web pages. After pressing Enter, notice the browser automatically inserted *http://* in front of the address you typed. The letters *http* stand for Hypertext Transfer Protocol, which is the communications standard used for transferring data within the Web.**

4. Move the mouse pointer over the underlined headings displayed at the left side of the USA Today page. Notice the pointer changes shape to a white hand with the index finger pointing upward when it is positioned over underlined text.

When the pointer takes this shape, it means you can click the left mouse button to jump to a related Web page (called a *hyperlink*).

5. Click the left mouse button over Scores. In a few seconds the scores page is displayed with recent sports scores.
6. Click the Back button on the toolbar to return to the previous page.
7. Click the Forward button on the toolbar to redisplay the scores page (the page viewed prior to clicking the Back button).
8. Notice the down-pointing arrow to the right of the Back and Forward buttons on the toolbar. Click the down-pointing arrow and then click a Web site name in the drop-down list to jump to a page previously viewed.
9. Click the mouse pointer in the Address bar, type **microsoft.com**, and then press Enter.
10. Click one of the hyperlinks on the Microsoft home page to jump to a topic that interests you.
11. Continue exploring Web pages by typing URLs in the Address bar, clicking hyperlinks, as well as the toolbar Back and Forward buttons.
12. When you have finished exploring the Web, click the Close button at the right end of the Title bar to exit Internet Explorer. If necessary, disconnect from your ISP if you are not continuing on to Tutorial 2.

Back button

Forward button

Close button

Conducting a Basic Web Search

In the previous Internet tutorial, Web sites were explored by keying the Web address (URL) for a specific company. Another method used to find information is by entering a keyword or a phrase and then browsing through a series of Web pages that were found. Several search engines are available to assist users with locating Web sites by topic. A search engine is a company that uses specialized software to continually scan the Web to index and catalog the information that is published. These companies have created Web sites where the user begins a search by typing the word or phrase about which they would like to find information. The search engine then lists the Web pages that contain the word or phrase as links, which are called hits. Some search engines maintain category indices where the user clicks through a series of categories and subcategories until they reach the desired list of Web pages.

In this tutorial, you will find information on the Web by entering keywords and then conduct another search by browsing through a list of categories.

Steps

1. Start Internet Explorer and then maximize the Internet Explorer window if it is not already maximized. If necessary, connect to your ISP and enter your user name and password.
2. Locate the Instant Search Box in the top right corner of the browser window.

> **The Instant Search Box allows you to execute a search using a search engine at any time, no matter what Web page you are currently on. Internet Explorer 7 uses Live Search as its default search engine. This is indicated by the text *Live Search* in the Instant Search Box.**

3. Click once in the Instant Search text box (the default text will disappear), immediately type **space station facts**, then press the Enter key. A list of hyperlinked Web pages displays in the Internet Explorer window that Live Search has indexed to the phrase you typed. *Note: If a dialog box appears asking you to enable Auto Complete, click No.*

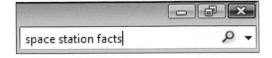

4. Click one of the links in the Internet Explorer window to view a related Web page.

5. Click the Back button to return to the search results list and then click another link to view another Web page.

> **Another way to search for information is to use a search engine's category index. In the next steps, you will type the URL for a search engine and then browse the category index.**

6. Click once on the URL currently displayed in the Address bar.

> **Clicking on the URL in the Address bar highlights it; anything you type next replaces the URL.**

7. Type **yahoo.com** in the Address bar and then press Enter.

> **Yahoo! is a popular search engine that maintains category indices and can also be used to search for a topic by keywords.**

8. Click the <u>More</u> hyperlink above the *Search* text box at the top of the Yahoo! page and then click *Directory*.

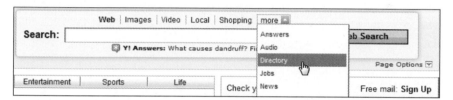

9. Scroll down the Yahoo! Web page and then click the <u>Science</u> hyperlink.

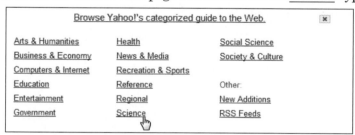

10. Scroll down the Yahoo! directory page for the Science category and then click the <u>Space</u> hyperlink.

- **Oceanography@**
- **Paleontology@**
- **Physics** (1895) NEW!
- **Psychology@**
- **Space** (1700) NEW!

11. Scroll down the Yahoo! directory page for the Science > Space category and then click the <u>Space Stations</u> hyperlink.

- **Space Environment** (73)
- **Space Physics** (29)
- **Space Stations** (54)
- **Spacecraft** (513) NEW!
- **Web Directories** (7)

12. Click <u>International Space Station (ISS)</u> on the Space Stations category page.
13. Click one of the links that is of interest to you on the International Space Station category page to read about this international project.
14. Click the Back button on the Internet Explorer toolbar, click another link from the International Space Station category page, and then view the Web page.
15. Close Internet Explorer.

If necessary, disconnect from your ISP if you are not continuing on to Tutorial 3.

URLs for Other Popular Search Engines	
Excite	http://www.excite.com
Google	http://www.google.com
WebCrawler	http://www.webcrawler.com

Conducting an Advanced Web Search

The number of Web sites that an individual will see in a list as the result of a search request can be overwhelming. It is not uncommon to see thousands of hits result from searching by a few keywords. The challenge when searching for information on the Internet is to reduce the number of hits to the smallest possible number. Including a search operator with the keywords refines a search by limiting the sites that are displayed based on where or how the keywords are placed. Search operators vary among search engines, so it is best to view links to advanced search information for a search engine prior to using operators.

In this tutorial, you will find information on the Web using Boolean operators, specifying a time period, and filtering by a domain in an advanced search page.

Steps

1. Start Internet Explorer. If necessary, connect to your ISP and enter your user name and password.
2. Type **google.com** in the Address bar and then press Enter.

   Search engines are constantly adding and removing Web pages from their databases and directories and changing their search page design. Therefore, the results you achieve throughout this tutorial may differ from what is shown in the figures or what is mentioned in the text.

3. Type **tesla** in the search text box and then click the Google Search button. In a few seconds, linked Web pages display; the total number of sites found from searching the index provided at the top of the search results list. The search engine has found over 220,000,000 results for "tesla," including the rock band Tesla, the scientist Nikola Tesla, and Tesla Motors. *Note: Search engine listings change daily so the number of results you receive will likely differ from 220,000,000.*

4. Scroll down the search results list and read the titles and descriptions of the Web pages found.

   In the next steps you will refine the list to display only those pages that contain information about the scientist Nikola Tesla.

5. Scroll to the top of the page and then click the Advanced Search hyperlink .

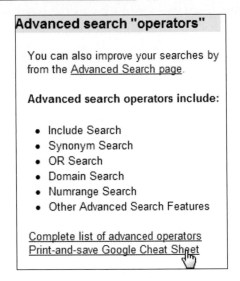

Web	Images	Video	News	Maps	more »	
tesla						Advanced Search
						Preferences
	Google Search		I'm Feeling Lucky			Language Tools

6. Click the Advanced Search Tips hyperlink at the top of the page.

Advanced Search   Advanced Search Tips | About Google

7. Scroll down the *Advanced search operators* section and click the Print-and-save Google Cheat Sheet hyperlink.

Advanced search "operators"

You can also improve your searches by from the Advanced Search page.

Advanced search operators include:

- Include Search
- Synonym Search
- OR Search
- Domain Search
- Numrange Search
- Other Advanced Search Features

Complete list of advanced operators
Print-and-save Google Cheat Sheet

8. Read the information about the options available for the Google search engine.

> When you type multiple words in the Google search box, all words are used to find results as if all your words were separated by the word AND. The more words you type, the more precise your search. You can also precede a word with a minus sign to exclude that word from the results. Let's specify "Nikola" and omit results with the words "band" or "motors."

OPERATOR EXAMPLE	FINDS PAGES CONTAINING...
vacation hawaii	the words **vacation** and **Hawaii** .
Maui OR Hawaii	either the word **Maui** or the word **Hawaii**
"*To each his own*"	the exact phrase **to each his own**
virus −computer	the word **virus** but NOT the word **computer**

9. Click in the Address bar, type **google.com**, and press the Enter key to return to the Google search page.

> Typing google.com in the Address bar takes you directly to the Google search page, which is quicker than clicking the browser's back button several times.

10. In the Google search box, type **nikola tesla -band -motors** and click the Google Search button. *Note: Take care to type the hyphens (or minus signs) immediately before band and motors.*

> **Your search results have been filtered. Instead of over 220,000,000 results, you now have just over 1,000,000. While that may seem like a lot, the majority of results should relate to the scientist and not the band or motor company. In the next steps, you will further refine your search by specifying a time period for published information and a domain filter.**

11. Click the <u>Advanced Search</u> link. Your search terms are pre-filled for you. Notice *nikola tesla* appears in the *with all of the words* text box while *band motors* appears in the *without the words* text box.

12. If necessary scroll down the Advanced Search page to the *Date* section. Click the down-pointing arrow next to the *Return web pages updated in the* text box and choose *past 3 months* from the list menu.

13. Locate the *Domain* section and type **pbs.org** in the text box.

> **This will filter your search results further to include only Web pages from the pbs.org domain that have been updated in the past three months.**

14. Scroll to the top of the page if necessary and click the Google Search button. Your search results will be filtered to just over 30 results, and the results should be more relevant to your search terms. *Note: The number of your results may vary. If you do not return any results, click Advanced Search and change the return Web pages updated in the textbox to a larger value, such as "Past Year."*

15. Close Internet Explorer. If necessary, disconnect from your ISP if you are not going on to Tutorial 4.

Shopping on the Web

The ability to shop at any time throughout the day, browse a variety of products within minutes, and compare prices among vendors with just a few mouse clicks is making online shopping a popular choice. **E-tailing**, the selling of retail goods on the Internet, is what most individuals think of when the term **e-commerce** is used. Companies that brought e-tailing to mainstream popularity are Dell Computers and bookseller Amazon.com. Most e-tailers use secure Web site servers that automatically encrypt personal data such as a credit card number as it is transmitted. This provides protection for both the consumer and the e-tailer. A secure Web site is indicated with a URL that begins with *https* rather than *http*. Encryption involves the use of Secure Sockets Layer (SSL) technology that scrambles information into an unbreakable code before it is sent over the Internet. To indicate that an active Web site is secure, Internet Explorer, Firefox, and Netscape display an icon of a closed lock on the right side of the Address bar.

In this tutorial, you will browse an e-tailer's secure Web site and identify the security and privacy features.

Steps

1. Start Internet Explorer. If necessary, connect to your ISP and enter your user name and password.
2. Type **newegg.com** in the Address bar and then press Enter.

   Newegg is an online retailer specializing in computer gear.

3. Click any one of the items shown on the home page.

   Clicking an item takes you to a details page where you can learn more about the item.

4. Click the ADD TO CART button. *Note: In the next steps you will proceed to check out in order to look at the visual clues that identify a secure Web server. However, you will not complete an actual transaction.*

5. Click the Checkout button. The shopping cart summary page displays and shows you the one item you have placed in your shopping cart.

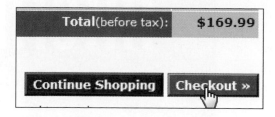

6. If necessary, scroll to the bottom of the page and click the Checkout button. The login page appears for existing members to log in.

> **New shoppers to the Newegg Web site without an account can create an account from this page.**

7. Locate the identifying features of a secure server. The URL begins with *HTTPS* and the closed padlock icon appears on the right side of the Address bar.

8. Find the *Security* section on the left side of the page and click the <u>Read More</u> hyperlink. A page of frequently asked questions (FAQs) relating to making online purchases appears.

> **Security is not just about keeping credit card information safe but is also about protecting a buyer's personal information. If an e-tailer does not have a link to a page that informs the buyer how information is stored and shared, then the site should be avoided.**

9. Click any of the FAQ hyperlinked questions to read about Newegg's policies.
10. If the Back button is enabled on the toolbar, click it to return to the Sign-In page. If the Back button is disabled, the Security page opens in a new window. Close the Security page window to return to the Sign-In page.

> **If you were actually going to complete your purchase, you would need to log in or create an account.**

11. Close Internet Explorer. If necessary, disconnect from your ISP if you are not going on to Tutorial 5.

> Cavaet Emptor! The trading principle, "Let the Buyer Beware" is just as applicable to electronic commerce as it is to face-to-face shopping. Buyers need to be prudent about verifying product and vendor reliability. The Better Business Bureau's site at http://www.bbb.org is a great place to start.

Downloading Information from the Web

If you find a Web site that contains information on a topic that you want to save for future use, you can either print a hard copy of the Web page(s) or you can save it as a file on your computer. If you want to save only a portion of the text on the Web page, select the text with the mouse and then copy it to the Clipboard. Once the text is stored in the Clipboard, it can be pasted into WordPad or Microsoft Word and then saved as a document. A graphic or another multimedia component on a Web page also can be downloaded and saved as a file.

In this tutorial, you will save an entire Web page as a file, select text from a Web page to copy and paste, and then save a graphic image as a file.

Steps

1. Start Internet Explorer. If necessary, connect to your ISP and enter your user name and password.
2. Type **loc.gov** in the Address bar and then press Enter.
3. Click the <u>AMERICAN MEMORY</u> link.

4. At the American Memory Home page, click the <u>Today in History</u> link.

5. Click the Page button on the Standard toolbar and then click Save As.

> **To successfully save the page, you will have to configure three options: the folder location in which the file will be saved, the name of the file, and the type of file. You will configure these three settings in the next few steps.**

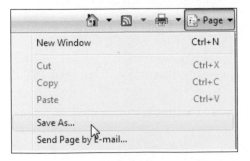

6. If you don't see a list of locations on the left side of the Save Webpage dialog box, click the Browse Folders button at the bottom of the dialog box.

7. On the left side of the Save Webpage dialog box, select *Desktop*.

This sets the download location to your desktop as indicated in the Save Webpage dialog box's Address bar. This will make it easy to find your file once it has been downloaded.

8. Verify that the *File name* text box reads *Today in History [today's date]*, set the *Save as type* option to *Web Archive, single file (*.mht)*, and then click the Save button.

A progress box appears as the Web page elements are downloaded and saved locally. To view the Web page at a later time, start Internet Explorer and press [CTRL]+[O]. Click the Browse button in the Open dialog box, navigate to the drive and/or folder where the Web page is stored, and then double-click the Web page name in the list box.

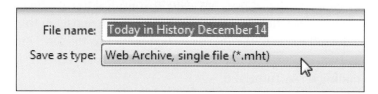

WARNING!
Be careful when downloading information from the Internet and be sure you are not violating someone's copyright. If in doubt, contact the author of the Web page and request permission before using material you have copied from a Web page.

I-beam pointer

9. With Today in History still the active page, position the mouse pointer slightly left of the first character in the first paragraph of text until the pointer changes to the I-beam pointer and then drag the mouse down and right to the end of the first paragraph as shown. *Note: Your text will vary from the text shown if you are viewing Today in History on a date other than December 14.*

> I leave you with undefiled hands, an uncorrupted heart, and with ardent vows to heaven for the welfare and happiness of that country in which I and my forefathers to the third or fourth progenitor drew our first breath.

10. Click the Page button on the Standard toolbar and then click Copy.

The selected text is saved to the Windows Clipboard. To save the text permanently, open a software application such as WordPad or Microsoft Word, paste the text, edit or format as required, and then save it as a document.

11. Click the Start button, click *All Programs*, click *Accessories*, and then click *WordPad*.
12. At a blank document window, click Edit on the Menu bar and then click *Paste*.
13. Click the Save button on the toolbar to open the Save As dialog box. Change the drive and/or folder as required in the Save In text box, type **Today in History** in the *File name* text box, and then click the Save button.
14. Click File and then click *Exit* to close the document and exit WordPad.

When WordPad closes, you should automatically be returned to the Internet Explorer window. If necessary, click the button on the Taskbar representing Internet Explorer to restore the window.

15. Click Back on the toolbar to return to the American Memory Home page.
16. Move the mouse pointer over any of the photographs in the main part of the page and then right-click. Click *Save Picture As* from the shortcut menu.

A graphic does not have to be saved as a file. Right-click a picture on a Web page and Copy it to the Clipboard. Paste the image into a document using the Edit, Paste command if you simply want to copy an image and do not need it saved as a separate file.

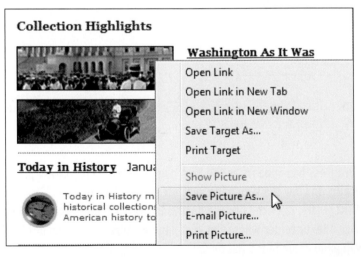

17. At the Save Picture dialog box, navigate to your desktop or other storage location as you did when you saved a Web page previously in this tutorial.
18. With the default name in the *File name* text box, click the Save button.
19. Close Internet Explorer. If necessary, disconnect from your ISP if you are not continuing on to Tutorial 6.

TUTORIAL 6

Internet

Reference Resources on the Web

A search engine can return a large number of hits as the result of a search request by keyword(s) or phrase even when search operators are included to reduce the list of Web pages. Although using the Internet to locate information is fast and very accessible, extra time needs to be taken to assess the reliability and accuracy of the online information. Information on the Internet can comprise opinions, stories, statistics, or facts. The context with which information is presented may be designed to inform the reader or persuade the reader to accept an opinion or buy a product or service. A considerable amount of time to filter through the hits to find the credible information can be avoided by using one of the many reference resources available on the Web. Reference resources are portals to information that has been evaluated prior to being linked through the resource site.

In this tutorial you will use two reference resource sites to locate information about global warming and earth sciences on the Internet.

Steps

1. Start Internet Explorer. If necessary, connect to your ISP and enter your user name and password.
2. Key **lii.org** in the Address bar and then press Enter.

   The Librarians' Index to the Internet contains over 7,800 Internet resources selected and evaluated by librarians. The index was originally funded by the U.S. Institute of Museum and Library Services and is now maintained through funding from the Library of California.

3. Click in the Search text box, type **"global warming"** and then click the Search LII.org button. *Note: Be sure to include the opening and closing quotes.*

4. Scroll through the list of Web links found. Click one of the links that interests you.
5. Click the Back button on the Internet Explorer toolbar to return to your original search results listing, scroll down until you see the *Regions of the World* category of links on the left side of the page, and click the

Polar Regions hyperlink. This narrows your search results to global warming in the polar regions.

Regions of the World	
International Governments	(4)
Maps	(2)
Polar Regions	(3)
More subtopics	

The Librarians' Index to the Internet and the Internet Public Library are just two of many reference resources. Go to your favorite search engine page and type reference resources to find more!

6. Type **ipl.org** in the Address bar and then press Enter.

   The Internet Public Library is hosted by the School of Information & Library Studies of the University of Michigan. The site contains a rich resource of library services to Internet users.

7. Click the <u>Science & Tech</u> hyperlink on the left side of the page.

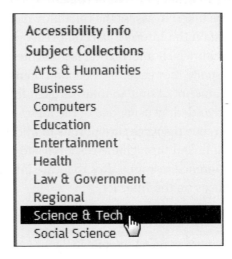

Accessibility info
Subject Collections
   Arts & Humanities
   Business
   Computers
   Education
   Entertainment
   Health
   Law & Government
   Regional
   Science & Tech
   Social Science

8. Click the <u>Earth Sciences</u> hyperlink in the main area of the page. Scroll down the page if necessary to see the link.

Earth Sciences
Branches of science related the Earth, its surface, and its atmosphere.

9. Scroll down the list of Internet resources provided for the Earth Sciences category and then click a link to a site that interests you.

10. Close Internet Explorer. If necessary, disconnect from your ISP if you are not going on to Tutorial 7.

Internet

Communicating Using Instant Messaging

Instant messaging (IM) is similar to an online chat with the exception that there are fewer participants engaged in a conversation that is not able to be viewed by everyone who is online. IM runs in the background while you are working on your computer. When a message arrives or one of your contacts goes online, a pop-up screen informs you. In a default installation of Microsoft Windows Vista, a download link to Windows Live Messenger is installed to the Start menu. After downloading and installing Windows Live Messenger, you need to have a .NET Passport in order to send and receive instant messages with other users. You also need the IM address of your friend added to your contacts list.

In this tutorial, you will install and open Windows Live Messenger, obtain a .NET Passport, add a contact to your contacts list, and send and receive a message to another student.

Note: Check with your instructor before completing this tutorial to find out which student in the class you will be partnered with for sending and receiving an instant message. Also, find out if Windows Live Messenger is already installed on your computer. If it is, skip to Step 12.

Download and Install Windows Live Messenger

Steps

1. Click the Start button and then click *Windows Live Messenger Download.* Internet Explorer launches and opens the Windows Live Messenger download page. You may be prompted to connect to your ISP by entering your user name and password.

2. Click the Get it free button.

3. At the File Download - Security Warning dialog box, click the Run button to download and install the program without saving it. The download may take some time, depending on your connection speed. Internet Explorer will alert you before running the installation program. *Note: If your Vista user account does not have permission to install software, you will see a different dialog box prompting you for an administrative password. You will need to type an administrative password to continue.*

4. In the Internet Explorer - Security Warning dialog box, click the Run button.

5. In the Windows Live Messenger Setup Wizard dialog box, click the Next button to begin the installation.

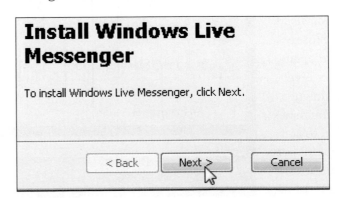

6. Read the information in the Terms of Use and Privacy Statement page of the Windows Live Messenger Setup Wizard dialog box, select the option stating *I accept the Terms of Use and Privacy Statement*, and click the Next button.

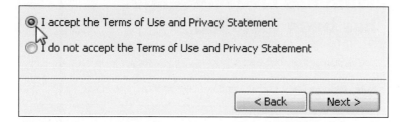

7. In the Choose additional features and settings page of the Windows Live Messenger Setup Wizard dialog box, remove the check marks in all of the checkboxes and then click Next.

Checking any of these boxes would result in changes being made to the default behavior of your computer or Internet Explorer. For the purposes of this tutorial, we will install Windows Live Messenger without any additional features or settings.

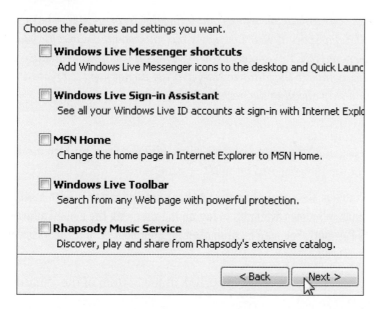

8. If the User Account Control dialog box appears, click the Continue button.

User Account Control in Windows Vista prohibits unauthorized users from making certain changes to the computer, such as installing software.

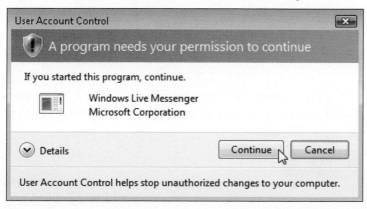

9. At the Windows Live Messenger has been installed page of the Windows Live Messenger Setup Wizard dialog box, click the Close button.

10. Exit Internet Explorer. The Windows Live Messenger window should now be visible.

Create a .NET Passport

Note: Check with your instructor before completing this tutorial to find out if you need to create a new .NET Passport, if your instructor has an account created for you, or if you may use your personal .NET Passport if you have one. If you need to create a .NET Passport account, complete the following steps. If you do not need to create a .NET Passport account, skip ahead to the next section.

Steps

11. If necessary, click the Start button, click *All Programs*, and then click *Windows Live Messenger* to launch the program.

> **If Windows Messenger has already been set up for a user with a .NET Passport account, Windows attempts to log on the user with the e-mail address of the .NET Passport. You may be prompted for your password if the password has not been stored.**

12. Click the Get a new account hyperlink at the bottom of the Windows Live Messenger window.

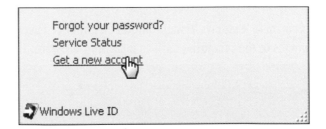

13. Internet Explorer opens the Get your Windows Live ID sign up page. (You may need to provide your user name and password to sign in to your ISP.) Click the Sign up button.

14. Type your desired name in the *Windows Live ID* text box and click the Check availability button to see if that user name is available. *Note: The Windows Live ID cannot contain spaces or special characters.* If your desired name is not available, type a different name and click the Check availability button again. Continue this process until you find a name that is available. Once you have decided on a name and verified it is available, write it down on a piece of paper followed by *@hotmail.com*.

You will later sign in to Windows Live Messenger using an e-mail address consisting of the name you just used followed by "@hotmail.com." This e-mail address is your .NET Passport.

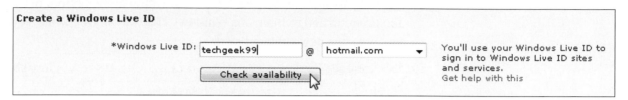

15. Continue to fill out the rest of the sign-up form and then click the I Accept button to create your account.
16. When the Congratulations page appears, exit Internet Explorer. The Windows Live Messenger window will once again be visible.

Use Windows Live Messenger

Steps

17. If necessary, click the Start button, click *All Programs*, and click *Windows Live Messenger* to launch the program.

Windows Live Messenger may be configured to automatically sign you in if it was previously installed. If you are automatically signed in, skip the next step and proceed to Step 19.

18. Enter your .NET Passport and password and then click the Sign In button. *Note: If you have a Hotmail or MSN account, you already have a Passport—sign in by typing your e-mail address and password.*

For the remaining steps, you will be working with your instant messaging partner. Decide between you which student will add the other as a contact, and only one student should complete Steps 19–20.

19. At the top of the Windows Live Messenger dialog box, click the Add a Contact button.

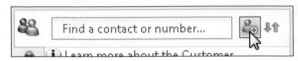

20. In the *Instant Messaging Address* text box, type the e-mail address of your tutorial partner and then click the Save button at the bottom of the window. You are returned to the main Windows Live Messenger window where you will see your new contact listed.

21. The student that did not add the contact should complete this step. At the Windows Live Messenger dialog box informing you that *[student name]* has added you to his/her contacts list, click OK to accept *Allow this person to see when you are online and contact you* and *Add this person to my contact list*.

22. In the *Online* section of the Windows Messenger window, double-click the e-mail address of the student with whom you have been partnered. A Conversation window opens in which you type message text to send and read the other person's replies.

23. With the insertion point positioned in the message text box at the bottom of the Conversation window, type **Instant messaging is fun!** and then click the Send button.

Your tutorial partner will receive an alert on his or her computer as soon as the message is received.

24. Send a few more messages back and forth to each other.
25. When you are finished using Windows Live Messenger, click the Close button on the Conversation window Title bar.
26. Click the Windows Live Messenger - Signed In icon on the Taskbar next to the current time and then click Sign Out at the pop-up menu.

Messenger icon

GLOSSARY

3D modeling program a program that allows users to create the illusion of depth in objects drawn on the computer

3G third-generation cellular technology that allows for the transfer of voice and nonvoice data

802.11 protocol a protocol for wireless LAN technology that specifies an over-the-air interface between the wireless client device and a server, or between two wireless devices, approved by the IEEE in 1997; also called Wi-Fi

802.11a protocol revision of the 802.11 protocol for wireless LAN technology, approved in 2001, which offers transfer rates of up to 54 Mbps when devices are at a range within 60 feet of the primary access point or hub, 22 Mbps at longer distances

802.11b protocol first major revision of 802.11 protocol for wireless LAN technology, approved in 1999, relatively low cost and with a faster transfer rate of 5.5 Mbps to 11 Mbps at a range up to 250 feet; popular in home and small office wireless networks

802.11g protocol approved in June 2003, this protocol for wireless LAN technology operates in the same frequency range as 802.11b but with transfer rates similar to 802.11a

A

Accelerated Graphics Port (AGP) bus a bus that increases the speed at which graphics (including 3D graphics) and video can be transmitted and accessed by the computer

acceptable use policy (AUP) a set of guidelines schools and other organizations develop to inform their internal users about standards of computer and Internet behavior and the procedure for reporting violations

access time the time a storage device spends locating a particular file

active-matrix display a type of monitor display in which separate transistors control each color pixel, allowing viewing from any angle; also called thin-film transistor (TFT) display

adapter an electronic circuit board that can be inserted onto the motherboard inside a computer to add new capabilities to a computer; examples include sound cards, graphics cards, and network interface cards; also called an expansion card

address a specific location in memory where an instruction or data is stored; the computer assigns an address to

each location so the instruction or data can be quickly located and retrieved when needed

adware software that tracks the Web sites that a user visits in order to collect information for marketing or advertising

algorithm a series of precise steps to solve a given programming problem

alpha product a prototype of software under development used by the development team for testing purposes

alphanumeric check a check made by database input forms to make sure that the value entered into a field contains only letters or numbers

alphanumeric data data that contains letters and numbers; may contain special characters

American Standard Code for Information Interchange (ASCII) a coding scheme used on many personal computers and on various midrange servers

amplifier an electronic device that receives signals along a network, amplifies the signals, and resends the amplified signals along the network; also called a repeater

analog signal an electronic signal composed of continuous waves transmitted at a certain frequency range over a medium, such as a telephone line

android a term used to describe a robot designed to seem human

antivirus software a software program for personal computers that seeks out and destroys any viruses found on a computer

applet a small application program, generally one created using the Java programming language, that performs specific functions; used to extend the capabilities of Web pages

application developer a person whose job it is to adapt software for use within a new system

application development the use of commercial software to develop an information system for a specific organization

application programmer a professionally trained programmer who specializes in developing new application software or updating existing application software

application programming software development that specializes in creating new or updating existing application software

application software programs that enable a user to perform specific tasks; examples of programs include word processors, database programs, spreadsheets, and desktop publishing

applied ethics the application of normative ethical beliefs to controversial real-life issues

arithmetic/logic unit (ALU) the part of the central processing unit (CPU) that carries out the instructions and performs the actual arithmetic and logical operations on the data; can perform arithmetic operations such as addition, subtraction, multiplication, and division and can also compare data items

artificial intelligence (AI) the science of using computers to simulate intelligent mental activities or physical behaviors such as problem solving, learning, and natural language processing

assembly language a low-level programming language that is derived directly from the binary instructions (machine language) understood by the CPU

asynchronous transmission a data transmission method in which control bits surround each byte of data; an extra bit, called a start bit, is added at the front of the character to signal its beginning and another bit, the stop bit, is added at the end of the character to indicate its end; and there is also the error checking bit called a parity bit

attribute the term for a field in a relational database

audio data relating to sound, including speech and music

audio data relating to sound, including speech and music

audio input the process of entering (recording) speech, music, and/or sound effects into a computer

audio mail sound attachments that can be sent with e-mails

audio perception the capability of a computer system to hear sounds in its environment and to understand what it is hearing; speech recognition is one example of this technology

audio port connects a sound card to external devices such as speakers, microphones, and headsets

auditing a review of monitoring data and system logins to look for unauthorized access or suspicious behavior

authentication the process of identifying an individual based on a username and password

automated clearinghouse (ACH) an automated entity established for the purpose of transferring funds electronically from one account to another account

auxiliary storage a type of storage that consists of devices and media used to record information and data permanently so it can later be retrieved, edited, modified, displayed, or printed; also called permanent storage, secondary storage, or external storage

avatar a virtual body given to a player in a game in order to create a virtual reality

AVI file format a Windows movie media format, identified with an .avi extension

B

backup and recovery plan developed by database administrators to ensure that data is backed up regularly and can be recovered in the case of loss

backup utility software that allows the user to make copies of the contents of disks or tapes

bandwidth the amount of data that can travel over an analog medium

banner a type of advertisement that takes up an approximately one-inch-high slice of a Web page; clicking on the banner activates a link to a vendor's site

bar code reader an electronic device that uses photo technology to read the lines in a bar code; the lines and spaces contain symbols that the computer translates into information

BASIC a programming language designed in the 1960s as a learning language for new programmers; acronym for Beginner's All-purpose Symbolic Instruction Code

basic input/output system (BIOS) a program that boots (starts) a computer when it is turned on and controls communications with the keyboard, disk drives, and other components

batch processing the accumulating of a large amount of data to process at once, rather than doing it immediately, as requests come into the system

bay a site within the system unit where a device, such as a floppy disk drive, hard disk drive, or CD-ROM drive is installed; also called a storage bay

beta testing one of the last steps in software development that involves allowing outside people to use the software to see if it works as designed

beta version a prerelease version of a piece of software distributed so that users can test it to evaluate features and to identify any existing bugs

binary numbers base 2 numbers written as strings of 1s and 0s

binary string sequence of binary symbols

biometric identifier an identifiable physical trait that can be measured by a biometric device and used to identify individual people

bit the smallest unit of data a computer can understand and act on; an abbreviation for binary digit

bit depth the number of bits used in a graphics expansion board to store information about each pixel; also called color depth

bitmap a storage technique in which scanned text or a

photo is stored as a matrix of rows and columns of dots

bitmap-based graphics program a computerized process of displaying images in which the program treats the image as a large collection of pixels, each of which is stored in its own memory location; the image is created by specifying the color of each pixel; also called a raster image-based graphics program

bits per second (bps) the number of bits (the fundamental digital unit, which can be either a 0 or a 1) that can be transmitted in a second's time; the usual measure of bandwidth

blind link a hyperlink that directs a Web browser to an unexpected result or location, such as a link that triggers an undesired download

blog frequently updated journals, or logs, containing chronological entries of personal thoughts and Web links posted on a Web page

blogosphere the collective world of all blogs, also referred to as Web-based journals or logs, containing chronological entries and Web links

Bluetooth a wireless technology that offers short-range connectivity with other Bluetooth devices through a small, temporary network that can transmit both voice and data

boot drive the disk drive that houses the operating system

booting the procedure for starting or restarting a computer

boot sector part of a floppy disk or hard disk that contains information about how the disk is organized and whether it is capable of loading an operating system

boot sector virus a virus designed to alter the boot sector of a disk so that whenever the operating system reads the boot sector, the computer will automatically become infected

breadcrumbs Internet navigation tool that defines a location within the hierarchy of a Web site

bridge hardware and/or software that allows for communication between two networks that are similar

broadband high-speed Internet connection

broadband medium a communications medium capable of carrying a large amount of data at fast speeds

browser software that allows users to move from one location to another on the Web and to access and retrieve Web pages; also called a Web browser

browsing accessing and moving about the Web using a browser; also called surfing

buffer a temporary storage place to which part of data to be displayed, printed, or transmitted is written

bug a term Grace Hopper coined meaning any kind of computer error

bus a collection of tiny wires through which data, in the form of 0s and 1s, is transmitted from one part of the computer to another

business intelligence (BI) the information gained from the effective use of online analytical processing (OLAP) systems

business systems analyst a highly trained professional who specializes in business information systems analysis, problem identification, and solution planning and who serves as a liaison between nontechnical business people and programmers

business-to-business (B2B) electronic commerce buying and selling of products and services between businesses over the Internet

business-to-consumer (B2C) electronic commerce buying and selling of products and services between sellers and customers over the Internet

bus topology a type of network topology in which all computers are linked by means of a single line of cable, called a bus, with two endpoints

bus width a measure of the size of a bus; determines the number of bits the computer can transmit or receive at one time

button a graphical element that, when selected with the mouse or keyboard, causes a particular action to occur within a software program

byte a combination of eight bits (0s and 1s) that represents a letter of the alphabet, a number, or a special character inside a computer; there are enough different combinations of bits (0s and 1s) in an 8-bit byte to represent 256 different characters

C

C a programming language developed in the 1970s; newer versions are used to write most of the software sold to the public

C# a new version of the C++ programming language under development by Microsoft

C++ an object-oriented version of the C programming language developed in the 1980s

cable modem a special type of modem that provides fast transmission speeds

cache memory a dedicated holding area in random access memory (RAM) in which the data and instructions most recently called from RAM by the processor are temporarily stored

carpal tunnel syndrome the condition of weakness, pain, or numbness resulting from pressure on the median nerve in the wrist; the syndrome is associated with repetitive motion, such as typing or using the mouse

CASE tool a software tool that aids in the project management of software development

cathode ray tube (CRT) monitor a large, sealed glass tube housed in a plastic case; the most common type of monitor for desktop computers

CD burner a device that uses lasers to record and read data to and from an optical disc; also called a CD-R drive

CD drive a drive that can read nearly any kind of data recorded on an optical disc, including text, graphics, video clips, and sound

CD-R an optical disc technology that allows a user to write data onto a compact disc; can be written on only once, cannot be erased, but can be read from an unlimited number of times; acronym for compact disc–recordable

CD-R drive a drive that uses lasers to record and read data to and from an optical disc, including text, graphics, video clips, and sound; also called a CD burner

CD-ROM an optical disc technology in which data is permanently recorded on an optical disc and can be read many times, but the data cannot be changed; acronym for compact disk–read-only memory

CD-RW an optical disc storage technology that uses an erasable disc on which a user can write multiple times; acronym for compact disc–rewritable

cell in a spreadsheet, the intersection of one row and one column into which text, numbers, formulas, links, or other elements may be entered; a 10- to 12-square mile area with its own antenna to receive and send cellular telephone signals

cellular technology an increasingly popular technology that allows people to communicate anywhere in the world without having to be connected via wired phone lines or cables

central processing unit (CPU) the part of a computer that interprets and carries out instructions that operate the computer and manage the computer's devices and resources; consists of components, each of which performs specific functions; also called the microprocessor or processor

certificate program intensive education courses offered primarily by large IT companies such as Microsoft and Cisco intended to train an individual for a particular job working with a specific type of product

chart a visual representation of data that often makes the data easier to read and understand; displays data in graphical rather than numerical form

chat room an online area, provided by an online service or an Internet host, where people can meet, exchange ideas and information, and interact socially

check box a dialog box feature that indicates an option a user can turn on or off; an option activated by clicking and thus adding a check mark; usually one of several options that can be selected

Children's Internet Protection Act (CIPA) legislation requiring public schools and libraries to install Internet filtering software on their computers

Children's Online Privacy Protection Act (COPPA) legislation aimed at protecting children under the age of 13 from privacy violations

chip a thin wafer of silicon containing electronic circuitry that performs various functions, such as mathematical calculations, storage, or control of computer devices

ciphertext unreadable, coded information produced by the process of encryption from user's personal or financial information; ensures that consumers' privacy rights will not be violated when they enter data to complete online transactions

client a smaller computer, terminal, or workstation capable of sending data to and from a larger computer (host computer) in a network

client/server architecture a type of network architecture in which a personal computer, workstation, or terminal (called a client) is used to send information or a request to another computer (called a server) that then relays the information back to the user's client computer, or to another computer (another client)

clip art professionally designed graphic images sold for use in word processing and other types of documents; collections are sometimes included in a software program

clock cycle the time between two ticks of a computer's system clock; a typical personal computer goes through millions or even billions of clock cycles per second

closed system a hardware or software system that must be serviced and supported by the original vendor

cluster a group of two or more sectors on a disk; the smallest unit of storage space used to store data

coaxial cable a type of wire that consists of an insulated center wire grounded by a shield of braided wire

COBOL a business application–oriented language developed in the 1960s; acronym for COmmon Business–Oriented Language

coding a term programmers use to refer to the act of writing source code

cognitive science a broad discipline dedicated to the study of the human mind

cold boot process of starting a computer by turning on the unit's power switch

collaboration software programs that enable people at separate PC workstations to collaborate on a single document or project, such as designing a new automobile engine; also called groupware

color depth the number of bits used in a graphics expansion board to store information about each pixel; also called bit depth

command-line interface a user interface, like the one created by the DOS operating system, that makes use of typed commands

comment a note programmers write in the source code; helps later readers comprehend the meaning of the program or line of code

commercial software programs intended for businesses or other organizations with multiple users

Common Gateway Interface (CGI) script a program used on Web sites to allow the tracking of traffic and the production of dynamic Web pages

communications (COM) port a port (opening) for connecting devices such as the keyboard, mouse, and modem to a computer; a port that transmits data one bit at a time; also called a serial port

communications device a device that makes it possible for a user to communicate with another computer and to exchange instructions, data, and information with other computer users

communications medium a medium, such as a telephone line, used for carrying data or information between computers and networks

communications satellite a solar-powered electronic device that contains a number of small, specialized radios called transponders that receive signals from transmission stations on the ground called earth stations, amplifies the signals, and then transmits the signals to the appropriate locations

communications software software that allows your properly equipped computer to communicate with other similarly equipped computers; software used to send and receive electronic messages, visit various Web sites, locate and retrieve information stored on other computers, electronically transmit large files, and much more

compact disc (CD) a plastic disc 4.75 inches in diameter and about 1/20th of an inch thick; uses laser technologies to store information and data

compiler a type of language-translating software that translates an entire program into machine language before the program will run; each language has its own unique compiler

completeness check a database accuracy element that requires every field to be filled in completely

computer an electronic device capable of interpreting and executing program instructions and data and performing the required operations to produce the desired results

computer codes of ethics standards for ethical use of computers put forward by computer professional organizations

computer engineering degree an educational degree focusing on hardware design

computer ethics the adapting of traditional ethical thought and behavior to issues involving computers and computer technology; computer ethics is a newly formed branch of applied ethics

computer graphic special effects (CG FX) special effects created for movies with computer graphics

computer information systems (CIS) degree an educational degree that is application-oriented, requiring both business and computer science courses; students learn programming, usually aimed at application development with existing software products rather than the creation of new software products

computer science degree an educational degree focusing on writing, or programming, new software

computer system system unit along with input devices, output devices, and storage devices

computer-aided design (CAD) software a sophisticated kind of productivity software providing tools that enable professionals to create architectural, engineering, product, and scientific designs

computer-aided manufacturing (CAM) a computer information system that directly manages factory production

computer-integrated manufacturing (CIM) a computer information system that manages production and connects the factory floor to every level of management

computerized facial recognition (CFR) a computer system capable of comparing facial images with a database of known individuals, thereby recognizing people

connectivity refers to the ability to link with other programs and devices

consistency check a database check that ensures data is accurate by checking it against known data

consultant an individual or a company with highly skilled IT workers that completes projects for other organizations

consumer profile a set of information about customers' lifestyle and buying habits that marketers use to target and sell their goods more effectively

context-sensitive Help message a help message that "senses" the user's needs based on what the user is doing

control unit the part of the CPU that directs and coordinates the overall operation of the computer system; interprets each program instruction in a program, and then initiates the action needed to carry out the instruction

cookie small programs placed on a computer's hard drive by Web sites designed to remember passwords and user IDs, avoiding the necessity of having to enter this data each time the site containing the cookie is visited

coprocessor a special type of dedicated processor designed to perform certain kinds of processing, such as processing large amounts of numerical data

copyright the legal protection of an individual's or business's original work, such as applications software, music, and books, that prohibits others from duplicating or illegally using such work or products; an artist or author whose work is copyrighted has the right to charge others for its use

core the essential components of a microprocessor's central processing unit (CPU)

crack the altering of a software product to remove copy protection

cracker a hacker with malicious or criminal intent

crash bug a run-time error that causes a program to stop running, or crash

credit account a customer's promise to pay for online purchases upon receipt of a periodic statement from the seller; when online purchases are made, each purchase is charged to the customer's credit account

credit card a small plastic card with a metallic strip containing owner information that enables the owner to make online and in-store purchases on credit

crossover a new design created as a result of combining the most successful variations (mutations) of potential design solutions

cross-platform compatibility the capacity of a software package to run on more than one operating system/type of computer

cross-platform operating system an operating system capable of being used on more than one type of computer

cryptographic coprocessor (crypto-coprocessor) a chip designed specifically to provide encryption and related processing

custom program a specialized software program a programmer writes to meet a company's special requirements; also called customized software

customer relationship management (CRM) all aspects of interaction a company has with its customers and suppliers; can help companies keep track of customers, develop detailed consumer profiles, and offer customers just the products they want to buy

customized software a specialized software program a programmer writes to meet a company's special requirements; also called a custom program

cyberwars attacks by groups of international hackers who attack sites in a competing country

D

data raw, unprocessed information

data browsing a type of information theft that equates to an invasion of privacy; the process of moving through a

database file, examining each record and looking for information

database a computer application in which data is organized and stored in a way that allows for specific data to be accessed, retrieved, and used

database administration a combination of application development, technical support, and technical training; includes maintaining and fixing databases

database administrator a critical job that involves the continuous management of a database management system (DBMS)

database approach a procedure for the development of databases; also called database management approach

database file a collection of related records

database management approach a procedure for the development of databases; also called database approach

database management system (DBMS) software that allows a user to create and manage a computerized database, and to create reports from stored data

database object an element within an object-oriented database, such as a report or a table

database response time the length of time it takes a database to respond to a request from a user; a critical measurement in rating the performance of any database

data compression a process of shrinking the storage size of a body of data by removing redundant information

data contamination the spread of incorrect information throughout a database and into other databases, diminishing the usefulness of the systems

data corruption the process of data becoming unreadable, incomplete, or damaged

data-destructive virus a virus designed to destroy data either by erasing or corrupting files so that they are unreadable or by formatting the entire drive so it is blank

data dictionary a descriptive listing of all the data values in an information system

data entry operator a person whose job it is to keep the information in a database current and accurate

data filter a condition that narrows down a large list of records

data integrity a measurement of database correctness and validity; also called data quality

data mining a technique programmers use to collate and extract meaningful data from a data warehouse; data mining software allows data warehouse users to see as much data detail or summarization as they need to aid them in making decisions

data model defines the structure of information to be contained in a database, how the database will use the information, and how the different items in the database relate to each other

data modeling provides a simulation of a real-world situation built into a software application; users can input numeric data into "what-if" scenarios to predict future outcomes

data processing the actions performed through transactions with a database; also called information processing

data quality a measurement of database correctness and validity; also called data integrity

data register a reserved location in main memory for storing data being processed or being used in a specific processing application

data transfer rate the speed at which data is transferred from memory or from a storage device to the CPU

data validation a strict process that ensures the entry of valid data into a database

data warehouse a collection of related databases that have been stored together so that needed data can be retrieved, analyzed, and readily available for decision making

dead code any source code within the final version of a released software product that is "commented out" and therefore not part of the actual working program

debit card resembles a credit card and, like a credit card, is used as an alternative to cash when making purchases

debugger a utility that helps a programmer remove errors from software

decision statement the decision points in a program and the different actions that can be performed depending on conditions

decision support system (DSS) an information system designed to model possible future outcomes and thus aid in the decision-making process of corporate management

decoding the activity of translating or determining the meaning of coded instructions

default option an option that has been programmed into a program by the software publisher under the assumption that that option is the one most likely to be chosen

defragmenting the process used by a defragmenter utility to reorganize files and unused disk space allowing the operating system to locate and access stored files and data more quickly

deliverable a document, service, hardware component, or software program that must be finished and delivered by a certain time and date in order to keep a project on schedule

demodulation the process of changing an analog signal into a digital signal

denial of service (DoS) attack a form of online attack, usually performed by hackers, in which a Web site is brought down by overloading it with false requests for data

design specification a document that specifically states how a program development project will be completed

desktop a screen on which graphical elements such as icons, buttons, windows, links, and dialog boxes are displayed

desktop computer a personal computer system designed to fit on the top of a desk

desktop publishing (DTP) software a type of software that enables a user to produce documents that closely resemble those done by printing companies

dexterity hand-eye coordination

diagnostic utility a utility program that assesses a computer's components and system software programs and creates a report identifying problems

dialog box an element in a graphical user interface that displays a rectangular box providing information to a user and/or requesting information from a user; usually displays temporarily and disappears once the user has entered the requested information

dial-up access a method for accessing the Internet in which a user can connect to the Internet using a computer and a modem to dial into an ISP or online service over a standard telephone line

dial-up modem a modem (electronic device) that converts digital signals into analog form so they can be sent using an analog communication medium

digital composed of discrete bits (1s and 0s) understood by computers

digital cable a technology capable of offering a wide selection of TV stations, typically more than 200, with the capability of expanding to 2,000 stations

digital camera a type of camera that records and stores images, including people, scenery, documents, and products, in a digitized form that can be entered into and stored by a computer

digital cash a system that allows a customer to pay for online purchases by transmitting a number from one computer to another computer; issued by a bank, each digital cash number represents a specified amount of real money

digital divide a term created to describe the gap between those who have access to computers and the Internet and those who do not

digital ink technology process in which a digitizer (a grid of tiny wires) is laid under or over an LCD screen to create a magnetic field that can capture the movement of a special-purpose pen and record the movement on the LCD screen; the effect is like writing on paper with liquid ink

digital media a digital form of media that can be stored on a computer

Digital Millennium Copyright Act of 1998 (DMCA) legislation updating copyright protection to bring it in line with the technical changes brought about by computer technology that generally prohibits people from taking action to break down software encryption programs and other safeguards that copyright holders have established to control access to their works, including DVDs, software, and digitized books and music

digital subscriber line (DSL) Internet service a high-speed Internet connection using telephone lines

digital versatile disc (DVD) an extremely high-capacity optical disc; also called a digital video disc (DVD)

digital video recorder (DVR) a digital TV cable box that allows for pausing and rewinding of live TV and quick, easy, intelligent TV recording for later viewing

digitizing the process of converting analog information to digital information; sometimes referred to as going digital

digitizing pen an electronic pen device, resembling a standard writing pen, used with a drawing tablet to simulate drawing on paper

direct access a storage technique that allows a computer to immediately locate and retrieve a program, information, or data similar to the way music stored on a CD-ROM is accessed

direct thermal printer a printer that uses heat to transfer an impression onto paper

disaster recovery plan a safety system that allows a company to restore its systems after a complete loss of data; generally includes procedures for data backup, remotely stored backup copies, and redundant systems

disk defragmenter a utility program that scans hard or floppy disks and reorganizes files and unused disk space, allowing the operating system to locate and access files and data more quickly

diskette a secondary storage medium consisting of a thin, circular Mylar wafer, sandwiched between two sheets of cleaning tissue inside a rigid plastic case; also called a floppy disk or disk

disk pack a vertically aligned group of hard disks mounted inside a disk drive on a large computer system; when activated, electromagnetic read/write heads record information and/or read stored data by moving inward and outward between the disks

disk scanner a utility that examines hard or floppy disks and their contents to identify potential problems, such as bad sectors

disk toolkit software that contains utility programs that let users identify and correct various problems on a hard or floppy disk

display device the screen, or monitor, of a personal computer; also called a monitor

display window a rectangular area of the screen used to display a program, data, or information

distance learning the electronic transfer of information from a college or publisher's host computer system to a student's computer at a remote site and the transmission of required responses from the student's computer to the host computer system; a course presented in this manner is called an online course

distributed database a relatively new type of database model where databases function in a networked environment, with each computer storing a portion of the total amount of data in the network

distribution management system a common application of information systems involving the transportation of goods from the manufacturer to the customer

divide-and-conquer approach a methodology for software development that breaks down large problems into small ones, and then tackles the smaller problems first

docking station a laptop computer accessory that provides additional ports plus (typically) a charger for the laptop's battery, extra disk drives, and other peripherals

document object model (DOM) a version of HTML that allows object-oriented Web page development

documentation any written manual, specification or commentary upon a computer system

domain name a portion of an Internet address, such as .com or .edu, that is used to segment Internet addresses into broad categories

domain suffix the last part of a URL, identifying the type of organization hosting the site

dot pitch the distance between the centers of pixels on a display

dot-com company a Web-based e-commerce company with a Web site in the .com domain

dot-matrix printer an impact printer that forms and prints characters in a manner similar to the way numbers appear on a football scoreboard

dots per inch (dpi) a measurement in which resolution (text and image quality) is expressed as the number of dots occupying one square inch

Double Data Rate SDRAM (DDR SDRAM) a type of random access memory (RAM) chip that can transfer data twice as fast as SDRAM because it reads twice as much data during each clock cycle

download to transmit data, such as a digitized text file, sound, or picture from a remote site to one's own computer via a network

downtime time in which the system is unavailable

draft quality a print quality acceptable for most in-house needs, but not for professional-looking documents

drawing program software that provides an intuitive interface through which a user can draw pictures, make sketches, create various shapes, and edit images

drawing tablet a tablet with wires under the surface that, when used with a digitizing pen, allows the user to create and capture drawings that can be entered and stored on a computer

driver a small program that enables the computer to communicate with devices connected to it, such as a keyboard or a printer

drop-down menu a menu containing various lower-level options associated with main menu options; also called pull-down menu

dual-core processor a central processing unit (CPU) chip that contains two complete processors along with their cache memory

dumb scanner a scanner that can only capture and input a scanned image; once entered into a computer, the image cannot be edited or altered

DVD drive a drive that uses lasers to record and read data to and from a DVD

DVD-R an extremely high-capacity disc capable of holding several gigabytes of data, such as a movie or the entire contents of a telephone book listing every resident in the United States; acronym for digital versatile disc–recordable

DVD-ROM an extremely high-capacity disc capable of holding several gigabytes of data, such as a movie or the entire contents of a telephone book listing every resident in the United States; acronym for digital versatile disc–read-only memory

DVD-RW a type of DVD that allows recorded data to be erased and recorded over numerous times without damaging the disc; acronym for digital versatile disc–rewritable

Dynamic HTML (DHTML) a general term used to describe a variety of new features in HTML programming that allow for more responsive, graphically interesting Web page development

Dynamic RAM (DRAM) a type of random access memory (RAM) chip that eventually loses its contents without a continuous supply of electrical energy

dynamic routing a capability of the Internet to send a given packet via a different route depending on traffic circumstances

E

earth station transmission stations on the ground

e-commerce venue a Web site where e-commerce transactions occur

educational and reference software programs that facilitate learning, such as software designed to enable a user to learn algebra, or that provide reference information, such as encyclopedias and dictionaries

electronic check (e-check) a payment method that directly initiates an electronic transfer of funds from the customer's checking account to the merchant

electronic commerce (e-commerce) a set of business Internet technologies in which business information, products, services, and payments are exchanged between sellers and customers and between businesses

electronic data interchange (EDI) companies' use of computer networks to buy, sell, or otherwise exchange information with each other electronically

electronic data processing (EDP) an old term for an information system

electronic funds transfer (EFT) a general term for the transfer of money over the Internet

electronic mail (e-mail) a text, voice, or video message sent or received remotely, over a computer network or the system by which such a message is sent

electronic office an information system dedicated to automating an office environment; also called an office information system (OIS)

electronic signature (e-signature) a code attached to an e-mail that uniquely identifies the sender of the message

electronic wallet (e-wallet) a software application that stores a user's personal, credit card, and shipping information; the application may store one set of user information or multiple sets that allow a user to choose which credit card or shipping information will apply to a certain purchase

e-mail a text, voice, or video message sent or received remotely, over a computer network or the system by which such a message is sent; short for electronic mail

embedded computer a specialized computer, usually housed on a single chip, that is part of a larger system, device, or machine

encryption the process of converting readable information, or plaintext, into unreadable information, or ciphertext, to prevent unauthorized access and usage

encryption key a special type of encryption code used to encrypt (encode) information

entertainment software category of programs that includes interactive computer games, videos, and music

entity a person, place, thing, or event in a database

ergonomics the study of the interaction between humans and the equipment they use

espionage virus a virus that does no damage, but allows someone to enter the system later for the purpose of stealing data or spying

e-tailer an individual or company that carries out business-to-consumer e-commerce over the Web

Ethernet protocol a bus topology type protocol that many local area networks use

ethics rules we use to determine the right and wrong things to do in our lives

e-ticket an airline ticket purchased over the Internet

executable statement a statement within a program that, when run by the program, performs an action

executing the CPU process of performing an operation specified in a program instruction

execution time (E-time) the time required for the arithmetic/logic unit to decode and execute an instruction

executive support system (ESS) an information system tailored to the needs of upper management

expansion bus a motherboard component that provides for communication between the processor and peripheral devices

expansion card an electronic circuit board that can be inserted onto the motherboard inside a computer to add new capabilities to a computer; examples include sound cards, graphics cards, and network interface cards; also called an adapter

expansion slot an opening in a computer motherboard where an expansion board can be inserted (installed)

expert system a sophisticated decision support system (DSS) data model that attempts to model an expert's knowledge of a topic

exporting the process of saving a data file with a different file format

Extended Binary Coded Decimal Interchange Code (EBCDIC) a coding scheme used mainly on large servers and mainframe computers

Extensible HTML (XHTML) a scripting language comprised of elements of HTML and XML, used in Web page programming

Extensible Markup Language (XML) a scripting language that not only defines the content of a Web page but also organizes data so that computers can communicate with each other directly, without human intervention

external modem a modem that works in the same fashion as an internal modem, but is a stand-alone device connected by cable to a computer's motherboard

external storage a type of storage that consists of devices and media used to record information and data permanently so it can later be retrieved, edited, modified, displayed, or printed; also called permanent, secondary storage, or auxiliary storage

extranet a network that makes certain kinds of information available to users within the organization and other kinds of information available to outsiders, such as companies doing business with the organization

F

facsimile machine an electronic device that can send and receive copies (facsimiles, or faxes) of documents through a telephone line; also called a fax machine

Fair Use the right by law to use copyrighted materials under certain conditions

fax an electronic document that is transmitted or received over a telephone line using a fax machine or fax/modem board

fax/modem card an expansion card that serves as a modem and provides many of the features of a standalone fax machine

fax program software needed to send and receive a fax; allows users to compose, send, receive, print, and store faxes

feasibility study a study conducted to investigate how difficult a project might be to complete and how much it might cost

fetching the CPU process of retrieving instructions or data from memory for execution

Fiber Distributed Data Interface (FDDI) a type of network software for ring networks dispersed over a large area and connected by fiber-optic cables; the software links the dispersed networks together using a protocol that passes a token over long distances

fiber-optic cable a cable consisting of optical fibers that allows data to be transmitted as light signals through tiny hair-like glass fibers

field in a table created by a database management system application, a location into which one kind of information about an entity, such as name or address, is entered

field the smallest element of data in a database

file a named body of data that resides on a storage medium

file allocation table (FAT) file a section of a disk that keeps track of the disk's contents

file compression the process of shrinking the size of a file so it occupies less disk space

file extension a period (.) and a set of characters following a file name that identifies the type of file

file manager an operating system function that performs basic file management functions, including keeping track of used and unused disk storage space and allowing a user to view stored files and to format, copy, rename, delete, and sort stored files

file processing manipulation of the data within a database

file server a special type of computer that allows other computers to share its resources

file specification an optional additional element in a URL, following the domain suffice, that indicates the name of a file or file folder

File Transfer Protocol (FTP) a transmission standard that enables a user to send and receive large files, such as reports, over the Internet

filtering program software that can prevent access to sites, keep track of sites visited, limit connection time, record keystrokes, prevent downloading, and allow users to view only those sites that have been accessed

financial electronic data interchange (FEDI) a form of EDI technology used to transmit payments and associated remittance information electronically among a payer, payee, and their respective banks

find a software program feature that allows a user to quickly locate a number or a particular type of text within a file

fingerprint scanner a biometric device that reads, records, and recognizes fingerprints

firewall software and hardware systems that place an invisible wall around the internal network, protecting it from unauthorized material from the Internet

flaming the act of transmitting negative comments to someone via the Internet

Flash a commonly used format for online, downloadable movies

flash memory a type of read-only memory that can be erased and reprogrammed quickly, or updated; also called flash ROM

flash ROM a type of read-only memory that can quickly be erased and reprogrammed quickly, or updated; also called flash memory

flat file database traditional data file storage system that lacks the ability to interrelate data in an organizational structure because it contains only one table or file

flat-panel display a type of computer monitor that allows display units to be smaller, thinner, and lighter so they can be used with small computers, such as notebook computers, personal digital assistants (PDAs), and other devices

floppy disk a secondary storage medium consisting of a thin, circular Mylar wafer, sandwiched between two sheets of cleaning tissue inside a rigid plastic case; also called a diskette or disk

flowchart a graphic representation of a programming algorithm

foot mouse a foot-controlled mouse that allows a user with carpal tunnel syndrome or other hand or wrist injuries to use a computer

form in a database management system, a document used for entering information to be stored in one or more linked records

FORTRAN a programming language developed in the 1960s and used primarily for the solving of math and science problems; acronym for FORmula TRANslator

forum an Internet application consisting of an electronically stored list of messages that can be accessed and read by anyone having access to the bulletin board; a user having access can post messages, read existing messages, or delete messages; also called a message board

frame a single still image; many frames, shown together in rapid succession, create the illusion of movement

frame rate the number of frames that a system is capable of producing and displaying per second; if this rate falls much below 20 frames per second, video begins to appear choppy

freeware a computer program that is provided free to users by its creator but for which the creator usually retains the copyright

frequency range a span of changes reflected in the transmission of voice or sound signals

front-end interface program the interface program of a database, through which the user enters data and requests information

full-duplex transmission the simultaneous transmission of information or data in both directions at the same time

function a section of code containing instructions for a specific purpose; also called a routine

functional specification a document that describes what an information system must do, but not exactly how it is supposed to do it

fuzzy logic system an artificial intelligence term that relates to the use of inexact conditions and criteria

G

Gantt chart a chart that identifies beginning and end times of tasks required for the completion of a system development project

garbage in, garbage out (GIGO) a database related proverb meaning that if errors are entered into a database, it will produce erroneous output; also refers to all situations involving incorrect user input into a computer

gateway hardware and/or software that allows communication between dissimilar networks

general-purpose computer a computer that allows the user to perform a range of complex processes and calculations

genetic algorithm an artificial intelligence design concept that uses tiny, evolutionary changes to solve a problem by trying many solutions, testing them, and selecting the best, then trying more variations of the best survivors of each successive generation

geosynchronous orbit the path of a satellite orbiting the earth at the same speed as the earth's rotation, making the satellite appear stationary when viewed from the ground

GIF file format a file format, indicated with a .gif extension, that provides compressed bitmap images with limited animation capability

gigabyte unit of memory equal to 1,073,741,824 bytes

Global Unique Identifier (GUID) an Internet tracking device using unique identification numbers that can be coded into both hardware and software

gold release the published, generally available version of software

grammar checker a part of a program or a standalone application that automatically searches for errors in grammar, usage, capitalization, or punctuation and suggests correct alternatives

graphic data still images, including photographs, mathematical charts, and drawings

graphical user interface (GUI) a computer interface that enables a user to control the computer and launch commands by pointing and clicking at graphical objects such as windows, icons, and menu items

graphics computer-generated pictures produced on a computer screen, paper, or film, ranging from a simple line or bar chart to a detailed, colorful image or picture; also called graphical image

graphics and multimedia software software that allows users to work with graphics, video, and audio files

graphics card a circuit board residing on the motherboard inside the system unit that converts the digital signals produced by the computer into analog signals and sends them through a cable to the monitor; also called a video card or video adapter

graphics coprocessor a chip designed specifically for processing image-intensive applications, such as Web pages and computer-aided design programs

graphics tablet a flat tablet used together with a pen-like stylus or a crosshair cursor; to capture an image, the user grasps a stylus or crosshair cursor and traces an image or drawing placed on the tablet surface

grid a matrix formed by the intersections of rows and columns, as in a spreadsheet

groupware communications software that allows groups of people on a network to share information and to collaborate on various projects, such as designing a new product or preparing employee manuals; also called collaboration software

H

hacker an individual who attempts to break into computer security systems

hacking code writing code without carefully planning and structuring the program

half-duplex transmission a transmission method in which transmissions can flow in both directions but not at the same time

hand geometry system a biometric device that recognizes individuals based on the structure of their hands

handheld computer a personal computer small enough to fit into a person's hand; also called handheld, pocket PC, or palmtop

hard copy a permanent, tangible version of output, such as a letter printed on paper

hard disk a secondary storage medium consisting of one or more rigid metal platters (disks) mounted on a metal shaft and sealed in a container, called a disk drive, that contains an access mechanism used to write and read data

hard drive a device for reading and writing to the magnetic storage medium known as a hard disk; consists of one or more rigid metal platters (disks) mounted on a metal shaft in a container that contains an access mechanism

hardware all physical components that compose the system unit and other devices connected to it, such as a keyboard or monitor; items peripheral to the computer itself

hardware design the specification of computer hardware such as CPUs, video cards, and memory chips; as a career, it is part electrical engineering and part programming and requires advanced skills

hertz a unit of measure that refers to the number of cycles per second

high-definition television (HDTV) a newer type of television technology that uses digital signals instead of analog signals to display high-quality pictures on the screen; a television with more lines and more pixels, a higher resolution, than a regular television

high-level language an English-like computer language used for writing application programs

hi-jacker a program that directs a Web page visitor's browser to a different Web address than the visitor intended to go to; usually directs visitors to advertisements

home page the first page usually displayed when a user accesses a Web site; often contains links to other pages at that site or to other Web sites

host computer a large and powerful computer to which smaller computers are connected in a network, and which manages all user activity occurring on the network; also called a network server

hot plugging the procedure of disconnecting one device and connecting another device to a computer while the computer is still running

hot swapping the capability of switching back and forth among various types of PC cards while a notebook or similar computer is running

hotspot a location that has one or more wireless access points

hub an electronic device used in a local area network that links groups of computers to one another and allows computers to communicate with one another; a hub coordinates the traffic of messages being sent and received by computers connected to the network

hub-and-spoke topology a network topology in which multiple computers and peripheral devices are linked to a central computer, called a host, in a point-to-point configuration; also called a star topology

hybrid database a type of database that combines more than one data model

hybrid topology a combination of networks having different topologies, such as a star network and a ring network

hyperlink an address that links to a document or to a Web page; also called a Web link

hypertext document a Web document created using a Web language, such as HTML or XML, that contains one or more hyperlinks (links) to other Web documents or sites

Hypertext Markup Language (HTML) a set of codes specifying typefaces, images, and links within text, used to create pages for the World Wide Web

Hypertext Transfer Protocol (HTTP) the communications standard used to transfer documents on the World Wide Web

hyperthreading a technology developed by Intel that allows its series of microprocessors to execute multithreaded software applications simultaneously and in parallel rather than processing threads in linear fashion, thereby greatly increasing processing speed

I

icon a graphic symbol that represents a software program, command, or feature

identify theft the stealing of an individual's personal information, such as social security number and/or credit card numbers, via hacking into a database on the Internet

if-then statement a decision statement in a programming language that decides upon two or more possible courses of action

image-editing program software that allows a user to touch up, modify, and enhance image quality

immersiveness a measurement of how convincing a virtual environment is, how "immersed" the user feels in the virtual reality

impact printer a printer that prints much like a typewriter, by striking an inked ribbon against the paper

implementation the phase of a project in which the actual work of putting the system together is done, including creating a prototype and completing the programming

importing the act of loading a file that uses a different data file type than the application normally requires

individual application software programs individuals use at work or at home

industrial espionage the stealing of corporate information

Industry Standard Architecture (ISA) bus the most common type of expansion bus that allows devices such as a mouse or modem to communicate with the processor

inference engine a software component of an expert system that processes input and a knowledge base to make logical conclusions

infinite loop a software bug that involves the creation of a loop with no endpoint, and which may cause the computer to crash

information data that has been processed to make it useful for a specific purpose, such as making a decision

information processing the actions performed through transactions with a database; also called data processing

information processing cycle a cycle during which a computer enters, processes, outputs, and/or stores information

information system (IS) a system involving hardware, software, data, people, and procedures that is usually used to help manage a company

infrared technology a communications technology that provides for line-of-sight wireless links between PCs and other computing devices, such as keyboards and printers

ink-jet printer a nonimpact printer that forms images by spraying thousands of tiny droplets of electrically charged ink onto a page; the printed images are in dot-matrix format, but of a higher quality than images printed by dot-matrix printers

input data that is entered into a computer or other device or the act of reading in such data

input device any hardware component that enables a computer user to enter data and programs into a computer system; keyboards, point-and-click devices, and scanners are among the more popular input devices, and a desktop or laptop computer system may include one or more input devices

instant messaging (IM) a form of communicating online in real time that includes a pop-up window that alerts a user when a message is received

instant messaging (IM) software software that allows for communicating online in real time that causes pop-up windows to interrupt users when a message is received

instruction register a memory location (register) where instructions being used for processing are stored

instruction time (I-time) the amount of time required to fetch an instruction from a register

integrated circuit a small electrical device consisting of tiny transistors and other circuit parts on a piece of semi-conductor material; also called a microprocessor chip

Integrated Services Digital Network (ISDN) line a special digital telephone line that can be used to dial into the Internet and transmit and receive information at very high speeds, ranging from 64 kilobits per second (64,000 bits per second) to 128 kilobits per second; a line that requires the use of a special ISDN modem

integrated software program software that is packaged together and is designed to work together seamlessly

intellectual property creative endeavors that are claimed as the personal property of the person who created them

intelligent agent a program or interface to a program that behaves intelligently, attempting to make complex operations easier and faster for a user by employing artificial intelligence techniques

intelligent scanner a scanner that uses optical character recognition (OCR) software to create an image that can be manipulated (edited or altered) with a word processor or other application program

interdependence the relationship between businesses and the outside vendors who help create, market, and distribute their products

interface a plug-in slot on a computer to which you can connect a device, such as a printer or, in the case of accessing the Internet, a telephone line; also called a port

internal modem a type of modem inserted into an expansion slot on the computer's motherboard

Internet a worldwide network of computers linked together via communications software and media for the purpose of sharing information; the largest and best-known network in the world; also called the Net

Internet Protocol (IP) a set of standards for the sending and receiving of information over the Internet

Internet Protocol (IP) address a numeric address, similar to a phone number, that locates a specific computer on the Internet; URLs are translated to IP addresses when connections are made

Internet service provider (ISP) an organization that has a permanent connection to the Internet and provides temporary access to individuals and others for free or for a fee

Internet telephony a combination of hardware and software that allows two or more people with sufficiently good connections to use the Internet to make telephone-style calls without long-distance telephone charges; also called Voice over IP (VoIP)

interpreter a type of language-translating software that reads, translates, and executes one instruction at a time

intra-business electronic commerce a Web-based technology that allows a business to handle transactions that occur within the business; although no revenues are generated, increased efficiency enables the business to save money by lowering its operating costs

intranet a network normally belonging to a large business or organization that is accessible only by the business or organization's members, employees, or other authorized users

iris recognition system a biometric device capable of identifying individuals through the unique patterns of their irises

J

Java a third-generation programming language used to write full-scale applications and small applications, known as applets, for use on the World Wide Web

Java Virtual Machine (JVM) part of the Java programming language that converts the general Java instructions into commands that a device or computer can understand

JavaScript a scripting language developed by Sun Microsystems

joining a process that allows a query to pull up data from more than one record source by matching data from fields in various record files

joystick an input device (named after the control lever used to fly fighter planes) consisting of a small box that contains a vertical lever that, when pushed in a certain direction, moves the graphics cursor correspondingly on the screen; it is often used for computer games

JPEG file format a file format, identified with a .jpg or .jpeg extension, for still images

jump drive a magnetic storage device that plugs into a USB port on a computer or other mobile device; also called a USB drive, thumb drive, or pen drive

just-in-time (JIT) a strategy that provides for the manufacture of products in time for delivery, and for the delivery of products at the exact time they are needed

just-in-time (JIT) distribution computerized distribution management system that allows companies to produce products to match market demand in order to shrink inventories and increase profits

K

kernel an operating system program that manages computer components, peripheral devices, and memory; maintains the system clock and loads other operating system and application programs as they are required

key an attribute that can be used to identify a set of information and therefore provide a means to search a database

keyboard an electronically controlled hardware component used to enter alphanumeric data (letters, numbers, and special characters); the keys on most keyboards are arranged similarly to those on a typewriter

keylogger a program that stores keystrokes in a file such as a credit card number or password for later analysis; also called a keystroke logger

keystroke logger a program that stores keystrokes in a file such as a credit card number or password for later analysis; also called a keylogger

keywords words used to tell a search engine what information to look for on the Web; also called search terms

kilobyte unit of memory equal to 1,024 bytes

knowledge base a specially structured database of information an expert system uses to make intelligent decisions

knowledge engineer an individual who creates knowledge bases

L

label printer a small printer designed to print adhesive labels

land flat, unburned area on a compact disc

landscape format a printing format in which a printed page is wider than it is tall

language translator a special type of program needed to translate (convert) high-level language programs into machine-language programs so they can be executed by the computer

laptop computer a computer small enough to be placed on a lap or carried by its user from place to place; also called a notebook computer

laser printer a nonimpact printer that produces output of exceptional quality using a technology similar to that of photocopy machines

law an external rule that if violated, is punishable by society

legacy database an older database that has been updated and maintained for years, and which may contain helpful, undiscovered information

legal software programs designed to help a user analyze, plan, and prepare a variety of legal documents, including wills and trusts

letter quality a print quality preferred for important business letters and documents; available with a variety of printers including laser printers

level 1 cache memory a type of cache memory that is built into the architecture of microprocessor chips, providing faster access to the instructions and data residing in cache memory

level 2 cache memory a type of cache memory that, in current processors, may be built into the architecture of microprocessor chips; on older computers, it may consist of high-speed SRAM chips placed on the motherboard or on a card inserted into a slot in the computer

level 3 cache memory a type of cache memory that is available on computers that have level 2 cache, or advanced transfer cache, and is separate from the microprocessor

line printer a line printer is a high-speed printer capable of printing an entire line at one time

Linux an operating system based on AT&T's UNIX and developed by a Finnish programmer named Linus Torvalds; original version is a nonproprietary operating system and is available for free to the public

liquid crystal display (LCD) a display device in which liquid crystals are sandwiched between two sheets of material

local area network (LAN) a computer network physically confined to a relatively small geographical area, such as a single building or a college campus

local area network (LAN) Internet connection a way to connect to the Internet by connecting users to an ISP on a direct wire at speeds 20 or more times faster than can be achieved through a dial-up modem

local bus a high-speed bus that connects devices such as disk drives to the CPU

locomotion broad movements such as walking

logic bomb virus a virus that is triggered by an event or the passing of a certain time; also called a time bomb virus

logic error in programming, an incorrect instruction stated in correct syntax

looping the process of repeating instructions in a computer program

low-level language a computer language that is closer in form to the thought processes computers use and less like natural language such as English, written in binary language consisting of 1s and 0s; language also called machine code

M

machine code a computer language that is closer in form to the thought processes computers use and less like natural language such as English, written in binary language consisting of 1s and 0s; also called low-level language

machine cycle a cycle a computer uses during which four basic operations are performed: (1) fetching an instruction, (2) decoding the instruction, (3) executing the instruction, and (4) storing the result

machine language a program consisting entirely of 0s and 1s that a computer can understand and execute quickly

Macintosh OS the first profitable graphical user interface released with Apple's Macintosh computers in 1984; it later became a model for other GUIs

macro a sequence of instructions designed to accomplish a specific task and generally executed by issuing a single command

macro virus a form of virus that infects the data files of commonly used applications such as word processors and spreadsheets

magnetic disk storage secondary storage that provides for the storage of programs, data, and information on a magnetic storage medium, such as magnetic disk or magnetic tape

magnetic storage device a storage device that works by applying electrical charges to iron filings on magnetic storage media so that each filing represents a 0 or a 1

magnetic tape storage a type of secondary storage for large computer systems that uses removable reels of magnetic tape; the tape contains tracks, each of which contains metallic particles that are magnetized, or not magnetized, to represent 0 and 1 bits

mail server a computer used to facilitate the sending and receiving of electronic mail messages

mailing list an Internet application that allows people interested in a topic to communicate via e-mail with others sharing their interests

main memory addressable storage locations directly controlled by the central processing unit (CPU) used to store programs while they are being executed and data while it is being processed; also called primary storage

main menu a horizontal or vertical bar in a software program that shows the highest-level command options; also called menu bar

mainframe computer a large, powerful, expensive computer system capable of accommodating hundreds of users doing different computing tasks

malware malicious software

management information system (MIS) an information system that turns raw data into information so that managers can make knowledgeable decisions

markup language a set of specifications describing the characteristics of elements that appear on a Web page, including headings, paragraphs, backgrounds, and lists

megabyte unit of memory equal to 1,048,576 bytes

memory access time the amount of time required for the processor to access (read) data, instructions, and information from memory

memory resident a characteristic describing programs, including operating systems, that remain in memory while the computer is in operation

mental interface systems that read the minds of their users by monitoring brainwave activity and react by controlling the computer

menu an on-screen set of options from which a user can make selections by clicking the option with a mouse or by typing one or more keystrokes

menu bar a horizontal or vertical bar in a software program that shows the highest-level command options; also called main menu

merchant account an account in which money is held until an online transaction has been completed and that requires e-tailers to pay a monthly fee to maintain this account plus a commission on each transaction

message board an Internet application consisting of an electronically stored list of messages that can be accessed and read by anyone having access to the bulletin board; a user having access can post messages, read existing messages, or delete messages; also called a forum

metadata information that helps explain the nature of other data

metalanguage a language for describing other languages

metropolitan area network (MAN) a wide area network limited to a specific geographical area, such as a city or town

micro payment a software system that enables buyers to purchase low-cost items such as newspapers over the Internet

microcomputer a single-user computer capable of performing its own input, processing, output, and storage; also called a personal computer (PC)

microprocessor the part of a computer that interprets and carries out instructions that operate the computer and manages the computer's devices and resources; consists of components, each of which performs specific functions; also called the central processing unit (CPU)

microprocessor chip a small electrical device consisting of tiny transistors and other circuit parts on a piece of semiconductor material; also called an integrated circuit

microwave system a communications technology that transmits data in the form of high-frequency radio signals through the atmosphere from one microwave station to another microwave station, or from a microwave station to a satellite and then back to earth to another microwave station

midrange server a powerful computer capable of accommodating hundreds of client computers or terminals (users) at the same time; also known as a minicomputer

mirrored hard drive a drive containing duplicate data from another hard drive so that if one fails, the data is not lost

mobile commerce (m-commerce) the carrying out of e-commerce activities through the use of small portable computers such as wrist or handheld computers

modem a hardware device that translates signals from digital to analog and from analog to digital, making it possible for digital computers to communicate over analog telephone lines

modem card enables computers to communicate via telephone lines and other communications media

modem port connects a modem card to a telephone line; the cable used to connect to a telephone line is a standard telephone cable with an RJ-11 connector

moderator an individual charged with maintaining order and civility in a virtual environment, such as a chat room

modular code code created in modules, with each module handling separate components of a program

modularity a measurement of how well written software is, based upon how well divided the source code is into modules

modulation the process of changing a digital signal into an analog signal

monitor the screen, or display device, on which computer output appears

moral realism a school of ethical thought that believes ethical principles have solid objective foundations and are not based on subjective human reasoning

moral relativism a school of ethical thought that believes ethical principles are not absolute and unchanging, but subjective and variable from society to society, from situation to situation, or from individual to individual

motherboard the main circuit board inside a personal computer to which other circuit boards can be connected; contains electrical pathways, called traces, etched onto it that allow data to move from one component to another

mouse an input device that, when moved about on a flat surface, causes a pointer on the screen to move in the same direction

mouse pad a rubberized pad with a smooth fabric surface that facilitates use of a mouse

mouse pointer a type of cursor resembling a small on-screen arrow, movements of which correspond to movements made with a mouse

MOV file format an Apple movie media format, identified with a .mov extension

MP3 file format a file format for storing digital sound files using a data compression system

MPEG file format a commonly used file format, identified with an .mpeg (or .mpg) extension, for storing compressed video files; the movie equivalent of the MP3 music format

MPEG2 file format the high-quality movie format DVD players use

multi-core processor a central-processing unit (CPU) chip that contains more than two separate processors on a single chip

multifunction device (MFD) a piece of equipment that provides a variety of capabilities including scanning, copying, printing, and sometimes faxing

multimedia the use of sound, images, video, and text mixed together to create a work or presentation

multimedia authoring software program that allows a user to create stand-alone multimedia products

multimedia database a database model that allows the storage of pictures, movies, sounds, and hyperlinked fields

multimedia developer a graphic artist, digital sound editor, or animation specialist who creates and enhances Web content with images, sounds, and movies

multimedia development the use of computers to create and enhance Web content with images, sounds, and movies

multipartite virus viruses that have the ability to attack in several different ways

multitasking the ability of an operating system to run more than one software program at a time; the use of different areas in Windows RAM makes this possible

multithreading a carefully designed program that enables several threads to execute at the same time without interfering with each other

multi-user computer system computer that can accommodate many users concurrently

multi-user operating system an operating system designed for use with large computer systems and capable of handling several users at the same time

Musical Instrument Digital Interface (MIDI) a type of data file for instrumental music

mutation random variations in the designs genetic algorithms generate

N

narrowband medium a communications medium capable of carrying a smaller amount of data at slow speeds

native format a file format that is specific to the application being used

natural interface an interface between human and machine that more closely approximates the normal communications between people

natural-language interface an interface that allows programmers to describe what they want a computer to do using natural (human) language rather than writing programs in highly structured programming languages

navigation the science of moving a mobile robot through an environment

Net short for Internet, a worldwide network of computers linked together via communications software and media for the purpose of sharing information; the largest and best-known network in the world

net neutrality a principle of even-handedness in the treatment of all network traffic

netiquette rules directing polite behavior online

NetWare a popular and widely used operating system developed by Novell, Inc. for microcomputer-based personal computers

network a group of two or more computers, software, and other devices that are connected by means of one or more communications media

network administration the operation and maintenance of a company network, including a LAN, WAN, network segment, intranet, or interactions with the Internet

network administrator the person whose job it is to oversee and maintain a company's network

network architecture the way a network is designed and built, just as an architect might design a new building or other facility

network firewall a combination of hardware and software that screens all communications entering and leaving networked computers to prevent unauthorized access

network interface card (NIC) expansion board that allows a computer to be networked

network operating system (NOS) an operating system in which a network server controls the flow of messages from client computers and also provides services such as file access and printing

network port connects a computer system to a local area network

network server a large and powerful computer to which smaller computers are connected in a network, and which manages all user activity occurring on the network; also called a host computer

network sniffer a software package that displays network traffic data such as which resources are being used or which Web sites are being visited

network topology the way computers and peripherals are configured to form networks

neural network an artificial intelligence technology that mimics the way nerve cells are connected in the human brain; information is supplied to the neural network to train it to recognize certain patterns, resulting in a program capable of making predictions, such as weather forecasts and fluctuations of stock values

newsgroup an online environment that allows users to exchange written information on a variety of subjects

niche information system an information system focused on a particular set of customers, for example a system designed for dental offices; also called a vertical market package

node a component connected to a network server, such as a personal computer or a printer

nonimpact printer a printer that uses electricity, heat, laser technology, or photographic techniques to produce output

nonprocedural language a programming language, such as a scripting language, that explains what the computer should do in English-like terms but not precisely how the computer should do it

nonresident a characteristic describing a program that does not reside in memory while the computer is running, but instead resides on a storage medium, such as a hard disk, until needed

nonvolatile memory a type of computer storage specifically designed to hold information, even when the power is switched off

normalization a process performed in a relational database to eliminate duplication of data (redundancy)

normative ethics determining a standard or "norm" of ethical rule that underlies ethical behavior

notebook computer a computer small enough to be placed on a lap or carried by its user from place to place; also called a laptop computer

nuisance virus a virus that usually does no real damage but is rather just an inconvenience

numeric data consisting of numbers only

O

object a programming term indicating a single element that contains both data and the code to manipulate the data

object-based graphics program a program that creates pictures by means of creating, editing, and combining mathematically defined geometric shapes; also called vector-based graphics program

object linking and embedding (OLE) a feature of Windows operating systems and applications that allows material from one application to be ported into a document created in another application and linked in such a way that when the material is updated in the originating application, it is automatically updated in the application into which it has been ported

object-oriented database a database that stores data in the form of objects; each object contains both the data related to the object and the actions that the user might want to perform on that object

object-oriented programming (OOP) a newer basis for programming language design developed in the 1980s

office information system (OIS) an information system dedicated to automating an office environment; also called an electronic office

online analytical processing (OLAP) system software that focuses on providing better ways to analyze the mass of data in large databases and massively distributed data systems, such as the Internet, in order to produce more useful results

online auction a peer-to-peer online transaction venue where consumers can place items for sale, bid on auctioned items, or (in some cases) buy items outright; an example is eBay

online banking the process of using a computer, a modem, and an Internet connection to conduct routine banking transactions; through this service, a user can make arrangements with the bank that will allow the user to pay bills, transfer funds among various accounts, and transact other financial activities

online catalog a virtual presentation of information about products and services similar to a traditional paper catalog; online catalogs can include multimedia such as voice, animation, and video clips

online gambling using a computer and Internet access to gamble online

online predator an individual who attempts to influence underage young people by conversing with them online

online shopping using a computer, modem, browser, and Internet access to locate, examine, purchase, sell, and pay for products over the Internet, either locally or worldwide

online shopping mall a collection of stores found at a single Web site sharing an electronic marketing environment, including servers, software, and payment systems

online store similar to a walk-in store, a seller's Web site where customers can locate, examine, purchase, and pay for products and services; also called a virtual store

online storefront an e-tailer's home page, a computerized version of a brick-and-mortar retail store, on which the e-tailer lists or shows products, descriptions, and prices of the merchandise

online superstore online stores that offer an extensive array of products, from candy bars to household appliances

online transactional processing (OLTP) a form of transactional processing used at e-commerce Web sites that require fast, always-on processing

open system a system that can be altered by a company's IT staff or by a third party

Open Systems Interconnection (OSI) Reference Model a set of communications protocols defined by the International Standards Organization based in Geneva, Switzerland, and adopted by the United Nations; also called OSI model

open-source software program software whose programming code is owned by the original developer but made available free to the general public, who is encouraged to experiment with the software, make improvements, and share the improvements with the user community

operating environment an onscreen visual interface on top of an underlying DOS kernel that makes using a computer easier

operating system (OS) a type of software that creates a user interface and supports the workings of computer devices and software programs that perform specific jobs

operational database a database that aids in the daily operations of an organization

optical character recognition (OCR) software that allows a captured image to be manipulated (edited or altered) with a word processor or other application program

optical disc a secondary storage medium on which data is recorded and read by two lasers: a high-density laser that records data by burning tiny indentations, or pits, onto the disk surface, and a low-intensity laser that reads stored data from the disk into the computer

optical mouse a type of mouse that contains no mouse ball and instead uses a light-based sensor to track movement; can be moved around on nearly any smooth surface, except glass, and thus no mouse pad is required

optical reader a type of optical scanner installed by many retailers at checkout stations

optical scanner a light-sensing electronic device that can read and capture printed text and images, such as photographs and drawings, and convert them into a digital form a computer can understand; once scanned, the text or image can be displayed on the screen, edited, printed, stored on a disk, inserted into another document, or sent as an attachment to an e-mail message; also called a scanner

option button a type of button used with a graphical user interface and resembling buttons on a standard radio that enables you to choose from among a set of options; also called a radio button

OS/2 an operating system produced by IBM in response to the popularity of Microsoft Windows and the Apple Mac OS operating system

output information that is written or displayed as a result of computer processing; also the act of writing or displaying such data

output device any hardware device that makes information available to a user, such as a monitor or printer

output medium any medium or material on which information is recorded, such as paper

outsourcing hiring a third party to handle a project, usually a consultant or a systems integrator

P

packaged software programs created and sold to the public on a retail basis by software development companies

packet switching the process of breaking up a message into parts called packets and directing the packets to their final Internet destination, where they are reassembled

painting program software that allows a user to create images in bit-map form and also to color and edit an image one bit at a time

Palm OS an operating system produced by Palm, Incorporated for use with the company's handheld personal digital assistants (PDAs)

parallel port a slot (opening) for connecting printers, scanners, and other devices; a parallel port can transmit data eight bits at a time

parallel processing a processing action in which two or more processors work concurrently on segments of a lengthy application, thus dramatically increasing processing capability

parallel transmission a transmission method in which a group of 8 bits representing a single byte plus one bit called a parity bit are transmitted at the same time over separate paths

parity bit an extra bit added to a byte, character, or word to ensure that there is always either a predetermined even number of bits or an odd number of bits; if data should be lost, errors can be identified by checking the number of bits

password a secret code of letters and numbers used to prevent access to a computer system by unauthorized people

patent an award made to inventors that allows them ownership of their invention; an inventor whose work is patented has the right to charge others for the use of the invention

pathname the entire URL (Web address) describing where information can be found

PC card a type of expansion board (card) developed for use with small computers such as notebook and other small computers; also called a PCMCIA card

PCI Express bus a computer bus standard for attaching peripheral devices to a computer's motherboard, providing faster data transfer rates than the original Peripheral Component Interconnect (PCI) bus

PCMCIA card a type of expansion board (card) developed for use with small computers such as notebook and other small computers; also called a PC card

PDF file format a popular platform-independent file format, identified with a .pdf extension, for the storage of high-resolution printable documents; PDF documents may contain text, graphics, video, and sound in the QuickTime video format

peer-to-peer (P2P) file sharing a way to use the Internet that allows people to download material directly from other users' hard drives rather than from files located on Web servers

peer-to-peer architecture a network design in which each PC or workstation composing the network has equivalent capabilities and responsibilities

peer-to-peer online transaction venue a Web site forum that allows individuals to sell, buy, trade, or share goods with each other over the Internet

pen computer a computer equipped with pattern recognition circuitry so that it can recognize human handwriting as a form of data input

pen drive a magnetic storage device that plugs into a USB port on a computer or other mobile device; also called a USB drive, jump drive, or thumb drive

performance monitor a set of operating system instructions that monitor the computer system's overall performance

Peripheral Component Interconnect (PCI) bus a type of bus that allows for the connection of sound cards, video cards, and network cards to a computer system

peripheral device a device, such as a printer or disk drive, connected to and controlled by a computer but external to the computer's central processing unit (CPU)

perl a popular script language that is similar to C, but with powerful text-processing abilities; acronym for Practical Extraction and Report Language

permanent storage a type of storage that consists of devices and media used to record information and data permanently so it can later be retrieved, edited, modified, displayed, or printed; also called secondary storage, auxiliary storage, or external storage

permanent storage medium a storage medium on which information and data can be permanently recorded, such as a floppy disk

personal computer (PC) a single-user computer capable of performing its own input, processing, output, and storage; also called a microcomputer

Personal Computer Memory Card International Association (PCMCIA) modem a modem that can be inserted into a PCMCIA slot in a notebook or other portable computer

personal digital assistant (PDA) a handheld, wireless computer, also known as a handheld PC or HPC, used for such purposes as storing schedules, calendars, and telephone numbers and for sending e-mail or connecting to the Internet

personal finance software programs that assist users with paying bills, balancing checkbooks, keeping track of income and expenses, and other financial activities

personal firewall a software-based system designed to protect a personal computer from unauthorized users attempting to access other computers through an Internet connection

personal information manager (PIM) software that helps users organize contact information, appointments, tasks, and notes

person-to-person payment system an Internet service that allows consumers to transfer money through a credit card or a bank account

petabyte a unit of memory measurement equal to approximately 1 quadrillion bytes

petaflop a measure of speed equivalent to 1 quadrillion calculations per second

phishing an activity characterized by attempts to fraudulently acquire another person's sensitive information, such as a credit card number

photo printer a unique high-quality ink-jet printer designed to print high-quality color photographs in addition to other types of print output

pipelining a technique for improving microprocessor performance that enables the computer to begin executing another instruction as soon as the previous instruction reaches the next phase of the machine cycle

pit a tiny indentation burned by laser into the surface of a compact disk to represent information, data, or programs

pitch the quality of sound reflected in the sound's loudness, intensity, and clarity

pixel the smallest picture element that a computer monitor or other device can display and from which graphic images are built

plagiarism the unlawful use of another's ideas or written work

plaintext readable information entered into a computer that is then converted to ciphertext, or unreadable, coded information in the process of encryption

platform compatible computers from one or more manufacturers; the two popular platforms for personal computers are PC and Macintosh

plotter a hard-copy output device used to output special kinds of hard copy, including architectural drawings, charts, maps, diagrams, and other images

plug-in a downloadable software addition, often used to distribute additional Web browser capabilities

polling protocol a network protocol that continually polls all workstations to determine if there are messages to be sent or received by each workstation

pop-up blocker a browser feature that blocks Web page pop-up windows

pop-up window a screen that jumps into the foreground of a Web page, usually during surfing; these windows are oftentimes advertisements

port a plug-in slot on a computer to which you can connect a device, such as a printer or, in the case of accessing the Internet, a telephone line; also called an interface

portable computer a computer small enough to be carried around

portable printer a battery-powered, small, lightweight printer that mobile workers easily can transport and use with various types of computer and communications devices such as notebook computers, personal digital assistants (PDAs), and smartphones

portal a Web site that offers a variety of Internet services, such as search engines, news, weather, sports, yellow pages, and online stores and shopping malls

portrait format a format in which a printed page is taller than it is wide

Post Office Protocol (POP) server a special type of server that holds e-mail messages until they are accessed and read by recipients of the messages

postage printer a small printer designed to print postage stamps

power-on self test (POST) chip a chip containing instructions that check the physical components of the computer system to make certain they are working properly when the computer is turned on

power spike a jump up or down in the level of power provided to a computer system, potentially damaging the hardware

power supply a source of electrical energy that enables the computer to function

presentation graphics software an application program that allows one to create a computerized presentation of slides

primary key a database key that uniquely identifies every record in a table

primary storage addressable storage locations directly controlled by the central processing unit (CPU) used to store programs while they are being executed and data while it is being processed; also called main memory

printer the most common type of hard-copy output device that produces output in a permanent form

print server a type of server that allows multiple users to share the same printer

print spooling a printing technique in which a document to be printed is placed in a buffer instead of being sent to the printer; the document is held in the buffer until the printer is ready to print it, thereby enabling the printer to print at its own speed and free the CPU to perform other tasks

privacy statement an e-tailer's written promise that the merchant will protect the confidentiality of any information revealed by a customer

problem-solving process the use of a logical series of steps in order to analyze a problem and find a solution

processing the manipulation of data by the computer's electrical circuits

processor the part of a computer that interprets and carries out instructions that operate the computer and manage the computer's devices and resources; consists of components, each of which performs specific functions; also called the central processing unit (CPU)

procurement the activity of searching for, finding, and purchasing materials, supplies, products, and services at the best prices and assuring that they are delivered in a timely manner

product developer a company that manufactures new hardware and software products for the general market

productivity software programs that allow users to perform specific tasks, such as creating documents, preparing income tax returns, managing finances, sending and receiving messages over the Internet, and designing new products; software that enables a user to be more "productive"; sometimes referred to as application software

program a set of instructions to be executed by a computer; types of programs include applications and operating systems

programming language a coding system, containing smaller vocabularies and simpler syntax than human (natural) languages; coding language used to write programs

programming language generation a group or type of programming language that was developed at the same time, in a particular chronological order

project management software category of programs that allow a user to plan, design, schedule, and control a project, thus facilitating the effective and efficient management of complex projects

project plan an estimate of how long a project will take to complete, along with an outline of the steps involved and a list of deliverables

prompt a symbol, character, or phrase that appears on-screen to inform the user that the computer is ready to accept input

proprietary software software owned by an individual or business that cannot be used or copied without permission; software that does not adhere to open standards but instead uses algorithms, protocols, file formats, and so on that were developed exclusively for the software by its developers to fulfill a certain purpose

protocol a set of rules and procedures for exchanging information between network devices and computers

prototype an initial "demo" version of a product or information system that allows people to get an idea of the final product's capabilities

pseudocode programming code that is more English-like than a programming language, and therefore easier to read, but is more structured and simplistic than English; algorithms often are written in pseudocode

public access network (PAN) a wide area network operated and maintained by a large company, such as AT&T, MCI, or US Sprint, that provides voice and data communications capabilities to customers for a fee

public key encryption a form of data encryption that uses two encryption keys, a public encryption key known by all authorized users, and a secret encryption key known only by the sender or the receiver

pull-down menu a menu containing various lower-level options associated with main menu options; also called a drop-down menu

pure-play e-tailer a company that depends on e-commerce as its single marketing and sales channel

Q

quality assurance (QA) the task of making sure that products meet quality standards before being released to the public

query a request for information from a database; allows users to ask questions designed to retrieve needed information

Query by Example (QBE) a standard for querying, or asking for particular information from, a database management system

query tools tools in a database management system that help users narrow down the amount of information that needs to be searched

R

radio button a type of button used with a graphical user interface and resembling buttons on a standard radio that enables you to choose from among a set of options; also called an option button

random access memory (RAM) a computer chip or group of chips containing the temporary, or volatile, memory in which programs and data are stored while being used by a computer

range check a database validity check that makes sure a field value entered by the user is within specified limits

rapid application development (RAD) a set of techniques and practices designed to increase the speed of software development

raster image an image composed of a collection of black, white, or colored pixels; the most commonly used file format is the Tag Image File Format (TIF or TIFF)

raster image–based graphics a computerized process of displaying images in which the program treats the image as a large collection of pixels, each of which is stored in its own memory location; the image is created by specifying the color of each pixel; also called a bitmap-based graphics program

read-only memory (ROM) a computer chip on the motherboard of a computer containing permanent, or non-volatile, memory that stores instructions

real-time dialog conversation taking place in the present moment; usually referring to Internet chat rooms

real-time system an information system that is in communication with real-world events directly and must operate fast enough to keep up with those events; examples include CAM, traffic control, and elevator systems

record in a table created by a database management system application, a row providing information about one entity, such as an individual or organization; a collection of related fields describing an event or situation

record locking a process a database uses to ensure that errors do not occur when two users access the same record

recovery a restoration of data from a backup

reduced instruction set computing (RISC) a shortened set of instructions that increases the speed and performance of a microprocessor

redundancy the duplication of data in different locations within a database

redundant system a duplicate system that is part of a disaster recovery plan; one part of a redundant system might be a mirrored hard drive that could be used to replace a damaged or corrupted hard drive

referential integrity a data validation test confirming that if a record is deleted from a database, no other record's validity will be affected

refresh rate the number of times per second a monitor's screen is redrawn

register a component of the arithmetic/logic unit (ALU) that temporarily holds instructions and data

relational database a type of database in which various tables can be linked (or related) in a way that allows retrieval of data from more than one table; tables must have a common data field, such as a product number

removable storage medium a secondary storage medium, such as a floppy disk or a CD-ROM, that a user can remove and replace with another medium

repeater an electronic device that receives signals along a network, amplifies the signals, and resends the amplified signals along the network; also called an amplifier

repetitive motion injury a category of injury that involves the overuse and subsequent damage of joints and nerves

report a database output that is often printed, such as a utility bill or a school transcript; a formatted body of output from a database

request for proposal (RFP) the solicitation of a plan for an information system sent to possible suppliers, inviting them to send representatives to determine what is required before quoting a price

resolution a measurement of the sharpness of an image displayed on a computer monitor or other output device; measured in dots per inch (dpi), both vertically and horizontally, with higher resolution achieved by more dpi

retinal recognition system a biometric device that uses the unique retinal patterns of individuals to identify them

ribbon an interface device in Microsoft Office 2007 that groups commands in a tab format instead of a menu bar

ring topology a network topology in which there is no host computer and each computer or workstation is connected to two other computers and communications are passed in one direction from the source computer to the destination; if one computer is not working, that computer is bypassed

robotics the science of creating machines capable of independent movement and action

rotating backup a system of maintaining multiple backup copies of data in which the oldest copy is erased and reused every time the system is backed up

router a hardware device that connects two or more networks

routine a section of code containing instructions for a specific purpose; also called a function

RPG a programming language commonly used in business environments; an acronym for Report Program Generator

RSA a popular public encryption technology used to transmit data over the internet; named for its developers, Rivest, Shamir, and Adleman

run-time error program mistake that occurs when an application is running

S

sampling the process of measuring the pitch, frequency, and volume of a sound

scanner a light-sensing electronic device that can read and capture printed text and images, such as photographs and drawings, and convert them into a digital form a computer can understand; once scanned, the text or image can be displayed on the screen, edited, printed, stored on a disk, inserted into another document, or sent as an attachment to an e-mail message; also called an optical scanner

screen projector a device that captures the text and images displayed on a computer monitor and projects those same images onto a large screen so the audience can see the text and images clearly

scripting language a large variety of languages that are interpreted rather than compiled; scripting languages are often used to write special functions into Web pages, as the transmission of a script is faster than a binary plug-in

scroll bar a rectangular bar at the side or bottom of a window that enables a user to see and work with other portions of the document by moving the small arrows at the tips of a scroll bar or by dragging the small box between the two arrows

search engine a software program that enables a user to search for, locate, and retrieve specific information on the Internet about any topic

search operators logic statement used by search engines to locate information on the Web; three of the most common are AND, OR, and NOT

search terms words used to tell a search engine what information to look for on the Web; also called keywords

secondary storage a type of storage that consists of devices and media used to record information and data permanently so it can later be retrieved, edited, modified, displayed, or printed; also called permanent storage, auxiliary storage, or external storage

secret key encryption an encryption method in which both the customer and the business use the same encryption key to encrypt and decrypt the data

sector a numbered section or portion of a disk similar to a slice of pie on which programs, data, and information are stored

Secure HTTP (S-HTTP) a protocol for transmitting individual messages securely over the World Wide Web

Secure Sockets Layer (SSL) an encryption protocol used for secure servers commonly found on sites that involve financial transactions, such as the use of credit card information

security measures methods used by a database management system to protect and safeguard data

SELECT command the basic query command supported by SQL, which asks a database to return records that match specified criteria

semiconductor a type of material that is neither a good conductor of electricity (like copper) nor a good insulator (such as rubber) and therefore does not interfere with the flow of electricity in a chip's circuits; most commonly made of silicon, a type of purified glass

sequential access a storage technology whereby stored data can be retrieved only in the order in which it is physically stored, just as musical selections on a cassette tape are recorded and accessed one after the other

serial port a port (opening) for connecting devices such as the keyboard, mouse, and modem to a computer; a port that transmits data one bit at a time; also called a communications (COM) port

serial transmission a data transmission method in which all the bits (0s and 1s) that compose the data are transmitted one bit after another in a continuous line

server a computer and its associated storage devices that users access remotely over a network

shareware software developed by an individual or software publisher who retains ownership of the product and makes it publicly available for a small "contribution" fee

shopping agent software that works for shoppers by locating Web sites that offer products specified by a user and does comparison-shopping to find the best bargain; also called a shopping bot

shopping basket a virtual location where a customer electronically places products for purchase at an online shopping site; also called a shopping cart

shopping bot software that works for shoppers by locating Web sites that offer products specified by a user and does comparison-shopping to find the best bargain; also called a shopping agent

shopping cart a virtual location where a customer electronically places products for purchase at an online shopping site; also called a shopping basket

signature verification system a biometric device that recognizes individuals via their handwriting

SIM card a storage medium used with some digital cameras for storing pictures

Simple Mail Transfer Protocol (SMTP) a communications protocol installed on the ISP's or online service's mail server that determines how each message is to be routed through the Internet and then sends the message

simplex transmission a directional protocol that allows transmissions to flow in only one direction; that is, messages can be either sent or received but not both

single sign-on (SSO) technology a security design that eliminates the problem of users having an ID and password for each application or system they access

single-user computer system computer that can accommodate a single (one) user at a time; the type of personal computer system found in homes and in small businesses and offices

site analysis a business or organization's ongoing evaluation of an e-commerce Web site and its activity

site license a contract that allows an organization to load or use copies of a piece of software on a specified maximum number of machines

situational ethics another name for the school of ethical thought called moral relativism

slide a document created using presentation graphics software that may contain text, graphics, images, sound, and other elements that can help capture and hold an audience's attention

slide show a group of slides compose a presentation; a slide show may include any number of individual slides

small computer system interface (SCSI) an abbreviation for small computer system interface, pronounced scuzzy; a parallel interface system used by some PCs and some UNIX systems for connecting peripheral devices to a computer; provides for faster transmission rates than standard serial and parallel ports; multiple devices can be attached to a single SCSI port

smart card a small plastic card that stores personal and financial data on a tiny microprocessor embedded in the card; when the card is inserted into an electronic card reader, information on the card is read and updated when appropriate

smartphone a device that allows users to transmit and receive phone calls as well as e-mail messages and photos and browse through Web sites

soft copy a temporary version of output, typically the display of data on a computer screen

software programs containing instructions that direct the operation of the computer system and the written documentation that explains how to use the programs; types include system software and application software

software development the creation of new software products for commercial sale; includes systems programming, application programming, multimedia development, and quality assurance

software development life cycle (SDLC) the phases involved in the process of creating, testing, and releasing new software products

software engineering the organized, professional application of the software development process by programmers and software engineers

software piracy the act of copying or using a piece of software without the legal right to do so

software suite a combination of applications programs (usually integrated) bundled as a single package; may contain applications such as word processing, spreadsheet, database, and possibly other programs

software worm a program that actively transmits copies of itself over the Internet, using up resources and causing other problems; also called a worm

Solaris a variation of the UNIX operating system designed for use on Sun servers

sort a feature of many application programs, such as word processing programs and database management systems, that enables the user to organize selected information in a particular way, as, for example, alphabetically or by date

sound card a type of expansion card that allows voice input by means of a microphone and sound output via speakers

sound digitizing card a computer hardware component capable of reproducing sound from a variety of digital file types

source code a computer program written in a programming language, but not yet turned into executable machine language by a compiler

spam an unsolicited e-mail message sent to computer users by a business or individual to promote products or services; similar to junk mail

spam blocker a utility program that allows users to block incoming unsolicited e-mail messages sent to computer users by a business or individual to promote products or services

speaker-dependent program a particular speech recognition program whereby the computer captures and stores your own voice as you speak words slowly and clearly into the microphone

speaker headset a miniature version of larger speakers frequently used with portable devices, including music CD players

speaker-independent program a particular speech recognition program that contains a built-in vocabulary of prerecorded word patterns; the computer can recognize only spoken words that match a word contained in the built-in list of vocabulary words

speakers computer devices that output sound; applications for which speakers are particularly important include computer games, multimedia distance learning programs, audio e-mail, and videoconferencing

special-function keyboard a type of keyboard designed for specific applications involving simplified, rapid data input

specifications a detailed set of requirements for a software product to be developed

speech recognition program a computer program capable of recognizing and capturing spoken words; usually speaker-dependent

spelling checker a part of a program or a stand-alone application that automatically searches for spelling errors and suggests correctly spelled alternatives

spoofing a practice by which a program masquerades as a legitimate source of data on a network in order to get a remote computer to accept its transmissions

spreadsheet software a productivity program that provides a user with a means of organizing, calculating, and presenting financial, statistical, and other numeric information; used to manipulate numbers electronically instead of using a pencil and paper

spyware software that tracks the activity of Internet users for the benefit of a third party

standard operating procedure (SOP) a set of instructions describing how to perform a task

star topology a network topology in which multiple computers and peripheral devices are linked to a central computer, called a host, in a point-to-point configuration; also called a hub-and-spoke topology

start bit a bit that signals the beginning of a character during asynchronous transmission

Static RAM (SRAM) a type of random access memory (RAM) that is faster and more reliable than the more common dynamic RAM

statistical quality control (SQC) system a methodology manufacturing companies use to maintain quality by vigilantly performing statistical analysis upon their production error rates

stealth virus a rare and sophisticated virus that attempts to "hide" from antivirus software by covering up its identifiable characteristics

stereoscopic vision vision that allows depth perception and the detection of movement

stockless inventory distribution a model for distribution management that involves daily deliveries to the customer

stop bit a bit that signals the end of a character during asynchronous transmission

storage a permanent recording of information, data, and programs on a permanent storage medium, such as CD-ROM, so they can be used again and again

storage bay a site within the system unit where a device, such as a floppy disk drive, hard disk drive, or CD-ROM drive is installed; also called a bay

storage device a hardware component that houses a secondary storage medium; also called secondary storage or storage medium

storage medium a medium, such as magnetic disk or optical disc, on which data is recorded (stored)

storage register special areas of main memory used to store program instructions being executed and data being processed

storing the activity of permanently saving instructions and data for future use

storyboard sketches of the pages or frames as they will appear in the final work; used to plan sequential page-based multimedia or movie-based multimedia

streaming an alternative to downloading a piece of music or a video; sends a continuous stream of data to the receiving computer, where it is immediately displayed; also called webcasting

structured programming a set of procedural rules for creating software that is written in a readable, standardized format, and which is broken into coherent structures

Structured Query Language (SQL) a standard for querying, or asking for particular information from, a database management system

style a special shortcut feature that allows text to be formatted in a single step

style error an error in writing source code that does not keep the program from working, but does make it more difficult to read

stylus a sharp, pointed instrument used for writing or marking

supercomputer fastest, most powerful, and most expensive type of computer designed for multiple users

supply chain a series of activities a company performs to achieve its goals at various stages of the production process; the value added at each stage contributes to profit and enhances the product's value as well as the company's competitive position in the market; also called a value chain

support contract a contract that allows users to contact the systems house for technical support, training, and sometimes on-site troubleshooting

surfing accessing and moving about the Web using a browser; also called browsing

surge protector a type of power strip that contains electronics that try to modulate and "smooth out" spikes in the power supply

switch a small hardware device that joins multiple computers together within one local area network (LAN)

synch byte bytes of data signaling the beginning and end of blocks of data during synchronous transmission

Synchronous DRAM (SDRAM) a high-speed, dynamic random access memory (DRAM) technology that can synchronize itself with the clock speed of the microprocessor's data bus

synchronous transmission a transmission method that provides a fast and efficient way of sending data in which blocks of bytes are wrapped in start and stop bytes called synch bytes

syntax the structure of a language

syntax error an error that violates the rules of a programming language; a compiler lists syntax errors when it attempts to translate a program from source code into machine language

system backdoor a secret, sometimes forgotten entry point into an otherwise secure system; oftentimes left behind by the original programmers, accidentally or on purpose

system bus connects the processor (CPU) to main memory, providing the CPU with fast access to data stored in random access memory (RAM)

system clock a small electronic chip inside a computer that synchronizes or controls the timing of all computer operations; the clock generates evenly spaced pulses that synchronize the flow of information through the computer's internal communications channels

system development life cycle (SDLC) a series of steps culminating in a completed information system; planning, design, implementation, and support

system software a type of software consisting of a set of programs that control the operations of a computer system, including starting the computer, processing applications, formatting disks, and copying files; software that controls all components and devices that compose the computer system

system unit the main part of a personal computer system that contains the motherboard and other components necessary for processing information

systems analysis the process of gathering requirements and developing a design for systems of distribution management, office information, management information, decision support, executive support, and factory automation

systems analyst the person whose profession it is to study and evaluate computer operations and procedures used to accomplish specific goals in order to plan and design a database system; may also be responsible for administering the database after it is built

systems integrator a company that specializes in installing, customizing, and supporting information systems

Systems Network Architecture (SNA) a networking program that uses a polling protocol for transmitting data; workstations are asked one by one if they have a message to transmit

systems programmer a professionally trained programmer who specializes in the development of systems software as opposed to application software

systems programming a highly specialized area of software development that involves writing instructions in C++, JavaScript, or other programming languages to accomplish a succession of tasks

T

T line a permanent connection between two points set up by a telephone company and typically leased by a business to connect geographically distant offices; always active and dedicated for use only by the leasing business that pays a monthly fee for use of the line

T1 line a high-speed telephone line that allows for both voice and data transmission and can carry data at a speed of 1.544 megabits per second

T3 line a high-speed telephone line capable of carrying data at speeds of up to 44.7 megabits per second

tab a subset of options, each of which is labeled as if it were a manila folder within a file drawer; the name of the subset of options is displayed in a tab at the top of the folder; clicking on the tab brings the particular group of options to the front of the dialog box

table in relational databases, a file consisting of rows and columns

tablet PC a type of notebook computer that has a liquid crystal display (LCD) on which the user can write using a special-purpose pen, or stylus

tactile perception the science of making a computer understand what it is touching

tape cartridge a secondary storage technology used with personal computers mainly for backing up the contents of a hard drive; the tape is housed in a small plastic container (the cartridge) that also contains a tape reel and a take-up reel

tape drive a device that records and reads data to and from a reel of magnetic tape; many large businesses and organizations use this sequential-access storage medium for backing up important programs and data

tax preparation software programs designed to aid a taxpayer in analyzing federal and state tax status and to prepare and transmit tax returns

technical sales a career involving educating potential customers about a product so that they want to buy it

technical servicing the installation and maintenance of hardware and software

technical support a career that involves responding to customers' phone and e-mail requests for assistance with computer-related products

technical training a career that involves teaching individuals how to use computer systems

technical writing a career that involves writing user manuals, training materials, and textbooks for hardware and software products

technician the person whose job is to repair and maintain computer equipment and systems and install software on a company's computers

telecommunications the combined use of computer hardware and communications software for sending and receiving information over communications media, including phone lines and other types of media

telecommuting an Internet application that enables workers to perform their work activities at home instead of at the workplace by using their computers, communications software, and a telephone line; also called teleworking

teleworking an Internet application that enables workers to perform their work activities at home instead of at the workplace by using their computers, communications software, and a telephone line; also called telecommuting

template a previously created and stored form

terabyte a unit of memory measurement equal to approximately 1 trillion bytes

teraflop a measure of speed equivalent to 1 trillion calculations per second

terminal an input/output device, consisting of a keyboard and monitor, typically used with multi-user computer systems; also called dumb terminal

terminator a device in a bus topology that absorbs signals so they do not reflect back down the line

testing harness a standard set of tests that a software product must pass before being released to the public

text output consisting of characters and numbers that can be used to create words, sentences, and paragraphs

text box a type of dialog box used for typing information that will allow the computer to continue or complete a task

text data alphabetic letters, numbers, and special characters, typically entered to produce output such as letters, e-mail messages, and reports

texture a bitmap used to cover the surface of a virtual object in a virtual environment such as a game

thermal dye sublimation printer a printer that produces images by heating ribbons containing dye and then diffusing the dyes onto specially coated paper or transparencies; also called a thermal dye transfer printer

thermal dye transfer printer a printer that produces images by heating ribbons containing dye and then diffusing the dyes onto specially coated paper or transparencies; also called a thermal dye sublimation printer

thermal printer an inexpensive printer that uses heat to transfer an impression onto paper; category of printer that includes direct thermal, thermal wax transfer, and thermal dye transfer printers

thermal wax transfer printer a printer that produces images by adhering a wax-based ink onto paper

thin-film transistor (TFT) display a type of monitor display in which separate transistors control each color pixel, allowing viewing from any angle; also called active-matrix display

threat a factor of risk assessment based on the severity of the effects of a security breach

throughput a measure of a computer's overall performance

thumb drive a magnetic storage device that plugs into a USB port on a computer or other mobile device; also called a USB drive, jump drive, or pen drive

time bomb virus a virus that is triggered by an event or the passing of a certain time; also called a logic bomb virus

title bar a rectangular area at the top of a window in which the window's name is displayed

token an electronic signal

token ring protocol a type of protocol that sends an electronic signal, called a token, carrying both an address and a message around a token ring network quickly

toner an ink-like powder used in a laser printer

toolbar a type of menu on which sets of icons are displayed that represent actions unique to the software and ones frequently employed by users; the number and kinds of icons often vary among programs and among different versions of the same program

top-down design envisioning a programming project in its entirety by viewing larger elements and then the smaller elements contained within them; often documented using an outline format

touch pad an input device that enables a user to enter data and make selections by moving a finger across the pad; also called a track pad

touch screen an input device that allows the user to choose options by pressing a finger (or fingers) on the appropriate part of the screen

trace electrical pathway etched onto a motherboard that connects internal computer components

track a numbered concentric circle on a magnetic disk, or groups of lines along the length of magnetic tape, along which programs and data are stored

track pad an input device that enables a user to enter data and make selections by moving a finger across the pad; also called a touch pad

trackball an input device consisting of a plastic sphere sitting on rollers, inset in a small external case, or in many portable computers, in the same unit as the keyboard; the user moves the ball with her fingers or palm to position an on-screen cursor

transaction a business activity central to the nature of an enterprise, such as the sale of a product, the flight of an airline, or the recording of a grade

transactional processing a type of data processing that is done continuously, as each activity occurs; used with smaller databases or with operational databases that require all information to be very current

transceiver a device that sends messages along the bus in either direction

Transmission Control Protocol/Internet Protocol (TCP/IP) protocol that governs how packets are constructed and sent over the Internet to their destination

transponder a device contained in a communication satellite that receives signals from transmission stations on the ground

Transport Layer Security (TLS) a newer encryption protocol used for secure servers; it may replace SSL

tree diagram a diagram that shows the links between the planned pages of hypertext page-based multimedia

Trojan horse virus a computer virus that gets the victim to install and use it by masquerading as a legitimate program

true color a term that refers to a graphics device using at least 24 bits to represent each pixel so that up to 16 million unique colors can be represented to accommodate the complex shades and hues of our natural world

trusted operating system (TOS) a security-hardened version of a standard operating system

tunneling a security technology a virtual private network uses to safeguard data that enables one network to send its data via another network's connections

tuple a record in a relational database

turnkey system an information system that is tailored to the customer's needs and thus is easy to use

tutorial a form of instruction in which students are guided step by step through the learning process

twisted-pair cable a communications medium consisting of two independently insulated wires twisted around one another: One of the wires carries the information while the other wire is grounded and absorbs any interference that may be present on the line

U

Unicode a data coding scheme that can accommodate a larger array of letters and symbols than ASCII; uses two

bytes, or 16 binary digits, and can represent 65,536 separate characters

Uniform Resource Locator (URL) an Internet address; also called Universal Resource Locator

uninstaller a utility program for removing (deleting) software programs and any associated entries in the system files

uninterruptible power supply (UPS) a device that provides a battery backup for a computer in the event of a blackout

Universal Product Code (UPC) a type of code printed on products and packages consisting of lines and spaces that a computer translates into a number; the computer then uses this number to find information about the product or package, such as its name and price, in a computerized database

Universal Serial Bus (USB) port a type of port that is widely used for connecting high-speed modems, scanners, and digital cameras to a computer; a single USB port can accommodate several peripheral devices connected together in sequence

UNIX an operating system developed by programmers at Bell Laboratories originally designed for large computer systems including minicomputers, mainframes, and supercomputers

USA PATRIOT Act antiterrorism legislation enacted in 2001 that allows law enforcement agencies to eavesdrop on private telephone messages and to intercept and read e-mail messages sent by individuals and groups

USB flash drive a magnetic storage device that plugs into a USB port on a computer or other mobile device; also called a thumb drive, jump drive, or pen drive

User Access Control (UAC) a protection system in Windows Vista that prompts the user for administrator-level credentials whenever an operation is attempted that might affect system stability or security

user ID a unique combination of characters (letters and numbers) identifying an individual computer user; also called a user name

user interface a set of instructions that allow the software to communicate with the user and, in turn, the user to communicate with the software; the manner in which the user enters data and commands and in which information and processing options are presented is controlled by the program's interface

user name a unique combination of characters (letters and numbers) identifying an individual computer user; also called a user ID

utility program a type of program that performs a specific and helpful task, such as checking for viruses, uninstalling programs, and deleting data no longer needed

utility software programs that perform specific tasks, such as managing a monitor, disk drives, and printers and removing viruses

V

value added network (VAN) a network in which a business uses the facilities of large communications companies to provide subscribers with additional services, such as providing subscribers with access to various network databases, electronic mail, and online advertising and shopping venues

value chain a series of activities a company performs to achieve its goals at various stages of the production process; the value added at each stage contributes to profit and enhances the product's value as well as the company's competitive position in the market; also called a supply chain

variable in a computer program, a data object used to hold values such as numbers or text

variant virus a virus that can alter itself to prevent antivirus software from detecting it

VBScript a script form of Visual Basic that can be used to create sophisticated Web pages

vector-based graphics program a program that creates pictures by means of creating, editing, and combining mathematically defined geometric shapes; also called object-based graphics program

vertical application software a complete package of programs that work together to perform core business functions for a large organization

vertical market package an information system focused on a particular set of customers, for example a system designed for dental offices; also called a niche information system

video consists of motion images, similar to those seen on a television or movie screen

video and audio editing software software that allows users to create and modify recorded video and audio clips

video card a circuit board residing on the motherboard inside the system unit that converts the digital signals produced by the computer into analog signals and sends them through a cable to the monitor; also called a graphics card or video adapter

video data moving pictures and images, such as a video-conference, film clip, or full-length movie

video digitizing card a piece of hardware that allows users to capture and digitize video images and sound from such sources as television, videotape recorders, and camcorders

video editing software software that allows users to edit sound and video and output it in various digital formats

video input an input technology that occurs by using a special type of video camera attached to the computer and plugged into a video capture card in an expansion slot, which converts analog video signals into digital signals

video port a port (connection) for connecting a monitor to the system unit; the port may be built into the computer's system unit or provided by a video card placed in an expansion slot

virtual private network (VPN) a type of wide area network (WAN) whereby a company has each branch office set up a local Internet connection through which company networking traffic is routed; uses encryption and other security technologies to ensure that only authorized users can access it and that the data cannot be intercepted

virtual reality (VR) a game-like form of interface that puts the user into a very realistic alternate world; used for 3D design work and gaming

virtual store similar to a walk-in store, a seller's Web site where customers can locate, examine, purchase, and pay for products and services; also called an online store

virus a program that is designed to harm computer systems and/or any users, typically sent via e-mail

Visual Basic (VB) a language developed by Microsoft in the 1990s that is popular with programmers who want to rapidly develop Windows interface software

visual perception the science of making a computer understand what it sees with an electronic eye (camera)

voice input technology that allows users to enter data by talking into a microphone connected to the computer

voice output technology that allows spoken words and sounds to be heard via a computer's speakers

Voice over IP (VoIP) a combination of hardware and software that allows two or more people with sufficiently good connections to use the Internet to make telephone-style calls without long-distance telephone charges; also called Internet telephony

voice recognition program programs that recognize pre-programmed words stored in a database; usually speech independent

voice verification system a biometric device that recognizes people via their voice patterns

volatile memory a type of computer memory whereby stored instructions and data are lost if the power is switched off

vulnerability a factor of risk assessment based on the likelihood of a security breach

W

warm boot process of restarting a computer while power is on; clears the memory and reloads the operating system

wave file format a noncompressed file type, identified with a .wav extension, used to reproduce any kind of sound

wearable computer a type of computer that can be worn on a person's body, thereby providing the user with access to mobile communicating capabilities and to information access via the Internet

Web administrator the person who is responsible for developing and maintaining a Web site; also called a Web master

Web authoring software software that helps users develop Web pages without learning Web programming

Web browser software that allows users to move from one location to another on the Web and to access and retrieve Web pages; also called a browser

webcam a digital video camera that captures real-time video for transmission to others via a Web server or an instant messaging tool

webcasting an alternative to downloading a piece of music or a video; sends a continuous stream of data to the receiving computer, where it is immediately displayed; also called streaming

webconference an online conference between two or more participants at different sites, using computer networks and webconferencing software

webconferencing software programs that make webconferencing applications possible

Web hosting service a company that allows individuals or other companies to use their Web server to store Web pages; examples include Internet service providers, communications companies, and online shopping malls

Web link an address that links to a document or to a Web page; also called a hyperlink

Webmaster the person who is responsible for developing and maintaining a Web site; also called a Web administrator

Web page an electronic document stored at a location of the Web; the document can contain text, images, sound, and video and may provide links to other Web pages

Web page trap a Web page specifically built to fire advertisements at users in a bewildering array in order to keep them from leaving the site

WebRing a managed ring of links between Web sites that allows a surfer to move through many topically similar sites

Web site a collection of Web pages associated with a given topic or company on a single host system

wide area network (WAN) a network that spans a large geographical area

Wi-Fi a protocol for wireless communication that specifies an over-the-air interface between the wireless client device and a server, or between two wireless devices; also called the 802.11 protocol

Windows 2000 a Microsoft operating system designed for use with business desktop and notebook computers and containing the power as well as many of the features of the earlier Windows NT

Windows 2000 Server a Windows-based operating system specifically designed for use on a network server

Windows Defender a protection system in Windows Vista that monitors for and defends against spyware and adware

Windows Firewall a protection system in Windows Vista that blocks other computers from gathering information or communicating with the system via unused network ports

Windows Longhorn Server the code name used for the server released following the 2007 release of Windows Vista

Windows Mobile an operating system, similar in appearance to the Windows XP operating system, used for personal digital assistants, smartphones, and handheld PCs

Windows NT Server one of Microsoft's earlier entries into the client/server market that supports multitasking operations

Windows Server 2003 Microsoft's server operating system that is available in four editions: Standard, Enterprise, Datacenter, and Web

Windows Server 200X (Longhorn) the server version of Windows Vista, designed to help IT professionals manage and maintain Windows-based networks; it includes a Network Access Protection tool that enables an IT administrator to define health requirements for the network, to restrict computers that do not meet these requirements from participating in the network, and to deploy installations and patches remotely; referred to as "Longhorn" during development

Windows Vista Microsoft's latest release of the Windows operating system for personal computers

Windows XP an operating system from Microsoft Corporation, released in 2001 and designed for the latest computers that are fast, powerful, and have lots of memory and hard disk space

Wired Equivalent Privacy (WEP) a security protocol for wireless networks

wireframe diagram a graphic created using three-dimensional vector techniques to show the underlying structure of a three-dimensional object on a two-dimensional surface

wireless access point a hardware device that transmits a wireless network signal to Wi-Fi-enabled devices

Wireless Application Protocol (WAP) a protocol commonly used with low-bandwidth, wireless systems, such as cell phone networks

Wireless Markup Language (WML) a standardized language included in the Wireless Application Protocol (WAP) that converts an HTML-coded page to Wireless Markup Language (WML), removes the graphics, and then sends the text to the wireless device, where it is displayed on the device's screen

wireless service provider (WSP) a business that provides wireless Internet access to subscribers using wireless Internet devices

wizard a programming feature that guides a user through a series of steps which allow the user to select content and layout options to be applied to a file

word a group of bits or bytes that a computer can manipulate or process as a unit

word processing software a type of computer application that allows the user to create, edit, manipulate, format, store, and print a variety of documents, including letters, memos, announcements, and brochures

word size the number of bits a processor can interpret and execute at a given time

workstation a high-performance single-user computer with advanced input, output, and storage components that can be networked with other workstations and larger computers

World Intellectual Property Organization (WIPO) a specialized agency of the United Nations dealing with intellectual property rights

World Wide Web (WWW) a global system of linked computer networks that allows users to jump from one site to another by way of programmed links on Web pages; also called the Web

worm a program that actively transmits copies of itself over the Internet, using up resources and causing other problems; also called a software worm

write once, read many (WORM) disk a type of optical laser disk that provides very high capacity storage that companies often use to store huge amounts of data, particularly images

WYSIWYG stands for "what you see is what you get"; the layout and content of the actual Web page can be seen within the Web authoring software

Z

zipped file a compressed file format, commonly used for the quick downloading of large files over the Internet

INDEX

3G technology, TI: C13
802.11a protocol, TI: C13
802.11b protocol, TI: C13
802.11g protocol, TI: C13
802.11 protocol, TI: C13

A

Accelerated Graphics Port (AGP)
  buses, 87
Accessibility for disabled, TI: E8
Access time, 126
Adapters, 83
Address, 79
Adobe Systems, Inc., 213
Aiken, Howard, 22
Aircraft: fly-by-wireless technology, 28
Allen, Paul, 170, 178
Almaden Research Laboratory, 142
Alphanumeric keyboards, 47–48
American Standard Code for
  Information Interchange (ASCII),
  64–65
Amplifiers, TI: C11
Analog transmission, TI: C3
Annan, Kofi, 17
Antiplagiarism software, 230
Anti-spyware, 188
Antivirus software, 184–185, TI: E6
Apple Computers Inc., 106
Apple I, 106
Apple II, 232
Apple Lisa, 106, 163
Apple Macintosh, 106, 171, 175–176
Application service providers (ASPs),
  242
Application software
  commercial, 204–205
  defined, 21, 155
  freeware, 206–207
  for home and individual use,
    207–211, 225–239
  installing, TI: B2
  open source software, 207
  shareware, 206
  suites, 223
  types, 203–204
Applied ethics, TI: E2
Architecture: networks classified by,
  TI: C6
Arithmetic/logic unit (ALU), 71–72
Artificial intelligence (AI): pattern
  recognition software, 242
ASCII, 64–65
Atkinson, Bill, 212
Attachments, TI: D2
Audio
  data, 14
  editing software, 233
  input devices, 61–63
  output, 102, 123–124
  ports, 85
  streaming, TI: D9–D10
Autorun file: manual activation, TI: B2
Auxiliary storage, 124

B

Backup utilities, 187
Bandwidth, TI: C1–C2
Bar code readers, 56–57
Basic input/output system (BIOS), 81
Bays, 67–68
Bell Labs, TI: C4
Bhutan, 157
Binary Automatic Computer (BINAC),
  62–63
Binary number system, 22, 64
Bit depth, 107
Bitmaps, 54
Bits (binary digits), 64, TI: C1–C2
Bits per second (bps), TI: C2
BlackBerry handheld devices, 34
Blackboard platform, TI: D4
Blogosphere, TI: D2
Blogs, TI: D2
BlueGene/L, 32
Bluetooth technology, 47, TI: C5–C6
Boost Technology, 88–89
Boot drives, 156
Booting computers, 157–159, TI: A8
Brain-computer interfaces, 52
Bricklin, Dan, 232
Bridges, TI: C12
Broadband medium, TI: C2, TI: D6
Broadband over Powerline (BPL), TI:
  D10
Browsers, 23, 236, TI: D7
Buffers, 160
Buses, 86–87, TI: C9
Bush, Vannevar, 62
Bus topologies, TI: C9, TI: C10
Buttons, 164–165
Bytes, 64

C

Cable modems, TI: C3, TI: D6
Cables
  connecting, TI: A8
  installing, TI: B3
  types of, TI: C2, TI: C3
Cache memory, 80–81, 159
CAD (computer-aided design) software,
  235
Cathode ray tube (CRT) monitors, 105
CD-R (compact disc, recordable) discs
  and drives, 134, 137
CD-ROM discs, 131, 133–135, 137
CD-RW (compact disc-rewritable) discs
  and drives, 135, 137
CDs (compact discs) and CD drives,
  131, 137
Cell microprocessors, 88
Cell phones, 28
Cells, TI: C5
Cellular technology, TI: C5, TI: C13
Central processing units (CPUs), 19, 24,
  69–70
Charting, 216
Chat rooms, TI: D2

Check boxes, 169
Children's Internet Protection Act
  (CIPA), TI: E7
Children's Online Privacy Protection
  Act (COPPA), TI: E4
Chips, 6
  in PCs, 24
  reconfigurable, 89
  transistors on, 54
Circuit boards, TI: B5
Circuits, 69–70, 75, 77
Clients, TI: C6, TI: C7
Client/server architecture, TI: C6, TI:
  C7
Clip art, 223
Clock cycle, 78
Clusters, 129
Coaxial cables, TI: C3
Cold boots, 157
Collaboration software, 203, 204,
  238–239
COM (Communications) ports, 85
Command icons, 168
Command-line interfaces, 162
Commercial software, 204–205
Communications, 10–13. See also
  Internet; Networks; Web
  media, TI: C3–C6
  software, 21, 235–240, TI: C12–C13
Communications (COM) ports, 85
Communications devices, 20. See also
  Modems
Communications satellites, TI: C5
Compact disc capacity, TI: A3
Compatibility issues, TI: A5
Compilers, 188
Computer-aided design (CAD) soft-
  ware, 235
Computer ethics, TI: E2, TI: E9
Computer jockeys, 140
Computers. See also Computer systems;
  Notebook computers; Personal computers (PCs)
  accuracy, 8
  categories, 23–32
  defined, 6
  embedded, 6, 33
  handheld, 23, 27–28, 33–34, 182,
    TI: A6–A7
  history, 7–8, 63–64
  mainframe, 23, 31
  midrange servers, 23, 29
  speed, 8, 32
  storage, 10
  supercomputers, 23, 32
  versatility, 9
  wearable, 26, 110
Computer systems
  components, 17–20
  types, 15–17
Consumer profiles, TI: E3
Consumer self-protection, TI: E4
Context-sensitive Help messages, 170
Control unit, 70–71

Cookies, TI: E3, TI: E4
Copper circuits, 75
Coprocessors, 72
Copyright, TI: E5
Cordless keyboards, TI: C5
Coverage: networks classified by, C8, T9, TI: C6
CPUs (central processing units), 19, 24, 69–70
Cross-platform operating systems, 180
Cryptographic coprocessors, 72
Cursors, 50
Customized software, 205, 212

D

Data, 13–14, 126, TI: C1–C3
Database management systems (DBMSs), 217–221
Databases, 217
Data processing, 15, 63–65
Data register, 72
DBMS (Database management systems), 217–221
D Data Inc., 141
DDR SDRAM (double data rate SDRAM), 79
Debian, 157
Decoding, 70–71
Default options, 167
Defragmenting, 186–187
Desai, Roger, 238
Desktop computers, 24–25. *See also* Personal computers (PCs)
Desktop publishing (DTP) software, 213
Desktops
    GUIs, 164–165
    Microsoft Windows Vista, 159
Diagnostic utilities, 185
Dialog boxes, 169
Dial-up access, TI: D5–D7
Dictionaries, 230
Digital cameras, 57–58, 233
Digital divide, TI: E7
Digital information, 6
Digital ink technology, 25–26
Digital interactions, 2–5
Digital Light Processing (DLP) projectors, 112
Digital Micromirror Devices (DMDs), 112
Digital subscriber line (DSL) Internet service, TI: C4, TI: D6
Digital transmission, TI: C3
Digital versatile disc-read-only memory (DVD-ROM) discs and drives, 135–136, 137
Digital versatile disc-recordable (DVD-R) discs and drives, 136, 137
Digital versatile disc-rewritable (DVD-RW) discs and drives, 136–137
Digital versatile (or video) discs (DVDs) and drives, 131, 137, TI: A3
Digitizing pens, 53
DIMMs (dual inline memory modules), TI: B6
Direct access, 126
Direct thermal printers, 118
Disabled persons: accessibility, TI: E8
Disk defragmenters, 186–187
Diskettes, 127

Disk packs, 138
Disk scanners, 186
Disk toolkits, 187
Display devices, 105, 110–112, TI: A6. *See also* Monitors
Display windows, 165–166
Distance learning, 202, TI: D4
Distributed computing, 242
Docking stations, 86
Document formatting, 211
Dot-matrix printers, 114–115
Dot pitch, 109
Dots per inch (dpi), 55, 58
Double data rate SDRAM (DDR SDRAM), 79
Downloading, TI: D2
Dpi (dots per inch), 55, 58
Draft quality printing, 115
DRAM (dynamic RAM), 79
Drawing software, 231–232
Drawing tablets, 53
Drivers, 160–161, TI: B3
Drop-down menus, 166–168
DTP. *See* Desktop publishing (DTP) software
Dual-core processors, 76
Dual inline memory modules (DIMMs), TI: B6
Dumb scanners, 55
DVD-ROMs (digital versatile disc-read-only memory) discs and drives, 135–136, 137
DVD-Rs (digital versatile disc-recordable) discs and drives, 136, 137
DVD-RWs (digital versatile disc-rewritable) discs and drives, 136–137
DVDs (digital versatile or video) discs and drives, 131, 137, TI: A3
Dynamic RAM (DRAM), 79

E

EarthLink, 106
Earth stations, TI: C5
EBCDIC, 64–65
Eckert, John P., 62–63
Editing, 210, 233
Educational software, 229–231
E-ink, 142
Electronic commerce (e-commerce), TI: D4, TI: E3
Electronic devices, 2–3
Electronic mail (e-mail), 235, TI: D1–D2
Electronic Numerical Integrator and Computer (ENIAC), 62
Electronic paper, 142
Embedded computers, 6, 33
Encryption software, TI: E4
Encyclopedias, 230
Entertainment software, 228
Entertainment via Internet, TI: D2–D4
Ergonomics, 110
E-shopping. *See* Electronic commerce (e-commerce)
Ethics, TI: E1–E2
Executing, 71
Execution time (E-time), 72
Expansion boards: installing, TI: B4–B6
Expansion buses, 86
Expansion cards, 83–84
Expansion slots, 83

Exposed bays, 67–68
Extended Binary Coded Decimal Interchange Code (EBCDIC), 64–65
External ports, TI: A4
External storage, 124
Extranets, TI: C9
EyeglassTek Covert Eyeglass Video Camera, 124

F

Facsimile/fax machines, 121–123
Fair Use right, TI: E5
FAT (file allocation table) files, 129
Fax/modem cards, 122–123
Fax programs, 123
Fetching, 70
Fiber-optic cables, TI: C2, TI: C4
Field programmable gate array (FPGA), 70
Fields, 217
File allocation table (FAT) files, 129
File compression utilities, 187
File extensions, 125
File managers, 161
File servers, TI: C6
File types, 125
Filtering software, TI: E7
Find feature, 219
Firewalls, 185, TI: C9
Flash drives/memory (flash ROM), 82, 130
Flat-panel displays, 105
Floppy disks and disk drives, 127–128, TI: A3
Fly-by-wireless technology, 28
Foot mouse, 50–51
Formatting
    floppy disks, 128
    numbers, 216
    text, 210–211
Formulas, 216
Frankston, Bob, 232
Freedom of speech issues, TI: E6
Freeware, 206–207
Frequency range, TI: C3
Full-duplex transmission, TI: C12

G

Gambling online, TI: E6
Games, 228
Garbage in, garbage out (GIGO), 8
Gates, Melinda, 170
Gates, William H. (Bill), 170
Gateways, TI: C12
General-purpose computers, 6
Gigabytes, 79
Global Positioning Systems (GPSs), TI: E3
Global Unique Identifiers (GUIDs), TI: E3
Government privacy threats, TI: E4–E5
Grammar checkers, 210
Graphical user interfaces (GUIs), 49, 163–164, 168–170, 171
Graphics. *See also* Video
    cards, 83, 84
    coprocessors, 72
    data, 14
    input devices, 57–58
    memory needs, TI: A3

output, 101
    presenting, 221–223
    software, 231–235
    tablets, 53
Grid computing, 242
Grids, 216
Groupware, 203, 204, 238–239
GUIs. *See* Graphical user interfaces
    (GUIs)

H

Hackers, TI: E5
Half-duplex transmission, TI: C12
Handheld computers
    buying, TI: A6–A7
    characteristics, 23, 27–28
    increase in use of, 33–34
    operating systems, 182
Handouts, creating, 222
Hard copy, 19, 101, 211
Hard disks and drives, 128–129, TI: A3,
    TI: B2
Hardware
    buying components, TI: A2–A5
    connecting components, TI: B3–B4
    Internet needs, TI: D4–D5
    network, TI: C11–C12
    overview of, 17–20, 47, 155
    wireless communications, TI: C5
Hate speech sites, TI: E6
Help messages: context-sensitive, 170
Hertz, 78
Hewlett, William, 30
Hewlett-Packard Corporation, 30
High Definition Digital Multilayer Discs
    (HD-DMDs), 141
High-definition television (HDTV),
    111–112
High-level languages, 188
High-resolution monitors, TI: A4
Holographic storage, 141–142
Home information infrastructure, 46
Host computers. *See* Servers
Hotspots, TI: C5
Hot swapping/hot plugging, 84, 87
Hubs, TI: C11
Human Genome Project, 9
Hybrid topologies, TI: C10–C11
Hypercard, 212
Hypertext Transfer Protocol (HTTP),
    TI: C13
Hyperthreading, 76

I

IBM
    OS/2 operating system, 176
    personal computers, 106
    super-fast transistors, 159
    Super Human Speech Recognition
        Initiative, 241
Icons, 163–164, 168
Icuiti DVD920, 124
Identity theft, TI: E5–E6
Image-editing software, 233
Impact printers, 113
Individual application software, 203
Information, 14
Information processing, 15
Information processing cycle, 15, 47
Infrared technology, TI: C5

Ink-jet printers, 115–117, TI: A5
Input, 15
Input devices, 15, 19, 59–60, 88–89, TI:
    A4. *See also specific devices*
Instant messaging (IM), TI: D2
Instant messaging (IM) software,
    236–238
Instruction register, 72
Instruction time (I-time), 71
Integrated Services Digital Network
    (ISDN) lines, TI: C4
Integrated software programs, 223
Intel Corporation, 54
Intellectual property, TI: E5
Intelligent scanners, 55
Internal bays, 67
Internal ports, TI: A4
Internet, 11–12, TI: D1. *See also* Distance
    learning; Electronic commerce (e-com-
    merce); Electronic mail (e-mail)
    access for disabled, TI: E8
    cell microprocessors, 88
    connecting to, 20, 21, 23, TI: D4–D7
    navigating, TI: D7–D10
    protocols, TI: C13, TI: D7
Internet2, TI: D10
Internet Protocol (IP) addresses, TI: D7
Internet service providers (ISPs), 21, 23,
    106, TI: D1, TI: D5
Internet telephony, TI: D9
Interpreters, 189
Intranets, TI: C9

J

Java Jacket, 26
Jobs, Steven, 106
Joysticks, 52
Jump drives, 130

K

Kernels, 158
Keyboards
    buying, TI: A4
    in notebook computers, TI: A5–A6
    types of, 47–48
    wireless, TI: C5
Keywords, TI: D8
Kilby, Jack S., 77
Kilobytes, 79
Krugle, 181
K-Team, 140

L

Label printers, 120
Land, 131
Landscape format, 113
Language translators, 188
Laptop computers. *See* Notebook com-
    puters
Large servers, 23, 31
Laser printers, 117–118, TI: A5
LCD. *See* Liquid crystal display (LCD)
    entries
LeBerge, Stephen, 240
Legal software, 227–228
Letter quality printing, 115
Line printers, 115
Links, 221
Linux, 181–182

Lipman, Sol, 134
Liquid crystal display (LCD) projectors,
    112
Liquid crystal displays (LCDs), 105
Local area networks (LANs)
    described, 10–11, TI: C6, TI: C8
    groupware, 203, 204, 238–239
    Internet connection, TI: D6
    protocols, TI: C12
    wireless, 34
Local buses, 87
Location tracking, TI: E3
Lotus Software, 232
Lucid dreaming, 240–241
Lucidity Institute, 240–241

M

Machine cycle, 70
Machine language, 64
Macintosh. *See* Apple Macintosh
MacPaint, 212
Macros, 216
Magnetic storage devices and media,
    126–130, 137–139
Mainframe computers, 23, 31
Main menus, 166
Malware, 188
Mauchly, John W., 62–63
McCaw, Craig, 170
Medicine, 206
Megabytes, 79
Memory, 19. *See also* Random access
    memory (RAM)
    buying, TI: A3
    capacity and computer type, 80
    managing, 159–160
    in notebook computers, TI: A6
    ROM, 81–82
    types of, TI: B6
Memory access time, 81
Memory residents, 158
Menu bars, 166
Menus, 166–168
Metropolitan area networks (MANs), TI:
    C9
Mice. *See* Mouse (mice)
Microcomputers. *See* Personal comput-
    ers (PCs)
Microprocessors, 19, 72–76, TI: A3
Microsoft Corporation, 170
Microsoft Office, TI: A2
Microsoft Windows, 157, 170–175
Microsoft Windows 95, 157
Microsoft Windows 98, 157
Microsoft Windows 2000, 171–172
Microsoft Windows Mobile, 182
Microsoft Windows Servers, 179–180
Microsoft Windows Vista, 174–175
    desktop, 159
    operating system, 157
    performance evaluation and
        improvement, 161–162
Microsoft Windows XP, 157, 172–174
Microsoft Word, 213
Microwave systems, TI: C5
Midrange servers, 23, 29
Minicomputers. *See* Midrange servers
MITS Altair, 170
Modem cards, 83, 84
Modem ports, 85

Modems: defined, 20, TI: C3
Monitors
    buying, TI: A4–A5
    ergonomics, 110
    in future, 141
    overview of, 103–105
    performance and quality factors, 105, 107–110
    refresh rates, 109–110
    resolution, 107–109
Moore, Gordon E., 54
Moore's Law, 54
Moral realism, TI: E1–E2
Moral relativism, TI: E1–E2
MoSoSo (Mobile Social Software), 238
Motherboards, 18–19, 68–69
Mouse (mice)
    buying, TI: A4
    head-mounted, 88–89
    overview of, 49–51
Mouse pads, 50
Mouse pointers, 50
Moving Pictures Expert Group Layer III (MP3), TI: D3–D4, TI: E5
Multi-core processors, 76
Multifunction devices (MFDs), 121–123
Multimedia software, 231–235
Multitasking, 160
Multithreading, 76
Multi-user computer systems, 16
Multi-user operating systems, 180
Murdock, Debra, 157
Murdock, Jan, 157
Music: online, TI: D3–D4, TI: E5
MyDropBox.com, 230
Mylonas, George, 206

N

Nanotechnology, 87–88
Nantero Inc., 88
Napster, TI: E5
Narowband medium, TI: C2
Natural-language processing (NLP), 241
Net. See Internet
Netware, 179
Network architecture, TI: C6
Network firewalls, 185
Network interface cards (NICs), 83, 84, TI: C11
Network ports, 85
Networks, 10–11
    classifications, TI: C6–C9
    hardware, TI: C11–C12
    servers, 29
    software, TI: C12
    telecommunications, TI: C1
    topologies, TI: C9–C11
NeXT Software, 106
Nodes, TI: C9
Nonimpact printers, 113
Nonresident operating system parts, 158
Nonvolatile memory, 81
Nonvolatile random access memory (NRAM) chips, 88
Normative ethics, TI: E2
Notebook computers, 25
    buying, TI: A5–A6
    modems, TI: C3
    monitors, 103
Novell Netware, 179

NTSC converters, 110–111
Number formatting, 216

O

Object linking and embedding (OLE), 223
OCR (Optical character recognition), 55
OLE. See Object linking and embedding (OLE)
On-demand computing, 33
Online education, 202, TI: D4
Online gambling, TI: E6
Online games, TI: D2–D3
Online help, 169–170
Open Source Development Labs, 178
Open source software, 207
    open source software programs, 177, 181
Operating environments, 171
Operating systems (OSs), 20
    Apple Macintosh, 171, 175–176
    choosing, 150, TI: A2
    drivers, 160–161
    file managers, 161
    function, 156–157
    handheld devices, 182
    installing or upgrading, TI: B1–B2
    Linux, 176–177, 178
    OS/2, 176
    performance monitors, 161–162
    security, 162
    servers, 177, 179–182
    Windows, 170–175
Optical character recognition (OCR), 55
Optical mouse, 50
Optical readers, 56–57
Optical scanners, 54–57
Optical storage devices, 131–137, 140, 141
Opt-in or opt-out cookies, TI: E4
Option buttons, 169
OTM Technology, 89
Output, 15
Output devices, 15, 19, 102. See also Monitors
    buying, TI: A4–A5
    multifunction, 121–123
    printers, 113–114
    screen projectors, 112
    television displays, 110–112
    wearable computers, 110
Output medium, 102–103
Output types, 101–102

P

Packaged software, 204–205
Packard, David, 30
PageMaker, 213
Painting software, 231–232
Palm OS, 182
Paragraph formatting, 210
Parallel ports, 85, TI: A4
Parallel processing, 75–76
Parallel transmission, TI: C3
Passwords, 162
Patents, TI: E5
Pattern recognition software, 242
PC architecture, TI: A3
PC Magazine, 142
PC (PCMCIA) cards, 84
PDAs (personal digital assistants),

27–28, 223
Peer-to-peer architecture, TI: C6, TI: C7
Peer-to-peer (P2P) file sharing, TI: D4, TI: D8–D9, TI: E5
Pen computers, 28
Pen drives, 130
Pentium processors, 72
Performance monitors, 161–162
Peripheral Component Interconnect (PCI), 87
Peripheral devices, 17–28, TI: A4
Permanent storage, 124
Permanent storage media, 126
Personal Computer Memory Card International Association (PCMCIA) modems, TI: C3
Personal computers (PCs)
    booting, TI: A8
    buying, TI: A1–A5
    characteristics, 23, 24–26
    commonly used operating systems, 150, 170–176
    history, 7–8, 106
    installing, TI: A7–A8
    Linux operating systems, 176–177, 178
    Macintosh operating system, 175–176
    upgrading decision, TI: B5, TI: B6
    Windows operating systems, 170–175
Personal digital assistants (PDAs), 27–28, 223
Personal electronic devices, 2–3
Personal finance software, 225–227
Personal firewalls, 185
Personal information managers (PIMs), 223
Petabytes, 80
Petaflops, 32
Phishing, TI: E5–E6
Photographic printers, 120, TI: A5
Pipelining, 75
Pitch, TI: C3
Pits, 131
Pixar Animation Studios, 106
Pixels, 54–55, 58, 107–108, TI: A4
Plagiarism, TI: E5
Plagiarism detection software, 230
Platforms, 156–157
Plotters, 119
Plug-and-play features, TI: B3
Point-and-click devices, 49–51, TI: A5–A6. See also Mouse (mice)
Point-and-click interface, 106
Polymorphous TRIPS architecture, 89
Pornography sites, TI: E6
Portable computers. See Notebook computers
Portable printers, 121
Portals, TI: D7
Portrait format, 113
Ports, 85–86, TI: A4, TI: B3
Postage printers, 121
Post Office Protocol (POP) servers, TI: C13
Power-on self test (POST) chip, 81
Power supply, 65–67
Presentation graphics software, 221–223
Primary storage. See Memory
Printers, 113–114, TI: A5, TI: B4. See also specific types
Printing, 211
Print servers, TI: C6

Print spooling, 160
Privacy, 74, TI: E2–E5
Privacy statements, TI: E3–E4
Processing, 15
Processors, 19, TI: A5
Productivity software
    database management, 217–221
    desktop publishing, 213
    personal information managers, 223
    presentation graphics, 221–223
    project management, 224
    spreadsheets, 214–216
    suites, 223
    word processing software, 208–211
Programs, 6
Project management software, 224
Prompts, 162
Property: protection issues, TI: E5
Proprietary software, 177, 205
Protocols, TI: C12–C13, TI: D7
Public access networks (PANs), TI: C9
Public information: availability, TI: E2

Q

Query by Example (QBE), 221
Query feature, 219, 221

R

Radio buttons, 169
Radio frequency identification (RFID)
  tags, 74
Random access memory (RAM), 78–80.
  See also Memory
    buying, TI: A3
    installing, TI: B5–B6
    managing, 159–160
Rave Wireless, 238
Read-only memory (ROM), 81–82
Real-time dialogue, TI: D2
Records, 217
Reduced instruction set computing
  (RISC), 75
Reference software, 229–231
Refresh rates, 109–110
Registers, 72
Relational databases, 219
Remington Rand Corporation, 63
Removable storage media, 126
Repeaters, TI: C11
Reports, 221
Research: via Internet, TI: D4
Research in Motion, 34
Resolution
    digital photoquality, 58
    measuring, 54–55
    monitors, 107–109, TI: A4
    printers, 115, 116, TI: A5
Ring topologies, TI: C10, TI: C11
Robots: surgical, 206
ROM (read-only memory), 81–82
Routers, TI: C11–C12
Run autorun.exe, TI: B2

S

Satellite systems, TI: C5, TI: D6–D7
Saving, 211
Screen projectors, 112
SDRAM (Synchronous RAM), 79
Search engines, 12, 181, 236, TI: D4

Secondary storage, 124, TI: A3
Sectors, 129
Secure Sockets Layer (SSL), TI: E4
Security
    antivirus software, 184–185
    firewalls, 185, TI: C9
    from identity theft, TI: E6
    operating system, 162
    transaction tips, TI: E4
    Windows Vista, 174, TI: E4
    Windows XP, 173
Semiconductors, 69–70
Sequential access, 126
Serial ports, 85, TI: A4
Serial transmission, TI: C3
Servers
    large, 23, 31
    midrange, 23, 29
    operating systems, 177, 179–182
    protocols, TI: C13
Service technicans: using, TI: B5
SETI@Home, 242
Setup utility, TI: B2
Shareware, 206
Silicon Valley, California, 30, 54
Silverman, Scott, 74
SIM cards, 120
SIMMs (single inline memory modules),
  TI: B6
Simple Mail Transfer Protocol (SMTP),
  TI: C13
Simplex transmission, TI: C12
Single-user computer systems, 16
Site licenses, 205
Situational ethics, TI: E1–E2
Sleep, learning during, 240–241
Slides, 221
Slide shows, 221, 222
Small computer system interface (SCSI),
  85
Smart cards, 57
Smart highways, 33
Smartphones, 28
Soft copy, 19, 101
Software. *See also* Application software;
  Graphical user interface (GUI);
  Operating systems (OSs); Productivity
  software
    antiplagiarism, 230
    antivirus, 184–185, TI: E6
    buying pre-installed, TI: A–2
    categories, 20–21, 23
    communications, TI: C12–C13
    creating, 212
    default options, 167
    fax programs, 123
    filtering, TI: E7
    installing, TI: B2
    Internet needs, TI: D4–D5
    network, TI: C12
    open-source programs, 177
    proprietary, 177, 205
    translators, 188–189
    utility, 20, 183–188, 190
    web authoring, 234
    webconferencing, 239–240
Software Arts, 232
Software companies: responsibilities, TI:
  E7–E8
Software piracy, 205
Solaris, 182

Sort feature, 219
Sound cards, 83, 84
Sound systems, 123–124
Spam blockers, 187–188
Speaker-dependent programs, 62–63
Speaker headsets, 123
Speaker-independent programs, 62–63
Speaker recognition programs, 62–63
Speakers, 123
Special-function keyboards, 48
Speech biometrics, 241
Speech recognition software, 241
Spelling checkers, 210
Spreadsheet software, 214–216
Spyware, 188
SQL. *See* Structured Query Language
  (SQL)
Stacks, 212
Star topologies, TI: C9, TI: C10
Static RAM (SRAM), 79
StickyDrive, 134
Sticky Inc., 134
Storage bays, 67–68
Storage devices and media, 15, 20,
  124–126
    capacity, 32, TI: A3
    electronic paper, 142
    holographic, 141–142
    large computer, 137–140
    magnetic, 126–129
    optical, 131–137
    tape, 130
Storing, 72
Streaming, TI: D9–D10
Structured Query Language (SQL), 221
Structured wiring, 46
Stylus, 25, 28, 53
Sun Microsystems, 182
Supercomputers, 23, 32
Surfing, TI: D7
Surge protectors, TI: A8
Sutherland, Doug, 26
Switches, TI: C11
Synchronous DRAM (SDRAM), 79
System buses, 86
System clocks, 77–78
System components: connecting, TI:
  B3–B4
System software
    defined, 20
    function, 155–156
    user-friendly, 190
System units
    components, TI: A3–A4
    described, 15–16, 18–19, 65
    installing devices inside, TI: B4–B6
    locating ports, TI: B3

T

Tabbed ribbons, 166
Tablet PCs, 25–26
Tabs, 169
Tape cartridges and drives, 130
Tax preparation software, 226–227
TCP/IP (Transmission Control
  Protocol/Internet Protocol), TI: C13
Technicans: using, TI: B5
Telecommunications, TI: C1
Teledesic project, 170

Telepathic technology, 52
Television displays, 110–112
Templates, 209, 222
Terabytes, 32, 80
Teraflops, 32
Terminals, 29
Terminators, TI: C9
Texas Instruments, 77
Text, 209–211
Text boxes, 169
Text data, 14
Thani, Hamid Bin Khalifa Al-, 140
Thermal printers, 118–119
Throughput, 159
Thumb drives, 130
Time (magazine), 178
T lines, TI: C4
Toner, 118
Toner cartridges, TI: B4
Toolbars, 168
Torvalds, Linus, 176–177, 178
Touch pads, 51
Touch screens, 49
Tracer, 88–89
Traces, 68
Trackballs, 51
Track pads, 51
Tracks, 129
Transistors, 54, 64, 159
Translators, 188–189
Transmeta Corporation, 178
Transmission Control Protocol/Internet
   Protocol (TCP/IP), TI: C13
Transponders, TI: C5
Transport Layer Security (TLS), TI: E4
Trelix, 232
True color, 107
Turnitin, 230
Tutorials, 230–231
Twisted-pair cables, TI: C2, TI: C3

U

Unicode, 65
Uniform (or Universal) Resource
   Locator (URL), TI: D7
Uninstallers, 186
United Nations Millennium Goals, 17
Universal Automatic Computer (UNI-
   VAC), 63

Universal Product Codes (UPCs), 56
Universal Serial Bus (USB) ports, 85, 87,
   TI: A4
UNIX, 180, 182. *See also* Linux
USB flash drives, 130
USB (Universal Serial Bus) ports, 85, 87,
   TI: A4
User Access Control (UAC), 174
User interfaces, 162, 173, 190. *See also*
   Graphical user interfaces (GUIs)
User names, 162
Users: networks classified by, TI: C9
Utility programs, 183–188, 190
Utility software, 20

V

Value added networks (VANs), TI: C9,
   TI: D5
Verichip implants, 74
Vertical application software, 203, 204
Video
   cards (adapters), 103, 105, 107
   data, 14
   editing software, 233
   glasses, 124
   input devices, 59–60
   memory needs, TI: A3
   output, 101
   ports, 85
   streaming, TI: D9–D10
   via Internet, TI: D3–D4
Video RAM (VRAM), 107
Virtual movie theaters, 124
Virtual reality (VR), TI: D3
Virus checkers. *See* Antivirus software
Viruses, TI: E6
VisiCalc (Visual Calculation), 232
Voice input programs, 61–63
Voice output systems, 124
Voice over IP (VoIP), TI: D9
Voice recognition programs, 61–62
Volatile memory, 79
VPens, 89

W

Warm boots, 157
Wearable computers, 26, 110

Web
   authoring software, 234
   navigating, 181, 236, TI: D7
   protocols, TI: C13
Webcams, 59
Webcasting, TI: D9–D10
Webconferencing software, 239–240
Weblogs, TI: D2
Web pages, 12, TI: D7
Web sites, TI: D7
Wide area networks (WANs), 11, TI: C6,
   TI: C8, TI: C9, TI: C12–C13
Wi-Fi. *See* Wireless communications
Windows. *See* Microsoft Windows
Windows Defender, 174
Windows Firewall, 174
Wired communications media, TI: C3
Wireless access points, TI: C5
Wireless application protocol (WAP), TI:
   C13
Wireless communications, TI: D6
   capability, TI: A6
   media, TI: C5–C6
   protocols, TI: C13
   technology, TI: C5
   threats to privacy from, TI: E3
Wireless devices, 33–34, 124
Wireless keyboards, TI: C5
Wireless local area networks (WLANs),
   34, TI: C5
Wizards, 209, 222
Word processing software, 208–211
Word size, 74
Workplace privacy threats, TI: E5
World Wide Web (WWW), 12. *See also*
   Web
Wozniak, Steve, 106
Write once, read many (WORM) disks,
   140
WYSIWYG, 234

X

Xerox Corporation, 142

Z

Zipped files, TI: D2
Z-learning, 240–241
Zuse, Konrad, 22

IMAGE CREDITS

Tech Insight A. *Page TI-B2:* © Paradigm Publishing, Inc.; *Page TI-B3:* © Paradigm Publishing, Inc.; *Page TI-B4:* © Paradigm Publishing, Inc.; *Page TI-A5:* Jim Craigmyle/Corbis; *Page TI-A6:* Don Mason/Corbis; *Page TI-A7:* © Hewlett-Packard Company; *Page TI-A8:* © American Power Conversion Corp. **Chapter 2.** *Page 46:* Corbis, Eric K. K. Yu/CORBIS; *Page 47:* Artiga Photo/Corbis; *Page 48:* (top) © Paradigm Publishing, Inc., (bottom) Saed Hindash/Star Ledger/Corbis; *Page 49:* (top) Ramin Talaie/Corbis, (bottom) Encore; *Page 51:* Courtesy of Microsoft Corporation; *Page 52:* © Lian-Li Industrial Company, Ltd; *Page 53:* istockphoto.com/Sharon Dominick, © Microsoft Corporation; *Page 54:* Roger Ressmeyer/CORBIS; *Page 56:* (top left) courtesy of Hewlett-Packard Company, (top right) Reuters/Corbis, (bottom) courtesy McKesson Provider Technologies; *Page 57:* Rick Friedman/Corbis, © Eastman Kodak Company; *Page 59:* Roy Morsch/Corbis, © Sintec Corp.; *Page 61:* Ramin Talaie/Corbis, Larry Williams/CORBIS; *Page 63:* Bettmann/CORBIS; *Page 67:* Encore; *Page 68:* © Lian-Li Industrial Company, Ltd; *Page 69:* Encore; *Page 78:* William Whitehurst/CORBIS; *Page 82:* James Leynse/Corbis; *Page 83:* istockphoto.com/jackson gee, (bottom, left to right) © NVIDIA Corporation, © Creative Technology Ltd, istockphoto.com/Marc Dietrich; *Page 84:* © Cisco Systems Inc., © NetComm Limited, U.S. Robotics; *Page 85:* © Paradigm Publishing, Inc. *Page 88:* Digital Art/Corbis, © 2005 Business Wire; *Page 89:* © Virtual Devices, Inc. **Tech Insight B.** *Page TI-B2:* Corbis; *Page TI-B3:* Corbis; *Page TI-B5:* © Hewlett-Packard Company. **Chapter 3.** *Page 100:* Roy McMahon/zefa/Corbis; *Page 101:* Corbis; *Page 102:* Corbis, Toru Hanai/Reuters/Corbis; *Page 103:* (left) Monica M. Davey/epa/Corbis, (right) Jim Craigmyle/Corbis; *Page 104:* ALBERT GEA/Reuters/Corbis, T & L/Image Point FR/Corbis; *Page 105:* Samsung Electronics/Handout/Reuters/Corbis; *Page 106:* Lou Dematteis/Reuters/Corbis; *Page 110:* (top to bottom) Najlah Feanny/Corbis, Forestier Yves/Corbis Sygma, Andrew Gombert/epa/Corbis; *Page 112:* © Microsoft Corporation; *Page 115:* © Printronix, © Hewlett-Packard Company; *Page 118:* © Hewlett-Packard Company, © Canon Inc; *Page 119:* © Hewlett-Packard Company, © Canon Inc; *Page 121:* (top to bottom) © Primera Technology, © DYMO, © Canon Inc; *Page 122:* © Canon Inc, © Panasonic Corporation; *Page 123:* © CNET Networks Inc, Corbis; *Page 130:* (top) © Paradigm Publishing, Inc., (bottom) © Maxell

Corporation Inc; *Page 135:* (left) © Memorex Products Inc, (right) © ePerformance; *Page 142:* courtesy Plastic Logic Limited 2007. **Tech Insight C.** *Page TI-C4: Page TI-C5:* Cisco Systems Inc., *Page TI-C6:* Corbis. **Chapter 4.** *Page 154:* Don Mason/Corbis; *Page 163:* Courtesy of Apple Computers; *Page 170:* Lynn Goldsmith/Corbis; *Page 177:* courtesy of Red Hat, Inc. © 2006 Red Hat Inc. All rights reserved.; *Page 178:* Kim Kulish/Corbis; *Page 180:* Microsoft product screen shot reprinted with permission from Microsoft Corporation.; *Page 182:* © Palm Inc; *Page 183:* © Hewlett-Packard Company, © Motorola, Inc., ©1995-2006 Symantec Corporation. **Tech Insight D.** *Page TI-D2:* Screenshots © Google Inc. and are used with permission; *Page TI-D3:* Apple Inc; *Page TI-D7:* Corbis; *Page TI-D8:* © 2006 Yahoo! Inc. YAHOO! and the YAHOO! logo are trademarks of Yahoo! Inc., Screenshots © Google Inc. and are used with permission; *Page TI-D10:* Michel Setboun/Corbis, © 1996-2006 Internet2 - All rights reserved. **Chapter 5.** *Page 202:* courtesy of the University of Phoenix © University of Phoenix, A. Sneider/zefa/Corbis; *Page 203:* © istockphoto.com/Marje Cannon; *Page 204:* © Paradigm Publishing, Inc.; *Page 207:* © 2006 Jupitermedia Corporation All rights reserved.; *Page 209:* C. Devan/zefa/Corbis; *Page 212:* Digibarn Computer Museum; *Page 213:* Erik Freeland/Corbis Saba; *Page 214:* © Paradigm Publishing, Inc.; *Page 221:* Corbis; *Page 224:* Jim Craigmyle/Corbis; *Page 225:* Corbis; *Page 226:* © istockphoto.com/Jill Fromer; *Page 227:* istockphoto.com/christine balderas; *Page 228:* Robert Glabraith/Reuters/Corbis; *Page 229:* By permission. From Merrriam-Webster's OnLine Dictionary © 2006 by Merriam-Webster, Incorporated (www.merrriam-webster.com); *Page 231:* © 2006 Apple Computer, Inc. All rights reserved.; *Page 232:* Louis Fabian Bachrach; *Page 234:* © Pinnacle Systems, Inc.; *Page 235:* Corbis; *Page 236:* Lars Langemeier/A.B./zefa/Corbis; *Page 237:* ©2006 Yahoo! Inc. YAHOO! and the YAHOO! logo are trademarks of Yahoo! Inc.; Screenshots © Google Inc., and are used with permission; *Page 240:* Jon Feingersh/Corbis; *Page 241:* Varie/Alt/Corbis; *Page 242:* Varie/Alt/Corbis. **Tech Insight E.** *Page TI-E1:* Gaetano/Corbis; *Page TI-E2:* Corbis, Kazuyoshi Nomachi/Corbis, Bettmann/Corbis; *Page TI-E4:* LWA-Sharie Kennedy/Corbis; *Page TI-E8:* Owen Franken/Corbis. **Appendix.** *Page A1:* Lawrence Manning/Corbis.